THE OBJECTIVE EYE

John Hyman

THE OBJECTIVE EYE

Color, Form, and Reality in the Theory of Art

THE UNIVERSITY OF CHICAGO PRESS
CHICAGO AND LONDON

John Hyman is a Fellow of the Queen's College, Oxford.

The University of Chicago Press, Chicago 60637
The University of Chicago Press, Ltd., London

Printed in the United States of America

15 14 13 12 11 10 09 08 07 06 1 2 3 4 5

ISBN: 0-226-36552-2 (cloth)

ISBN: 0-226-36553-0 (paper)

Library of Congress Cataloging-in-Publication Data

Hyman, John.
Color, form, and reality in the theory of art / John Hyman.
p. cm.
Includes bibliographical references and index.
ISBN: 0-226-36552-2 (cloth : alk. paper)—ISBN: 0-226-36553-0 (pbk. : alk. paper)
1. Visual perception. 2. Art—Psychology. 3. Composition (Art). 4. Color in art. I. Title.
N7430.5 .H96 2006
701'.15—dc22

2005029205

♾ The paper used in this publication meets the minimum requirements of the American National Standard for Information Sciences—Permanence of Paper for Printed Library Materials, ANSI Z39.48-1992.

For my father

The longer you work, the more the mystery deepens

of what appearance is, or how what is called

appearance can be made in another medium.

Francis Bacon, 1974

CONTENTS

ILLUSTRATIONS

PREFACE

THE MOST FUNDAMENTAL QUESTIONS we can ask about pictorial art seem childish when we put them down on paper. To say this is not to make any sort of apology for writing about them. On the contrary, they seem childish because they are the kind of questions we want answers to until our curiosity is pruned into a conventional shape. How do the marks on a picture's surface represent the objects that we see in them? Are they copies or facsimiles of things, or are they like reflections in a mirror? What is the difference between a picture and a written text? Are pictures in some sense more "natural" than words? Can absolutely anything be represented in a picture? For example, can a picture represent a thought or a feeling, or a sound or smell, or must the things it represents have shapes and colors? Why are some pictures said to be more realistic than others? Is it because they are especially truthful or, on the contrary, because they deceive the eye?

Some of the deepest philosophers addressed these questions—notably, Plato, Descartes, and Wittgenstein. In due course we shall see what they had to say. But they are the exceptions. For while the idea of a picture has always played a prominent role in philosophical thought about the mind, for most of its history philosophy has not paid much attention to the nature of pictorial art as such. The topic has been addressed by theologians from time to time, especially during the iconoclastic controversy in the eighth century. The principal question then was whether the portrayal of Christ is consistent with the doctrine of the incarnation. If God cannot be circumscribed or represented in a picture but a man can, does an icon of Christ deny his divinity, or does iconoclasm deny his humanity? History delivered its answer on the first Sunday of Lent in 842, when the icons were solemnly reinstalled. But philosophy was not advanced much, if at all, by the debate.

Then, rather suddenly and unexpectedly, the philosophical study of pictorial art flourished in the second half of the twentieth century as it had never done before. The initial impetus was provided by Ernst Gombrich's path-breaking book *Art and Illusion,* and the results that emerged were mainly influenced by the scientific study of vision, by ideas that originally stemmed from seventeenth-century epistemology and metaphysics, and by the advances in logic and the philosophy of language that provided philosophy in the twentieth century with its main driving force. During the same period, some of this philosophical work in turn influenced historians of art. But inevitably the reception of philosophy by writers in other disciplines tends to gloss over the detail or to ignore the broader theoretical ideas that inform and direct philosophical debate. In this book, I have moved these ideas to the foreground while trying to ensure that the argument is readily intelligible at every step to readers without any philosophical training.

This book is intended for all readers interested in the visual arts. But it is a work of analytical philosophy, from beginning to end, and therefore unlike most theoretical writing about art in several ways. To begin with, the problems I address only partly resemble the problems addressed in art history and visual studies, even when the broad topic headings—"form and color," "word and image," "representation," and so on—are the same. Consequently, some of the texts I discuss may be new to experts in these areas; and some of the authors generally acknowledged as canonical in visual studies do not appear here. Even the style in which I write is a sign of the intellectual tradition in which I work. My hope is that these things will not be disorientating and that the arguments that make up the substance of the book are sufficiently interesting to reward the reader unfamiliar with analytical philosophy for venturing across the tracks.

Finally, like most analytical philosophers, I am interested in advancing arguments and not in surveying the literature. However, having said that, I do discuss the historical sources of some ideas in considerable detail because many of the ideas we find convincing today were originally designed to answer specific intellectual needs, which differ substantially from our own. This means that it can be easier to distinguish what is sound from what is erroneous in our own thought if we are aware of its history. Intellectual communities can preserve ideas as assiduously as religious communities preserve customs and even costumes from a different climate and a different age. So we can sometimes shake ourselves free from ideas that are confused or mistaken by seeing that the purposes they served when they were invented are ones we no longer have.

The main topics treated in this book are the nature of colors and shapes, their representation in pictorial art, and the concept of realism in art theory.

But the most important decision I took when I planned it was to write an integrated study of color and depiction. It is surprising that this has not yet been attempted. Pictures consist of colors distributed on a plane. (I am including the achromatic colors black, gray, and white.) So it makes as much sense to think about pictures without thinking about colors as it would to think about music without thinking about sounds. Nevertheless, this is how philosophers generally proceed. Perhaps the reason is that the two topics have traditionally been placed under different headings in the syllabus. For at least since Hegel, philosophers have regarded the nature of pictorial art as a topic in aesthetics, while the theory of colors belongs to metaphysics. In any event, colors are difficult properties to understand, and a philosophical study of depiction that does not examine colors explicitly is bound to involve assumptions about them that not all of its readers can be expected to share—and perhaps ones they would do well to reject.

There is another reason to combine these topics. Ever since Kant placed the problem at the center of the *Critique of Pure Reason,* philosophers have struggled to define the extent to which the constitution of the human mind influences our knowledge and experience of the world; and the theory of colors has been one of the main battlefields for contending solutions to this problem. But the very same problem occupies a central place in the theory of art. It was a crux in *Art and Illusion,* where Gombrich famously labeled it with the phrase "the beholder's share." Comparing paintings with the inkblots Hermann Rorschach used to explore the unconscious mind, Gombrich pointed out that "it is always hard to distinguish what is given to us from what we supplement in the process of projection." And he argued—more persuasively than anyone else had done since Descartes—that drawing this distinction correctly is the key to understanding how pictures represent.

So the main topics I shall be concerned with are color and shape, depiction and realism in art. But when philosophy keeps its feet on the ground it depends on friction to make progress. Accordingly, I have organized the book around four myths, drawn from philosophy and science, that have captured the imagination of many historians of art. Chapters 1–3 are concerned with the doctrine that colors exist only in the mind and not in the physical objects we perceive. In chapters 4–7, I examine the idea that we can explain how pictures represent by analyzing the experience they produce in a spectator's mind. In chapters 8 and 9, I discuss the twin claims that a painting is a kind of text and that "realism" is an honorific term, which we bestow on art in a familiar style. Finally, in chapter 10, I criticize the idea that perspective is a successful technique for depicting space because it reproduces the geometrical structure of the retinal image—the picture from which our perception of space is naturally derived. I shall not attempt to summarize the positive ideas that I defend; but I shall say something about what, taken together, they imply.

Whereas philosophers and psychologists are fascinated by illusions and by images in the mind or in the eye, artists have more often said that they are interested in nature, reality, and truth. For example, Lorenzo Ghiberti wrote in his autobiography that he had sought to imitate nature as far as he could. Picasso described Velazquez as the true painter of reality. Gainsborough summed up his approach to painting with the remark, "I like the truth and daylight." And Van Gogh said that his aim in painting was to be simply honest before nature. But when we discover how differently their intentions were realized in paint, the appearance of unanimity vanishes before our eyes. And this makes it tempting to dismiss these remarks as lazy repetitions of stock phrases, which a sophisticated art theory will debunk.

This is the conclusion many philosophers have reached. They have preferred to believe that the most artists can imitate is the effect of nature on our senses; that truth and reality are outmoded ideas; that daylight is not what it seems; and that simple honesty is for simple folk. The extraordinary claim in Hegel's *Lectures on Fine Art,* that the essential principle of painting is subjectivity of mind, is accepted by the majority of philosophers today. I doubt whether any of this is right. The visible world is infinitely complex and diverse; every significant work of art is also a confession; and the perfectly objective eye does not exist. Nevertheless, as George Orwell said, it is possible to be more objective than most of us are. One kind of excellence in art is to be just that. The individuality and limitless variety of painting do not support the Hegelian view. On the contrary, they show how diverse the evidence against it is.

~

Orwell also said somewhere that the experience of writing a book is like a long bout of some painful illness. This one was long, but it was less painful than it might have been, thanks to the hospitality of two academic sanitoriums I shall never forget.

I began it during the tenure of a Getty Scholarship at the Getty Research Institute in Los Angeles and completed it during the tenure of a fellowship at Wiko, the Wissenschaftskolleg zu Berlin. I could not have been more fortunate. The Getty Center is an extraordinary place—perched on its magic mountain above LA—and the friendly and stimulating company of my colleagues there was both instructive and delightful. I should like to take this opportunity to thank them, the excellent staff at the Getty Research Institute, and its formidable director, Thomas Crow. My year in Berlin was no less enjoyable and no less instructive. Dieter Grimm and Wolf Lepenies presided over the company with exceptional grace. I thank them, the Wiko's wonderful staff, and my colleagues, including the large company of biologists, who set a standard of rigor and lucidity the rest of us scrambled to approach.

My greatest debts are to the friends and colleagues who have encouraged, criticized, and assisted my work in various ways. In particular, I am indebted to Frederika Adam, Maria Alvarez, George Benjamin, Hanoch Ben-Yami, Anthony Burton, Jonathan Dancy, John Elderfield, Barbara Finley, Hanjo Glock, Ketty Gottardo, Tina Koch, Jacqueline Lichtenstein, Steven Lukes, Stephen Mulhall, Michael Podro, Siegbert Prawer, Joseph Raz, Klaus Rehkämper, Christopher Timpson, and Yvonne Zipter. I am especially grateful to Susan Bielstein for her encouragement and expertise; to Peter Hacker and Charles Harrison for their astute advice on several fundamental points; and to Max de Gaynesford, who went over every page with a fine-toothed comb and persuaded me to reorganize the whole book. Above all, I owe a special debt to my father, David Hyman, for his unquenchable curiosity and enthusiasm: *bis hundert und tzvantzig*!

Finally, I should like to thank the Governing Body of the Queen's College, Oxford, and the Faculty of Philosophy, both of which generously relieved me of my duties and allowed me to be absent for two years.

INTRODUCTION

THE MAIN AIM of this book is to clarify the concept of depiction, the concept we use when we describe a configuration of lines or colors as a picture of a kind of object, event, or scene—such as a man, a battle, a forest, or a god. This concept is used constantly in art history and theory and in our most innocent and unsophisticated thought and conversation about art. But it is one thing to use a concept and another to understand it clearly; and when a concept is not understood clearly its more ambitious use in theoretical writings will be confused.

There are two reasons for thinking that clarifying the concept of depiction is a timely exercise. First, after half a century of sustained work on the topic, it is now possible to map out a terrain with some confidence, which the pioneers explored with different methods and conflicting results. Second, it was once thought that art in the twentieth century was effecting a "gradual withdrawal from the task of representing reality," as Clement Greenberg put it, and hence that the concept of depiction would soon be of purely antiquarian interest, like the eighteenth-century concept of the picturesque. But we can now see in retrospect that this is a misleading view of twentieth-century art. On the contrary, many artists in the twentieth century explored the limits of pictorial art with the same intense curiosity as the philosophers did—even though in some cases (I am thinking especially of Kasimir Malevich and Piet Mondrian) they also held a view Wittgenstein once held about the limits of language, that what lies outside them matters more than anything they contain.

A history of the numerous and varied forms this exploration took would be coterminous with the history of twentieth-century art; and although these are not sharp categories, a number of broad themes in this protean tradition can be defined. For example, the image fragmented; the cityscape or landscape drained of pictorial content by abstraction; the image consumed by the paint or graphic marks of which it is made; the image as a reiterated sign, depleted of significance by repeated use; the quasi-image/quasi-replica; the image defaced, blurred, or erased. By pursuing these and several other themes, artists from Picasso and Braque to Gerhard Richter charted the borderlands of pictorial art and populated it with examples. So although philosophers reflect on art discursively, whereas artists make concrete instances of it, the task I have attempted in this book resembles a task that many artists in the twentieth century set themselves. Few of the works of art to which I shall refer were made in the twentieth century. But my argument is informed by the same desire to define the limits of pictorial art.

In the whole body of philosophical literature, from Plato to the present day, there are two main contending doctrines about depiction. The first, which Plato states in the *Cratylus*, says that a picture represents an object by copying its form and color. The second, which appears much later in the history of philosophy and as a reaction to the first, says that a picture represents an object by producing a special kind of experience in a spectator's mind. The original source of the second doctrine is in Descartes's *Optics*. Pictures, Descartes argues, do not cause us to see the things they represent because they are likenesses. On the contrary, we call them likenesses because they cause us to see these things. He writes as follows: "The problem is to know simply how [pictures] can enable the soul to have sensory perceptions of all the various qualities of the objects to which they correspond—not to know how they can resemble these objects."[1]

Now when we consider these opposing doctrines in the broad intellectual context of philosophy as a whole it is striking how familiar the relationship between them is. For when Socrates asks Euthyphro whether a pious act is pious because it is loved by the gods or whether, on the contrary, a pious act is loved by the gods because it is pious, when Aristotle insists that we desire an object because it seems good to us and Spinoza replies that an object seems good to us because we desire it, when Augustine asks whether things are beautiful because they please us or whether they please us because they are beautiful, the problems about piety, goodness, and beauty these philosophers address and the problem about depiction have precisely the same form.

Each of these problems is about defining the relationship between a property some of the objects we perceive seem to possess—such as beauty or pictorial content—and a response that objects that seem to possess this property arouse. The question is this: which of these two things, the response or the property, explains the other? Which of them comes first—not chronologically, but theoretically? Do we desire an object because it seems good to us, as Aristotle maintained? Or was Spinoza right in claiming that we deem a thing to be good because we strive for it, wish for it, long for it, or desire it? Do beautiful things please us because they are beautiful, as Augustine and Aquinas held? Or was Hume right in claiming that we "gild" or "stain" the objects we admire "with the colors borrowed from internal sentiment"? In each case, to use Gombrich's phrase, what is "the beholder's share"?[2]

Let us consider the case of beauty in more detail. In the theory of values, these two opposing views, which assign theoretical priority to the response or to the property, are commonly known as subjectivism and objectivism, respectively. Subjectivism is the doctrine that if an object has some value, positive or negative, this can only be because of the response it arouses or the reaction it provokes in a particular individual or group of individuals. Whereas objectivism is the doctrine that the value of an object is independent of any such reaction or response. Until the eighteenth century, most philosophers were objectivists about beauty; and for as long as objectivism predominated, so did the theory that beauty consists in a certain kind of mathematical order or perfection—specifically, in the proportionality of an object's parts.

The original source of this theory was the discovery, attributed by tradition to Pythagoras, that the consonant musical intervals correspond to simple arithmetical ratios between the lengths of a vibrating string.[3] This astonishing discovery governed philosophical thought about beauty for two thousand years. For if musical harmonies can be explained by measurements and calculations, it seems that beauty is no more dependent on our sensibilities than the geometry of a right-angled triangle. Perhaps the allure of beauty is so subtle and entrancing that we cannot generally perceive its abstract skeleton with a mathematician's penetrating eye. But if the mathematical theory of beauty is correct, this skeleton is hidden in the harmonies we love and described by the canonical systems that define a beautifully proportioned face or body.

Both Plato and Aristotle accepted these ideas. As did Vitruvius, Boethius, and Augustine; Alberti, Lomazzo, and Dürer; Poussin and Leibniz. But the mathematical theory of beauty was attacked with particular force, and eventually with spectacular success, in the seventeenth and eighteenth centuries—first by Descartes, Hobbes, Spinoza, and Pascal and then by Voltaire, Hume, and Kant. The two main arguments were as follows.

First, it is obvious that taste varies. For example, the shapes of Greek vases made in the fifth century B.C. are quite unlike the shapes of vases made in China in the Song Dynasty; and the taste of one age or society is often considered crude or mannered by another. But why do these differences exist? Are there unvarying laws beneath the differences, which a new Pythagoras may eventually discover? Do different cultural traditions and changing tastes simply make people sensitive to some instances of these laws, and not to others? In the seventeenth and eighteenth centuries, many philosophers found this suggestion quite implausible and argued that the variety of taste proves that the mathematical theory is absurd. Voltaire, for example, writes as follows:

> Ask a toad what beauty is, absolute beauty, the *to kalon*. He will answer that it is his female, with two large round eyes sticking out of her little head, a large and flat snout, a yellow belly, a brown back. Ask a Negro from Guinea; for him beauty is a black oily skin, sunken eyes, a flat nose. Ask the devil; he will tell you that the beautiful is a pair of horns, four claws, and a tail. Finally, consult the philosophers: their answer will be grandiloquent nonsense; they will ask for something conforming to the archetype of the beautiful in essence, to the *to kalon*.[4]

Each creature, Voltaire claims, however despised, has its own beauty. Only philosophers believe in the existence of a universal abstract pattern, which everything that is beautiful conforms to.

The second argument against the mathematical theory was that if it were true, we would be able to deduce that something is beautiful by taking measurements and making calculations. But it was widely acknowledged that this is impossible to do. There was not a consensus among writers who opposed the theory on the role that reasoning plays in the exercise of taste. Some agreed with Pascal that "the thing is not repellent [or attractive] for the reasons which one finds later, but rather one finds these reasons later because the thing was repellent [or attractive]": reason, as Shakespeare puts it, panders will.[5] Others agreed with Hume's view that "critics can reason and dispute more plausibly than cooks or perfumers."[6] But it was generally accepted that the acid test of beauty is the pleasurable experience it produces in our minds: "I must feel the pleasure directly, in the contemplation of the object," Kant claims, "and I cannot be talked into it by any grounds of proof."[7]

Ostensibly, objectivism about beauty lost favor for these reasons. But philosophical arguments find favor when they harmonize with cultural trends. In this case, a gradual but profound change occurred in European taste, which made the mathematical theory seem more like an antiquated predilection for symmetry than a convincing philosophical idea. Thus Burke denied that beauty has "anything to do with calculation and geometry"; and Sterne satirized the men he called the "connoisseurs": "Their heads, Sir, are stuck so full of rules and compasses . . . that a work of genius had better go to the devil at once, than stand to be prick'd and tortured to death by 'em."[8] So by now the ground was well prepared and subjectivism was bound to flourish. But considered as a philosophical theory, and not merely as an expression of taste, subjectivism faces problems of its own.

On the one hand, subjectivism makes nihilism and relativism difficult to resist. Many subjectivist philosophers have fought shy of these radical ideas. Hume, for example, claims that "beauty and deformity . . . are not qualities in objects, but belong entirely to the sentiment."[9] But he is not a nihilist. Nihilism may be irrefutable; but Hume claims that we cannot be convinced that beauty does not exist because the love of beauty is too deeply rooted in our nature: "The reflections of philosophy are too subtle and distant to take place in common life, or eradicate any affection. The air is too fine to breathe in, where it is above the winds and clouds of the atmosphere." Again, relativism may be intellectually attractive; but Hume argues that the joint verdict of discerning critics is "the true standard of taste and beauty," and he insists that it would be a plain mistake to rank the minor Scottish poet John Ogilby as Milton's equal, just as it would be "to declare a mole-hill to be as high as Teneriffe, or a pond as extensive as the ocean."

But how convincing are these moderate ideas? In the first place, if taste varies, why should we defer to an elite—even if it is not just class and money posturing as savoir-faire? Is it not more egalitarian and more plausible to acknowledge that nothing is beautiful in and of itself, but only relative to one individual or another? Second, if we accept that beauty is not a quality in objects, should we really believe that it exists at all? Is it not simpler and more honest to overcome our nostalgia for a world in which Abraham could eat at the same table as the angels and beauty seemed as real to men as bread? In a scene in Turgenev's *Fathers and Sons*, the warm evening light piercing a clump of aspen trees, and making their trunks glow like pines, seems to Nikolai Petrovich to embody a deeper truth than the arguments of the young nihilist

Bazarov. But to another kind of sensibility the opposite view is equally convincing. For example, the Portuguese poet Fernando Pessoa wrote the following lines:

> Has a flower somehow beauty?
> Is there beauty somehow in a fruit?
> No: they have colour and form
> And existence only.
> Beauty is the name of something that does not exist
> Which I give to things in exchange for the pleasure they give me.[10]

This is the radical response to the qualified subjectivism Hume defends. But there is also a conservative response. For suppose we concede to the subjectivist that beauty is not something whose presence we detect by taking measurements and making calculations and that perceiving beauty is intrinsically enjoyable. It does not follow that we can define a pleasant feeling that is peculiar to beauty just by the way it feels. In fact there does not seem to be a special thrill or throb or tingle whose occurrence could provide us with a test of beauty; and mere talk of pleasure is obviously too vague. Amusement is a pleasant feeling. But a school orchestra's performance may amuse a discerning critic without seeming beautiful at all. So how can the sentiment Hume postulates be defined?

The objectivist will be ready with an answer. Her answer will be, first, that the sentiment can only be defined in terms of a thought that gives it an articulate shape and a direction—the thought that the thing seems beautiful; and second, that this thought is true if, and only if, the thing is as it seems to be. But if we accept this answer, the objectivist will surely claim that we have implicitly accepted her position, namely, that an object is not beautiful because it would please a discerning critic: on the contrary, it would please a discerning critic because he would perceive its beauty.

Thus, in the case of beauty, neither objectivism nor subjectivism appears to be a stable position. Objectivism pushes us toward subjectivism. And subjectivism either pushes us further toward relativism or nihilism or back toward objectivism. Now as we shall see, each of these four positions has an analogue in the theory of color, and the arguments that make them either attractive or difficult to sustain are analogous as well. Color is the topic I shall turn to now. For just as philosophers have debated whether beauty is objective or subjective, they have debated about colors in the same way. Do the colors we predicate of objects depend on the experiences that occur when we perceive them, or do these experiences depend on the colors of the objects we perceive? Is an apple red because of the visual sensation it produces in us when we see it, or does it produce this sensation in us because it is red?

All pictures—whatever kind of substance they are made of—consist of colors distributed on a plane. So this is the right way for a study of depiction to begin. But colors are difficult properties to understand. Sight is inconceivable without them, but it is hard to explain exactly how they are related to our visual perceptions and to the objects we perceive. The task of explaining this will occupy three chapters. In chapter 1, I shall discuss the popular doctrine that our experience of color is an illusion, and nothing in reality has any color at all. In chapter 2, I turn from nihilism to relativism. And in chapter 3, I shall examine subjectivism about color in its modern form. The second and third parts of the book are directly concerned with pictures—the second part being about depiction in general and the third about the idea of realism in pictorial art. But in these parts of the book, too, the contest between subjectivism and objectivism will be a major theme. The problem of defining the beholder's share, which Gombrich placed at the center of art theory, runs through the entire book from beginning to end.

COLOR

1

GALILEO'S MYTH

> The implicit acceptance of mythical concepts is a habit that never completely relaxes its hold. Today it is even more heavily overlaid than in ancient Greece with the terminology of rational disciplines. This makes it more difficult to detect and therefore more dangerous.
>
> W. K. C. Guthrie

IT IS WIDELY BELIEVED that physical objects are not really colored. This doctrine was already stated by Democritus in the fifth century B.C.: "Colors, sweetness, bitterness, exist by convention," he wrote, "in reality, there are atoms and the void."[1] It became an orthodoxy in the seventeenth century, under the joint aegis of Galileo and Descartes. And the orthodoxy was cemented into place by Sir Isaac Newton, who made it a permanent feature of the modern scientific picture of the world. Nevertheless, the orthodox doctrine is a myth. Myths often contain truths, but they are truths in fancy dress or in disguise. So it is possible to discard a myth without losing hold of the truths that it contains, for we can reformulate them in transparent terms. The historical roots of the myth about colors have by now been thoroughly documented and are well understood.[2] But unfortunately there is nothing like a consensus on how best to demythologize this part of science. Too often, philosophers who attempt it deserve to be reminded of Alexander Herzen's trenchant remark: "We are not the doctors. We are the disease."

The original modern statement of the myth about colors occurs in Galileo's writings, in particular in *The Assayer,* and it is supported there with two main arguments, both of which still resonate today. First, Galileo points out that our general concept of matter compels us to attribute shapes, sizes and locations to material objects, but it does not compel us to acknowledge that they have colors, smells, or tastes:

> whenever I conceive of any material or corporeal substance, I am necessarily constrained to conceive of that substance as bounded and as possessing this or that shape, as large or small in relationship to some other body, as in this or that place during this or that time, as in motion or at rest, as in contact or not in contact with some other body, as being one, many, or few—and by no stretch of imagination can I conceive of any corporeal body apart from these conditions. But I do not at all feel myself compelled to conceive of bodies as necessarily conjoined with such further conditions as being red or white, bitter or sweet, having sound or being mute, or possessing a pleasant or unpleasant fragrance. . . . I think, therefore, that these tastes, odours, colours, etc., so far as their objective existence is concerned, are nothing but mere names for something that resides exclusively in our sensitive body, so that if the perceiving creature were removed, all of these qualities would be annihilated and abolished from existence.[3]

This argument is unconvincing. It is true that we can conceive of matter that has no color, no taste, and no smell. In fact, matter of this kind exists. But it does not follow that colors, tastes, and smells do not really exist outside the creatures that perceive them. For the fact that water has no taste does not imply that in reality wine has no taste either; and the fact that hydrogen is colorless does not imply that chlorine is really colorless as well. Compare mass and electric charge. We can conceive of particles that have no mass or no electric charge. Indeed there are such particles. But it does not follow that mass and electric charge are "nothing but mere names for something which resides exclusively in our sensitive body." The fact is that photons have no mass, but leptons and quarks do; and neutrons have no electric charge, but protons and electrons do. There is simply no reason to accept that the only real properties of a material substance are the ones that it is inconceivable or unimaginable that it should lack.

Galileo's second argument is by analogy:

> a piece of paper or a feather, when gently rubbed over any part of our body whatsoever, will in itself act everywhere in an identical way; it will, namely, move and make contact. But we, should we be touched between the eyes, on the tip of the nose, or under the nostrils, will feel an almost intolerable titilla-

> tion—while if touched in other places, we will scarcely feel anything at all. Now this titillation is completely ours and not the feather's, so that if the living, sensing body were removed, nothing would remain of the titillation but an empty name. And I believe that many other qualities, such as taste, odour, colour, and so on, often predicated of natural bodies, have a similar and no greater existence than this.

This argument is also unconvincing. It is true that a tickle is a sensation, which can only occur in the living body of a sentient animal. It is also true that the experiences of tasting sweetness and seeing red could not occur if there were no sentient animals alive to have them. And it is true that we should not predicate *tasting sweetness* and *seeing redness* of a grape. But it does not follow that we should not predicate *sweetness* or *redness* of it either. If every perceiving creature were removed, every perception would be annihilated and abolished from existence. But we cannot infer that the colors and tastes we predicate of natural bodies would vanish too.

Hence, these arguments fail, both individually and in conjunction. But taken together they point in the direction of an idea that is still widely entertained, namely, that we do not need to assume that tasting sweetness and seeing redness are perceptions of qualities that bodies actually possess, in order to explain why these experiences occur. This idea, as we shall see, is the main reason why it is still widely believed that tastes and colors exist only in the mind.

Why do I say that Galileo's arguments point in this direction? The first argument is in effect a plea for parsimony, or theoretical economy. It says: let us not acknowledge the existence of any qualities in matter unless it is irrational to deny them—that is, unless the science of matter, or a rationally compelling argument of some sort, demands that we acknowledge they exist. And the second argument says this: all that we need to predicate of a feather, in order to explain the tickling feeling it produces, is motion and contact; and the same is true of the things we describe as "red" and "sweet." "I cannot believe [Galileo writes] that there exists in external bodies anything, other than their size, shape, or motion . . . which could excite in us our tastes, sounds, and odours." Hence, the qualities that we need to predicate of things, in order to explain the experiences they produce, do not include being red or being sweet.

If we accept both of these points—the point about theoretical economy and the point about how sense experience can be explained—we are not bound to accept the conclusion Galileo draws, namely, that "if ears, tongues, and noses be taken away, the number, shape, and motion of bodies would remain, but not their tastes, sounds, and odours." For there may be other effects, apart from our perceptions, which we need to postulate tastes and colors to explain. And there may be other compelling reasons, apart from the effects they are capable of explaining, to accept that sweetness and redness are qualities that inhere in matter. And besides, there is a difference between refusing to assume that colors do inhere in matter and accepting the conclusion that they do not. Nevertheless, the argument I have reconstructed sets an agenda; and I shall examine it in detail later in this chapter.

Galileo's opinion about colors is still widely held today. For example, John Gage, who has made the place of color in art the main theme of his work, claims that "Newton . . . showed that colour was indeed illusory." Many student textbooks on visual perception treat this claim as an established fact. For example, Stephen Palmer states that "colour is a psychological property of our visual experiences when we look at objects and lights, not a physical property of those objects and lights." And similar claims appear in many learned articles as well. For example, in an important article on color vision in monkeys, Samir Zeki claims that color "is a property of the brain, not of the world outside."[4]

Remarks like these imply that our visual experiences are infused with colors that seem to inhere in the visible objects we perceive but that these objects do not in fact possess. So, if we take the ordinary statements in which we attribute colors to physical objects at face value—for example, "bananas are yellow" or "the t-shirt I am wearing now is red"—these statements are uniformly false. How should we set about deciding whether to accept this challenging idea? To begin with, we need to ask what conception of color is implicit in ordinary statements of this kind. We need to begin with this question because the thought that something we say is either true or false must always presuppose an interpretation of it, or a way of understanding what it means. And sometimes what is presupposed is false, inaccurate, or incomplete. Truth, as W. V. O. Quine says, depends both on language and on extralinguistic fact.[5] We should not assume that our grip on either element is absolutely sure.

"Bananas are yellow" and "the t-shirt I am wearing now is red" are of course relatively simple color statements, and the basic conception of color that is implicit in them is gradually elaborated as we learn to think about primary colors and complementary colors, surface colors and aperture colors, metameric pairs, and so on. But although it is elaborated, it is not abandoned, just as our basic conception of shape is gradually elaborated, but not abandoned, when we study geometry at school. So we must begin with the simplest examples and examine the basic conception of color they embody; but we must not forget that we can be misled if we assume that all color statements are the same.

In particular, we need to bear in mind that red and yellow are "gross" colors. In other words, like all of the dozen or so colors for which most languages have names, they encompass a vast number of discriminable shades and they are therefore easy for most human beings to recognize without comparing the object whose color is in question with a sample. Furthermore, bananas and t-shirts are what J. L. Austin liked to call moderate-sized specimens of dry (or dryish) goods, which many colored things, such as the sea and the sky and the planet Mars, are not. Finally, the color of a banana or a t-shirt depends on its tendency to reflect light of certain wavelengths and to absorb light of other wavelengths; but although this is true of many colored objects, it is not true of them all. For example, the color of stained glass depends on its tendency to filter light rather than on its reflectance. And the color of a flame depends on the light it produces, rather than on the way it interacts with light radiating from another source.

As we shall see, some philosophical doctrines about colors cannot be properly assessed unless we bear these points in mind. But in this chapter, we shall be concerned only with our basic conception of color. The argument will be simple. I shall begin by explaining this basic conception of color—the conception that is implicit in every color predication that we make. Then I shall argue that colors are thought to be illusory because of a misunderstanding about this conception of color. The claim that the colors we predicate of physical objects do not really exist is, I shall argue, a confused way of stating a simple and important insight about how our experiences of color are produced—an insight that marks the transition from the Aristotelian optical theory that predominated in the medieval period to the modern optical theory that was inaugurated by Galileo, Kepler, and Descartes.

~

Our basic conception of colors is rooted in one fundamental principle, namely, that an object's color is part of its appearance, in other words, that it is part of how it looks. An object's appearance, in this sense, is not the sum of its visible properties. It is a subset of its visible properties. For example, a man's rough age is typically visible. We can typically tell roughly how old a man is by seeing his face. But a man's rough age is not part of his appearance. For example, being roughly sixty, as opposed to looking roughly sixty, is not part of how a man who looks roughly sixty looks. By contrast, if a man is pale, being pale is part of his appearance. The idea of a man's appearance is already implicit in the thought that he is pale in the way that the idea of an object's taste is already implicit in the thought that it is sweet. So there is no need to say that a man *looks* pale in order to refer to his appearance. The statement that he *is* pale does this already.

The statement that a man *looks* roughly sixty is therefore analogous to the statement that a man *is* pale. But this does not prevent it from being analogous to the statement that a man looks pale, in one sense of the phrase "looks pale." For the statement that something looks pale can mean either that it has a pale color or that it seems to have a pale color. For example, the statement that anemic boys look pale means that anemic boys have a pale color, whereas the statement that ruddy boys look pale in blinding sunlight means that ruddy boys seem to have a pale color in blinding sunlight. Similarly, the statement that honey tastes sweet means that honey has a sweet taste, whereas the statement that boiled fish tastes sweet to a man who has eaten salty food means that boiled fish seems to have a sweet taste to a man who has eaten salty food. "Looks roughly sixty" is analogous to "looks pale" when "looks pale" is equivalent, as it sometimes is, to "has a pale color." Indeed, it is precisely because the idea of a man's appearance is already implicit in the statement that he is pale that "looks pale" sometimes means "has a pale color." This is, one could say, a pleonastic use of the verb "looks."

So an object's color is part of its appearance, which is to say that it is part of how it looks. But we should not equate appearance and illusion because some appearances are deceptive or illusory, while others are not. An object's appearance is illusory in a certain respect if it appears to possess a certain property that it does not in fact possess. For example, if a fruit looks ripe but is not ripe, or if it looks red but is not red, or if it looks round but is not round, these appearances are illusory. But appearances are not deceptive or illusory as such. Indeed, the primary notion of something's being apparent is that it is manifest, evident, or obvious and not that it is misleading or false, although it is of course also true that we often compare the way things appear with the way they actually are. Hence, some appearances are mere appearances while others are not. The moot question is which category of appearances colors belong to. I shall come to this question in due course.

I am proposing that the fundamental principle, from which any attempt to explain our basic conception of colors must proceed, is that an object's color is part of how it looks. Similarly, the smell of a thing is how it smells, and the taste of a thing is how it tastes. I do not want to insist that these principles are self-evident—that is, that everyone who understands them will perceive immediately that they are true. For what is self-evident to one person may need to be proved to another. But once they are recognized as true, it will be clear that there is a fundamental difference between an object's color or smell or taste, on the one hand, and its shape, on the other. For example, if an egg is white and round, then being white is part of its appearance but being round is not. Looking round is part of its appearance—that is, it is part of how it looks.

But being round, as opposed to looking round, is not. Hence, the statement that an object has a certain color already involves the idea of its appearance, in a way that the statement that it has a certain shape does not. So there is an intrinsic tie between color and sentience, as there is between smell or taste and sentience, which does not exist between sentience and shape.

Compare sourness. We cannot have a clear conception of what sourness is unless we understand that it is a smell or taste; and we cannot understand what a smell or a taste is unless we have some conception of a sentient animal with the corresponding sense. This is not a condition on the existence of sour things. It does not mean that the existence of sourness entails the existence of sentient animals or that lemons will cease to be sour when sentient animals become extinct. It is a condition on having a clear understanding of the concept of sourness and not a condition on the concept's application. Just the same can be said about color. If lemons are yellow they will not cease to be yellow when sentient animals become extinct. But we cannot understand what color is without some notion of the sense of sight.

The last introductory point I shall make is this: if the color of a thing is part of how it looks and the smell or taste of a thing is how it smells or tastes, then being yellow and being sour are comparable to properties such as looking like a lemon and tasting like vinegar because these are all properties that belong to the way a thing looks, tastes, or smells.[6] It will be helpful, when we try to unfold our basic conception of colors, to compare colors with other properties that are part of how a thing looks or smells or tastes but where this status is marked explicitly in the predicates that signify these properties—in other words, where the predicates wear this feature of their meaning on their sleeve.

~

So much by way of introduction. Now since an object's color is part of how it looks, the basic conception of colors, the conception that is implicit in the simplest color statements that we make, involves the following related principles. Each principle captures one aspect of the intrinsic tie between color and sentience, which I commented on in general terms above.

First, colors, like smells and tastes, are properties that only perceptible objects can possess. For example, nothing that is invisible can be yellow and nothing that cannot be smelled or tasted can be sour. For the color of a thing is part of how it looks and the smell or taste of a thing is how it smells or tastes; and nothing can look, smell or taste a certain way if its physical nature is such that it cannot be seen or smelled or tasted, by any sentient animal at all. Invisible objects can of course have shapes. For example, the shape of an atom of hydrogen is a sphere and the shape of a molecule of CH_4 is a tetrahedron. But a hydrogen atom does not look like a sphere and a molecule of CH_4 does not look like a tetrahedron because they are too small to look like anything at all. Hence, they are also too small to be colored.

Second, an object's color, smell, or taste, unlike its shape, cannot affect what happens—it cannot influence the course of history—except as a consequence of being perceived. For how a thing smells or tastes can only make a difference to the course of events by being smelled or tasted; and how a thing looks can only make a difference by being seen. In this respect, sourness and yellowness are like beauty. Beauty can change the course of history: Pascal's example was Cleopatra's nose. But although the beauty of an object does not itself depend on whether it is perceived, its consequences do. The *esse* of beauty is not *percipi*, but its *efficere* is. In the same way, sour milk that is not smelled or tasted is still sour; and being yellow does not depend on being seen. But the behavior of sentient animals is the bottleneck through which colors, smells, and tastes affect the world.[7]

Third, the final arbiter of an object's color, smell, or taste is the corresponding sense. This is probably the meaning of Aristotle's dictum that the senses are never mistaken about their proper objects. We are not infallible judges of the colors of the things we see or of the tastes and smells of things we taste and smell. But a mistaken judgment about the taste or smell or color of something is corrected by tasting or smelling or looking at it again or by deferring to someone else who has tasted or smelled or seen it. There cannot be a litmus test for sourness, a chemical test that can overturn the verdict of the senses, because sourness is a matter of how things smell or taste; whereas there is such a test for acidity, of course. So smelling or tasting things is the acid test of how they smell or taste. Similarly, whatever instruments we have at our disposal, looking at things is the acid test of how they look.

Fourth, colors, like smells and tastes, are basic properties, relative to the sense with which we perceive them. In other words, whatever else we perceive by the sense of smell—for example, that a fruit is rotten or that a child is ill—we perceive by smelling smells; whatever else we perceive by taste, we perceive by tasting tastes; and whatever else we perceive by sight, we perceive by seeing colors—including the achromatic colors, of course. For example, I cannot see the shape of a banana except by seeing its spatial boundaries, however fleeting and uncertain this experience may be. And I cannot see its spatial boundaries except by seeing the differences of color that make it visibly distinct from its surroundings. That is why, as James Clerk Maxwell pointed out, all vision is color vision.[8]

Finally, colors, like smells and tastes, are perceptible qualities of the objects that possess them. For it is, tautologically, possible to see how a thing looks and to smell or taste how a thing smells or tastes. Hence, colors are visible, if they exist at all.

These five points create, in summary form, an analysis of the basic conception of color that is implicit in the simplest color statements we make. According to this conception, only visible objects can have colors; colors are inert, in the sense that they cannot influence what happens, except as a consequence of being seen; they are subject to the epistemic jurisdiction of the senses, in the sense that the acid test of an object's color is to look at it; and they are the basic visible properties of the world. This is not a set of factual assumptions about colors. It is an exposition of the language side of the double dependency Quine referred to when he said that truth depends on both language and extralinguistic fact. In other words, it is part of an explanation of what our simplest color statements mean.

It does not follow from this analysis that any such statement is true. There cannot be an ontological proof for the existence of colors, and I have not tried to provide one. But if a simple affirmative color statement is true, then the object referred to has a property of this kind.

~

The myth about colors stems principally from the second point in the analysis above, and I shall say something more about this now. I have already said that according to our basic conception of colors, an object's color is inert. Strictly speaking, this principle needs to be qualified. For the color of the dye in which a cloth is soaked affects the color of the cloth, rather as the sourness of vinegar affects the sourness of a vinaigrette and the beauty of Cleopatra's nose contributes to the beauty of her profile. Strictly speaking, therefore, we ought to say that an object's color can only make a difference other than to the appearance of something by being seen; that the way something tastes can only make a difference other than to the taste of something by being tasted; and that an object's beauty can only make a difference other than to the beauty of something by being perceived. From now on, I shall take this qualification as read.

With or without the qualification, the principle that colors are inert is very widely accepted by philosophers today. It was challenged recently by Peter Hacker on the grounds that "we correctly explain why my hut is cool in the summer while yours is hot by reference to the fact that yours is black and mine is white."[9] But the challenge is unsuccessful. It is true that we can explain why my hut is cooler than yours by saying that it is paler and that dark huts heat up in the sunshine more than pale ones. But this is not because a dark hut's heating up more than a pale one is a consequence of its darker color. It is because having a darker color correlates with having a tendency to heat up more. And this correlation exists because the color and the tendency have the same cause, namely, the absorption of light.[10]

It follows immediately from the principle that colors are inert that the theoretical role played by colors in the sciences is strictly limited, as scientists themselves are keenly aware. Many explanations of animal behavior refer to colors—in ethology, anthropology, sociology, and daily life. For example, my niece may choose to wear one pair of socks rather than another because it is pink. But explanations in physics, chemistry, and physiology do not refer to colors. These sciences do explain facts about colors, for example, why the sky is blue or what causes color blindness. But they do not explain phenomena by means of facts about colors. The boundaries between the sciences are shifting and permeable, of course. But since an object's color is part of how it looks, it is a property that science can have no reason to refer to in its explanations, except when the field of study includes the thought and behavior of animals that see colors.

In particular, we cannot expect the colors of visible objects to play a role when physics, chemistry, and physiology explain how color experiences are produced. But I emphasize that this is not a result we owe to these sciences themselves. As a matter of historical fact, it took Newton's experimental work in optics to drive the point home. But it is essentially an a priori philosophical insight and not a discovery of natural science. That is why, despite the wholly speculative nature of his atomism, Galileo could write with such conviction: "I cannot believe that there exists in external bodies anything, other than their size, shape, or motion . . . which could excite in us our tastes, sounds, and odours." And it is why Descartes, who argued that atomism is self-contradictory, expressed exactly the same thought, with equal vehemence.

Size, shape, and motion are, as we now know, too limited a repertoire of concepts to explain the nature of light or the physiology of vision. And neither Galilean atoms nor Cartesian *res extensa* exist. Indeed both of these notions are fraught with logical difficulties. Descartes equates matter with extension and, therefore holds that the existence of a vacuum is a logical impossibility, while Galileo holds that the ultimate constituents of matter are unextended atoms, whose relative positions in solid bodies are preserved by *horror vacui*. Hence, it cannot have been a real understanding of the nature of matter that enabled Galileo and Descartes to deny that our experiences of color are caused by colors themselves, several decades before Newton discovered the correlation between the color of a light-ray and its index of refraction and centuries before the chemistry of photoreception was understood. But neither was it prescience or luck.

~

A thorough historical treatment of Galileo's myth about colors would consider several ideas besides the ones I have mentioned.[11] But its main intellectual foundation was the combination of the a priori insight I have discussed and the first speculative steps in the modern science of matter. Both of the principal seventeenth-century theories of matter have been discarded but the a priori insight has not. On the contrary, the more we know about color perception, the more salient it becomes. And it is still the main reason why philosophers and natural scientists deny that physical objects really have colors—in addition to sizes, shapes, spectral reflectances and whatever other properties the scientific explanation of our perceptions needs to invoke.

For example, Bernard Williams claims that "in understanding, even sketchily, why things appear variously coloured to various observers, we shall find that we have left behind any idea that . . . they 'really' have one colour rather than another. In thinking of these explanations, we are in fact using a conception in which colour does not figure at all as a quality of things."[12] Thomas Nagel claims that "the hypothesis that objects have intrinsic colours in addition to their primary qualities . . . provides a poorer explanation of why they appear to have colours . . . than the hypothesis that the primary qualities of objects and their effects on us are responsible for all the appearances."[13] And John Mackie claims that predicating colors of physical objects "forms no part of the explanation of what goes on in the physical world in the processes which lead on to our having the sensations and perceptions that we have." "Physics," Mackie concludes, "gives us no reason for taking colours as primary qualities. . . . And the philosophical principle of economy of postulation then supplies a reason for not introducing supposedly objective qualities of kinds for which physics has no need."[14]

It is clear how our response to these arguments should begin. It should begin with a concession, followed by a reminder. We should concede that there is no need to accept that colors are qualities that physical objects really possess in order to explain how our experiences of color are produced. And we should add the reminder that this is not a discovery of modern physics: it is implicit in the basic conception of color that our simplest color statements presuppose. But this initial response does not concede that these simple color statements may be uniformly false or that our experience of colors cloaks the physical objects we perceive in a glamorous disguise. These ideas, whatever else can be said in their favor, are certainly not implicit in our basic conception of color, as we have seen. So, it is true that a sketchy grasp of optics is more than enough to dispose of the idea that we can explain why things appear variously colored to various observers by predicating colors of them. But we cannot infer that these predications are always either false or misleading—that is, that these things do not, or do not "really," have colors.

The skeptical conclusion therefore depends on the next step in the argument—the one that involves the philosophical principle of economy of postulation. This is the step that is meant to entitle us to withhold assent to the predications physics does not specifically license us to make. And this is the step we must contest.

More than one reason can be given for contesting it. For example, it has been argued that the physical sciences are themselves products of a specific set of social structures and power relations, which are no more capable of disclosing the true structure of reality than any other local ideology.

None of the arguments to this effect that I have seen appear convincing. In one way or another, they all seem to commit a genetic fallacy—the fallacy of confusing a question about the historical sources of ideas and a question about their truth or validity. It is true that some philosophers purport to renounce these very standards—of truth and validity—themselves. But they face the unenviable task of defining an alternative standard to sustain and measure the value of intellectual exchange—which none has yet managed to do in a remotely plausible way. In theory, they could alternatively also renounce any claim on our attention except for the claim of force. But force plays a smaller role in metaphysics than it did in the days when heretics were burned.

The most telling reason for denying that the principle of economy of postulation provides a reason to deny colors exist is that if we examine this idea with care, we shall find that it relies on a false assumption. Let us begin with a question about the principle's jurisdiction. Which qualities, quantities, and relations should it encourage us to relinquish, and which is it powerless to touch? For example, the label on my t-shirt says that it was made in China. But physics does not sanction the hypothesis that anything is a t-shirt or was made in China. Should this encourage us to abandon the idea that some things are "really" t-shirts rather than socks, or that some t-shirts are "really" made in China rather than in France? Perhaps it should. But the larger question, which we would need to decide in order to settle these others, is what it is about a quality that places it within the remit of the principle of economy of postulation.

To postulate something is to grant it hypothetical existence for a theoretical reason—which means, in the simplest case, for the purpose of explaining an observed effect. For example, a planet with approximately Neptune's orbit was postulated to explain the anomalous orbit of Uranus; and observations subsequently confirmed that it exists. A particle with the same mass as an electron but the opposite charge was postulated by Paul Dirac and discovered experimentally at a later date. Newton postulated universal gravitation—an attractive force between any pair of bodies—to explain the orbits of the planets and their satellites, the paths of projectiles, and the tides. And so on. We normally speak of postulating individual objects, kinds of objects, or forces—as these examples illustrate. But we can just as well speak of postulating a property. For example, postulating universal gravitation is equivalent to postulating gravitational mass.

The principle of economy of postulation applies wherever postulation occurs. Without a way of measuring how economical a theory is, it is tantamount to the imprecise but reasonable demand that we prefer relatively simple explanations to relatively complex ones and relatively parsimonious explanations to relatively extravagant ones.[15] So, on the one hand, Mackie is wrong to gear the principle to physics alone. Physics is not the only science there is, and the properties invoked in explanations in the biological and social sciences do not dissolve or vanish under the more exacting scrutiny of physics. Hence, if physics gives us no reason for predicating a quality of an object, it does not follow that there is no scientific reason for doing so at all. But, on the other hand, the principle of economy of postulation applies wherever an object, a property, or a force is introduced with the specific purpose of explaining an effect. Hence, it applies in physiology, anthropology, and political science—and for that matter in the quotidian explanations that do not form part of any science at all—in the same way as it does in physics.

In general then, and not only in physics, a property will fall within the remit of the principle if the justification for predicating it of an object is that doing so contributes to explaining some effect—which may be, but need not be, on our senses. But we cannot demand economy of postulation if nothing is postulated, and so the principle cannot touch predications that are not meant to be justified in this way. That is not to say that such predications are unimpeachable. No predications are. It is only to say that whatever method we can use to decide whether or not we should accept them, it cannot be estimating theoretical or explanatory costs and gains. For example, I know how to decide whether my aching tooth is the first or second molar (I prod them); and I know how to decide whether 139 is prime (the Sieve of Eratosthenes). I also know that I can make mistakes when I employ these methods and I can check the judgments they lead me to make. But if I do not predicate primeness of 139 or aching of my molar to explain effects, invoking the principle of economy of postulation cannot be the right way to challenge these predications.

It follows that if we claim that colors are subject to the principle of economy of postulation, we are making an assumption about the grounds on which we predicate them of physical objects. We are assuming that—like gravitational mass, electric charge, élan vital, repressed desire, and so on—the role that colors play in our intellectual lives is theoretical or explanatory and hence that predicating them of physical objects can be justified, if it can be justified at all, only in terms of theoretical or explanatory gain. But what reason is there for accepting this assumption? No doubt, there are many cases in which a color is postulated to explain an observed effect. For example, if a white shirt comes back from the laundry pink, it is reasonable to suppose that there was something red in the same wash. But if I predicate a color of an object I can see, what could I be postulating this color to explain?

The answers to this question in the passages quoted above are that the colors of physical objects are postulated to explain (as Williams, Nagel, and Mackie put it) "why things appear variously colored to various observers," to explain "why they appear to have colors," or to explain "our having the sensations and perceptions that we have."

Before I comment on these claims directly, I shall make a preliminary point, to draw out something they imply. The point is that if colors *are* postulated to explain these things, it should be possible by now to say what observations would verify or falsify the hypothesis that they exist and to test the hypothesis experimentally once and for all. It is true that this is often not a simple matter. The existence of Neptune was confirmed quite easily, when Johann Galle found an unknown disk within a degree of Urbain Le Verrier's predictions one night in 1846 and then observed its new position on the following night. But the telescope he used was not a simple instrument. Again, the existence of Dirac's positron was confirmed by the shape and direction of the paths of particles in a cloud chamber at CalTech. This was also a sophisticated piece of machinery, which it took considerable theoretical knowledge to design. But what about colors?

Nagel claims that "the hypothesis that objects have intrinsic colours in addition to their primary qualities . . . provides a poorer explanation of why they appear to have colours . . . than the hypothesis that the primary qualities of objects and their effects on us are responsible for all the appearances."[13] But there is surely something faintly absurd about this. It is not as if we were debating the relative merits of the Ptolemaic and Copernican systems in the 1550s, designing experiments to test the phlogiston theory in the 1770s, or figuring out what testable predictions follow from supersymmetric gauge theories in the 1990s. If it really is a hypothesis that objects have intrinsic colors in addition to their primary qualities, why hasn't this hypothesis been tested? Nagel's use of the phrase "a poorer explanation" and Mackie's appeal to the principle of economy of postulation acknowledge that the decisive experiments have not yet been conducted since we prefer one theory to another because it is simpler or more parsimonious only until one of the two has been disproved. But why not? Have the physicists not applied themselves to the problem seriously enough? Or does the necessary technology not yet exist?

There are two possibilities, neither of which is one of the two I have just mentioned. The first is that the existence of colors *is* hypothetical, but the hypothesis is unfalsifiable and therefore, in a sense, unscientific. The second is that the so-called hypothesis that objects have intrinsic colors is not in fact a hypothesis at all. The first is that colors, like gods, lie too far beyond the ambit of experience for their existence to be decided by experimental science. The second is that, like aches, they lie too securely within it. The first is that predicating a color of a physical object is too fanciful to be tested experimentally. The second is that it is not fanciful enough. The first is that colors are primitive science or pseudoscience. The second is that they are not science at all. These seem to be the only serious answers that we have.

So the larger choice we face about colors is this: we can hold that we predicate colors of physical objects in order to explain why things appear to have colors or why we have the sensations and perceptions that we have and, therefore, hold also, as a corollary, that these qualities are metaphysical—that is, that they are qualities the very thought of which, in Kant's phrase, "oversteps the limits of all experience."[16] Alternatively, we can hold that these statements have no intrinsic explanatory purpose at all and, in particular, that when we predicate colors of the objects we perceive, we are not postulating qualities to explain the experiences occurring in our minds. These are the two alternatives we face. The first view supports the idea that our experience of colors is a pervasive and inescapable illusion, while the second implies that this idea itself is an intellectual myth—an illusion of reason and not a discovery of science.

The choice, I suggest, is an easy one to make. The doctrine that colors are postulated to explain our perceptions cannot be the right way to explain the purpose of our simplest color predications because it contradicts the basic conception of color they presuppose. In particular, it contradicts the principle that colors are inert—that they cannot influence what happens except as a consequence of being seen—because, as we have seen, this implies that our perceptions cannot be explained by the colors of the objects we perceive. And it contradicts the principle that colors are subject to the epistemic jurisdiction of the senses—in other words, that the acid test of an object's color is to look at it—because if I predicated a color of my t-shirt in order to explain the experience I have when I perceive it, then the right way of deciding whether it is red would be to identify the properties that cause the phenomena I am seeking to explain.

Hence, the assumption that the skeptical argument relies on, namely, that colors are postulated to explain experiences, is false. And the reason why no scientific instrument has been built that could test whether colors actually exist is not that colors are occult and impossible to detect. It is that the only "instruments" that can detect them are sentient animals themselves.

~

Galileo's claim, that "if the perceiving creature were removed, all of these qualities would be annihilated and abolished from existence," is still widely accepted. But in fact it is the opposite of the truth. For when the last sentient animal dies, lemons will not suddenly lose their yellow color and their sour taste. But if all of these qualities were removed, sense perception would be annihilated and abolished from existence. Perhaps the purely intellectual cognition that angels are officially held to enjoy would still be possible. But if nothing had any taste we could not taste anything; if nothing had any smell we could not smell anything; if nothing had any color we could not see anything; and so on. This follows directly from the principle that tastes, smells, colors, and so forth are basic properties, relative to the sense we perceive them with: whatever else we taste we taste by tasting tastes; whatever else we smell we smell by smelling smells; whatever else we see we see by seeing colors; and so on.

This does not amount to a reductio ad absurdum of Galileo's claim. It merely shows that if we are mistaken in believing that sensible qualities exist, our naive conception of the senses is mistaken, too. In fact there is a sense, although it is a limited sense, in which the claim that sensible qualities do not exist is unassailable. Returning to the specific case of colors, it is possible to show that the arguments that support the claim that bodies do not have colors are fallacious or that their premises are false. But if we use the word "prove" in the narrow sense in which to prove something is to deduce it from non-question-begging premises, it is not possible to prove either that bodies have colors or that they do not. This is not a regrettable limitation on the powers of reason. It is a direct consequence of the basic conception of colors that our simplest color judgments presuppose.

It is impossible to prove that bodies do have colors, in this narrow sense of "prove," because such a proof would need to show either that Galileo's claim is self-contradictory or that a phenomenon whose existence is not in question cannot possibly be explained except by postulating colors. But the doctrine is not self-contradictory, and since an object's color is part of how it looks, the only phenomena that colors can explain are the thought and behavior of animals that actually perceive them. But of course an argument that purported to prove that colors exist, and that was founded on the premise that some animals actually perceive colors, would be question-begging in a rather obvious way.

This is exactly what we should expect. For since it is part of our basic conception of colors that they are subject to the epistemic jurisdiction of the senses, seeing colors is how we know that they exist. Kant's remark about beauty, which I quoted in the introduction, expresses a similar idea: "I must feel the pleasure directly, in the contemplation of the object, and I cannot be talked into it by any grounds of proof." So it is impossible to prove that my t-shirt is red, in the narrow, logical sense of prove that excludes the "proof of the pudding." But by the same token, it is impossible to prove that it is not red. And it is impossible to prove that no bodies have colors—again, unless our basic conception of colors is self-contradictory, which there is no reason to accept.[17]

This explains why Galileo and his followers could only argue for the nonexistence of colors on the relatively weak—and finally unconvincing—grounds that there is no need to postulate colors in order to explain why our experiences of seeing them occur. The argument is simple, as we have seen. The first premise is that we have no reason to believe (and good reason to deny) that the colors of physical objects explain why they appear to have colors. The second premise is that the colors we predicate of physical objects are postulated to explain why they appear to have colors. And the conclusion drawn from these premises is that we have no reason to believe (and good reason to deny) that the colors we predicate of physical objects exist. I have argued that the defect in this argument is that the second premise is false and that we can see that it is false if we think carefully about the reason why the first premise is true.

When the myth about colors is presented as a matter of absorbing what the scientific study of color perception has taught us it seems difficult to contest because the physical sciences are generally believed to contain the most accurate and objective record in our culture of the structure of the natural world. I share this belief myself. But it needs to be balanced by an acknowledgment—and not just in a general hand-waving sort of way—that mythical notions are quite often woven into the fabric of natural science, where, as Guthrie puts it, they are overlaid with the terminology of rational disciplines and therefore difficult to detect. We shall see this again, more than once, in later chapters.

One of the ways in which this happens is due to the double dependence of science, pointed out by Quine, on language and extralinguistic fact. The myth about colors is a case in point. For if we imagine that colors are postulated to explain perceptions, and if the insight that colors cannot explain perceptions is thought to be a scientific discovery, science will seem to be at odds with the simplest color statements that we make. But both of these steps are bad philosophy and not good science. Colors cannot be impugned for failing to explain our perceptions because this was never something they were meant to do. On the contrary, it is something that our basic conception of color actually excludes; and it is bad practice to sack employees for failing to do things that are inconsistent with their job descriptions.

There is one final question to consider. "I cannot believe," Galileo wrote, "that there exists in external bodies anything, other than their size, shape, or motion . . . which could excite in us our tastes, sounds, and odours." As we have seen, the insight contained in this remark, that our experiences of perceiving sensible qualities are not caused by these qualities themselves, does not support Galileo's skepticism about the existence of colors or contradict the ordinary color statements we naively make. But now the question naturally arises, what significant doctrine does it contradict?

The answer to this question is straightforward. "Colour," Aristotle wrote, "moves the transparent medium, for example, the air, and this, being continuous, acts upon the sense organ."[18] The hypothesis that light is transmitted by a medium was rejected by most scientists during the fertile medieval period in optics; but the idea that colors cause changes in the eye was not. It prevailed until the seventeenth century, when it was demolished by Galileo and Descartes. Galileo's skepticism about the existence of colors outside the sensitive body and Descartes's skepticism about their existence outside the mind are, I suggest, an exaggerated statement of their opposition to this residue of Aristotle's theory of vision, which mixes scientific speculation with conceptual confusion as thoroughly as they did themselves. Perhaps the enormous intellectual effort involved in freeing science from Aristotelianism excuses the exaggeration; but the same excuse does not exist today.

2

FRAMES OF REFERENCE

> If one chooses, one may replace the expression "frame of reference" by "frame of reference of an observer." However, nothing is added to the theory of relativity by any such linguistic transformation.
>
> R. B. Angel

IN ONE OF HIS famous lectures at CalTech, Richard Feynman made fun of philosophers who are prone to say, "Oh, it is very simple: Einstein's theory says all is relative!" I cannot remember hearing a philosopher say this—although perhaps they did in Pasadena in the sixties. But colors have been described as relative to observers, relative to the circumstances in which they are observed, relative to languages, and even as relative to "the human perceptual standpoint" or, less chauvinistically, "the perceptual point of view."[1] As this variety of relativisms suggests, the blanket claim that colors are relative and the blanket denial of this claim are equally unhelpful. We need to ask what, if anything, are colors relative to. This is the first question I shall address in this chapter. The second question is whether the relativity of colors, such as it is, implies that they are less real than shapes or intervals in time.

To begin with, it is a familiar truth in physics that we cannot talk sensibly about spatial and temporal quantities in nature except in the context of a frame of reference, in which they can be measured or observed. For scientific purposes, a frame of reference can be defined as a system of coordinates attached to a body of reference. The system of coordinates may be a set of orthogonal Cartesian axes or a different system. But every system of coordinates is a purely conceptual structure and therefore, as Einstein put it, a free invention of the human mind. By contrast, a body of reference is a physical object, which serves as a conventional standard of rest—such as the earth, the sun, or the "fixed" stars. In combination, these things provide a numerical name or label for each position where an object can be located. So measuring velocity, for example, requires these things: a coordinate system attached to a body of reference and a set of instruments with which to take the measurements, such as a clock and a ruler or a radar.[2]

Now if we compare this with the task of identifying an object's color, what do we find? First, we find that the role of the coordinate system is played by the system of concepts that is used to identify a color, for example, by stating its name. This system of concepts may only distinguish a dozen or so gross colors: red, blue, green, yellow, black, white, and so on. Or it may be considerably more sophisticated, like the color systems invented by Philipp Otto Runge and James Clark Maxwell, which are among the ancestors of the standard systems used in the printing and manufacturing industries today (plate 1).[3] Next, the relative motion of the observer and the object is generally ignored—although light from the distant stars is shifted toward red, because lightwaves are lengthened when the source recedes from the observer. Finally, we do not use instruments analogous to clocks and rulers to detect gross colors because our system of gross color concepts has evolved for use by trichromatic human beings without the aid of samples. But charts are used to identify specific shades, and a color chart is used as a standard for comparison, which is how a ruler is used too: the ruler provides a sample of a specific length, like the sample of each shade of color on a chart.

Let us take this comparison a step further. As I have said, we cannot talk sensibly about spatial and temporal quantities, except in the context of a frame of reference. But it does not follow that these quantities are relative to a frame of reference, for two reasons. First, there may be a privileged frame, which can serve as the measure of reality and truth—for example, a frame in which the so-called fixed stars are at rest. Accordingly, earth may not appear to be in motion, but perhaps it truly is in motion, if it is in motion relative to the fixed stars. Second, the measurement of a spatial extension or a temporal duration may produce the same result in every frame of reference, whichever body of reference we decide to use. For example, special relativity tells us that both the distance in space and the duration of the interval in time between two events are relative to an inertial frame—that is, a frame of reference in which Newton's laws of motion hold true. But it is one of the postulates of special relativity that the speed at which light travels through a vacuum is the same in every inertial frame.

Now returning to colors, we find that the same is true. That is, we cannot identify an object's color except in the context of a frame of reference. But since we generally ignore the relative motion of the observer and the object, the only part of the frame of reference we are generally aware of is the part that is analogous to the coordinate system—that is, our system of color concepts. So the first question about the relativity of colors I shall consider is whether colors are relative to systems of color concepts. I shall then consider the relativity of colors to conditions of observation and, finally, relativity to observers themselves. I shall not discuss relativity to "standpoints" or "points of view," since these terms are very vague and seem to involve some combination or other of the factors I have mentioned.[4] For simplicity, I shall confine my remarks to gross colors, except at the points where this can be misleading.

~

Where the relativity of gross color to a system of gross color concepts is concerned, the relevant facts are these. The colors most English speakers learn to identify by name, and recognize without the use of samples, are tightly constrained by the physiology of the human visual system. As recently as forty years ago, it was widely assumed that colors are carved out of an undifferentiated visual flux by words, or by habits of mind instilled by learning words. For example, Quine claims that "whether some arbitrary interval in the spectrum is *a* color [e.g., red] . . . depends on the casual matter of there being a word for it; and this matter of vocabulary varies from culture to culture."[5] But the evidence does not support this nominalist view.[6] On the contrary, our gross color vision is naturally organized around a set of focal areas, which are centers of variation for each of the gross colors—for example, the range of shades that qualify as paradigmatic examples of the color red. The boundary lines we draw between gross colors are more variable and fluid. But of course they cannot be located very close to the focal areas.

In effect, our perception of gross colors is a product of the relative salience of some differences in spectral reflectance, by comparison with others. For example, the difference in wavelength between 425 and 475 nanometers is the same as the difference between 475 and 525 nanometers. But if the wavelength of light projected onto a screen is gradually changed from 425 to 475 nanometers, there will be very little noticeable change in its color. It will become a slightly brighter shade of blue. Whereas if the light is gradually changed from 475 to 525 nanometers it will change markedly, from blue to green. A bell curve that plots the spectral sensitivity of a single photoreceptor shows how this phenomenon can arise, because the same difference in wavelength will correspond to a greater difference in response on the two steep sides of the curve than on the top. Of course, the mechanisms that explain why our sensitivity

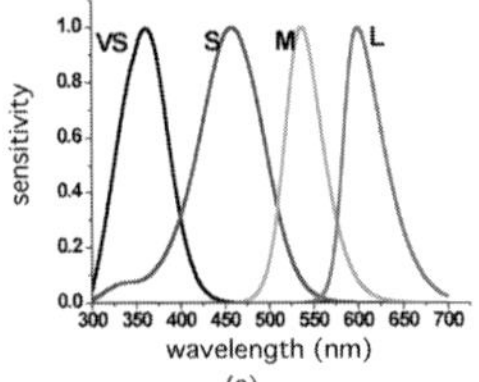

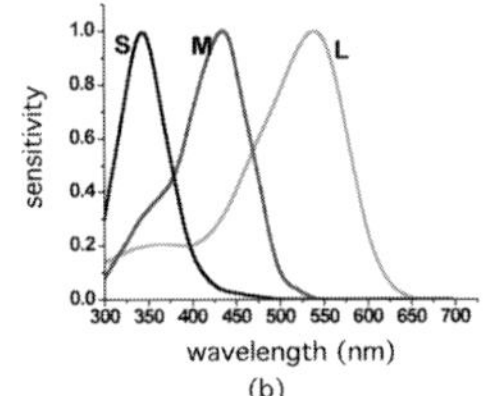

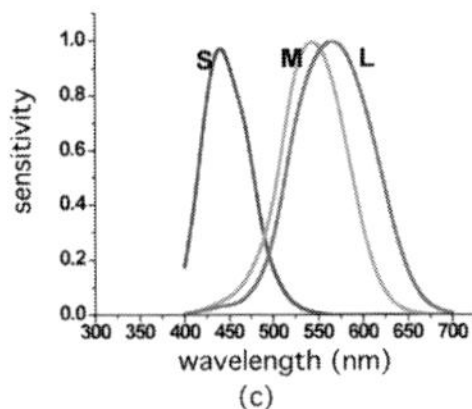

1. Photoreceptor spectral sensitivities of a human, a honey bee (*Apis melifera*) and a blue tit (*Parus caeruleus*). (*VS* = very short; *S* = short; *M* = medium; *L* = long.)

to a fixed difference in wavelength varies along the visible spectrum are very complex. And besides, several of the gross colors we perceive are not spectral colors. So this is a highly simplified model. But it shows how a stimulus varying at a constant rate can elicit an abrupt change in response even in a simple mechanism.

The focal areas at the heart of gross colors and the boundary areas that separate them are, then, the places where we are relatively insensitive and relatively sensitive, respectively, to similar differences in reflectance. However, other vertebrates have color vision, and so do butterflies and bees; and color vision differs from one species to another (fig. 1). In the first place, the photoreceptors of birds and bees are sensitive to lower wavelengths of light than human photoreceptors are. Second, normal human color vision is trichromatic: it depends on three kinds of photoreceptors, each containing a photopigment with a characteristic spectral response curve. Ungulates, such as pigs, sheep, and horses are dichromatic; while birds, and some fish and amphibians, are tetrachromatic. Third, the boundaries we draw between gross colors are a complex function of the spectral response curves of our photoreceptors. So trichromatic animals whose photoreceptors have different spectral response curves from ours will perceive these boundaries in different places from us and will no more be able to see the boundaries we perceive than we are able to see theirs.

Hence, the set of gross colors that English-speakers learn to name is anthropocentric, in the sense that it reflects the color focuses and the approximate boundaries between gross colors that most trichromatic human beings perceive. It is not specifically Anglocentric, or less so than many philosophers and anthropologists once thought. But it is anthropocentric, in a deeper sense than the imperial system of measurements is—with its inches, feet, and yards. For if two objects have the same dimensions in the imperial system, they have the same dimensions in the metric system, or in a system based on the body of a cat. But two objects that are both red or both green need not have the same gross color from a set that is tailored to fit the visual system of another species.

In order to decide whether gross color is relative to a system of color concepts, it will be useful to imagine that the gross color of an object is identified with our familiar anthropocentric system of gross color concepts and, also, with a system devised for a dichromatic species, such as the horse. We shall ignore questions about the conditions of observation and questions about the color experiences or behavior of observers. For the moment, we are only interested in the alleged relativity of gross color to systems of color concepts.

Now imagine that a grassy bank is found to be green when the anthropocentric system is being used and that it is found to be a color that encompasses some shades of red, some shades of green, and some shades of brown when an equine system is used. It may seem as if we could argue as follows: We have seen that there can be two reasons to deny that a spatial or temporal quantity is relative to a frame of reference. First, there may be a privileged frame of reference, such as the fixed stars; and second, measurement may produce the same result in every frame of reference, as it does in the case of the velocity of light. Presumably, the same is true of a quality, such as gross color. But in this case, "measurement" has produced two different results: first green and then an equine gross color, for which we have no name. And there is no reason, apart from chauvinism, to prefer the human system of color concepts. Hence, gross color is relative: it varies from one system of color concepts to another.

If this argument were sound, we should have to say that nothing is green or red without qualification but only relative to a system of color concepts. But in fact the argument is fallacious. For although we found that the grassy bank has two colors—first green and then a nameless equine color—this is not like finding that two measurements of an object's velocity have yielded inconsistent results. It is like finding that an object is located in two overlapping regions. For example, Barnsley is in the Catholic Diocese of Hallam and in the Anglican Diocese of Sheffield. Certainly, these are different regions, but one and the same town can be in both. Hence, we should not say: Barnsely is inside the Diocese of Hallam relative to the Catholic Church, and outside it relative to the Anglican Church. We should say without qualification that it is inside the Diocese of Hallam—and add, if we wish, that this is a Catholic diocese. Similarly, we should not say that the color of the grassy bank is green relative to the anthropocentric system but not relative to the equine system. We should say that it is green without qualification—and add that this is an anthropocentric color.

If we return to the idea of a frame of reference, we shall see why we have obtained this result. We saw that a frame of reference consists of a system of coordinates and a body of reference and that the system of coordinates is a conceptual construct, whereas the body of reference is a physical object. When a physical quantity is said to be relative to a frame of reference, this does not mean that it varies depending on the system of coordinates that is used to measure it. It means that it varies depending on the body of reference that is used as a standard of rest. For example, according to special relativity, if the length of a rod is one meter in an inertial frame in which it is at rest, then its length will be less than one meter in an inertial frame in which it is in motion.[7] But the length of the rod will not differ depending on whether the coordinate system is a set of orthogonal Cartesian axes, an oblique Cartesian system, in which the axes are rectilinear but not orthogonal, or a system in which the axes are curves. As Wittgenstein laconically observed, by a new notation no facts of geography are changed.

Admittedly, the anthropocentric system of gross color concepts is not a coordinate system. If we use it to identify an object's color, this is more like locating a town in a diocese than like giving coordinates in longitude and latitude or an Ordnance Survey grid reference. However, the basic role of the system of concepts in a frame of reference is the same, whether it is mathematical or not. The gross color of an object is therefore not relative to a system of color concepts.

~

I shall turn now from the reference frame to the conditions in which an object's color is observed. The questions here are whether colors are relative to illumination, to the extent and quality of the atmosphere between an object and an observer, or to the background against which an object is seen. For example, suppose that the color of a mountain appears to change from white at midday to pink at dusk; that a distant range of hills looks bluish, by comparison with one that is closer; or that a yellow pigment looks more saturated on a blue ground. Should we say that the colors of these things are relative? For example, should we say that the mountain is white at midday and that it is pink at dusk? Or should we deny these things and privilege one kind of illumination, one distance, and one kind of ground? Should we say that the mountain looks pink at dusk, but that broad daylight reveals its true color, and that proximity reveals the true color of the hills?

I shall begin by making two preliminary observations. First, we cannot deny that an object's color is relative to the conditions in which it is observed unless we can distinguish between the color it looks in various conditions and the color it is. And we cannot draw this distinction unless we can define the conditions in which the color it looks *is* the color it is. A blithe mention of "standard conditions" achieves nothing. For the question is whether there really are such standard conditions and, if so, what they are. Second, we cannot define the conditions in which the color an object looks is the color it is unless one system of color concepts or another is in play. This need not be our familiar system of gross color concepts—red, green, blue, yellow, et cetera. But "the color it is" is just an empty phrase, unless a range of colors has been defined. It is tempting to point at an object and imagine that "the color it is" simply refers to THIS. But the question of what color something is is a question about the identity of its color. And as Wittgenstein pointed out, one does not define a criterion of identity by emphatic stressing of the word "this."

Now as a matter of fact, in many cases, although not by any means in all, we follow the principle that the gross colors of objects are the gross colors they appear to have in daylight. Of course, our color perception is responsive to subtle changes in the intensity and color temperature of light, to its direction and the degree to which it is diffused. But each of our gross colors encompasses so many shades that these subtle changes do not generally affect the gross colors we perceive. In other words, the loose definition of "standard conditions" we implicitly accept corresponds to the broad range of shades of color each gross color includes. But there are many anomalous cases. That is to say, there are many cases in which this principle cannot easily, or cannot possibly, be applied. And it follows that there are many cases in which the distinction between the gross color an object looks and the gross color it is is difficult or impossible to sustain.

For example, J. L. Austin asks: "What is the real colour of the sky? Of the sun? Of the moon? . . . We say that the sun in the evening sometimes looks red—well, what colour is it really? (What are the 'conditions of standard illumination' for the sun?)"[8] As this passage suggests, we often confine ourselves to the question of what color an object looks in one set of conditions or another and discard the question of its real color. And for ordinary purposes, it does not matter whether the idioms we choose appear to relativize the color a thing is or the color it looks—for example, whether we say that the sun in the evening sometimes is red or that it sometimes looks red or whether we say that the hills become bluish at a distance or that they look bluish at a distance. For this is precisely the distinction we no longer make. But the fact that we do not or cannot make this distinction in some cases does not imply that we do not or cannot make it in any cases. And the fact that the daylight principle cannot be used to fix *the* color of an object *simpliciter* does not imply that it cannot be used to fix the gross color of a broad range of colored objects or that it is a kind of fiction, which misrepresents the facts.

In general, then, we tend to be absolutists about gross color—that is, we tend to assign specific gross colors to objects without relativizing these colors to the conditions in which they are observed—first, when standard conditions can be easily defined and, once defined, identified from one occasion to another; and second, when we are more interested in the relatively stable properties of visible objects than in their variable relationship with light. But our conceptual habits tend to be as relaxed and fluid as the case allows, and in this case the latitude is large. So the question of whether gross colors are relative to the conditions in which they are observed does not have the same answer, or even a definite answer, in every case.

Three further points should be noted. First, fine shades of color are less stable than gross colors in varying illumination, as a small boat is less stable than a big one in rough weather. Daylight or "clear gray"—a phrase Cezanne used to describe the kind of weather that he wanted for a sitting—is a sufficiently precise definition of the standard illumination for the gross colors of moderate-sized dry goods. But color systems that distinguish several thousand hues are commonly used in conjunction with a more precisely defined standard light source—for example, a tungsten-filament lamp with a specific color temperature.

Second, as we approach the limit of barely discriminable shades, the definition of a shared system of named or numerically labeled shades becomes less feasible because individual differences make it more difficult for us to agree on the correct use of a standard chart. At the limit, where no system of color concepts is in use, we can still decide whether two color samples are indistinguishable by a given observer in a given light; but the question of what color a sample is simply cannot be raised if no system of color concepts is in play. Hence metamers—that is, matching samples with different reflectances—are relative to observers and conditions of observation. But it is a mistake to infer that the same is true of gross colors. This inference ignores the cardinal principle that specific colors cannot be identified except by means of specific color concepts.

Finally, when we cannot distinguish straightforwardly between the colored object and the illumination, we have no option but to say that the object's color changes with the light. For example, the sky may be uniformly blue at midday and streaked with red and pink at dusk. It makes scant sense to ask which of these is its true color because the color of the sky *is* the color of sunlight that has passed through the atmosphere's diffusing filter.

~

Are colors relative to observers? To begin with, our perceptions of objects obviously depend on both their nature and our own. Returning to an example we considered earlier, if a trichromatic human observer and a horse both see a grassy bank, the gross colors they will see are different: the human observer will normally see the anthropocentric color green, whereas the horse will normally see a color that encompasses some shades of red, some shades of green, and some shades of brown. And the difference between these gross colors will be due to the difference between the human and the equine visual systems.

However, we should not infer that the gross color of the grassy bank is green relative to a trichromatic human being but not relative to a horse. For as we saw earlier there is no reason to deny that it has both colors. Indeed, it is tempting to say that in principle an object has as many gross colors as we care to define, as long as it lies within their boundaries. But the point of defining a gross color is that it can be identified without comparing the object with a sample, and a gerrymandered color cannot satisfy this requirement. So it is better to say that the class of objects with the same gross color encompasses a great family of reflectances—which has, as large families do, some degree of indeterminacy at the margins—and that objects with various reflectances may have the same gross color from an anthropocentric system, while having different gross colors from a system designed for another species.

We should therefore be pluralists about gross color—that is, we should acknowledge that the gross colors we are familiar with are not the only ones it is possible to perceive. But we should not relativize gross colors to observers. For what varies from one kind of animal to another is not the color of the grassy bank but the color that is normally perceived, when it is seen. It is true that a grassy bank normally *looks* green to a man but not to a horse; but we should not infer that it *is* green relative to a man but not a horse. The mistaken idea that we should make this inference stems mainly from forgetting the cardinal principle that we cannot identify an object's color except in the context of a frame of reference. For if we ignore the role of the frame of reference, then instead of thinking, correctly, that the grassy bank is green and that green is a gross color relative to a trichromatic human being, we produce an elision of this thought in our minds and think, instead, that the grassy bank is green relative to a human being.

Thus if we ignore the role of the frame of reference, the idea that colors are relative to observers becomes hard to resist. But once we remember that the frame of reference is indispensable, it is clear that far from the color of an object being relative to observers, observers qualify as such only relative to specific frames of reference. Of course, it is obvious in general terms that only some animals qualify as observers of colors from the mere fact that only some animals are sighted. The less obvious point—although it is surely not much less obvious—is that which animals qualify as observers depends on the frame of reference that is being used. Naturally, a normal trichromatic human being qualifies as an observer relative to the anthropocentric system of gross colors because the system evolved to fit his grip. In general, if we assume, for simplicity, that the gross color of an object is to be identified by unaided observation, an animal will qualify as an observer in the context of a given frame of reference if, and only if, the gross colors that the system provides for are the gross colors which that animal perceives.[9] For the anthropocentric system, standard tests for color vision can be used to decide which people qualify and which do not.

In a sense, we can therefore say that there is a preestablished harmony between qualified human observers and the anthropocentric reference frame in which gross colors are observed. There is nothing mysterious about this, and nothing that should make us wonder whether colors can be real. The mistake is to confuse this with a preestablished harmony between qualified observers and the facts.

That there is this latter kind of preestablished harmony is the substance of Democritus's famous remark, which I quoted at the beginning of chapter 1: "Colours, sweetness, bitterness, exist by convention: in reality, there are atoms and the void." This remark invokes the antithesis between *nomos* (law, convention, custom) and *phusis* (nature), which occupied a central place in philosophical and political debate in Athens in the fifth century B.C.[10] But we do not need to understand the intellectual context of the remark in order to perceive its force. For we are not infallible judges of physical reality; and it must therefore be possible to distinguish between the properties we are severally or jointly willing to predicate of a physical object and the properties it really does possess. In effect, Democritus is claiming that this condition is not satisfied in the case of colors and tastes, and many philosophers have agreed. For example, Hume writes: "The appearance of objects in daylight, to the eye of a man in health, is denominated their true and real colour, even while colour is allowed to be merely a phantasm of the senses."[11]

More recently, Bernard Williams has expressed the same idea, although he follows Democritus in referring to agreement between observers, where Hume refers to the qualified observer in general. "Our distinctions between what seems green and what is green," Williams writes, "are essentially based on agreement within the range of human experience."[12] And P. F. Strawson claims, in a similar vein, that where the ascription of colors is concerned, "the standard of correctness [is] intersubjective agreement."[13] If this is true, our agreement that something is green—at least if it is reached in favorable circumstances—is sufficient to guarantee that it is green. And this dependency of colors on agreement implies that they are not properties that objects really possess.[14]

I shall criticize this doctrine in a moment, but before I do so I shall make a few preliminary remarks and note a point of qualified agreement with

Williams's view. It would clearly be a mistake to say that what is right is never fixed by agreement. For it is, in the case of social norms. For example, the right way to pronounce a word is the way it is generally pronounced by native speakers and the right way to express appreciation is often to clap. Thus we can say about rules of pronunciation, and about various forms of polite behavior, that the right way of doing something is the way that is agreed on in the relevant group. We can even say that the *esse* of a social norm is *percipi*, as long as *percipi* means "being acknowledged" and not "being observed." But—this is the point on which I agree with Williams and many others—where what we agree on determines what is right, the only kind of truth we can intelligibly aspire to is essentially a truth about ourselves. Or, to put the same point in a different way, agreements are the only realities that agreement can produce.

It is self-evident that conventions exist by convention; but it is not self-evident that colors do as well. If we say that they do, we are not bound to hold that the case of colors and the case of politeness are exactly alike. Presumably human nature leaves us with a freer hand to vary social norms, and individual responses are correspondingly determined to a greater degree by custom.[15] But we are bound to hold that if trichromatic observers agree in favorable circumstances that something is green, then it follows, as a matter of logic, that it is.

The claim that agreement fixes the truth about an object's color and the claim that colors are relative to communities of observers are in essence one and the same. Hence, we should expect to find that the former claim projects a feature of our system of gross color concepts onto the colored objects we perceive, just as the latter has been shown to do. And in fact we do find this. As we have seen, our system of gross color concepts is essentially based on our shared disposition to find some differences in spectral reflectance more salient than others. But if a system of concepts is essentially based in this way on agreement in experience, it does not follow that the same is true of the facts this system of concepts used to state. Crimes are defined by laws; and in a democracy laws are fixed by agreement. But the fact that a man has broken the law is not. If it were, the jury's verdict could not be mistaken, and it would be logically impossible to convict an innocent man. But this is not impossible, however favorable the circumstances are in which he is tried.

The same is true in the case of colors. Our anthropocentric system of gross color concepts is fixed by agreement, tightly constrained by the nature of our visual system. Hence, in questions of law—for example, where the approximate boundaries of a gross color lie—we are authoritative. In fact, this is true in a quite literal sense, since if we include our ancestors among ourselves, we are the authors of the concepts that we use, just as we are the authors of our laws. But we are not authoritative in questions of fact. Like every other kind of judgment that we make, our judgments about what seems green and what is green cannot be tested by a jury of angels: human jurors are the only ones we have. But we cannot bestow colors on objects merely by agreeing that they possess them, however sober and responsible we are. In general, that takes a lick or two of paint.

So, where questions about the colors of physical objects are concerned it is reasonable to accept the judgment of qualified and disinterested observers—as it generally is, in questions of fact. But mistakes are conceivable in the most favorable circumstances; no one's impression is irrefragable; and agreement cannot remove the logical possibility of a mistake. In many cases it is true that the broader the agreement we secure, the more confident we are entitled to be that we are right. But there are no circumstances in which a consensus about an object's color is logically guaranteed to be the truth—however extensive the consensus is. Of course, we can if we wish define "favorable circumstances" to mean circumstances in which the consensus of qualified observers is true. But this maneuver does not exclude the logical possibility of error: it merely transfers it to the question of whether these circumstances obtain. We can pull the rug across one gap; but the result is that we expose the other.

It does not follow that we should always feel doubtful about our judgments of color. We should not—any more than we should always feel doubtful about our judgments of shape. Nor does it follow that there are no circumstances in which we could not seriously entertain the possibility that we were wrong. No doubt, there are such circumstances—as there are with shapes. But the question here is not about what ought to satisfy us that an object has a certain color, or even about what ought to convince us absolutely that it does. It is whether there are any circumstances in which the opinion of normal observers—that is, normal trichromatic human beings—carries a logically impervious guarantee of truth. If we distinguish carefully between questions about our color concepts and questions about the facts we use them to state, it is clear that there are no such circumstances—regardless of how much agreement is secured.

It follows that there are both similarities and differences in the way in which judgments about color and judgments about space and time are made. On the one hand, as I noted earlier, we are able to make primitive spatial and temporal judgments without using a ruler or a clock, just as we are able to make judgments of gross color by unaided observation. For example, we can often say which of two past events occurred before the other, or whether two objects are roughly equidistant from a third. These judgments cannot be described as measurements, if the term "measurement" is reserved for the case where an observation is expressed with actual numbers. But they are evidently judgments about space and time.

Furthermore, rulers and clocks refine our ability to make these kinds of judgments by providing samples of lengths and temporal durations, and color samples refine our ability to make color judgments in a similar way. Some philosophers are still inclined to think that we decide on an object's length by an objective technique, namely, measurement, whereas we decide on its color by appealing to the verdict of the mob. But as David Armstrong pointed out long ago, the use of a standard chart to decide on an object's color is no more reliant on the senses or on agreement than the use of a ruler to decide its length. It is true that we have to see that the object's surface has the same color as the sample on the chart, but we also have to see that the object being measured coincides with the points on the ruler.[16]

At the same time, there is an equally important difference between colors and distances or durations, which Armstrong does not mention. For the measurement of space and time can be cut loose from any reliance on perception, in a way that the observation of an object's color cannot. For example, a clock is an instrument that ticks out equal intervals of time; and it need not be designed to match an intuitive sense of temporal duration. But a spectrophotometer cannot decide an object's color, as opposed to its reflectance, unless it has been calibrated to match the sorting behavior or the color judgments of an animal that sees them. As we saw in the last chapter, this follows from the fundamental principle from which this discussion of color set out, namely, that an object's color is part of its appearance—that is, that it is part of how it looks. It is part of the point that I summarized there by saying that colors are subject to the epistemic jurisdiction of the senses.

Hence, where colors are concerned, human observers staff the highest court of appeal; whereas questions about temporal duration can be referred to clocks.[17] This is surely one source of the common intuition that Democritus was right. For it is tempting to say: "Since there is no implacable machine to overturn the verdict of our senses, we have a free hand! These things are up to us!" But this is a mistake. We might just as well say: "Since there is no god Chronos to overturn their verdict, how long it takes to boil an egg is up to the clocks!" It is true that agreement among observers leaves us in no doubt that grass is green, and agreement among clocks leaves us in no doubt that eggs are boiled in five minutes at sea level. But the statement that grass is green is not a covert generalization about observers, any more than the statement about eggs is a covert generalization about clocks.[18]

~

I shall turn now from the question of whether colors are relative to concepts, conditions of observation or observers, to the question of whether the relativity of colors, such as it is, impugns or diminishes their reality. The most stringent view we can take on this question is that if a property is relative to a frame of reference, we are immediately bound to exclude it from a scientific conception of the real world. This view was famously expressed by Hermann Minkowski, in the 1908 paper in which special relativity was given its four-dimensional formulation: "Henceforth, space by itself, and time by itself, are doomed to fade away into mere shadows, and only a kind of union of the two will preserve an independent reality."[19] More prosaically, although special relativity relativizes the spatial and temporal intervals between two events to an inertial frame, there is a function of these two quantities, called the "space-time interval," which is the same in every inertial frame.

However, despite Minkowski's poetic remark, special relativity does not imply that space or time is an illusion. If we imagine that it does imply this, we are confusing the distinction between absolute and relative and the distinction between reality and illusion. For example, special relativity does indeed imply that simultaneity is relative to an inertial frame; but far from implying that simultaneity is an illusion, it provides a well-defined method for deciding whether two events are simultaneous. Some philosophers have argued that time is an illusion: that no man is really born before his children and that no battle really begins before it ends. But whatever can be said in favor of this doctrine, special relativity does not imply that it is true.

A more moderate view is that if a property is found to be relative to a system of concepts or to observers, we can no longer hold that it is real. I accept this view, simply because it is obvious, as I have said already, that we are not, even collectively and even in the most favorable circumstances, infallible judges of physical reality. At most, we are infallible judges—in a limited range of circumstances—of our own thoughts and sensations and of the meanings of the things we say. Hence, we are bound to accept that the properties really possessed by the physical objects we perceive cannot depend on the properties we think they possess, the properties they seem to us to possess, or the terms in which we choose to describe them. For example, if a grassy bank really does have one gross color rather than another, its gross color cannot depend on the system of gross color concepts that we use or on the gross colors we perceive.

If this moderate view is correct, it is precisely the claims about the relativity of colors that impugn their reality that turn out to be false. The chromatic color of a light source is relative to the inertial frame in which it is observed, and in many cases, the color of an object is relative to the atmosphere or light in which it is observed. But gross colors are not relative to systems of concepts or to observers. The thought that they are is a confused way of registering the fact that our system of gross color concepts is anthropocentric, that is, that the colors it defines are gross colors relative to trichromatic human beings.

This anthropocentric system of gross color concepts provides us with a way of identifying gross colors that reflects the characteristics of our visual system and, thereby, of the environment in which it evolved, as plainly as the B.C./A.D. reference frame for dates reflects the recent history of mankind. The significance of the gross colors we perceive is therefore very local. All but a tiny part of the cosmos is indifferent to colors in general; and since the class of animals that perceives the same gross colors as a normal trichromatic human being is tiny by comparison with the class of sighted animals, the significance of these particular colors is more limited still. For example, if a bull is enraged by a matador's cape, the explanation cannot be that the cape is red, since a bull literally cannot see red.

However, the contrast between local and global is not the same as the contrast between illusion and reality. Like our visual system itself, our system of color concepts has evolved to perform a variety of related tasks, in a variety of related circumstances. Naturally, these tasks and circumstances are human tasks and human circumstances. Of course, the same is true of all of the concepts that we use, including the most rarified parts of mathematics. But some tasks are more limited in scope and more provincial than some others. My local midwife is as competent as the Minister of Health, but her expertise is more specific and the domain in which she works is smaller. Something similar could be said about colors and shapes. Neither has a greater claim to reality, but one exerts its influence on a much larger stage.[20]

~

It is time to wrap up this discussion of the relativity of colors. In the last chapter, I examined the main argument that is thought to support the doctrine that colors are illusory, the argument that stems from the idea that the colors of objects do not explain the experiences of color that occur when we perceive them. In this chapter, I have considered whether the same conclusion can be derived from premises that, in one way or another, revolve around the supposed relativity of colors. The arguments that suggest that it can be so derived are more varied and perhaps more complex, but they are not more cogent. In general terms, they depend on a failure to appreciate the significance of the fact that colors cannot be identified except in the context of a frame of reference; on a failure to distinguish with sufficient care between systems of concepts and the facts or truths they are used to express; and on a tendency to slide between a number of distinctions: between reality and illusion, between absolute and relative, between natural and conventional, and between global and local explanatory force.

The truth that lies behind these errors is that our color concepts are anthropocentric. This is the fact that, seen through a distorting lens, seems to diminish the reality of the colors we perceive. Thus, suppose we confine ourselves, for simplicity, to a single dimension of variation in color. As we have seen, there is a striking contrast between the constant rate of change in wavelength from one end of the visible spectrum to the other and the broad bands of approximately homogeneous color we perceive. Wavelengths of light do not vary continuously: the ancient motto *natura non facit saltum* is not true. But the imperceptible jumps that nature makes progress across the boundaries between gross colors at an even rate; and our perception of the gross colors in the visible spectrum is explained by the unequal salience—that is, salience to us—of equal intervals along her path. It follows that there is no independent sanction for our system of gross color concepts—independent, that is, of ourselves. In Plato's extraordinary phrase, our color concepts do not "carve nature at the joints"—or rather, they do, but this is human nature, and not the nature of the visible objects we perceive.[21]

This train of thought seems to me to be correct, and Plato's phrase provides an apt way of saying where it leads. The mistake is to infer that colors are not real. For Plato's metaphor is not about reality and illusion: it is about explanatory force. The fact it records, in this particular case, is that our system of gross color concepts can be used to explain the behavior of human beings and of other animals that perceive the same gross colors as we do but that it cannot be used to explain the behavior of the colored objects we perceive. Of course, we noted this fact and examined its significance in the previous chapter. But as we saw there, it does not support the doctrine that colors are not real or that they are properties of our experiences, which we project onto the visible objects we perceive.

3

PERCEIVING POWERS

THE THEORY OF COLORS defended in John Locke's *Essay concerning Human Understanding* is familiar in outline to many historians of art because Ruskin appealed to it in the first volume of his *Modern Painters* to prove that color is less important in painting than form: "The artist who sacrifices or forgets a truth of form in the pursuit of a truth of colour," he concludes, "sacrifices what is definite to what is uncertain, and what is essential to what is accidental."[1] Notice that Ruskin does not say, "sacrifices what is real to what is illusory, and what is in the body to what is in the mind." For whereas Descartes claims that colors "are clearly and distinctly perceived when they are regarded merely as sensations or thoughts," Locke maintains that they are "real qualities in the subject," meaning by "the subject" not the person seeing a physical object but the physical object that he sees (2.8.10).[2] This seems to readmit into the physical world those flimsy qualities that Galileo and Descartes had expelled, but actually it does not. For Locke argues that these "real qualities" are merely powers to produce sensations in our minds.

This delicate adjustment to his predecessors' doctrine is attractive for two reasons. First, by reducing colors to properties he believes modern science can accommodate rather than eliminating them from his catalog of the physical world, Locke avoids having to defend the blunter claim that our simplest color statements are uniformly false. Second, Locke's theory explains the intrinsic tie between color and sentience in a lucid and simple way.[3] For it implies that colors are subjective, in the sense explained at the beginning of this book. As I said there, a subjectivist about beauty maintains that if an object is beautiful, this can only be because of the response it tends to arouse or the reaction it tends to provoke in a particular individual or group. Locke holds that colors are subjective, in this sense. For example, he holds that the red color of an apple is its power to produce the sensation of red in the mind of a sentient being. Hence, what color it is depends on what sensation it produces, when it is seen.

Locke's theory of colors can be taken in two ways. Taken in one way, it is basically a terminological variant of the ostensibly bolder view of Galileo and Descartes that the colors we innocently predicate of physical objects do not exist. Taken in the other way, it purports to explain our basic conception of colors, in a manner that allows these innocent predications to be true. I shall argue that the first interpretation conforms more closely with Locke's own position, although the second corresponds to a view that is commonly held (and sometimes attributed to Locke himself) by neo-Lockeans today. I shall then argue that the neo-Lockean view is untenable and that the doctrine that colors are subjective is untrue.

~

Locke's *Essay* is the principal modern source of the doctrine that colors are powers or, as we say now, dispositions. Some of Locke's remarks about color contradict some others, and it is not a simple task to decide on the best line of fit. However, his key idea is that colors are powers to produce sensations: "*colours* . . . and other the like sensible qualities . . . are in truth nothing in the objects themselves, but powers to produce various sensations in us" (2.8.14).[4] The concept of power is twofold. An active power is an ability to cause a certain kind of change; a passive power is a liability to undergo a certain kind of change. So the exercise of an active power is an action *by* a substance, and the exercise of a passive power is a change *in* or *to* a substance. Colors, Locke maintains, are active powers; but they are active powers of a particular sort, namely, ones whose exercise consists in producing sensations in our minds.

This claim immediately raises two questions: first, how do objects cause these sensations to occur? and, second, what exactly are the sensations themselves? Locke's answer to the first question is that objects cause sensations of color "by the bulk, figure, texture, and motion of their insensible parts" (2.8.10). These microphysical properties affect the light that colored objects reflect, and the impact on our eyes of this reflected light produces "some motion . . . thence continued by our nerves . . . to the brains, or the seat of sensation, there to *produce in our minds the particular ideas we have of them*" (2.8.12).[5]

It is harder to pin down Locke's conception of the sensation caused by a colored object. Sometimes, he seems to think of it as the awareness of the object itself—clothed in its appearance by the mind. At other times, he seems to think of it as cognitively empty—as a kind of blank sensory effect.[6] But whichever idea predominates in the *Essay*, Locke did not think of the sensation caused by a colored object as the perceptual awareness of a "real quality"—a quality that it really does possess. He makes this negative claim, somewhat obscurely, in the following way: "The *ideas, produced* in us *by* these *secondary qualities, have no resemblance* of them at all. There is nothing like our ideas, existing in the bodies themselves. They are in the bodies, we denominate from them, only a power to produce those sensations in us" (2.8.15).

Locke's use of the word "resemblance" here is misleading, whichever conception of sensation he has in mind, for a perception of a quality is not an idea that resembles the quality perceived. For example, shape is a primary quality; so in Locke's view there *is* something resembling our ideas of shape in bodies themselves. But a perception of the shape of a lump of sugar does not resemble a cube. The thought that it does stems from the confused notion that a perception is itself a kind of image or picture, coupled with the idea that pictures resemble the objects they represent. Nevertheless, the thought expressed in Locke's remark is clear. Colors are not visible properties of the objects that possess them; and my sensation of color does not have a better claim to be described as a perception than the tickle a feather causes in my nose.

Officially, then, Locke does not deny that the colors we seem to perceive in bodies really exist—unlike Galileo and Descartes. His official position, to take one of his own examples, is that sensations of sweetness and whiteness are not really in the manna; but its sweetness and whiteness, which are powers to produce these sensations, are. These powers are not, of course, in the manna in the way that soup is in a tin, or in the way that salt is in a soup: they are in the manna in the sense that they are properties that it really does possess. They are, as he puts it, "real qualities in the subject," that is, in the physical objects and substances to which we attribute colors and tastes (2.8.10).[7] But Locke is aware that the real qualities he admits into the physical world are not the ones we innocently have in mind when we describe something as sweet or white;

and he believes that the qualities we do have in mind are fictions. That is why he sometimes strays from his official line and writes, for example, "sweetness and whiteness are not really in the manna" (2.8.18).

Locke's theory of colors therefore entails as radical a revision of our thought about the natural world as Galileo's or Descartes's. For a philosopher who denies, as these two both did, that physical objects are colored need not object to the claim that they have powers to produce sensations of color, unless he also denies that powers or sensations of color exist; and he need not object to transferring the names of colors to these powers. Locke holds that colors, properly conceived, are "real qualities in the subject"; but the proper conception of colors he envisages is not the one that our simplest color judgments presuppose, and these judgments—unlike the subtler ones philosophy enables us to make—are, in his view, uniformly false.

However, it has recently become common for philosophers to hold both that colors are powers or dispositions to produce sensations of color and that they are visible properties of bodies, which we normally perceive when these experiences occur. For example, John McDowell accepts Locke's doctrine that colors are "powers to produce various sensations in us"; but he claims that this doctrine is consistent with regarding these sensations as "perceptual awareness of properties genuinely possessed by the objects that confront one."[8] The attraction of this view is that, if it is true, we can accept Locke's doctrine without opposing it to our innocent conception of the natural world, as Locke himself did. On the contrary, we can see it as teasing out what is already contained in this conception by placing in clear view a connection it already embodies, between the concepts of color and perception.[9]

According to the neo-Lockean view, therefore, the sharp dissonance that was held to exist between appearance and reality by the great philosophers and natural scientists of the seventeenth century—by Galileo, Boyle, and Newton, no less than by Descartes and Locke—modulates into harmony. Both harmony and dissonance have their attractions, but I shall argue that in this case the attempted reconciliation fails. I shall give two reasons. The first is epistemological: it has to do with our knowledge or awareness of colors; and the second is semantic: it has to do with the meanings of color words.

The first reason is that powers are potencies, not acts. The idea of a power is about what can potentially occur or what would occur in certain circumstances: it is not about what is actually occurring. But we cannot see *cans* or *woulds*, any more than we can taste them or feel them on our tongues. We can see the exercise of a power—that is, the corresponding act. For example, we can see a strong man shift a heavy weight. And we can also see the physical constitution that gives him the ability to shift it—his bulging muscles and his bulky frame. But as Locke acknowledged, our eyes cannot encounter the ability itself: his strength is not something we can see. Hence, if colors were powers, abilities, or dispositions, they would not be visible properties of bodies, and none of our experiences of color would be perceptions.

Some philosophers have rejected this argument. Barry Stroud, for example, denies that colors are powers or dispositions, but he does not accept this argument because (taking the example of a passive power) "a reasonably informed person who watches what goes on in a teacup can see a lump of sugar to be soluble, or see that it is soluble."[10] However, this remark misses the point of the objection. We talk of seeing objects and properties and of seeing *that*—as in, for example, "I can see the white color of the sugar" and "I can see *that* the sugar is white." But these things cannot be equated. For example, I may see that the bite on Flora's ankle is itching when I see her scratching it. But a bite is visible whereas an itch is not. Again, it is easy enough to see that it is dark. But if we concede this we can still maintain that the phrase "darkness visible" is contradictory, as Milton intended it to be.[11] The point of the objection is not that if colors were powers we could not see that something is red: it is that we could not see colors themselves—for example, the red color of the t-shirt I am wearing now.

Once this is understood, it is clear that the rebuttal fails. For although there can be no objection to saying that a reasonably informed person can see that a lump of sugar is soluble, that a man is strong or that he is a skillful draftsman, it does not follow, and it is not true, that she can see a lump of sugar's solubility, or a man's strength, or his skill. We can see that something is possible, say, that this pair of shoes would fit into this box; and we can see that something is probable or inevitable, say, that this bridge will probably collapse or that this lump of sugar will inevitably dissolve. But we cannot see powers or dispositions themselves. Like probabilities, they can be known but they cannot be sensed.[12]

The second reason why the doctrine that colors are powers cannot be reconciled with the principle that they are visible properties of the objects we perceive is that active powers can only be defined by specifying what they are powers to cause. Hence, if colors were powers to produce sensations, the use of the predicate "*x* is red" would have to be explained as follows. The predicate, we would have to say, is applied in the first instance to sensations, and it is applied to objects in the public realm by causal analogy—in the way that spinach is described as a healthy food because it contributes to the health of someone who eats it, and a thumbscrew is described as a painful instrument because it has the function of causing pain. We would have to say that its use is transferred—as it is in both of these cases—from effect to cause. This is certainly Locke's view: "*Flame* is denominated *Hot* and *Light; Snow White* and *Cold;* and *Manna White* and *Sweet,* from the *Ideas* [i.e., the sensations] they produce in us" (2.8.16). But this is simply a dogma, which our experience of teaching and learning language uniformly disproves. On the contrary, "red" is applied in the first instance to red bodies, surfaces, and light and is applied by analogy to sensations. For example, a red afterimage is described as red because seeing a red afterimage is like seeing a reddish mark or patch of light.[13]

Most contemporary philosophers acknowledge that the use of color words to describe sensations derives from their use to describe nonmental objects, and not vice versa. But neo-Lockeans deny that this order of precedence in the use of color words implies that colors are not dispositions. For example, Colin McGinn argues that if we hold that colors *are* dispositions, "we are explaining the instantiation of a quality in terms of the production of experiences [that] consist in representing the world as having certain qualities . . . so naturally we shall need to use predicates of the external world in specifying them."[14] But although McGinn is right to deny that there is anything inherently absurd in explaining the instantiation of a quality in terms of the production of experiences that consist in representing the world as having certain qualities, this observation does not rebut the objection to the neo-Lockean view.

Suppose, for example, that a drug has the disposition to cause hallucinations of seeing wild animals. We identify this disposition by specifying the experience that substances that possess it cause; and since an experience of seeing wild animals represents the world as having certain qualities (i.e., as containing wild animals in the vicinity of the affected person), we use predicates of the external world to specify this experience—namely, "*x* is wild" and "*x* is an animal." The application of these predicates to the public realm comes first of all; but this does not prevent their use to specify the experience from being prior to their use to identify the disposition. For they are applied first to wild animals, then to experiences of seeing wild animals, and finally to drugs that cause these experiences to occur. In effect, we arrive at the idea of the disposition in two stages: first we specify the experience in terms of the qualities it represents the world as having and then we identify the disposition in terms of this experience.

The difficulty arises when the disposition is itself the very quality that the experience is supposed to represent the world as having, as it is, by hypothesis, in the case of colors. In this case, we cannot arrive at the idea of the disposition (i.e., the color) in these two stages because at the first stage the experience needs to be specified in terms of the quality it represents the world as having and this quality is the disposition (i.e., the color) itself. So if we hold that colors are dispositions we cannot consistently maintain both that the public use of a predicate such as "*x* is red" comes first and that its use to specify the experience of seeing the color red is prior to its use to identify the disposition to cause this kind of experience to occur. The doctrine that colors are dispositions to produce the experience of seeing colors—that is, experiences of seeing these dispositions themselves—sets these two requirements on a collision course. Hence, this rebuttal of the objection fails.

These arguments converge on the same conclusion, namely, that if colors are visible properties of the objects we perceive, they cannot be powers. Like several other philosophical ideas inherited from the seventeenth century, the doctrine that colors are reducible to dispositions has been made more palatable to philosophers—or at least those with an eirenic disposition—at the cost of being made less bold. But the exchange turns out to be unfeasible. If an object's color is part of its appearance—that is, if it is part of how it looks—the doctrine that colors are dispositions must be false.

This conclusion should not come as a surprise. For we anticipated it (in chapter 1) when we first considered the basic principle that an object's color is part of its appearance, that is, that it is part of how it looks. As we saw there, this principle implies the property attributed to an object by saying that it is yellow is like the property attributed to it by saying that it looks square or looks like a banana. And similarly, if the smell or taste of a substance is how it smells or tastes, the property attributed to it by saying that it is sour is like the property attributed to it by saying that it smells burnt or tastes like vinegar. But the verbs "looks [square/like a banana]," "smells [burned]," and "tastes [like vinegar]" are not causative verbs like the verbs "boiled," in the sentence "Joe boiled the milk," and "broke," in the sentence "Sam broke the vase." They are copular verbs, like "is [pretty]," "becomes [tired]," and "stays [still]." Hence, the question of how something smells or tastes cannot be the same as the question of what it causes, and neither can the question of its color.

~

For a relatively brief period in the history of philosophy, many philosophers denied that objects and events have spatial and temporal properties independently of their relationship with sentient beings. Kant, the preeminent advocate of this doctrine, claimed that "if the [perceiving] subject . . . be removed, the whole constitution and all the relations of objects in space and time, nay space and time themselves, would vanish."[15] But this astonishing doctrine (to which I shall return in chapter 10) was based on the mistaken belief that geometry and arithmetic are bodies of a priori knowledge about space and time; and there is no immediate prospect of it flourishing again, in either philosophy or science.

Colors are different. Galileo's claim that "if the perceiving creature were removed, all of these qualities would be annihilated and abolished from existence" is accepted by many philosophers and scientists today; and the philosophers who deny this and prefer to maintain with Locke that colors are "real qualities in the subject" commonly claim either that colors can be reduced to the dispositions of physical objects to produce sensations of color, as Locke himself did, or that they can be reduced to the physical properties that underlie these dispositions, such as microphysical structures or reflectances.[16] ("Reduced to" here means identified with, not merely correlated with.) I shall make some final observations about these two kinds of reductionism before returning to the general question of how colors and experiences of color are related.

Galileo and Descartes were perfectly comfortable with the thought that our simplest color statements are uniformly false. For example, Descartes says that our tendency to think that colors are in bodies is the result of confusions that begin in childhood.[17] Both kinds of reductionism are designed to avoid acknowledging the existence of properties that physical science abjures, without explicitly embracing this affront to common sense. But they are both inconsistent with the principle that colors are visible properties of the objects that possess them, if they exist at all. We have already confirmed this in the case of Locke's doctrine, that colors are "powers to produce various sensations in us." It is equally true of the claim that colors can be reduced to reflectances, to the microphysical structures that explain reflectances, or in general to whichever properties of objects are thought to explain why our experiences of color occur. For since these properties are invisible, these claims invariably imply that colors are invisible as well.

On the one hand, an object's reflectance is invisible because it is a disposition. It is the object's disposition to reflect light of certain wavelengths and to absorb light of other wavelengths. And as we have seen, since dispositions are potentialities we cannot see them. It is possible to see that an object has a certain kind of reflectance. For example, I can see that a piece of charcoal absorbs light of all the wavelengths in the visible spectrum because I can see that it is black. But seeing that something has a property cannot be equated with seeing the property itself, and powers are not properties that can be seen.

On the other hand, the microphysical structures of bodies that explain their reflectances are invisible simply because they are so small. I have heard it proposed in all seriousness that our experiences of color are a blurry record of these microphysical structures, which are too fine-grained to be resolved by the naked eye. This might have been an excusable error when the microscope was a recent invention, but today it shows a deplorable ignorance of the scales involved. The naked eye can resolve a grain of sand at five meters, just. But if we think of the microstructure that explains color as a kind of texture or granularity, it is ten thousand times finer. Moreover, if the structure that explains color were visible, the structure that explains the eye's refractive properties would also be visible, and this would prevent us from seeing anything beyond our eyes at all.

It follows that reductionism about colors, whichever form it takes, cannot be regarded as a satisfactory explanation of the basic conception of colors that our simplest color statements presuppose. It is a separate question how best to define the physical properties of objects that correspond to our experiences of seeing specific colors, but this problem in optics does not concern us here.

~

In the introduction, I presented the conflict between subjectivism and objectivism by means of a series of questions: Is an act pious because the gods approve of it, or do the gods approve of it because it is pious? Is an object beautiful because of the response that it arouses in us when we perceive it, or does it arouse this response in us because it is beautiful? Is sugar sweet because of the experience it produces in us when we taste it, or does it produce this experience in us because it is sweet? Is an apple red because of the experience it produces in us when we see it, or does it produce this experience in us because it is red?

All of these questions invite us to define what Gombrich called "the beholder's share." They invite us to choose between a claim like Aristotle's, "We desire the object because it seems good to us, rather than the object's seeming good to us because we desire it," and one like Spinoza's blunt riposte: "In no case do we strive for, wish for, long for, or desire anything, because we deem it to be *good,* but on the other hand we deem a *thing* to be good, because we *strive* for it, wish for it, long for it, or desire it."[18] But although these remarks have a magnetic force, it may be possible to resist them both. For one lesson we can learn from the theories of color I have examined is that the alternatives presented by these questions have generally been understood in ways that make them less symmetrical than they look. As I shall explain in a moment, this has encouraged some philosophers to search for a kind of equality of status, or reciprocity, which would deny precedence either to the property or to the response.

The asymmetry I have just mentioned is due to the different ways in which the word "because" can be meant and understood. On the one hand, the "because" in "an apple is red because of the experience it produces in us when we see it" is treated as an analytical "because" by the philosophers who accept this proposition.[19] That is to say, the proposition as a whole is about what kind of property redness is. For example, "an apple is red etc." is not meant to explain what causes an apple to be red. It is meant to express the idea that phenomenalism about colors is true: roughly speaking, that colors are the possibilities for experience that bodies, surfaces, and light possess.

On the other hand, the word "because" in "a red apple produces an experience of redness in us because it is red" is treated by the philosophers who accept this proposition as a causal "because," so that the proposition purports to say how the experience of color is produced. Understood in this way, this proposition was accepted by Aristotle, who held that the red color of an apple is an irreducible quality, which modifies the air between the apple and the eye, and also by the twentieth-century philosophers who held that the red color of an apple is reducible to the microstructure of its skin, which modifies the ambient light to an observer's eye.

Now since the "because" is equivocal in this way, some philosophers have argued that it is possible to hold both that our experiences of color normally occur because of the colors of the objects we perceive and that these object have these colors because of the experience they produce. David Wiggins defends this view, both about colors and about values. "Maybe it is the beginning of real wisdom" he writes, "to see that we may have to side against both Aristotle and Spinoza here and ask: 'Why should the *because* not hold both ways round?'"

> Surely it can be true both that we desire *x* because we think *x* is good, and that *x* is good because *x* is such that we desire *x*. It does not count against the point that the explanation of the "because" is different in each direction. . . . There is an analogy for this suggestion. We may see a pillar-box as red because it is red. But also pillar-boxes, painted as they are, *count* as red only because there actually exists a perceptual apparatus (e.g., our own) that discriminates, and learns on the direct basis of experience to group together, all and only the actually red things.[20]

These remarks are suggestive, but what precisely do they suggest? Consider first the claim that we may see a mailbox as red because it is red. It may be perfectly correct to say, for example, "The pillar-box does not look red because of a trick of the light: it looks red because it is red." This statement may be true if it is simply meant to rule out the abnormal explanation and to insist that we are perceiving the mailbox's true color. But if it is meant to explain how the perception of color is produced, then it is false. For as we saw in chapter 1, the color of a pillar-box does not cause this perception to occur. In this respect, as in the others we have noted, the color of an object differs from its shape. In order to explain why an apple looks round, we need to refer to the apple's shape, because the shape of the apple affects the structure of the ambient light to the observer's eye; and this in turn explains why it looks round. By contrast, the apple's color does not affect the ambient light at all. Hence, Wiggins's remark—that we may see a pillar-box as red because it is red—is true if it means that the color of a pillar-box is a quality we can perceive. But it is false if it means that the color causes our perceptions.

Consider next the claim that pillar-boxes, painted as they are, count as red only because there actually exists a perceptual apparatus (e.g. our own) and so forth. In this case, it is the phrase "count as red" that is problematic. Does it mean the same as "are red"? Or does it mean the same as "are counted or classified as red"? In other words, is Wiggins claiming that pillar-boxes, painted as they are, would not be red if a perceptual apparatus like ours did not exist? Or is he making the more modest claim that they would not be classified as red in these circumstances? These claims are certainly quite different. Being red is not like being a token or a gift—where *being* and *being counted as* are roughly the same. But whereas the second claim is evidently true—nothing would be classified as red, if no creatures could discriminate red things and learn to group them together—the first is false. For if it were true, we should have to say that pillar-boxes, painted as they are, will cease to be red when the last creature with our kind of perceptual apparatus dies.

Hence, on the one hand, the quoted passage as a whole may be intended to suggest both that the red color of a pillar-box is a quality we can perceive and that if its color could not be perceived, it could not be classified as red. In this case, the passage is true. But the truth is a meager one, which cannot advance us far toward real wisdom. On the other hand, the passage may be intended to suggest both that our experiences of color are normally caused by the colors of the objects we perceive and that the colors we perceive would not exist if no animals were able to perceive them. In this case, as we have seen, it is doubly false.

This, I submit, indicates the right way to side against both Aristotle and Spinoza. Rather than asking why the "because" should not hold both ways round, as Wiggins does, we should deny that it holds either way round. In the case of goodness, it is not generally true that we desire *x* because it seems good to us or that *x* seems good to us because we desire it. And in the case of color, it is never true that an apple is red because of the experience it produces in us when we see it or that it produces this experience in us because it is red. We can deny precedence either to the property or to the response not because each explains the other in some sense of the adaptable word "explain" but because, in general, both have the same explanation. For example, if I desire an apple because of its sweet taste, then it seems good to me for the same reason. And if an apple is red because of the microstructure of its skin, then it makes me see its red color for the same reason. On this point, as we have seen, Galileo was right against Aristotle. The invisible structure of matter causes us to see an object's color: its color does not have this effect on us itself.

If this is the right way to think about colors, subjectivism is false. For if an apple is red, this is not because of the experience it tends to produce in any individual or group. But is objectivism true? Is it true that an apple's color is independent of the experience it produces? Here we need to distinguish. On the one hand, there are no circumstances in which the opinion of observers about an apple's color, or the experience it produces in their minds, carries a logically impervious guarantee of truth. On the other hand, colors are subject to the epistemic jurisdiction of the senses. In other words, there is no appeal beyond the experience of color that could overturn its verdict. If this is right, the correct view about colors can be described as a qualified objectivism, since colors are in this sense logically independent of our perceptions of color but not epistemically independent of them. Experience is the highest court of appeal where the colors of objects are concerned, but it does not and cannot fix the facts.

DEPICTION

4

ART AND IMITATION

The essence and the definition of painting is the imitation of visible objects by means of form and colours.

Roger de Piles

DEFINING A CONCEPT can be rather like the task of defining the boundaries of a state. Instead of locating it in a hierarchy of concepts, like a Linnaean tree, we try to map the boundary lines that separate it from its neighbors. Indeed these boundaries sometimes seem to be held in place by the pressure exerted on each other by neighboring concepts, like the pressure exerted on each other by contending states.[1] In the case of depiction, there are two such conceptual pressures, and we therefore need to examine two pairs of opposed or contrasting concepts: first, the concept of a picture of an object and the concept of a copy or replica, and second, the concept of the experience of seeing a picture of an object and the concept of the experience of seeing the object itself, face to face. Both of these pairs of concepts generate borderline cases—cases that mark, with unavoidable inexactness, the limits or boundaries of pictorial art.

First, there are musical imitations—of birdsong, for example. Some philosophers have argued that musical phrases that imitate birdsong are representations—like pictures, but in the medium of sound. Others have insisted that they are just mimicry, reproducing sounds to the extent that the instruments used and the conventions of musical form allow but not representing them at all.[2] Second, there are photographs. Some hold that photographs are pictures drawn by light—the pencil of nature, in Fox Talbot's phrase—while others deny that photographs represent the things we see in them at all. For example, Roger Scruton argues that "photography is not a representational art" because "the photograph is transparent to its subject."[3] In other words, seeing something in a photograph is rather like seeing it through a windowpane.

Each of the two main theories of depiction focuses on one of these pairs of concepts and tries to define the boundary that corresponds to it. The resemblance theory is the earlier of the two and was unchallenged by philosophers until Descartes. It says that a picture is a work of imitation and that the difference between a picture and a copy or replica is that a picture is a marked surface that imitates the visible forms and colors of the kinds of objects it depicts but not their internal structures. The illusion theory, which was originally advanced by Descartes, says that a picture is a marked surface that produces the experience that is normally caused by seeing an object of the kind depicted—that is, that it imitates the effect of a visible object on the senses rather than the object itself. These basic ideas have been elaborated and qualified in various ways, with the result that many variations on both theories exist.

In the next four chapters, I shall examine these two theories in detail, devoting two chapters to each of them. I shall begin by making some preliminary remarks about the resemblance theory and by considering four objections to it. The first objection is that many pictures represent things that have neither form nor color—for example, states of mind such as fear or lust and abstractions such as charity or truth. The second is that resemblance is a relation, and the relata of relations must be particular things that actually exist. But a picture may depict a man without depicting any man in particular, and it may depict a centaur, although no such animal exists. The third is that the resemblances we perceive when we look at pictures are resemblances between the objects we see in them and the objects we see around us in the world: they are not resemblances between the marks or pigments that make up the picture and the objects these marks depict. The fourth is that the resemblance theory implies that artists strip away the varnish of knowledge and interpretation from their perceptions of the world and record the innocent impressions of form and color, which it is thought this operation will reveal.

I shall argue that these objections can help us to refine the resemblance theory and to define the proper limits on its scope but that they should not persuade us to abandon it entirely. The traditional formulations of the theory are misleading, and the theory needs to be thoroughly overhauled. But if the dross is discarded and the scope of the theory is narrowly defined, it captures a truth about pictures, which a plausible approach to understanding pictorial art must include. It does not contain the whole truth about depiction that philosophical argument can discover. But it contains an important part of it; and it is the part we need to get straight first. Once we have got it straight, we may prefer to regard the epigraph to this chapter as an acceptable epitome of a subtle matter. Or we may prefer to be less economical with the truth. This choice will matter relatively little, once we know what the truth is.

The argument in these four chapters as a whole will emphasize the truthful part of the resemblance theory and the erroneous part of Descartes's illusion theory, and the theories in the recent literature that stem from it. The reason for this emphasis is that I am mainly interested in criticizing the idea that the theory of response is the cornerstone of the theory of pictorial art. This idea began life in Descartes's *Optics*, it was carried over into aesthetics by Hegel, who argued that subjectivity of mind is "the essential principle of painting," and it continues to govern the more abstract reaches of art theory, as we shall see.[4] In a different climate of opinion, I might have approached these theories from the opposite direction. The more balanced judgment, which is set out at the end of chapter 7, is that both sides mix truth with falsehood and exaggeration, as many philosophical theories that prosper do.

~

In the *Cratylus,* Plato says that a picture represents an object by copying its form and color. But the passage that is mainly responsible for the way in which the resemblance theory has been regarded by its critics is in book 10 of the *Republic.*[5]

The general term that Plato uses there to refer to representation in the arts is *mimesis;* and he defines "*mimesis* as a whole" as intentionally making an appearance (*phainomenon, phantasma*) that resembles something of a certain kind but is not something of that kind itself. His principal thought is that the appearance is like the original object but less real. Shadows and reflections are compared in this way to the things they are shadows and reflections of, and a painting of a bed is compared to a bed made by a craftsman. So, what does a painter who creates a representation of a bed make? "The painter also makes a bed, after a fashion, does he not?—Yes, he does, but only the appearance of one" (596e). The painter does not make nothing, but what he makes is merely an appearance. He is, Socrates says ironically, "in a sense a maker of these things, and in a sense not" (596d). And in the sense in which he does create the things he represents, anyone with a mirror can do the same:

> Don't you see that you yourself could make all these things in a way? . . . Take a mirror and carry it about everywhere. You will quickly make the sun and all the

> things in the sky, and quickly the earth and yourself and the other animals and artifacts and plants and all the objects of which we just now spoke.—Yes, he said, the appearance of them, but not the reality and the truth. (596d)

We cannot be sure how seriously Plato meant the analogy between painting and mirroring to be taken, or how damning he intended it to be. Analogies inevitably involve both likeness and difference, and the only likeness we can be sure Plato intends is that the sun, the earth, and so on in a picture, like mirror images of these things, are merely appearances of them and not the real things themselves. He does not mention the fact that a mirror image of a man must be an image of some man in particular, whereas this is not true of a picture. Or that the painter's control of the "appearance" he creates is limited only by his materials and skills, whereas the man carrying a mirror can choose only where to place it. Or that a painting is a marked surface, whereas a reflection is not. He does not mention these facts. But neither does he contradict them—either expressly or by implication.

Nevertheless, Plato's analogy has encouraged philosophers to believe that if the resemblance theory were true, pictures would necessarily portray objects that actually exist, pictorial art would be as unimaginative as forging banknotes, and the artist's medium would be invisible, so that only the objects represented could be seen. As we shall see, these ideas are due in large part to the hostile imagination of the theory's critics, although it is also true that they can draw support from Plato's text without grossly distorting either the tenor of his writing or the similes he chose to use.

~

The first objection to the resemblance theory is that many pictures represent things that have neither form nor color, such as states of mind, abstractions—for example, the triumph of virtue over ignorance—and the Holy Ghost. Hence, we cannot explain why a picture represents one of these things in terms of resemblances in form and color.

This objection cannot be swept aside, but a qualification will suffice to meet it. It will help us to formulate the qualification, if we consider a remark made by Alberti, on the first page of his treatise on painting: "No one would deny that the painter has nothing to do with things that are not visible. The painter is solely concerned with representing what can be seen."[6]

Strictly speaking, this is false. But it is approximately true, and the truth to which it approximates obviously involves the fact that a picture can represent one thing by representing another. For example, it can represent grief by representing the facial expression, posture, or demeanor of a grieving person; it can represent veracity by representing a female figure with a peach in her hand; and so on. The truth to which Alberti's remark approximates is that the painter is solely concerned with representing what can be seen, or what can be represented by representing what can be seen. The use of the preposition "by" here is the one that introduces a phrase of means, a possible answer to the question "how . . . ?" in the specific sense of "by what means . . . ?"

Now the preposition "by" has been used by philosophers interested in the nature of human action to single out a special class of so-called basic or primitive actions—"the ones we do not do by doing something else," in one well-known formulation. For example, I wrote this "a" by depressing a key on my computer's keyboard, and I depressed the key by moving the fourth finger on my left hand. But I did not move my finger by doing something else, and so moving my finger was, on this occasion, a basic action. There is room for debate about which actions count as basic, but it is undeniable that there are basic actions, since otherwise no finite means would exist to perform an action, and we would be perpetually stymied if we tried to act. Similarly, the representation of some objects in pictures must be basic for pictorial representation to occur at all.

The question therefore arises, how can we define the class of basic representations? In order to answer this question, we need to know how A (e.g., a facial expression) and B (e.g., an emotion) are linked when B is depicted by depicting A. The corresponding question about actions is not difficult to answer. There are two kinds of link. One kind is forged by a convention, because a convention can make an instance of one kind of action count as an instance of another. For example, when someone makes a bid at an auction by raising her hand, a convention makes the action of raising her hand count as the action of making a bid. The other kind of link is causal, because the result of one action can cause an event that then counts as the result of another action by the same agent. For example, when someone kills a man by stabbing him, the result of the stabbing is the knife's penetrating the man's body, the result of the killing is the man's death, and the first of these two events causes the second. Thus, a basic action is one whose occurrence does not depend on the existence of a convention and whose result is not caused by the result of another action by the same agent.[7]

In the case of representations, the answer also turns on convention and causation, but for a different reason. If a picture represents B by representing A, A is a sign of B. A man's facial expression, posture, or demeanor may be a sign of grief, a female figure with a peach signifies veracity, and so on. And the relevant kinds of signification depend either on the existence of a convention or on the fact that B causes A. Thus, veracity can be represented by a female figure with a peach in her hand because of the existence of an iconographic convention; and the representation of anger, grief, and shame depend on the fact that a man's facial expression, posture, and demeanor are affected by his emotional state. Hence, basic representation does not depend on either of these kinds of signification, and basic representation is what the resemblance theory is meant to explain.[8]

The resemblance theory therefore presupposes that whatever a picture represents, it represents by representing visible objects, their relations to each other, and their parts; and it is the representation of these visible objects—the ones that are not represented by representing something else—that the theory is intended to explain. Of course, the word "object" here is not to be equated with one of the philosophical terms of art, "body" or "material object." A picture can depict the sky, a river, a flame, a shadow, or a rainbow; and none of these things fits the traditional notion of a body. Nor should we assume that a visible object in a picture is bound to belong to some familiar kind of object with a familiar name. At the limit, we may be forced to describe it more or less purely in terms of color and form—for example, as grayish-pink and yellow and shaped like a piece of molten wax.

The second objection turns on the claim that resemblance is a relation. By a relation, I mean a way in which one thing can stand to another thing or several things can stand to one another.[9] For example, there are relations of comparison, such as *being hotter than* or *being wiser than;* spatial and temporal relations, such as *being inside, being west of,* or *being earlier than;* cognitive relations, such as *witnessing* or *being acquainted with;* and relations that result from actions, such as *being the father of, being the author of,* or *being the owner of.*

Before we consider the objection, it will be helpful to have some typical statements that involve relations before us. Here is an example of each of the kinds I have mentioned: "The sun is hotter than the moon," "Paris is west of Moscow," "John is acquainted with Jim," "Scott is the author of Waverley." In each case, the verb phrase that expresses the relation—"is hotter than," "is west of," "is acquainted with," and "is the author of"—is flanked by proper names that refer to the objects that are said to be thus related. These names can be replaced by descriptive terms such as "earth's satellite," "the capital of France," or "the man who is standing by the window." But, like proper names, these terms identify particular people, things, or places. Even the sentence "John is acquainted with a fireman," which does not purport to identify John's acquaintance, implies that there is a particular fireman with whom John is acquainted. For one cannot be acquainted with a fireman, but with no fireman in particular.

The objection is as follows. A portrait represents a particular man, woman, child, dog, and so on. For example, one of Frans Hals's portraits represents Johannes Hoornbeek, and there is a portrait by Guercino of Count Filippo Aldrovandi's dog. But a picture may represent a man or a dog without representing any man or dog in particular; or it may represent a centaur or a satyr, despite the fact that no such animals exist. Hence, we cannot explain why these kinds of pictures represent the things they do by claiming that they resemble them. For if resemblance is a relation, nothing can resemble a man, but not any man in particular, and nothing can resemble a kind of animal that does not exist.

The reply to this objection is as follows. It is true that the verb "represents" and the verb phrase "is a picture of" are sometimes used to express relations and sometimes not. For example, "It is a picture of a bridge," ". . . a shop," ". . . a battle," ". . . a river" can be read in either way. Read in the first, relation-involving way, each question—"Which bridge?" "Which shop?" "Which battle?" "Which river?"—has an answer, even if we do not know what it is; or, what generally comes to the same thing, the sentence can be continued with a "namely" rider: ". . . namely, the Rialto," ". . . namely, Gersaint's shop," ". . . namely, Agincourt," ". . . namely the Styx." Read in the second, non-relation-involving way, the question "which . . . ?" and the "namely" rider are both out of place. It is useful to mark this distinction clearly, and to a degree we do. Neither use of "represent" predominates. "Portray," however, is typically used to express a relation, whereas "depict" is not.[10]

But this does not disprove the resemblance theory because the verb "resembles," along with many other verbs and verb phrases, has exactly the same dual use. The best known case of such a verb is "is," which can either express identity (e.g., "the morning star is the evening star") or occur in a sentence as part of a predicate (e.g., "the morning star is a planet"). The first kind of "is" is widely believed to express a relation, and the second is generally agreed not to.[11] The same can be said of the verb phrase "is like" or the verb "resembles"; "*x* is like *y*" and "*x* resembles *y*" are two-place predicates, and if the variables are replaced by names, the resulting sentences do relate the individuals named: for example, "Seattle is like Toronto" or "Harry resembles John." But the sentences "SoHo is like a village" and "Socrates resembles a satyr" do not relate anything to anything. They are comparable not to "Cicero is Tully" or "The morning star is the evening star" but, instead, to "Cicero is a statesman" or "The morning star is a planet."

Hence, the statement that a picture (or a part of one) resembles a man does not imply that there is a particular man whom it resembles, and the statement that it resembles a satyr does not imply that satyrs exist. Satyrs have a distinctive appearance, which it is easy to describe, and if something has the same appearance as a satyr, then it resembles one. The fact that satyrs are mythical creatures does not prevent this from occurring. In Plato's *Symposium*, Alcibiades says that Socrates resembles a satyr. This may have been unkind, but it was not absurd.[12]

The third objection is that the resemblances we perceive when we look at pictures are resemblances between the objects they depict and the objects we see around us in the world. In Maupassant's novel, for example, Suzanne is struck by the resemblance between Bel-Ami and the figure of Christ in a painting her father has just bought. But the resemblance she is struck by is not between Bel-Ami and a canvas: it is between Bel-Ami and the figure of Christ in Markovitch's painting. Hence, this kind of resemblance cannot explain the fact that Markovitch's painting portrays Christ or the fact that it depicts a man with light-brown hair and a calm expression in his eyes.

Similarly (the objection continues), it is the man we can see in Hals's portrait that resembles Johannes Hoornbeek, or is thought to do so, and not the marks on the surface of the painting. It may be tempting to reply that the man in Hals's painting cannot be said to resemble Hoornbeek because he *is* Hoornbeek. But this would be a mistake because the phrase "The man in Hals's painting" has the kind of dual use we noted a few paragraphs ago. It can be used to describe the content of a painting—that is, to say what it depicts. But it can also be used to refer to the man whom it portrays. For example, if the phrase is being used in the first way, to describe the content of the painting, "The man in Hals's painting is dead" is false and "The man in Hals's painting is holding a book" is true. But if the phrase is being used in the second way, to refer to Johannes Hoornbeek, then "The man in Hals's painting is dead" is true and "The man in Hals's painting is holding a book" is false, unless Hoornbeek was buried holding a book and his body is miraculously well preserved.

There are (the objection concludes) exceptional cases in which part of the surface of a painting resembles what it depicts. For example, there are many self-portraits in which the artist holds a palette, and here of course the paint on the palette and the paint that represents this paint are exactly the same kind of stuff. But this is the exception rather than the rule, and we must always take care not to confuse the marks on the surface of a painting with the objects they depict. If a portrait of a man is a good likeness, the man depicted resembles the man portrayed. But it does not follow that the marks on the surface of the painting also resemble the man portrayed. Again, if an apple in a painting is unmistakably a Cox's Orange Pippin, it is the depicted apple that has the characteristic appearance of a Cox's Orange Pippin and not the part of the painting that depicts it.

This argument has considerable force. It may seem odd to claim that if a portrait is a good likeness, the man depicted resembles the man portrayed. It may seem as if the man depicted is a third entity, which has been rustled up, in addition to the painting and the sitter, in a moment of philosophical extravagance. But the claim is innocuous, and it will only create this impression if we mistakenly suppose that the verb "depict," like the verb "portray," expresses a relation. "The man portrayed" picks out a man in terms of a relation to a portrait, just as "the author of Waverley" picks out a man in terms of a relation to a book; and it invites a "namely" rider, for example, "the man portrayed, namely, Johannes Hoornbeek." "The man depicted" is quite different because the verb "depict" is not being used to express a relation, and the phrase does not invite a "namely" rider. But this does not make the phrase a puzzling one, and we are generally able to decide whether a statement in which it occurs—for example, "The man depicted has a calm expression in his eyes"—is true or false without much difficulty.

The objection is serious because the distinction that it fastens on—between the marks on the surface of a painting and the objects they depict—has often been mishandled in art theory. For example, many casually written histories of Renaissance painting include inaccurate descriptions of perspective, which are sometimes merely careless but sometimes confused: "The parallel lines orthogonal to the picture plane meet at a point on the horizon." "The squares of the pavement diminish in size at a regular rate." And so on.[13] If my interpretation of the painting is correct, it is also the distinction that Magritte refers to, in *La trahison des images* (fig. 2). The painting's title mischievously implies that every picture is a deceiver, a false friend. The truth is less dramatic: "Ceci n'est pas une pipe" is true if the pronoun refers to the painting, and false if it refers to the object it depicts. Hence, it is the words, or our grasp of their meaning, that is intended to betray us and not the prosaic image they describe.[14]

So it is true that the resemblance theory can appear plausible because we have confused the surface of a painting and its content—that is, the objects or the scene that it depicts. But the fact that the theory can appear plausible for the wrong reason does not imply that it is false. And the fact that the resemblances we tend to be struck by when we look at pictures are only perceptible once we have already perceived what they depict does not imply that these are the only resemblances that exist. It is true that we can often look straight through the surface of a painting, although many painters force us to slow down. Augustine was struck by this point: "When you see a picture," he wrote, "the matter is ended: you have seen it, and you praise. When you see letters, this is not yet the end, because you also have to read."[15] And so was Wittgen-

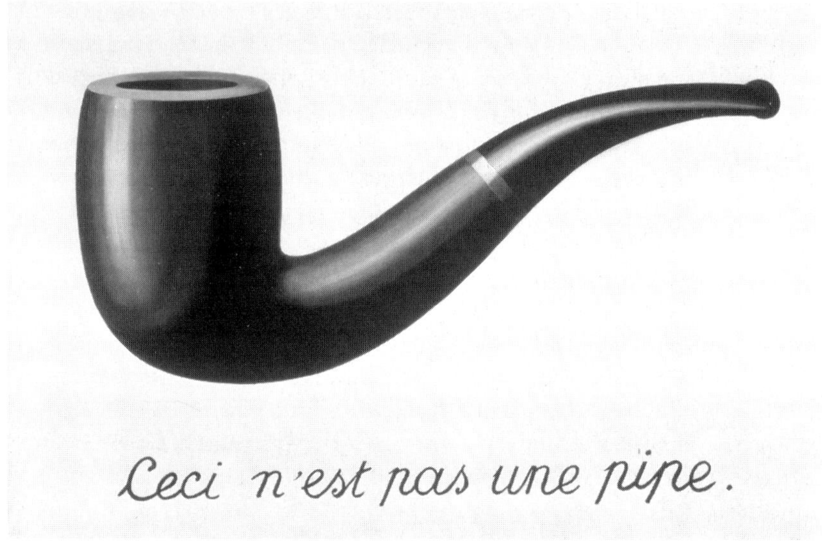

2. Réné Magritte, *La trahison des images*, 1928–29. Oil on canvas. Los Angeles County Museum of Art.

stein: "I might get an important message to someone by sending him the picture of a landscape. Does he read it like a blueprint? That is, does he *decipher* it? He looks at it and acts accordingly. He sees rocks, trees, a house, etc. in it."[16]

These comparisons are not wholly convincing because it is not always necessary to decipher a blueprint or a text. But the principal point both authors make is true. For although we cannot see what a picture represents without seeing the marks of which it is composed, we can learn to perceive a depicted scene as spontaneously as we perceive the world around us—without attending to the marks on the surface, as such, in the least. Moreover, if we find it difficult to identify an object in a painting—the mousetrap in the Mérode altarpiece, for example—this is generally not because the marks on the surface are hard to decipher (fig. 3). On the contrary, we distinguish the thing from its surroundings, and perceive it as a discrete object, before being puzzled by it. It is evidently a wooden contraption of some kind—but what kind?

So there is typically no need for us to attend first to the marks on a picture's surface in order to perceive its content. But if the pictorial content of a design can be explained by resemblances in form and color between parts of the surface and the objects they depict, it does not follow that we should expect these resemblances to strike us. The content of a picture may depend on them, without the chalk, the ink, or the paint—the "disinterested" paint, as

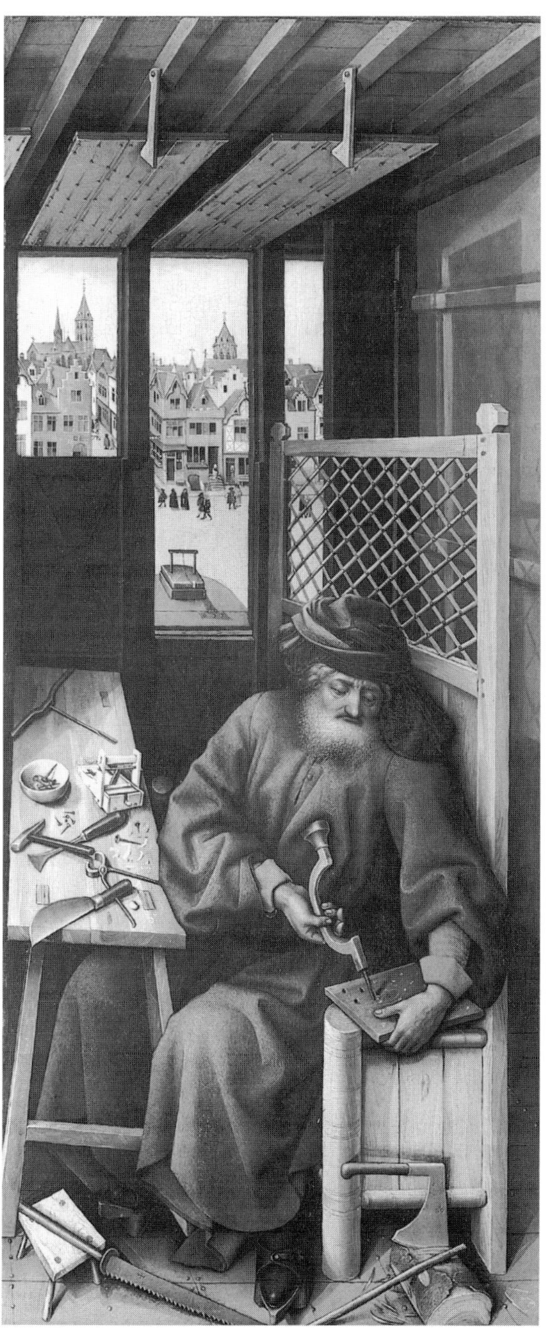

3. Robert Campin and assistant, *The Annunciation Triptych (Mérode Altarpiece)*, ca. 1425. Oil on wood. The Cloisters Museum, Metropolitan Museum of Art, New York. Right wing.

Clement Greenberg nicely called it—attracting the spectator's attention when she perceives it.

The fourth objection to the resemblance theory, which we find in Nelson Goodman's book *Languages of Art,* is that it presupposes a false theory of visual perception. Following Gombrich, Goodman calls this theory the "myth of the innocent eye," and he assails it with such a fierce barrage of rhetoric that it is hard to discern the enemy in the smoke. But the theory is in fact one that was consistently defended by empiricist philosophers from Locke onward, namely, that strictly speaking all we can ever see are flat patterns of light and color and that we identify the objects that surround us, and their various qualities, by interpreting this brilliant panorama.[17] Goodman argues that if the resemblance theory were true, an artist would need, somehow or other, to strip away the varnish of thought and interpretation in order to record the pristine patchwork of colors that lies beneath it. But since this operation, which Goodman calls "purification rites" and "methodical disinterpretation," is impossible, the resemblance theory is false.[18]

Goodman is right to reject the myth of the innocent eye. Our visual experience does not normally present us with a patchwork of colors, unless we are looking at a quilt. It presents us with the familiar kinds of colored objects disposed in space that we describe when we report what we can see. It is true, as we saw in chapter 1, that we can see objects only by seeing colors; but it is false that strictly speaking all we really see are colors themselves. Compare action again. Whenever we lift or move an object, we lift it or move it by lifting our arms or moving our bodies in some way. But it does not follow, and it is not true, that strictly speaking all we can ever lift or move are our own limbs.

This is not a trivial point because the myth of the innocent eye has been accepted by many philosophers, psychologists, and art theorists—and by painters too. Monet, for example, offered the following advice: "When you go out to paint, try to forget what objects you have before you, a tree, a house, a field, or whatever. Merely think, here is a little square of blue, here an oblong of pink, here a streak of yellow, and paint it just as it looks to you, the exact colour and shape, until it gives your own naïve impression of the scene before you."[19] There is no record of this remark in French; but if the translation is accurate, Monet probably intended the phrase rendered in English as "your own naïve impression" to refer to the colorful mosaic that was supposed to be the raw material of visual experience. In England, John Ruskin and later Roger Fry were committed to the very same idea. Indeed, Ruskin states it plainly in the passage from *The Elements of Drawing* where the phrase "the innocence of the eye" occurs: "The whole technical power of painting," he writes, "depends on our recovery of what may be called the *innocence of the eye;* that is to say, of a sort of childish perception of these flat stains of colour, merely as such, without consciousness of what they signify."[20] And in Germany, the father of physiological optics, Hermann von Helmholtz, declared: "We must look upon artists as persons whose observation of sensuous impressions is particularly fine and exact, and whose recollection of the memory images of these impressions is particularly true."[21]

These remarks were all written in the nineteenth century. But the myth persists, especially in relation to impressionist painting. For example, Merleau-Ponty claims that impressionism "tries to capture, in the painting, the very way in which objects strike our eyes and attack our senses. Objects are depicted as they appear to instantaneous perception, without fixed contours, bound together by light and air."[22] And Meyer Schapiro, who is generally scrupulous in his treatment of philosophical ideas, comments on one painting by Monet that "the painter has introduced many touches that translate intense sensations of color. They have been adroitly selected to produce effects like those of uninterpreted sensation" and says of another that "priority [is] given to the uninterpreted sensation and its material counterparts: the accented touch, the stroke of colour."[23]

So the myth of the innocent eye needed, and still needs, to be attacked. Nevertheless, Goodman's objection to the resemblance theory is unconvincing because it imputes guilt by association. For although the resemblance theory and the myth of the innocent eye dovetail neatly and have often been combined, there is no reason to accept that the former implies the latter. If the essence of painting is, as Roger de Piles claims, the imitation of visible objects by means of form and colors, it follows that these are qualities an artist must be able to perceive. But it does not follow that they are all he is able to perceive. Hence, the charge that the resemblance theory implies this is unjust. And one cannot condemn a theory because it has been seen in bad company.[24]

~

In conclusion, none of these four objections to the resemblance theory proves that it ought to be abandoned. But they are all instructive, and the main lessons are these. First, the defensible residue of the resemblance theory is not a comprehensive theory of pictorial art. Nothing beyond the basic representation of visible objects falls within its scope. Second, it is a theory of depiction. It purports to define the relationship between the visible objects depicted and the marks and colors on a picture's surface and not the relationship between these marks and colors and the person, object, place, or event, if any, that is portrayed. Third, it is not a theory of pictorial perception. And finally, it is also not a theory of artistic perception. For it does not purport to define either the kind of experience that occurs when we look at pictures and see what they represent or the kind of experience an artist needs to have or should be encouraged to cultivate. So each of the objections we have considered points to a retrenchment: each limits the theory's scope. But the simple idea, that an artist depicts an object by imitating its form and color, has so far survived. In the next chapter, I shall explain how this idea can be explained in detail, within these relatively severe constraints.

5

ART AND OCCLUSION

The question as to the origin of the art of painting is uncertain . . .
but all agree that it began with tracing an outline around a man's shadow.
Pliny the Elder

AS WE HAVE SEEN, the relationship between Plato's theory of depiction and Descartes's is similar to the relationship between the objectivist and subjectivist positions in the theory of value. Plato's doctrine, that a picture represents an object by copying its form and color, is objectivist. He does not refer to the response or reaction that a picture produces in a spectator's mind but to a resemblance in form and color between the marks that a picture is composed of and the objects these marks represent. By contrast, Descartes's position is subjectivist: "The problem," he claims, with characteristic vigor and directness, "is to know simply how [pictures] can enable the soul to have sensory perceptions of all the various qualities of the objects to which they correspond—not to know how they can resemble these objects."

In this chapter, I shall argue that there is a strict and invariable relationship between the shapes and colors on a picture's surface and the objects that it depicts, which can be defined without referring to the psychological effect the picture produces in a spectator's mind, and that Descartes's claim is therefore false. I shall begin by quoting his criticism of the resemblance theory at length, so that his reasons for rejecting it are stated plainly, in his own words:

> In no case does an image resemble the object it represents in all respects, for otherwise there would be no distinction between the object and its image. It is enough that the image resembles its object in a few respects. Indeed the perfection of an image often depends on its not resembling its object as much as it might. You can see this in the case of engravings: consisting simply of a little ink placed here and there on a piece of paper, they represent to us forests, towns, people, and even battles and storms; and although they make us think of countless different qualities in these objects, it is only in respect of shape that there is any real resemblance. And even this resemblance is very imperfect, since engravings represent to us bodies of varying relief and depth on a surface which is entirely flat. Moreover, in accordance with the rules of perspective they often represent circles by ovals better than by other circles, squares by rhombuses better than by other squares, and similarly for other shapes. Thus it often happens that in order to be more perfect as an image and to represent an object better, an engraving ought not to resemble it.[1]

Descartes makes three claims in this passage. The first, that an image cannot resemble the objects that it represents perfectly, does not in itself mark a departure from the resemblance theory. It has been made by many writers, including Plato, and I shall discuss it toward the end of this chapter. The same is true of Descartes's second claim, that an image need only resemble what it represents in a few respects. But one point about this claim should be noted. We might suppose, as Plato does, that an image must resemble what it represents in form and color. But Descartes ignores color and illustrates this claim with an engraving. Perhaps this is because it is possible to depict an object's form without depicting its color. But it is probably because he denies that physical objects have colors at all; and this stricture obviously includes both pictures and the kinds of objects they depict. In any event, Descartes says that an image must resemble what it represents in a few respects ("en peu de choses") but he only considers shape.

Descartes's final claim is that even in respect of shape the resemblance between an image and the object it represents is often imperfect. He supports this with two observations, one concerning the shapes of bodies and the other, two-dimensional shapes. First, he points out that "engravings represent to us bodies of varying relief and depth on a surface which is entirely flat." So, for example, the parts of an engraving that depict a cylindrical tower and its conical roof cannot possibly resemble these things in shape because a figure on a plane cannot be cylindrical or conical. Then he adds that "in accordance with the rules of perspective [engravings] often represent circles by ovals better than by other circles . . . and similarly for other shapes." Thus, even part of an engraving that depicts something with a two-dimensional shape—the facade of a building or the surface of a table, for example—will not have exactly the same shape as the thing it depicts if the artist has used foreshortening to represent them.

The sheer simplicity of these observations is disarming; and they prove incontrovertibly that the vague idea of copying an object's shape cannot explain how the inky marks on the surface of an engraving depict the forest or town we see in it. This much must be conceded from the start. But as we shall see, the precise sense in which a picture can resemble a three-dimensional body in respect of shape is not difficult to explain because three-dimensional bodies have two-dimensional aspects or appearances, which inky marks on paper can record. For example, a circular tabletop has an elliptical aspect or appearance, when it is seen along an oblique line of sight. The difficult question is whether this aspect or appearance is in the visible object we perceive or whether it belongs to "the beholder's share." We have already seen that it is hard to define exactly how the appearances of the objects we perceive are related to these objects themselves and to our perceptions of them. As we shall see now, this topic has caused as much confusion in the case of form as it has in the case of color.

~

The word "form" expresses several distinct concepts, which range around the focal idea of the disposition or arrangement of an object's parts. Thus, in one sense (corresponding to the Greek *eidos*) an object's form is an essence or structure, which makes it the distinct object that it is. This is the sense in which God is described as having formed man from the dust of the ground. And in another sense (corresponding to the Greek *morphē*) an object's form is the shape by which it can be known or recognized, either as an individual or as an instance of a kind. This is the sense in play when Queen Constance, in Shakespeare's *King John,* says that grief for her dead son "stuffs out his vacant garments with his form." Since a form is a disposition of an object's parts it is always a product of complexity. Nothing that is absolutely simple has a form.

The elliptical appearance of a tabletop belongs in the family of *morphē* or shape. It is a perfectly familiar property. But the term "apparent shape," by which it is commonly known, is tendentious because it suggests that the tabletop's real shape is not elliptical and, hence, that its elliptical appearance is an illusion. I shall call the tabletop's elliptical appearance its "occlusion shape." The following example explains why. Directly ahead of me, through the window on the far side of my desk, I can see the bare branch of a lime tree. If I close one eye and look straight at the tip of this branch, making sure that the

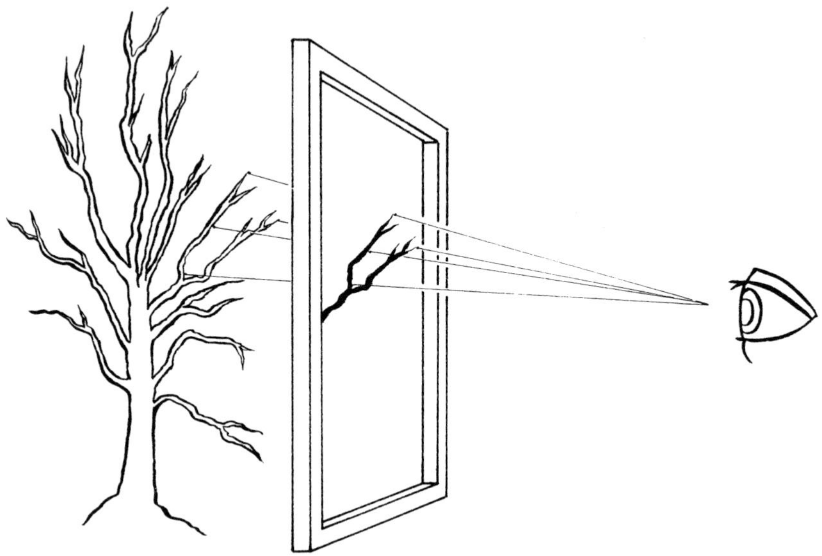

4. A branch of a tree seen through a window.

windowpane is perpendicular to my line of sight, the shape of the mark I would need to make on the windowpane in order to occlude the branch precisely is its occlusion shape, relative to my line of sight (fig. 4). Notice that this shape is relative to my line of sight and not to the particular position of my eye along it. The shape of the mark I would need to make in order to occlude the branch precisely will not change if I take a step back along this line. Its size will change of course but not its shape.

The concept of occlusion shape goes back to Euclid's *Optics,* which begins by postulating a thick cone of rays connecting the eye with an object that is seen. The apex of the cone is in the eye and its base is on the visible surface of the object. Of course this cone of rays is an idealization, since the visible surface of an object may have any shape and the direction in which light travels is affected by refraction. But an object's occlusion shape is the shape of a perpendicular cross section of this so-called cone or solid angle. It is therefore possible to identify the occlusion shape of an object, relative to a given line of sight, by measurement and calculation. But it is also possible to see it, as I can see the occlusion shape of the branch now. Since few occlusion shapes have names, discursive treatments of the topic tend to concentrate on a few simple geometrical examples. But we can see, recognize, and record an unlimited variety of occlusion shapes and not merely these few.

An object's occlusion shape is relative to a line of sight: it depends on the object's three-dimensional shape and its orientation relative to this line. It is also affected by refraction, as the example of a straight stick half immersed in water shows: the stick is straight but its occlusion shape is crooked. And it is affected by reflection if the reflecting surface is curved. Parmigianino's *Self-Portrait in a Convex Mirror* illustrates this effect (fig. 5). Hence not even a sphere has the same occlusion shape from every angle, regardless of the medium that surrounds it and how it is seen. But although an object's occlusion shape is relative, it is real. The term "apparent shape," which suggests a contrast with an object's real shape, is a misnomer for two reasons. First, an object's apparent shape is the shape it appears to have. But an object's occlusion shape is a two-dimensional shape, and most objects do not normally appear to have two-dimensional shapes because they do not normally look flat. Second, we can distinguish between the apparent occlusion shape of an

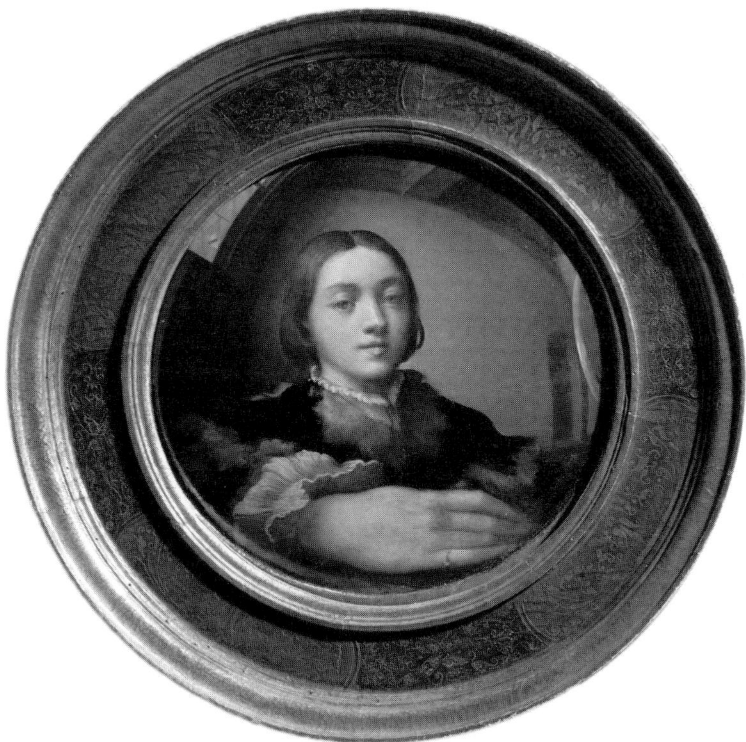

5. Parmigianino, *Self-Portrait in a Convex Mirror*, ca. 1524. Oil on wood. Kunsthistorisches Museum, Vienna.

object and its real occlusion shape. For example, the profile of a man's nose may look sharper or rounder than it really is because of his hat or the way he wears his hair.

Despite these simple and familiar facts, occlusion shape has been treated as a standard example of illusion by philosophers since Plato, and as we shall see in a later chapter, psychologists and art historians have been confused about it, too. In the twentieth century, several generations of philosophers were taught to believe in the existence of sense data by being asked what is really elliptical when a coin looks elliptical despite really being circular, or what is really crooked when a straight stick is half immersed in water. More recently, the idea of a point of view has become a standard trope with which to introduce a distinction between reality and appearance, and occlusion shape has become a standard trope with which to introduce the idea of a point of view.[2] The common opinion is that three-dimensional shapes are, in Locke's phrase, "real qualities in the subject" and that occlusion shapes are in the eye of the observer.

Two arguments have contributed to this confusion. The first is that a circular tabletop cannot also be elliptical. Hence, if it looks elliptical, this appearance cannot be veridical, and the experience of perceiving it is therefore an illusion. The reply to this argument is that no inconsistency is involved in supposing that the tabletop is circular and that a cross section of the solid angle it subtends to an observer's eye is elliptical, and there is no reason why both properties should not be perceived or, indeed, perceived at once. The second argument is that two observers looking at the same object will often perceive different occlusion shapes. Hence, these different shapes cannot be predicated of the same object. They can only be predicated of the effects the object produces in the each person's mind. The reply to this argument is that an occlusion shape is relative to a line of sight, and a single object can therefore have two different occlusion shapes, relative to two different lines of sight. Again, there is no reason why each of two observers should not perceive the occlusion shape of a single object, relative to her own line of sight.

A variation on the second argument is that the occlusion shape seen by an observer changes as she moves around an object without the object itself undergoing any visible kind of change. Hence, this changing occlusion shape cannot be predicated of the object. The reply to this argument is obvious from the last. It can also be pointed out that as Columbus sailed away from the harbor in Cadiz he could see the distance to the harbor growing steadily—without the harbor moving by an inch. But this does not show that the changing distance Columbus seemed to perceive was not real or that it was merely a fea-

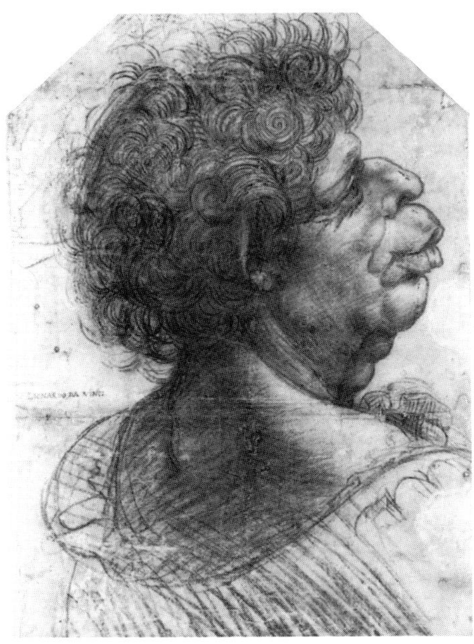

6. Leonardo da Vinci, *Bust of Grotesque Man in Profile,* ca. 1503–5. Charcoal or black chalk. Christ Church, Oxford.

ture of his thoughts and sensations. It shows that the distance between two objects depends on both of their positions, which is surely something we already knew.

In short, an object's occlusion shape depends on its three-dimensional shape and its orientation relative to a line of sight. But this relativity does not imply that an object's occlusion shape is nebulous, merely apparent, or unreal or that it is a property of our perceptions and not of the physical objects we perceive. The answer to the question, "What is really elliptical when a coin looks elliptical despite really being circular?" is that the face of the coin is really circular and its occlusion shape, relative to an oblique line of sight, is really elliptical. And there is no reason why it should not look as it really is in both respects, which by and large it does.[3]

~

We can now use the idea of occlusion shape to explain how pictures represent the objects we see in them. Consider a drawing of a man's head (fig. 6). The head may be bulbous or narrow, the nose may be Roman or snub, and the chin may be a rounded curve or a jutting wedge. These are just examples. In his *Libro di pittura* Leonardo names ten types of nose in profile and describes

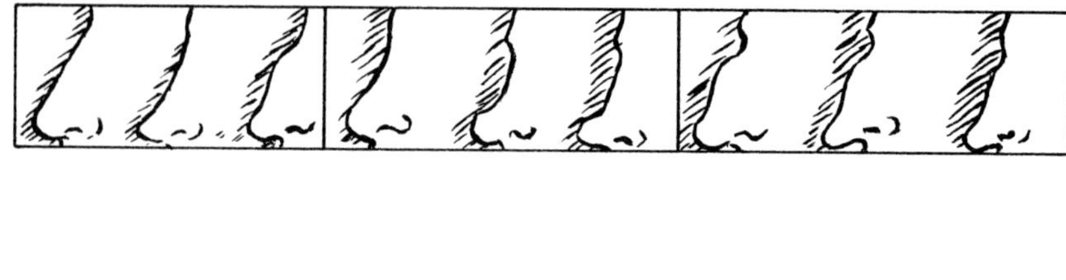

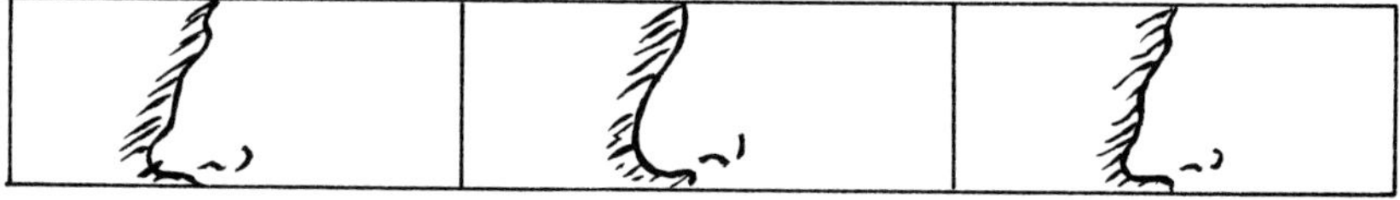

7. Leonardo da Vinci, *Noses in Profile.* Based on Vatican, Codex Urbinas Latinus 1270, 108v.

eleven characteristics of noses in full face (fig. 7). But even if we cannot find the right words to describe them, the shapes of the head, the nose, and the chin are the shapes they are represented as having—they are the shapes that the artist has given them. And their occlusion shapes are the occlusion shapes they are represented as having.

Since an object's occlusion shape is relative to a line of sight, to depict an object's occlusion shape is to depict the object relative to a line of sight. This line is not itself depicted or marked on the surface of the picture. (If it were, it would be represented by a point.) But it is implicit in the way the object is depicted, and I shall call it an implicit line of sight. We should not think of an implicit line of sight as the line of sight of an implicit spectator. Many poems have an implicit speaker, whom the reader is invited to imagine uttering the lines or thinking the thoughts they express. Similarly, as we shall see later, the content of a picture is sometimes represented as being seen by an individual. Sometimes, but not always. The implicit spectator is not an essential feature of pictorial art as such, but the association between an object in a picture and an implicit line of sight is.

As well as distinguishing the implicit line of sight associated with an object in a picture from the line of sight of an implicit spectator, we also need to distinguish it from the line of sight of an actual spectator.[4] For suppose that a picture depicts something spherical, such as a ball. Setting aside refraction, the occlusion shape of a sphere is circular, relative to every line of sight. But if a spectator is looking at the picture along an eccentric line of sight, the occlusion shape of a depicted sphere will be elliptical, relative to the spectator's line of sight, just as an actual sphere would be occluded by an elliptical patch on a screen placed obliquely to her line of sight. Hence the implicit line of sight associated with an object represented in a picture need not be the same as an actual spectator's line of sight.

With these preliminaries in place, the main point can be stated quite concisely. Suppose a drawing depicts a man's head. The shape of the smallest part of the drawing that depicts this head and the occlusion shape of the head that it depicts must be identical. (I say the smallest part because if a small part of a drawing depicts a head, then a larger part that includes this part also depicts a head.) The same is true of every other object, or part of an object, that is depicted. Hence, if O is a depicted object and P is the smallest part of a picture that depicts O, the general principle can be stated as follows: the occlusion shape of O and the shape of P must be identical. This general principle, which I shall call the occlusion shape principle, is a precise statement of the basic and indispensable thought that a picture represents an object by defining its form.

It is not difficult to imagine Socrates patiently eliciting the occlusion shape principle from Meno. But it would be an exaggeration to describe it as an explicit statement of something that anyone who has grasped the concept of a picture already knows. A remark of Wittgenstein's suggests a different conception of it, which is closer to the truth: "If we wish to draw boundaries in the use of a word, in order to clear up philosophical paradoxes, then alongside the actual picture of the use (in which as it were the different colors flow into one another without sharp boundaries) we may put another picture that is in certain ways like the first but is built up of colors with clear boundaries between them."[5] A precise definition is not a perfect record of the boundaries of an imprecise idea—precisely because of its precision. But it can make an area of thought more tractable and fallacies easier to expose.

In particular, the occlusion shape principle shows that Descartes's final objection to the resemblance theory is partly right and partly wrong. It is true that engravings depict bodies of varying relief and depth on a flat surface and that they often represent circular surfaces by ovals rather than by other circles, square surfaces by rhombuses rather than by other squares, and so on. Furthermore—this is an important point, which we shall return to more than once—the occlusion shape principle does not enable us to infer what kind of object is depicted from the shape of the mark that depicts it, beyond its occlusion shape and the occlusion shapes of its parts. For example, if part of a drawing depicts a duck's bill or a rabbit's ears, the principle cannot tell us which; although of course it does tell us that if the drawing can be seen either as a picture of a duck or as a picture of a rabbit, the duck and the rabbit must have the same occlusion shape, relative to the implicit line of sight (fig. 8).

But Descartes was wrong to conclude that "the problem is to know simply

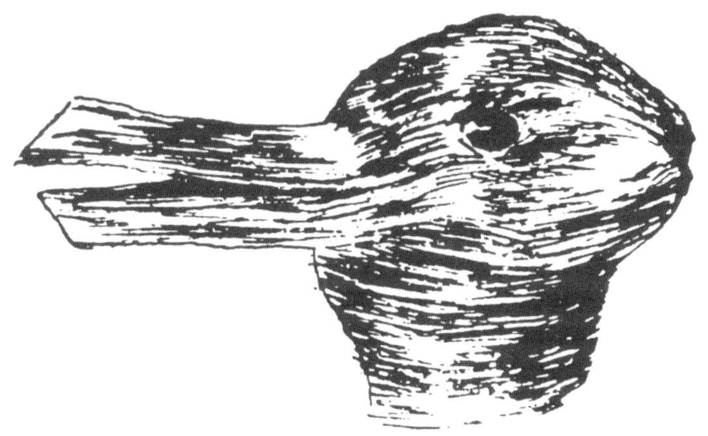

8. Duck-Rabbit. Originally published in *Fliegende Blatter,* October 23, 1892.

how [pictures] can enable the soul to have sensory perceptions of all the various qualities of the objects to which they correspond—not to know how they can resemble these objects." For although the occlusion shape principle is modest, it implies that there is, after all, a precise relationship between the marks on a picture's surface and the objects they depict, which does not depend on the picture's psychological effect on a spectator.

The technical and imaginative achievements of pictorial art are rooted in its nature. To say this is to state the obvious. But a corollary of this fact—and one on which the value of a philosophical theory of depiction largely depends—is that we cannot claim to have fully understood the ways in which artists have enlarged or transformed the resources of pictorial art to express meaning until we have understood how specific innovations exploit the possibilities that are inherent in pictorial art as such. We need to see the shape of the whole tree, from the crown to the root. This is a rather abstract claim, but a small number of examples will convey what I have in mind. Each of the four devices I shall mention has its own complex history, each has been elaborated in many ways, and each has an extensive literature of its own. But it is satisfying to discover that a single principle, which applies to pictorial art in general, underlies them all.

The occlusion shape principle implies that whatever a picture depicts, it depicts relative to an implicit line of sight. This immediately suggests several lines of development. First, the view of an object along a specific line of sight can acquire a particular resonance or meaning. For example, the *en face* view was a conventional sign of majesty in European art for many centuries, although it could express many other things instead—passivity or insolence, for example. And the *en face* convention could in turn endow a profile with peculiar piquancy or force. For example, in Giotto's fresco of *The Betrayal of Christ,* the drama is accentuated by discarding the conventional view of Christ and showing the protagonists' noses confronting each other like daggers (fig. 9). By contrast, the profile had a decorum of its own, which was associated in particular with its use on coins and medals. But Titian's portrait of *François I,* which was probably based on a medal, softens the convention by showing the king turning spontaneously to one side, as if to face someone outside the frame (fig. 10).[6]

Second, novel views of objects—that is, views associated with novel lines of sight—can be introduced by combining views along established lines of sight. For example, quasi-frontal views were often first composed by com-

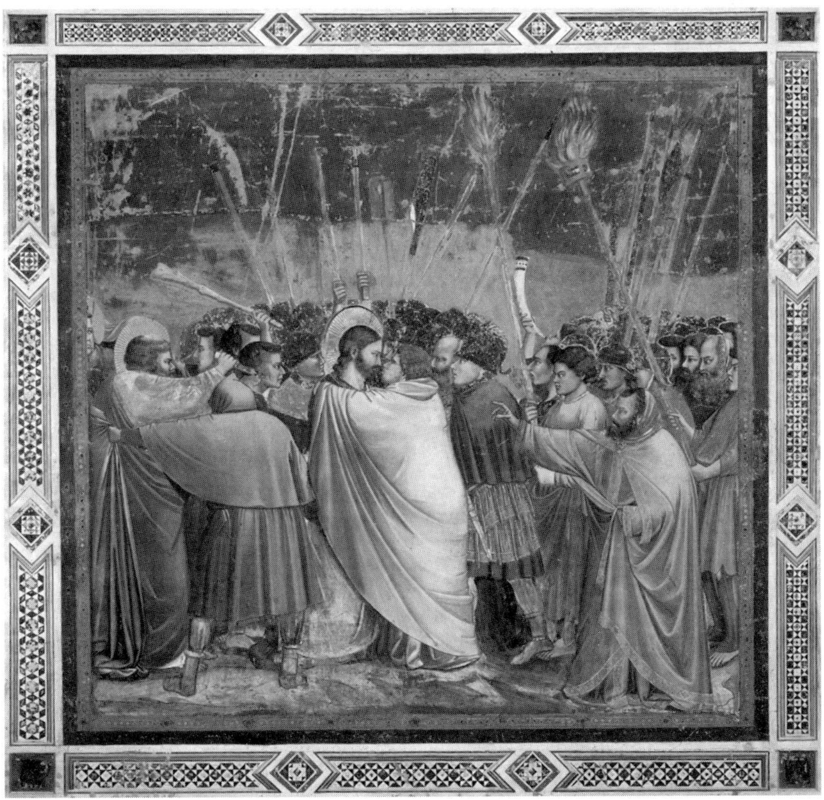

9. Giotto, *The Betrayal of Christ,* ca. 1305. Fresco. Arena Chapel, Padua.

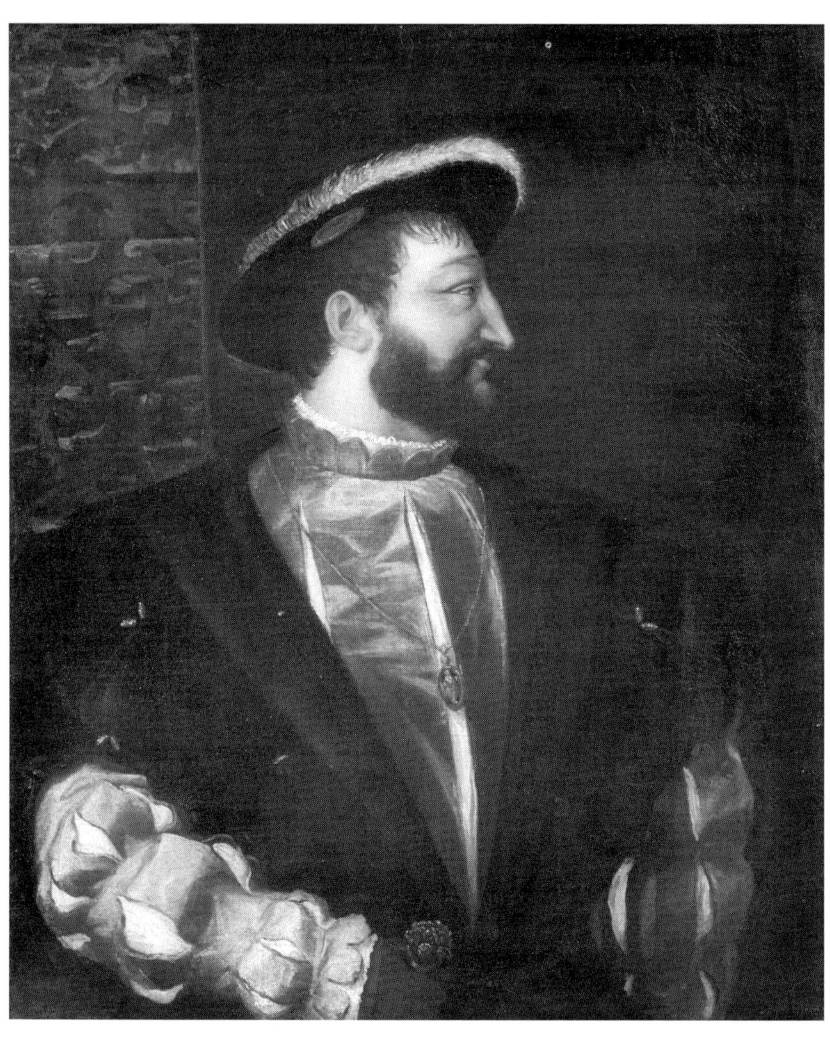

10. Titian, *François I*, 1538. Oil on canvas. Musée du Louvre, Paris.

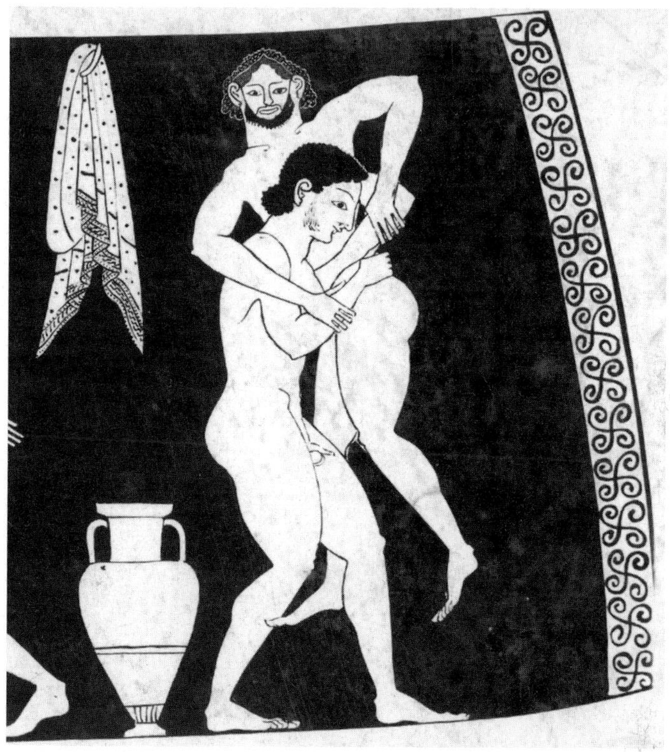

11. Amphora, ca. 515 B.C. Attributed to the Andokides Painter. Staatliche Museen zu Berlin, Antikensammlungen.

bining two profiles or oblique views, so that the composite image divides along a vertical axis. This is how the Andokides Painter and Euphronios produced frontal views of a wrestler's and a symposiast's face, and it is how Giotto produced a frontal view of a mourner in his *Dormition of the Virgin* (figs. 11–13). The same method of composition was used by Master Bertram to produce a frontal view of a pavement, in which the axis is deliberately hidden by the curl of drapery at the front (fig. 14).[7]

In each of these cases, the method of composition produces a vertical axis, although there is no reason to suppose that this axis is part of the way in which the method was conceived or understood.[8] But in other cases, the method of combination does not have this effect. For example, Greek vase painters depicted a chariot in quasi-three-quarter view by the same method of combination (fig. 15). The wheels of the chariot are shown obliquely, that is, in true three-quarter view, the horses' bodies are shown in profile, set diagonally on

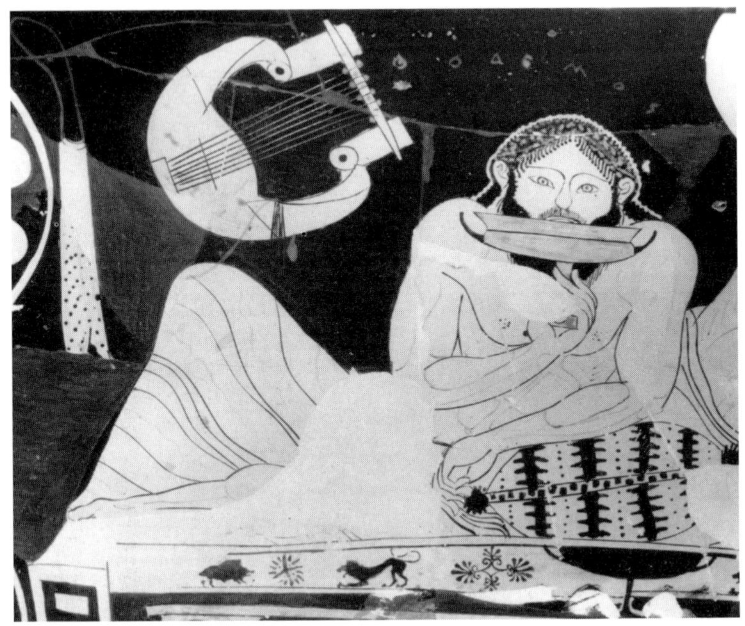

12. Calyx crater, ca. 515 B.C. Attributed to Euphronios. Antikensammlung, Munich.

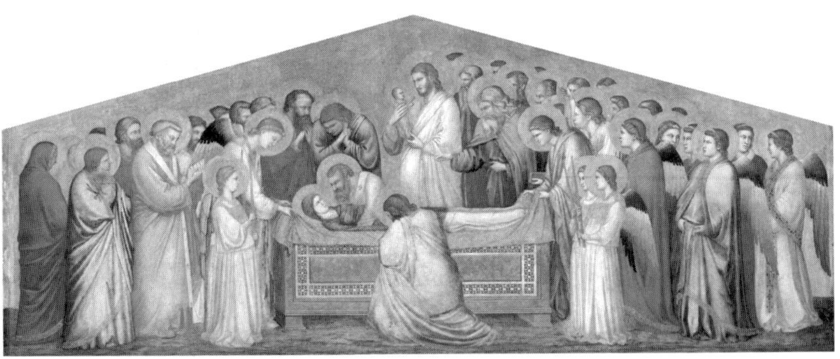

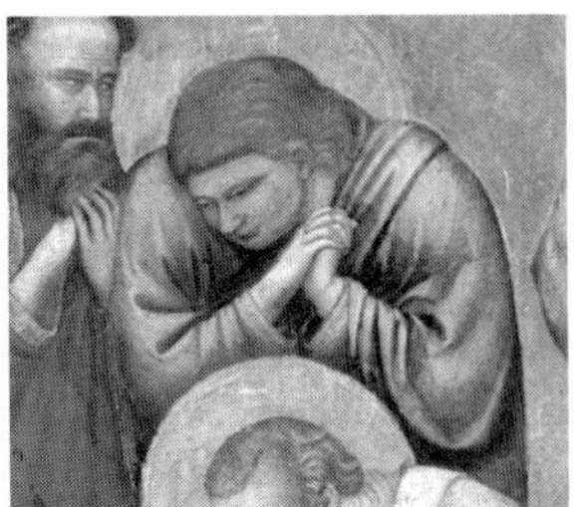

13. Giotto, *Dormition of the Virgin,* ca. 1310. Tempera on wood. Staatliche Museen zu Berlin, Gemaldegalerie. Detail of mourner.

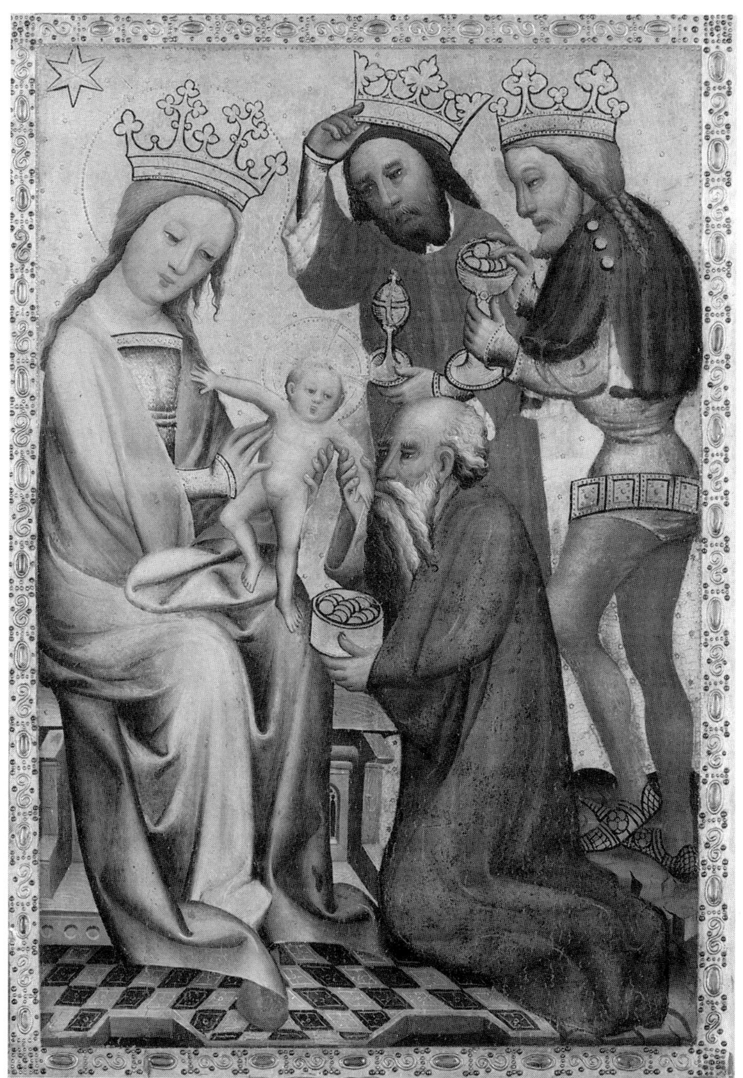

14. Master Bertram, *Adoration of the Magi,* 1383. Panel from the *Grabow Altarpiece.* Tempera on wood. Hamburger Kunsthalle, Hamburg.

the surface of the vase, while their necks and heads are alternately shown in profile and turning to their right, across the implicit line of sight. We intuitively summarize this complex spatial information as a unified three-quarter view. Interestingly, Picasso's double view of a face is a recent invention of essentially the same kind (fig. 16). The New York dealer Julien Levy reports Picasso as explaining it like this: "'Is this woman with one eye, or three eyes a development of cubism?' I asked Picasso. 'Not at all,' he answered. 'This double-profile, as it is called, is only that I keep my eyes always open. Every painter should keep his eyes always open. And how does that arrive at seeing truthfully, one eye or two eyes, you may ask? It is simply the face of my sweetheart, Dora Maar, when I kiss her.'"[9]

A third line of development moves in the opposite direction. Instead of combining views along distinct lines of sight, the lines of sight associated with distinct parts of the depicted scene can be coordinated or played off against each other. The simplest examples to describe—although they were by no means simple to conceive or execute—are the Renaissance system of perspec-

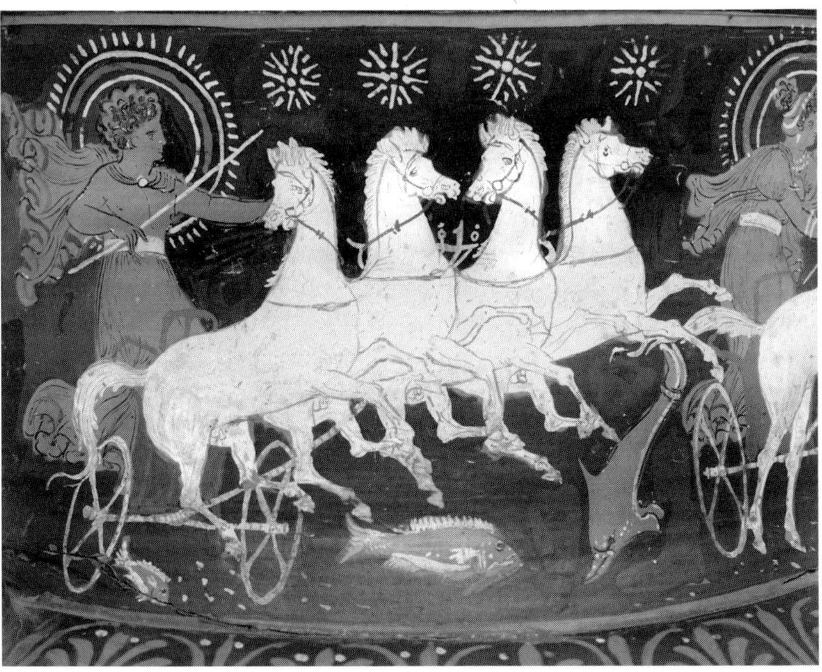

15. Apulian volute crater, ca. 330 B.C. Name vase of the Underworld Painter. Antikensammlung, Munich. Detail of neck.

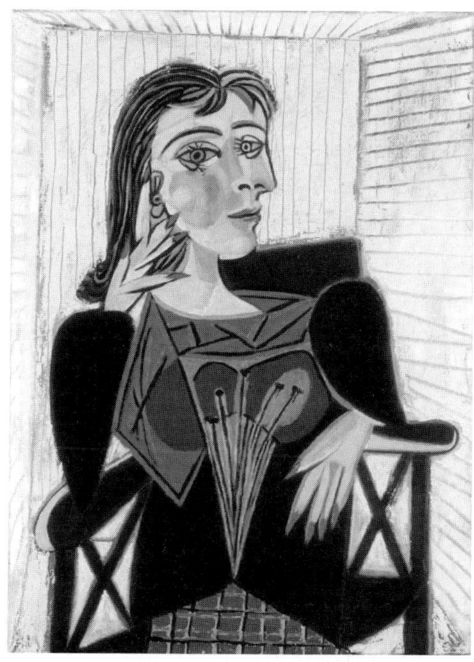

16. Pablo Picasso, *Portrait of Dora Maar,* 1937. Oil on canvas. Musée Picasso, Paris.

tive and the use of multiple implicit points of view. For example, in an orthodox use of perspective, the lines of sight associated with each part of the depicted scene are made to intersect, so that the entire scene is coordinated by this implicit point of view. In other words, the visible surface of each object in the depicted scene forms part of the base of a single visual cone. By contrast, in Masaccio's fresco of *The Trinity,* the architecture and the supporting figures are depicted as if seen from below, but the figures of the Father and the Son are depicted frontally, without any foreshortening at all (fig. 17).[10]

Fourth, whatever a picture depicts, it depicts as visible, but it may not depict it as actually being seen. When it does so, an implicit point of view is embodied in an implicit spectator, who may or may not be represented and who may be an individual or a type. For example, compare the drawings Dürer made of himself in 1484 and in 1493 (figs. 18, 19). Nothing in the earlier drawing indicates whose view of the child is represented, and the pose does not immediately suggest what the inscription records, that the artist and the subject are the same person. The later drawing, by contrast, evidently shows the artist, absorbed in the act of drawing himself—and so the view of the young man it depicts is represented as his own. Boucher's *Marquise de Pom-*

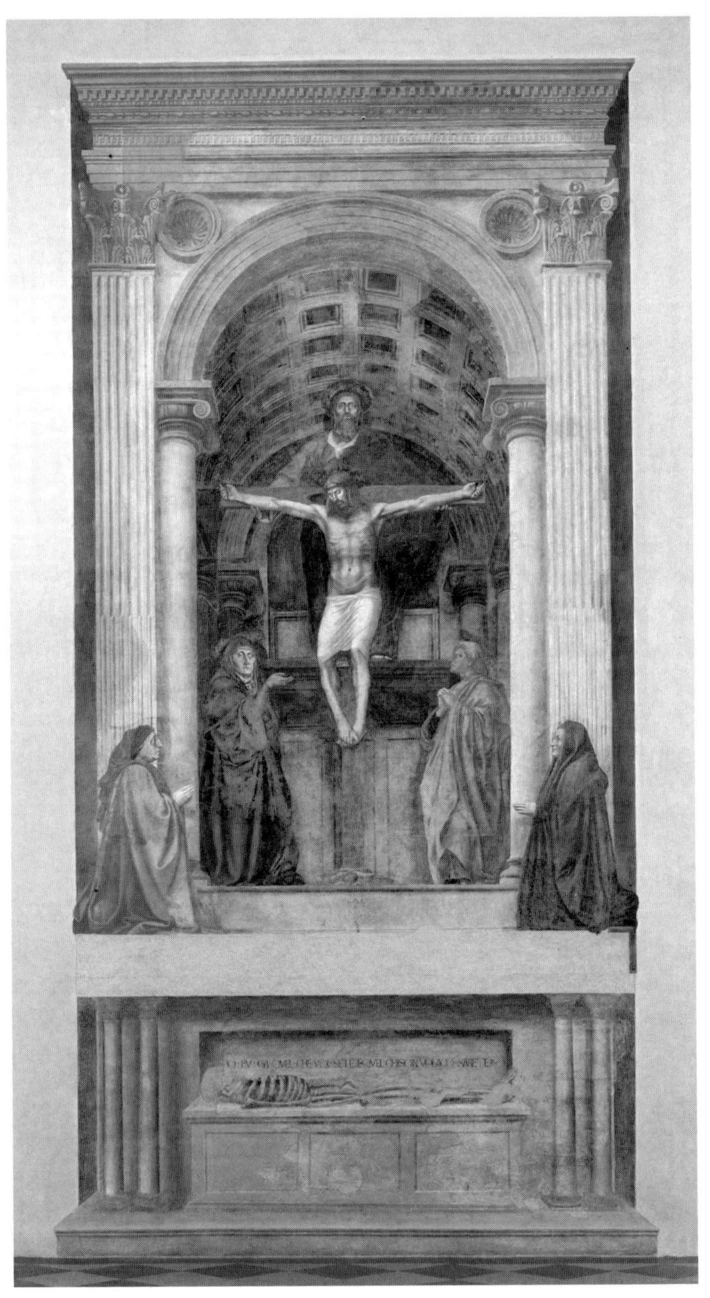

17. Masaccio, *Trinity,* ca. 1425. Fresco. S. Maria Novella, Florence.

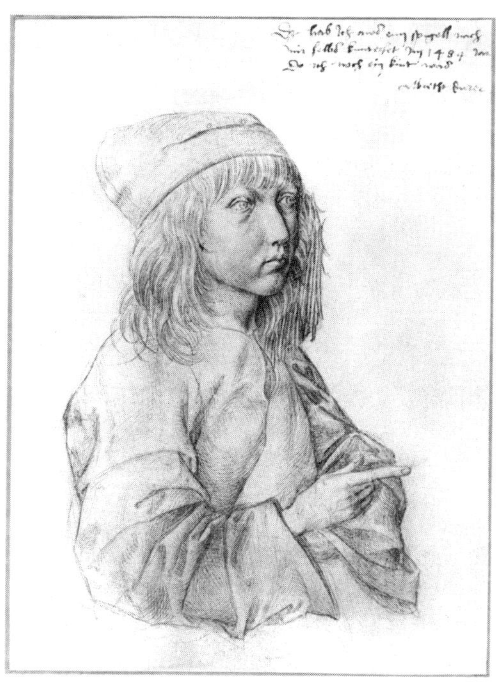

18. Albrecht Dürer, *Self-Portrait at the Age of Thirteen*, 1484. Silverpoint on prepared paper. Albertina, Vienna.

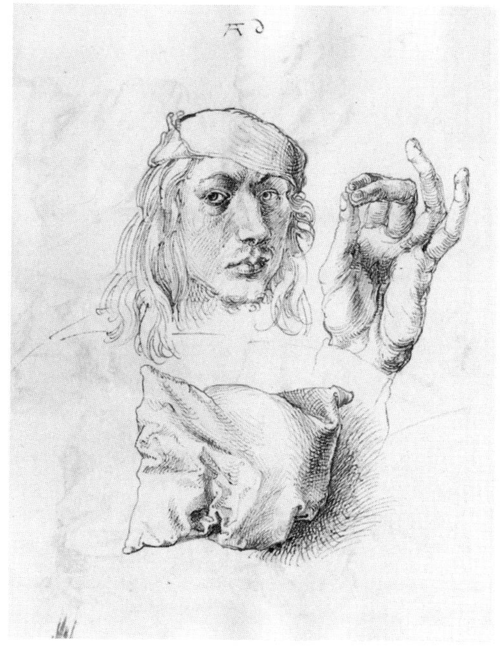

19. Albrecht Dürer, *Self-Portrait with a Cushion*, 1493. Pen and brown ink. Robert Lehman collection, Metropolitan Museum of Art, New York.

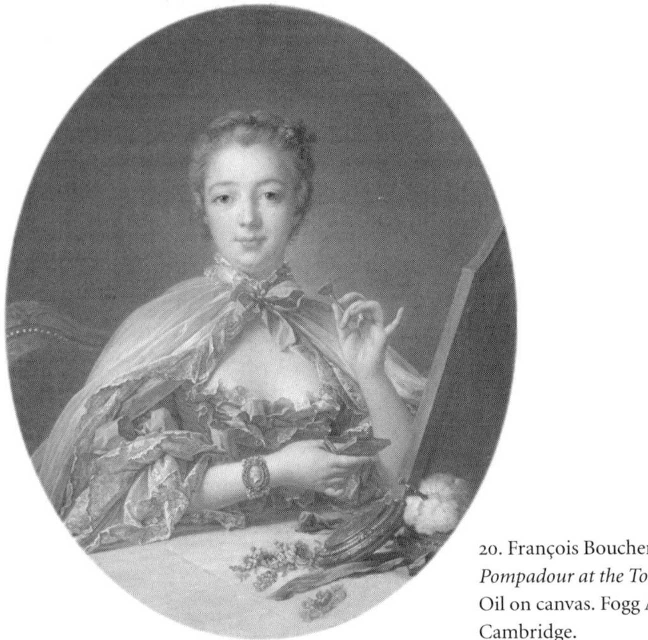

20. François Boucher, *Marquise de Pompadour at the Toilet-Table*, 1758. Oil on canvas. Fogg Art Museum, Cambridge.

padour at the Toilet-Table uses the same device in a strikingly different way (fig. 20). In this case, the artist has represented the subject's view of herself, as she brushes powder onto her face, before her mirror. Here of course the subject and the artist are not identical. But the painting expresses the conceit that the artist and his subject use their brushes to similar effect and that painting a portrait is therefore also a cosmetic exercise.[11]

In these two examples, the implicit spectator is the person portrayed. But this is not the only possibility. For example, Renoir's *La Loge* depicts a man and a woman in a box at the theater (fig. 21). The man, seated in shadow behind the woman, leans back and looks across the theater with his opera glasses, his casual pose suggesting that hers may not be quite so effortless. She holds her opera glasses in one hand, which rests on the ledge of the box, while her other hand rests in her lap. She faces slightly to the left, but she looks slightly to *her* left, so that her eyes are shifted marginally to the right of the implicit line of sight. Her body is still and her expression is neither vacant nor absorbed—as if where she looks matters less than where she does not look. If the composition encourages us to imagine that the view we see is the view of an implicit spectator, whose gaze she is aware of but reluctant to engage, the figure behind her suggests what kind of person's gaze this is.[12]

I have indicated a few salient landmarks in a vast terrain, which the visual

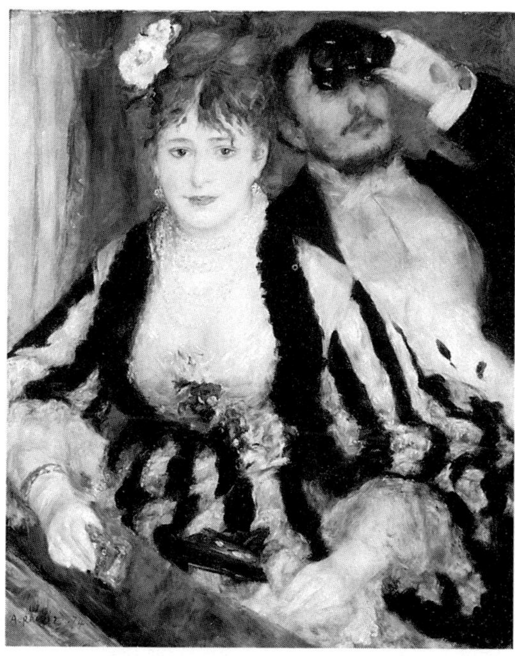

21. Pierre-Auguste Renoir, *La Loge*, 1874. Oil on Canvas. Courtauld Institute Gallery, London.

imagination, intellectual rigor, and technical skill of successive generations of artists have disclosed. But despite the fundamental importance of the occlusion shape principle in the theory of art, there is an important exception to it, namely, anamorphosis. Anamorphic pictures—and anamorphic parts of orthomorphic pictures—are, in Shakespeare's words, "perspectives which, rightly gazed upon, / Show nothing but confusion,—ey'd awry, / Distinguish form."[13] One of the best-known examples, which matches this description well, is the anamorphic depiction of a skull at the bottom of Holbein's portrait of Jean de Dinteville and Georges de Selve, *The Ambassadors* (figs. 22, 23).

From the sixteenth century onward, anamorphic pictures were often intended to be seen both "rightly" and "awry"—so that the trick could be enjoyed. But anamorphosis as such has a much longer history. The earliest mention of it is in Plato's *Sophist* (235d–236a), and it was sometimes used in Byzantine church decoration to compensate for distortions that would otherwise appear in pictures because of the curvature of the support.[14] For example, in the main dome of the Hagia Sophia in Thessalonica, the legs of the Apostles are deliberately elongated because, whereas the upper parts of the figures lie at an obtuse angle to the spectator's line of sight, their lower parts are more nearly vertical, and so the anamorphosis ensures that the apostles' bodies will appear well-proportioned when the dome is seen from below (fig. 24).

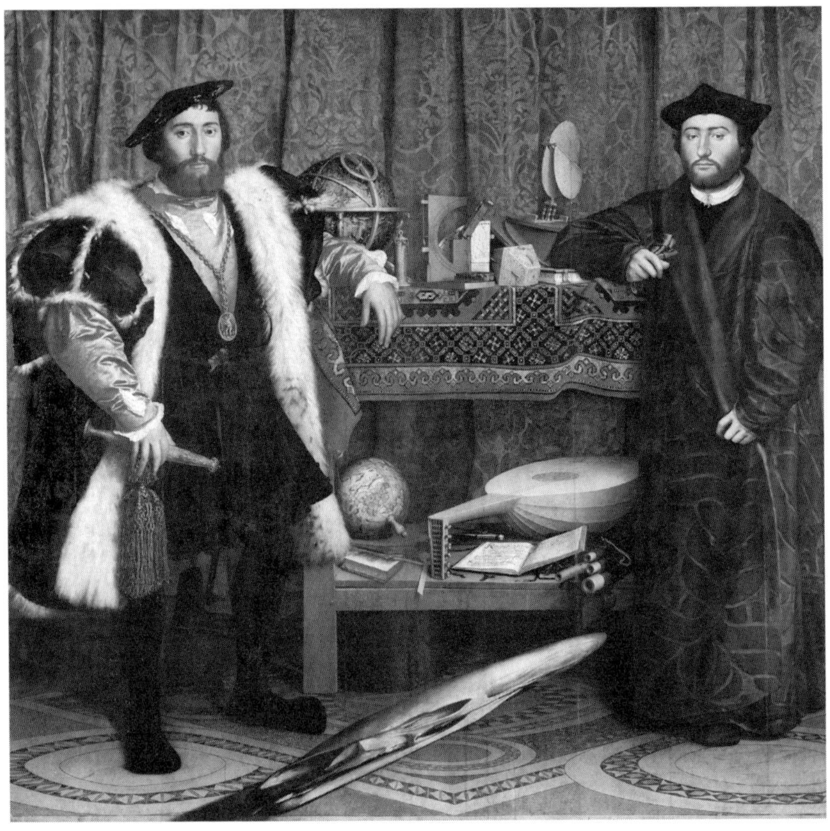

22. Hans Holbein the Younger, *The Ambassadors*, 1533. Oil on canvas. National Gallery, London.

Pictures of this kind are exceptions to the occlusion shape principle, because the occlusion shape of an Apostle's leg and the shape of the smallest part of the mosaic that depicts it are not identical. The second shape is an elongation of the first. It is as if the artists responsible for the cupola, instead of folding an orthomorphic figure of each apostle over its curved surface, projected these figures onto it from below (fig. 25). This is not a radical departure from the basic method of depiction, and like the other devices mentioned above, it embodies the idea that whatever a picture depicts, it depicts relative to an implicit line of sight. But unlike these other devices it is also calculated to accommodate—or to exploit—the fact that a spectator sees the surface of a picture along a specific line of sight.

Anamorphosis therefore requires a modification of the occlusion shape

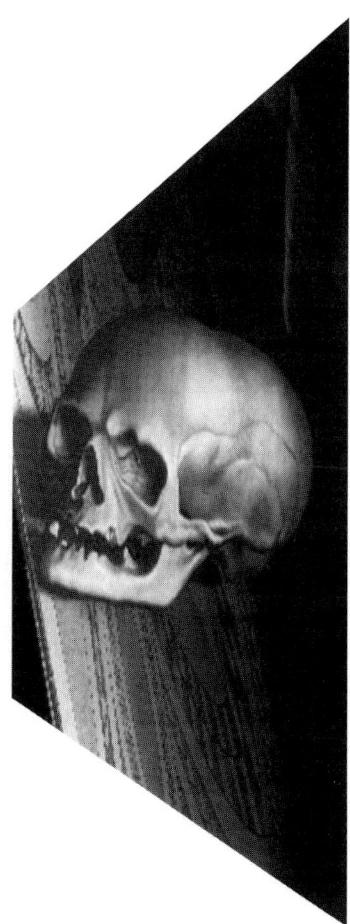

23. Detail of the skull in *The Ambassadors* with the anamorphosis corrected.

principle, which can be stated as follows: if O is a depicted object and P is the smallest part of a picture that depicts O, the occlusion shape of O and the occlusion shape of P, relative to the intended line of sight of the spectator, must be identical. I shall call this the anamorphic occlusion shape principle. Notice that this principle refers to the *intended* line of sight of the spectator. It cannot refer instead to her actual line of sight. For the occlusion shape of P will change as a spectator moves back and forth between a centric and an eccentric line of sight. But the occlusion shape of O—that is, the occlusion shape that O is represented as having—will not change, since the content of a picture does not vary as we move around it.

This reference to the intended line of sight also indicates why the anamor-

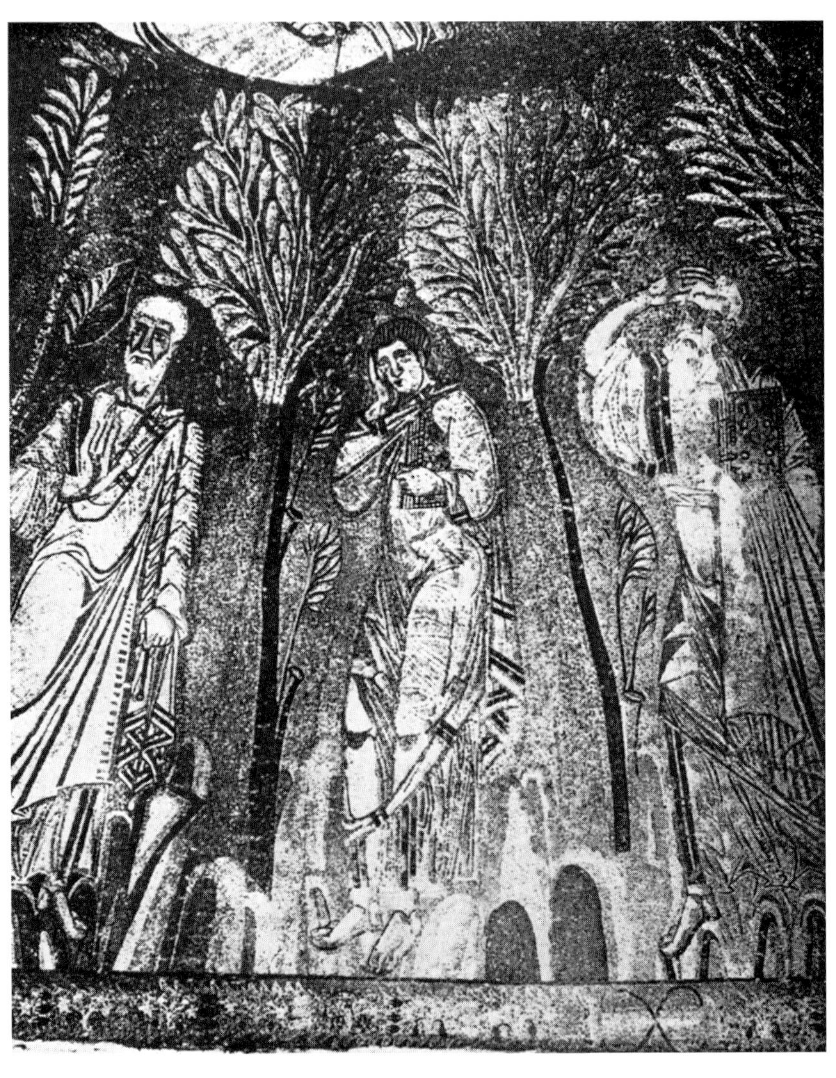

24. *The Ascension*, late ninth century. Mosaic. Hagia Sophia, Thessaloniki. Detail of apostles.

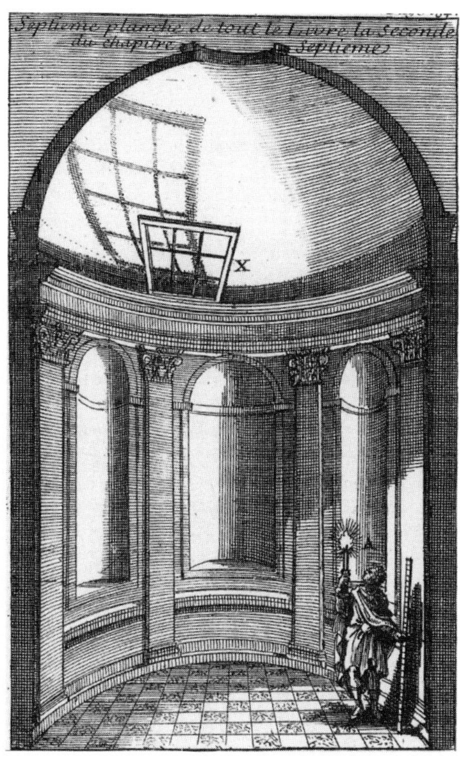

25. *A Shadow Cast on the Interior of a Dome.* Illustration from Bernard Lamy, *Traité de Perspective.* Paris, 1701.

phic occlusion shape principle cannot be applied universally. The reason is that if the occlusion shape of O is identified with the occlusion shape of P, it cannot be fixed with more precision than the spectator's line of sight. But the idea of fixing the position of the spectator is, again, a fifteenth-century innovation. Hence, if the anamorphic principle were applied universally, we should have to conclude that the occlusion shape of O is indeterminate in most orthomorphic pictures, which it is not. In theory, we could add a rider to the anamorphic occlusion shape principle, stipulating that the normal or intended line of sight for orthomorphic pictures is at right angles to the part of the picture's surface occupied by P. But since the shape of P is the same as its occlusion shape, relative to this line of sight, this stipulation would in effect reintroduce the occlusion shape principle by the back door.

The theory of depiction has to acknowledge the exceptional nature of anamorphosis somehow or other, just as the theory of meaning has to find a place for irony and hyperbole, without being stymied by them. The best way of doing this is to maintain the occlusion shape principle explicitly and to treat anamorphosis as an exception to it because anamorphosis was invented by artists faced with a problem that made the spectator's line of sight an issue for the first time. A theory of depiction that reflects this fact is preferable to one that does not. It is both unnecessary and unrealistic to stipulate that the normal or intended line of sight for orthomorphic pictures is at right angles to the picture plane. It is unnecessary because the occlusion shape principle does not require it. And it is unrealistic because in reality the only constraint on the spectator's line of sight is that she should be able to perceive the surface of the picture and the scene that the picture represents.[15]

The concept of occlusion size is similar to the concept of occlusion shape, except that occlusion shape is relative to a line of sight, whereas the occlusion size of an object will vary depending on the position of the eye along this line. But again, this relativity does not imply that an object's occlusion size is nebulous or unreal or that the experience of perceiving it is an illusion. For example, if I hold out my hands in front of me and extend one arm further than the other, the greater occlusion size of the nearer hand will be evident, if I attend to it; and if I pick up a glass of water from the table and lift it toward my lips, I can see its occlusion size increase. The relative occlusion size of my hands depends on their relative size and their relative distance from my eyes and the same is true of the glass when it is on the table, and when I have lifted it toward my lips. These properties are perfectly objective. We can perceive them accurately or inaccurately and we can correct our mistakes by taking measurements and making calculations.

However, like occlusion shape, occlusion size has commonly been regarded by philosophers as an illusion. For example, in the third *Meditation*, Descartes writes as follows:

> I find in my mind two wholly diverse ideas of the sun; the one, by which it appears to me extremely small draws its origin from the senses . . . the other, by which it seems to be many times larger than the whole earth, is taken up on astronomical grounds, that is, elicited from certain notions born with me, or is framed by myself in some other manner. These two ideas cannot certainly both resemble the same sun; and reason teaches me that the one which seems to have immediately emanated from it is the most unlike.[16]

The contrast between these two ideas is entirely specious. For the sun does not appear to be extremely small to me when I look at it. It may appear to have the same occlusion size as a small coin held at arm's length from my eye. And this estimate may be accurate or inaccurate. But the sun does not appear to be the same size as a coin. Indeed it does not appear to be any particular size at all.

Hume does not accept that my idea of the sun's true size depends on any notions I am born with, but he agrees that our visual experience of occlusion size is an illusion: "All objects seem to diminish by their distance: But tho' the appearance of objects to our senses be the original standard, by which we judge of them, yet we do not say, that they actually diminish by the distance; but correcting the appearance by reflexion, arrive at a more constant and establish'd judgement concerning them."[17] Evidently, Hume thinks of an object's diminishing occlusion size as a change in the size that it appears to be, but again, this is mistaken. For if I hold out my hands in front of me and extend one arm further than the other, my hands will not appear to differ in size; and if I lift a glass toward my lips, it will not appear to grow in size, and the volume of water will not appear to swell. The contrast that we need to draw here, in order to describe what I perceive, is not between a constancy in their real dimensions and a variation in "the appearance of objects to our senses." It is between a constancy in size and a variation in occlusion size, both of which are equally real and both of which I can perceive.

Just as the occlusion shapes of the objects represented in a picture are the occlusion shapes they are represented as having, so are their occlusion sizes. And just as the concept of occlusion shape can be used to define the relationship between the shapes of marks on the surface of a picture and the shapes of the objects they depict, the concept of occlusion size can be used to define the relationship between the sizes of marks on the surface of a picture and the sizes of the objects they depict. Thus, if O_1 and O_2 are two depicted objects and P_1 and P_2 are the smallest parts of an orthomorphic picture that depict O_1 and O_2, the relative occlusion size of O_1 and O_2 and the relative size of P_1 and P_2 must be identical. I shall call this the relative occlusion size principle. Like the occlusion shape principle, it is only applicable to orthomorphic pictures, but a corresponding principle for anamorphic pictures can be readily defined. Thus, in the case of an anamorphic picture, the relative occlusion size O_1 and O_2 are represented as having and the relative occlusion size of P_1 and P_2, relative to the intended viewing position must be identical.

~

Just as the shapes of the objects in a picture are the shapes they are represented as having, so are their colors. However, we cannot simply equate the colors of the materials used to make a picture with the colors of the objects it depicts. For example, a drawing can be made on green paper with a gray wash heightened with white without attributing any of these colors to its subject. We can often say something, if only something negative, about the color of an object in a picture, even in the case of a drawing or a print. For example, we cannot say that Saint Eustace's horse in Dürer's print is gray or that it is not gray or that it is dun or that it is not dun, but we can say that it is not piebald. So its color is not completely indeterminate. But now suppose the objects in a picture are, in fact, given determinate colors. Must these be the same as the colors of the pigments that depict them? And if not, is there any fixed relationship at all between the colors on the surface of a picture and the colors that the artist used them to depict?

Wittgenstein struggled with these questions in his *Remarks on Colour*.[18] Early in the discussion, he writes: "It isn't from the outset clear how shades of colour are to be compared and what 'sameness of colour' means" (I, §59). And it must be admitted that this has not become much clearer by the end. One remark appears to suggest that if paint is used to depict an object's color, this in itself implies that the paint and the object have the same color, in one sense: "Grey or a weakly illumined or luminous white can in one sense be the same color, for if I paint the latter I may have to mix the former on the palette" (III, §244). However, other remarks suggest that—in another sense, possibly—the opposite is true. For example, there is the following laconic remark: "There is gold paint, but Rembrandt didn't use it to paint a golden helmet" (III, §79). And yet other remarks seem mainly intended to throw cold water on the question: "Imagine a painting cut up into small, almost monochromatic bits which are then used as pieces in a jig-saw puzzle. Even when such a piece is not monochromatic it should not indicate any three-dimensional shape, but should appear as a flat colour-patch. Only together with the other pieces does it become a bit of blue sky, a shadow, a highlight, transparent or opaque, etc. Do the individual pieces show us the *real colours* of the parts of the picture?" (I, §60). Wittgenstein's tone here, if I have interpreted it correctly, implies that they do not; and the emphasis on the phrase "real colors" seems to imply that there is something suspect about the very idea of "real colors" in this context. It recalls J. L. Austin's pointed question: "We say that the sun in the evening sometimes looks red—well, what colour is it *really*?"[19]

My own view is that it is possible to be more systematic than Wittgenstein is here. For there are two compelling reasons to reject the simple claim that the colors of pigments must be the same as the colors of the objects they depict. Both relate to seminal inventions made by Greek painters in the fifth century B.C., first, shading and, second, the use of optical fusion to blend different pigments applied separately to a painting's surface.

By shading, I mean the representation in pictures of the variations in brightness on an object's surface that are caused not by variations in its pigmentation but by an obstacle between the surface and a light source or by the orientation of the surface relative to a light source. So I am referring to a technique used by artists and not the phenomena in nature that it is used to depict. And for the moment I shall ignore the distinction between the two kinds of shadows I have mentioned. The distinction is an important one in the history of art, but for the moment I am only concerned with the difference between pictures that represent some kind of shadow, whatever its cause may be, and pictures that ignore shadows altogether.[20] In this broad sense of the term, "shading" refers generally to the representation of the varying effect that light has on an object, depending on its direction and intensity and, sometimes, its color temperature as well.

As I shall explain, the invention of shading changed the relationship between a color represented in a picture and the color on the picture's surface that represents it. But in order to describe this change precisely, we need to distinguish between surface colors and aperture colors. When we predicate colors of physical objects, we are sometimes interested in their relatively stable properties and sometimes in their changing relationship with light. The concepts of surface color and aperture color formalize this distinction. For example, suppose we are looking at a uniformly painted wall with a cast shadow lying across it. In general, that will be exactly how it will look. The shadow will not look as if it is a darker shade of paint: it will look as if it is a cast shadow on a uniformly painted surface because we are generally able to see both the uniformity in pigmentation and the variation between the relatively bright part and the shaded patch. And of course neither the uniformity in pigmentation nor the variation in brightness is an illusion. They are distinct, but related, properties of the same surface, both of which we normally perceive.

However, if we look through a cardboard tube at a part of the wall where there is a sharp transition from light to shadow, the uniformity in pigmentation will tend to disappear. The reason is obvious: the tube prevents us from seeing the shadow as a shadow by preventing us from seeing the wider scene, and so the colors we perceive only depend on the light reflected by the two parts of the wall. These colors are called aperture colors because they are the colors we see through a small aperture, such as a cardboard tube. An object's pigmentation is called its surface color.

Now the relationship between the colors on the surface of a painting and the colors they depict depends on whether shading has been used. And we can use the distinction between surface color and aperture color to explain how the two cases differ. For example, shading was not used in Egyptian painting until the Ptolemaic period. Consequently, for most of the history of Egyptian painting, the surface colors of depicted objects were the same as the surface colors of the parts of the painting that depict them, and a difference in surface color between two parts of a painting's surface corresponds to a difference in surface color between the corresponding parts of the depicted scene (plate 2). By contrast, when shading is used, the aperture colors of the various parts of

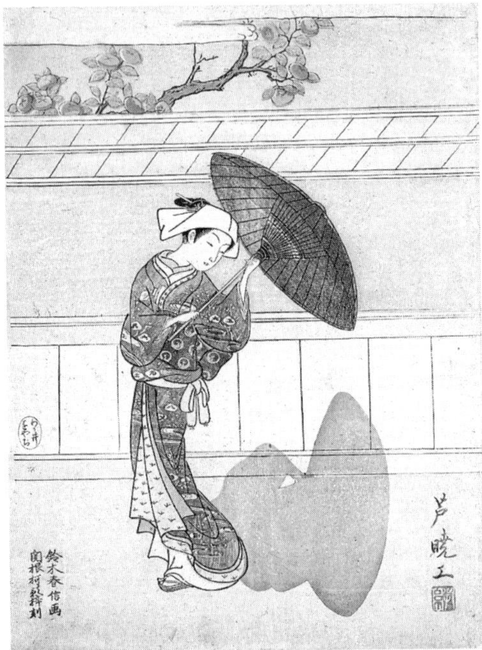

26. Suzuki Harunobu, *Casting a Shadow,* ca. 1766. Woodblock print.

a painting's surface are the same as the aperture colors of the various surfaces they depict, as long as the painting itself is suitably lit; and differences in surface color on the painting's surface do not always correspond to differences in surface color in the depicted scene. For example, in Filippo Lippi's *Annunciation,* the pink wall behind the Virgin is uniform in surface color but the part of the painting that depicts the wall is not (plate 3). The same is true of the pale surfaces on which the shadow falls in a print by Suzuki Harunobu—a rare example of a cast shadow in eighteenth-century Japanese art (fig. 26). The sharp boundary of the shadow makes it especially salient, and it seems to announce itself as the main subject of the print.

The second invention I referred to was the use of optical fusion to blend different colors on a picture's surface. This technique is commonly associated with pointillism, but paintings in tempera that are composed of tiny strokes and dabs of paint exploit the same effect, and so does fine hatching in a print or drawing. The technique was also used—in coarse grain, so to speak—by Byzantine mosaicists. For example, in the Catholicon in Daphni, a row of alternately colored tesserae is used to depict a penumbra on the Virgin's cheek (fig. 27). Here we are obliged to deny that the colors depicted are the same as the colors that depict them because the gradual transition from the shaded edge of the cheek to its bright surface is depicted by means of a sharp transition in color along the toothed line dividing the dark tesserae from the lighter ones. When shading is combined with optical fusion, as it is in this case, the aperture colors that parts of the picture's surface *appear* to have from a suitable distance—in this case, a distance at which the spectator can see the penumbra—are the same as the aperture colors of the surfaces they depict.

The depiction of colors is a complex subject. I have only mentioned a few

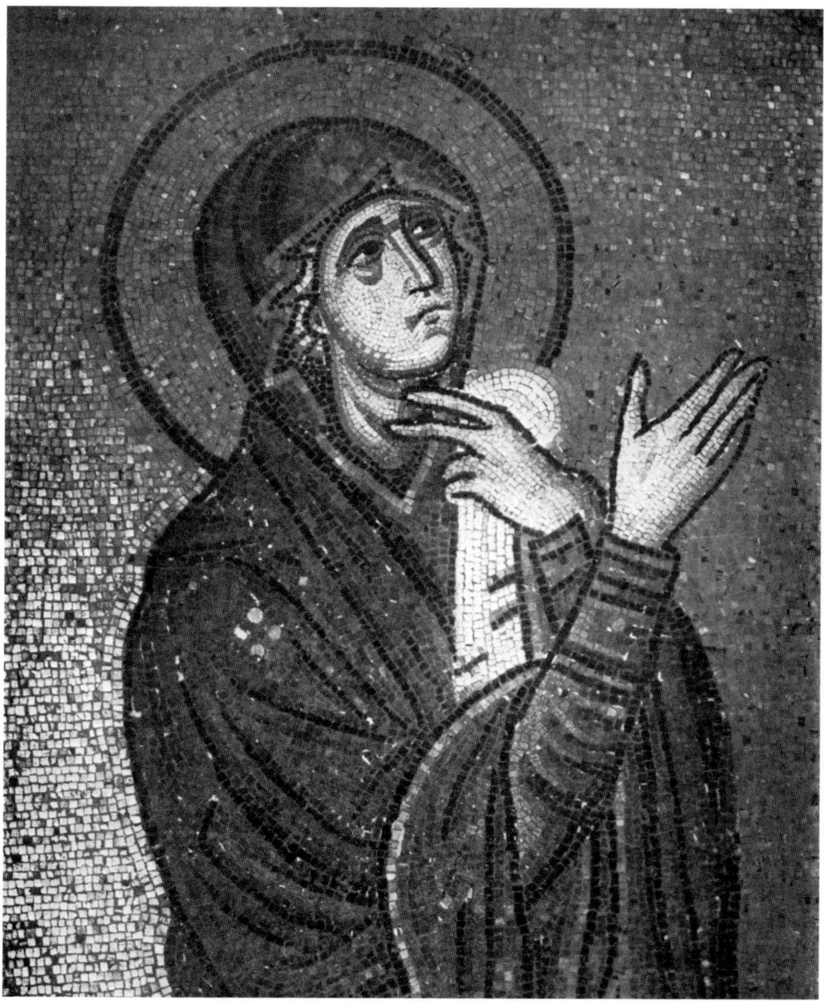

27. *Virgin from Crucifixion,* late eleventh century. Mosaic. Catholicon, Daphni. Detail of Virgin.

basic examples, and even here I have simplified the facts. However, these simple examples demonstrate two things. First, the relationship between the colors of the objects in a picture and the colors that depict them cannot be explained by means of a single comprehensive principle. And second, in the case of color, as in the case of form, it is sometimes possible to define a precise relationship between the marks on a picture's surface and the objects they depict that does not depend on the picture's psychological effect. Optical fusion is an exception, but shading is not—because optical fusion, unlike the variations in brightness that shading represents, is itself a psychological effect. Descartes's remark—that the problem is to know simply how pictures can enable the soul to have sensory perceptions of all the various qualities of the objects to which they correspond—is attractively simple. But when we study the depiction of colors with some care, we see that it masks important differences and that there is no reason to accept this blanket claim in the case of color any more than there is in the case of form.

~

The principles we have defined so far concern identities: now it is time to turn to differences.[21] As we have seen, Descartes claims that "in no case does an image resemble the object it represents in all respects, for otherwise there would be no distinction between the object and its image." Socrates makes the same claim in the passage from Plato's *Cratylus* to which we have already referred. "An image," he says to Cratylus, "which reproduced all the qualities of the thing imitated would no longer be an image." And he continues as follows:

> Let us suppose the existence of two objects: one of them shall be Cratylus, and the other the image of Cratylus. And we will suppose, further, that some God makes not only a representation such as a painter would make of your outward form and color, but also creates an inward organization like yours, having the same warmth and softness; and into this infuses motion, and soul, and mind, such as you have—in a word, copies all your qualities, and places them by you in another form. Would you say that this was Cratylus and the image of Cratylus, or that there were two Cratyluses?[22]

Although it is clear which of the two answers Socrates expects, neither of them is satisfactory. As we all know today, what Socrates describes is called a clone—from the Greek word for a twig. But is the general proposition about images true? Is it true that an image cannot have all of the qualities of the thing imitated—its inward organization as well as its outward form and color?

The answer is that this claim is true if it is qualified. The qualification is necessary because one picture may represent another and, more generally, because ink or pigment may represent ink or pigment. For example, a portrait by Botticelli shows a young man holding a small fragment of a painting, the size and shape of a large medal (plate 4). But the part of the portrait that represents the fragment is itself a small painting in tempera and gold leaf and, therefore, has the same inner structure as the object that it represents, as well as its form and color. As a matter of fact, it actually is a fragment of a trecento painting, which has been inserted into a hole cut in the larger panel. It is therefore true that there is no distinction between the object and its image in this case; but this does not prevent the image from being an image—that is, an image of an image—as long as it is not considered as a self-sufficient whole. Similarly, the bright blob of lead white pigment on the artist's palette in Hogarth's portrait of the artist painting the comic muse is depicted by a blob of lead white pigment, which "resembles the object it represents in all respects," or did until it began to dry and age (fig.28). But again, it depicts a blob of pigment only in the larger context. If we excised it from the painting it would cease to depict anything at all.

So the claim that an image cannot have all of the qualities of the thing imitated needs to be qualified, and the qualification we need is that there must be differences between *whole* pictures and the objects that they represent.[23] But how can we define these differences? The answer to this question is that the visible relation between a picture's content and its surface, which the various principles we have formulated define, needs to be balanced by a *visible* difference. The reason for this is that the pictorial content of a design has to be visible: not visible to anyone, regardless of her visual acuity, experience or education, but visible, in suitable conditions, to a spectator with the requisite acumen and visual skills. But if the only differences between a picture of a kind of object and an instance of that kind of object were invisible ones—such as differences in internal structure or in smell—then no degree of acumen, acuity, or visual skill would enable a spectator to see that the object was a picture or, a fortiori, that it depicted such and such a scene.

It follows that there must be a visible difference between a picture's content and its surface. It must be possible to see that a picture has a range of properties—such as the flatness of the surface, the shape of the support, the substance of the pigment, the form of the brushstrokes or impasto—which cannot be attributed to the objects that it represents. And here we find a fundamental difference between a picture and a copy or an imitation. A copy or imitation is judged better or worse depending on the degree to which it resembles what it is a copy or an imitation of. But a picture by its very nature must differ visibly from what it represents. If, for example, it is evident that a picture is made of pigments bound by oil or glue, whereas its subject is made of flesh and blood, or that a picture is evenly lit, whereas its subject is partly in

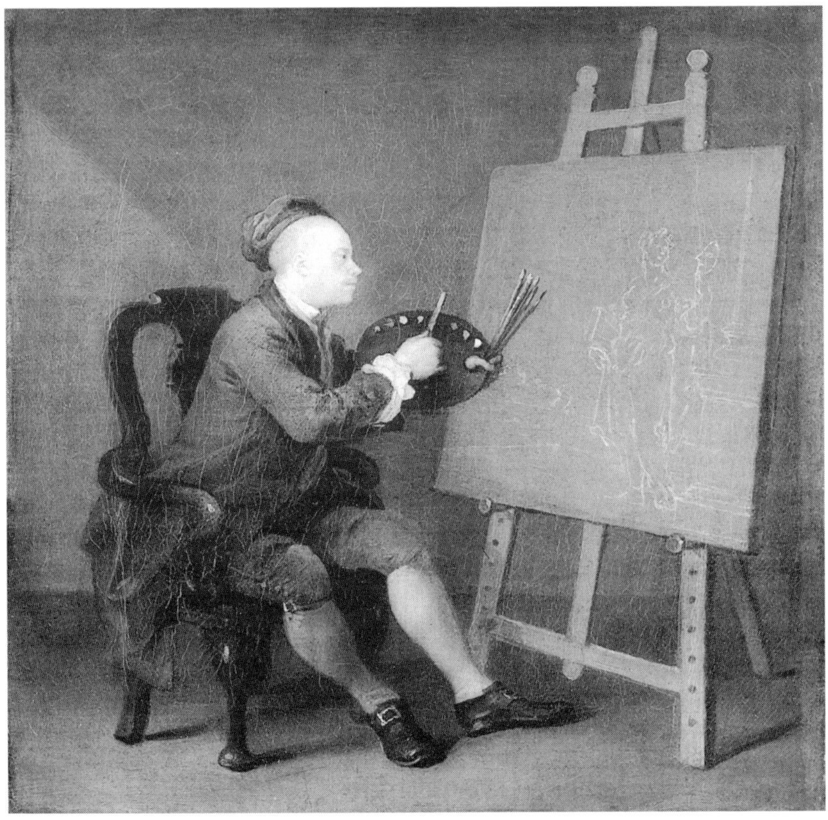

28. William Hogarth, *Hogarth Painting the Comic Muse,* ca. 1757. Oil on canvas. National Portrait Gallery, London.

shadow, or that the shape of part of a picture is circular, whereas the shape of the object it depicts is spherical, these differences cannot be accounted defects in the picture.

The principle that there must be a visible difference between a picture's content and its surface is easily stated and quite simply proved, but if we merely state it, in these relatively abstract terms, we risk missing its importance in the theory of art. For it does not simply mark an ideal limit, like the distinction between a portrait of a man and a copy made by a god. It draws a line within appearances themselves, and not between appearances and internal structures, and so it cannot fail to affect the practice of making and perceiving pictures.

Like the occlusion shape principle, the visible difference between a pic-

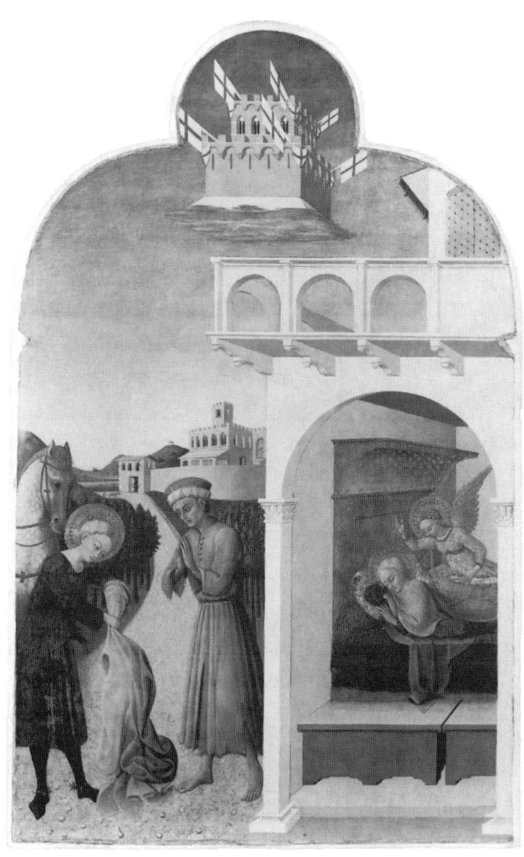

29. Sassetta, *St. Francis Meeting a Poor Knight*, ca. 1437–44. Panel from *The Life of Saint Francis*. Tempera on wood. National Gallery, London.

ture's content and its surface underlies a range of pictorial effects, which depend in this case on various analogies that an artist can establish between the content of a picture and its surface because they are visibly distinct. In the first place, there are effects that depend on the nature of the colored matter itself—gold, pigment, glass, dirt, blood, and so forth. For example, as Michael Baxandall has pointed out, Sassetta's choice of the costly pigment ultramarine to depict the cloak Saint Francis gives to a poor knight enhances the symbolic importance of his gift and accentuates the modesty of his pose (fig. 29).

Second, there are effects that depend on the manner in which the color has been applied to the support. For example, a scroll painting by the Japanese painter Isshi Bunshu depicts a grapevine with a liquid ink that spreads visibly on the paper (fig. 30). The painting accompanies the following poem, whose loose calligraphic strokes trail vertically beside the glistening fruit:

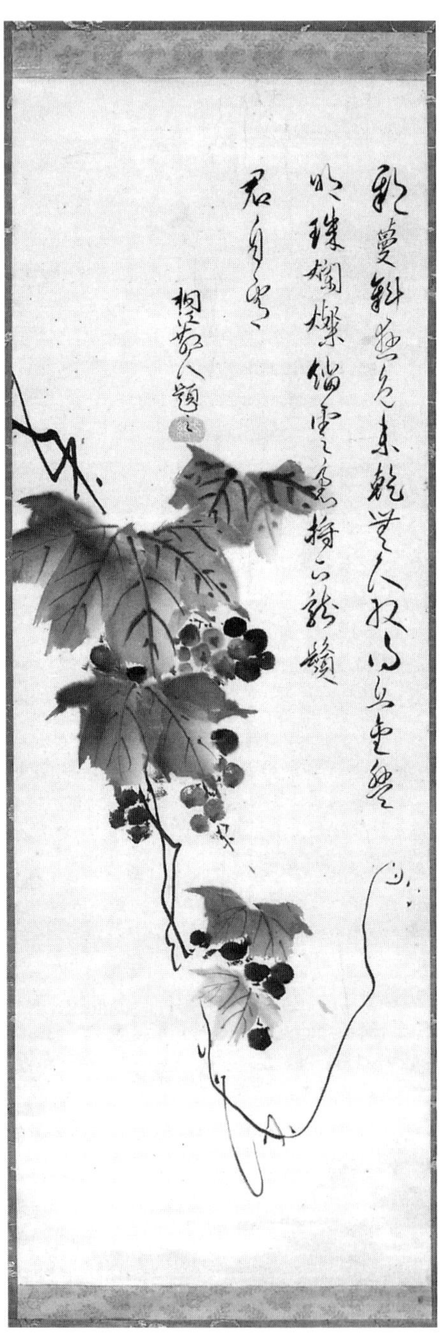

30. Isshi Bunshu, *Grapes,* ca. 1634. Ink on paper. Arthur M. Sackler Gallery, Smithsonian Institution, Washington, D.C.

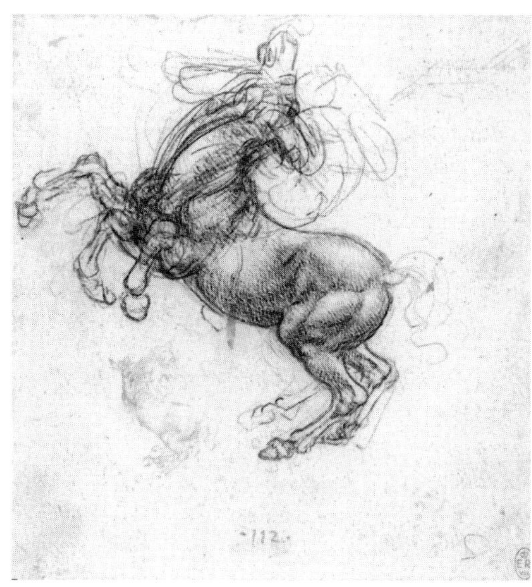

31. Leonardo da Vinci, *Rearing Horse,* ca. 1502–4. Red chalk. Royal Library, Windsor Castle.

New vines dangle aslant, their color not yet dry,
No one has taken them to place on a golden plate.
Shining gems glisten and gleam among dark clouds,
Pluck down a dragon whisker and see for yourself.

Third, there are cases where the significant thing is the activity of applying the color to the support, to the extent that this is visible in the result. For example, speed and vigor of execution commonly convey a sense of motion—perhaps by a kind of metaphor, which transfers the motion of an artist's hand into the image (fig. 31). In several pastel drawings made in the 1880s in which Degas depicts a woman drying herself, the trace of the pastel rubbing against the paper's surface subliminally registers the motion of the towel against the woman's skin.

Fourth, artists have often played with the relationship between the picture and its frame or decorative border—often by creating a visual parallel between the frame and part of the picture's subject or by subverting the convention of the frame. For example, the tondo of a cup decorated by the Colmar Painter shows a boy running with a hoop and a tray of food, the hoop echoing the line of the picture's frame (fig. 32). And another tondo, by Peithinos, shows Peleus seizing Thetis, whom he can only win, according to the myth, by holding her tightly as she changes shape. His hands are securely locked together, repeating the form of the meander border (fig. 33). There are also sev-

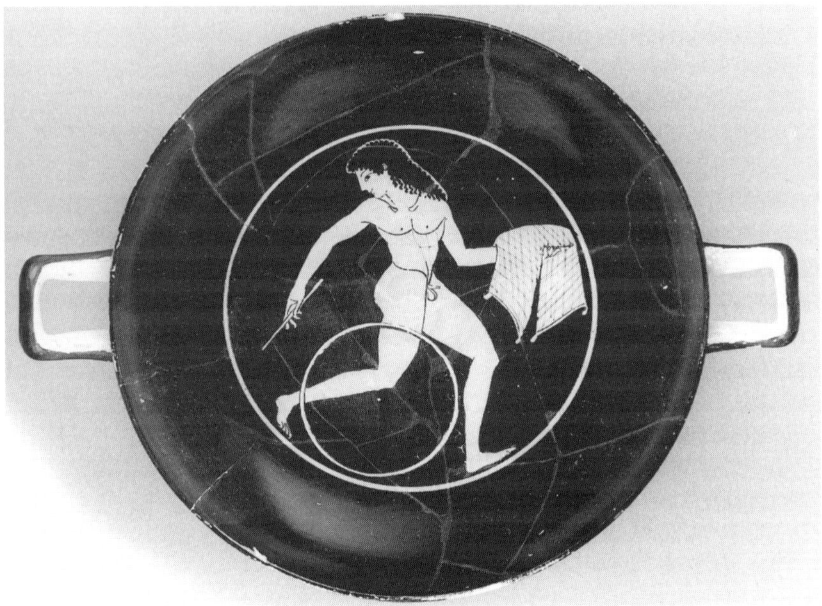

32. Kylix, ca. 500 B.C. Attributed to the Colmar Painter. Ashmolean Museum, Oxford.

eral examples in Greek vase painting of subjects breaking out the frame, but perhaps none is as striking as a fresco Giandomenico Tiepolo painted for the villa his family owned in Zianigo, showing a kestrel scattering a flock of sparrows (fig. 34). One of the poor little birds is evidently so frightened that it has flown right out of the picture—a breach of decorum, perhaps, but an excusable one in the circumstances, and no more surprising than jumping out of one's skin would be.

Finally, the principle that there must be a visible difference between a picture's content and its surface points to a distinction that our experience of art compels us to acknowledge between pictures that are designed to distract attention from the surface and those that, on the contrary, invite it. This distinction has sometimes been treated crudely—for instance, by Clement Greenberg, who claims that "realistic" European art "dissembled the medium" and praises "modernism" for celebrating it. And it has sometimes been misunderstood—for instance, by Richard Wollheim, who denies that trompe l'oeil paintings are representations on the grounds that they "repel attention" to the surface. (Both of these ideas will be discussed in later chapters.) But serious criticism is bound to examine the extent to which, the means by which, and the purposes for which artists have either emphasized and drawn attention to

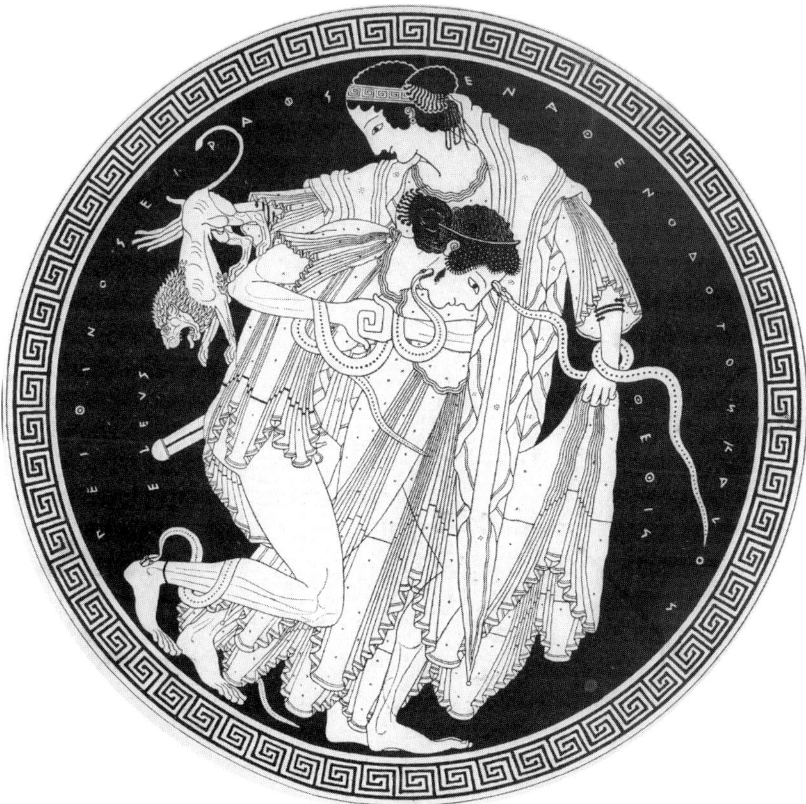

33. Kylix, ca. 490 B.C. Attributed to Peithinos. Staatliche Museen zu Berlin, Antikensammlungen.

the qualities of the surface of a picture or, on the contrary, diverted the viewer's attention from them. And so it has, ever since Plato.

~

The basic principles of pictorial art defined in this chapter are the defensible residue of the resemblance theory of depiction. These principles do not imply that a picture is an imitation of the objects that it represents if the idea of an imitation is burdened with the associations that critics of the theory have traditionally objected to. For they do not imply that pictures necessarily portray objects that actually exist or that pictorial art is slavish copying. But of course these propositions were never seriously advanced, either expressly or by implication. They appear in the literature because (as Christopher Ricks once put it) brickbats cannot be made without straw men. Nor do these basic

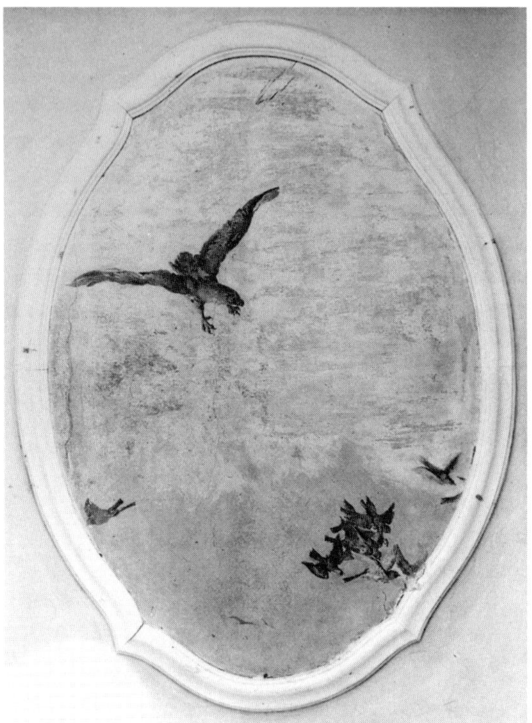

34. Giandomenico Tiepolo, *A Kestrel Scattering a Flock of Sparrows*, ca. 1791. Fresco. Ca' Rezzonico, Venice.

principles either support or oppose the judgments about artistic value that the concept of imitation was once used to express—such as Alberti's proposition that artists should aim at beauty rather than at likeness, or Leonardo's insistence that artists who depend on pattern books instead of imitating nature herself "labor in vain." As for the comparison between paintings and reflections—which Plato, Alberti, and Leonardo all proposed—we shall return to this important topic more than once. In the next chapter, and then again in chapter 10, I shall argue that the careless use of the comparison—by philosophers, psychologists, and historians alike—has had an extensive and enduring influence on the theory of art.

6

ART AND OPTICS

IN THE PREVIOUS CHAPTER, we saw how far it is possible to define the basic principles of pictorial art in objective terms, that is, without referring to the psychological effect a picture produces in a spectator's mind. I shall now begin to examine the idea that the nature of pictorial art can be explained subjectively by defining this effect. This idea has been widely canvassed during the past forty years or so, since the publication of Gombrich's book, *Art and Illusion.* But its original source is in Descartes's *Optics,* which was written in the early 1630s and which was, along with the *Discourse on the Method,* the *Meteorology,* and the *Geometry,* the first of Descartes's writings to appear in print.

Descartes argues in his *Optics* that progress in the theory of vision depends on a radical transformation in the way we conceive of pictures. This argument is a decisive moment in the history of science because it marks the beginning of modern physical optics.[1] But it is also the single most radical and imaginative step that has been taken in the theory of pictorial art. In the next chapter, I shall discuss the resurgence of Descartes's ideas in twentieth-century art theory. But I shall devote this chapter to examining these ideas in their original context. My reason for doing so is partly to avoid obscuring their very radical character, their oddness and their ingenuity, and partly because a clear understanding of the purpose that they were designed to serve will bring their strengths and weaknesses to light.

Descartes's principal idea about pictorial art is that in order to explain how a picture represents an object—he mentions an engraving of a battle or a storm—we only need to think about the picture's physiological and psychological effects. "The problem," he says, "is to know simply how [pictures] can enable the soul to have sensory perceptions of all the various qualities of the objects to which they correspond—not to know how they can resemble these objects." He accepts that there is often some resemblance in shape between a part of a picture and an object of the kind it represents. But he denies that this is of any theoretical significance at all. It plays no part in explaining why the picture represents that kind of object. Depiction, according to this view, is rooted in response. An engraving is a tangle of inky marks: the rest is in the eye or, strictly speaking, in the soul of the beholder.

In the last chapter, I commented on Descartes's claim, in the fourth discourse of the *Optics,* that pictures need only resemble the forests, towns, or people they represent in respect of shape and that "even this resemblance is very imperfect." But I did not explain why Descartes attempted to disprove the resemblance theory. His reason was that he believed its truth was presupposed by a conjecture about the nature of vision that commanded widespread assent and that the *Optics* was intended to disprove. This is the hypothesis that vision is the result of perceiving images, which transmit the appearance of visible objects to the eye. The importance of this hypothesis, from Descartes's point of view, was ultimately due to its metaphysical implications. For it seemed to him that if the hypothesis were true, the physical world would in fact be the colorful place we are presented with in our experience of it, and matter could not be the purely geometrical substance he imagined.[2]

Descartes was therefore bound to deny that the imagist hypothesis is true. But he did not deny that the objects we see do in fact produce images of themselves on our retinas or that these images cause our perceptions. Instead, he transformed the very concept of an image. The received view about images was, he says, "confined to the requirement that they should resemble the objects which they represent." But Descartes turns this view upside down. Images, he argues, do not cause us to see the things they represent because they are likenesses. On the contrary, we call them likenesses because they cause us to see these things, that is, because they produce perceptions of them in our minds. It follows that according to Descartes's view, a retinal image cannot be thought of as a surrogate for the objects that it represents. It is simply a mechanical stimulus that produces a distinctive kind of psychological effect.

It is not difficult to appreciate how startling and paradoxical this view about pictures seemed to Descartes's contemporaries. It still seems paradoxical. However, I believe it is substantially correct, where optical images are concerned. Descartes's mistake, I shall argue, was to claim that we must think about optical images and pictures—such as paintings and engravings—in just the same way and to extend his conception of optical images to pictures.

~

The first discourse of the *Optics* begins with a disclaimer, which was necessary because Descartes was unwilling to publish the details of his physical theory. He says that he will not attempt to explain the "true nature" of light: his aim is only to "use two or three comparisons in order to facilitate that conception of light that seems most suitable for explaining all those of its properties that we know through experience and then for deducing all the others that we cannot observe so easily."[3] The first of these comparisons, which is the most interesting from our point of view, is between the action of light on our eyes and the pressure of a blind man's stick on his hand:

> No doubt you have had the experience of walking at night over rough ground without a light, and finding it necessary to use a stick in order to guide yourself. You may then have been able to notice that by means of this stick you could feel the various objects situated around you, and that you could even tell whether they were trees or stones or sand or water or grass or mud or any other such thing. It is true that this kind of sensation is somewhat confused and obscure in those who do not have long practice with it. But consider it in those born blind, who have made use of it all their lives: with them, you will find, it is so perfect and so exact that one might almost say that they see with their hands, or that their stick is the organ of some sixth sense given to them in place of sight. In order to draw a comparison from this, I would have you consider the light in bodies we call "luminous" to be nothing other than a certain movement, or very rapid and lively action, which passes to our eyes through the medium of the air and other transparent bodies, just as the movement or resistance of the bodies encountered by a blind man passes to his hand by means of his stick.[4]

Descartes did not invent this analogy—Galen mentions that the Stoics "say that we see by means of the surrounding air as with a walking-stick"—but uses it in ingenious and diverse ways.[5] For example, in the sixth discourse, he uses it to explain why the inversion of the retinal image does not make us see things upside down. He points out that if a man holding two sticks crosses his arms, it does not feel as if the part of the ground he prods with the stick in his right hand is to his right or that the part of the ground he prods with the stick in his left hand is to his left (fig. 35). His sense of left and right is not impaired. Similarly, if the rays of light cross inside our eyes, there is no reason to expect our visual experience of the world to be inverted.

However, the first discourse is where we need to start. Here, Descartes uses the walking stick analogy to show how elegant and plausible a mechanical theory of light and color can be—although bearing his disclaimer in mind, he is mostly careful to speak in tentative and hypothetical terms.

In the first place, he explains how the instantaneous transmission of light might occur. Since "the action by which we move one end of a stick must pass instantaneously to the other end," he says, there is no need for us to find it strange that "light can extend its rays instantaneously from the sun to us."[6] Of course, we now know that light is not transmitted instantaneously, and one could argue that since Descartes was content to postulate matter too subtle to be detected, he might have entertained the possibility of a delay that was too brief to be observed, as several earlier philosophers had done. Be that as it may, Descartes follows Aristotle on this point: "if the distance traversed were short," Aristotle wrote, "the movement might have been unobservable, but where the distance is from extreme East to extreme West, the strain upon our powers of belief is too great."[7]

Second, Descartes uses the analogy to challenge the assumption that our experience of light and color displays the true nature of objects that seem luminous or colored to us and to introduce his own mechanical theory of color. He argues as follows: since I do not suppose that the sensations I feel in

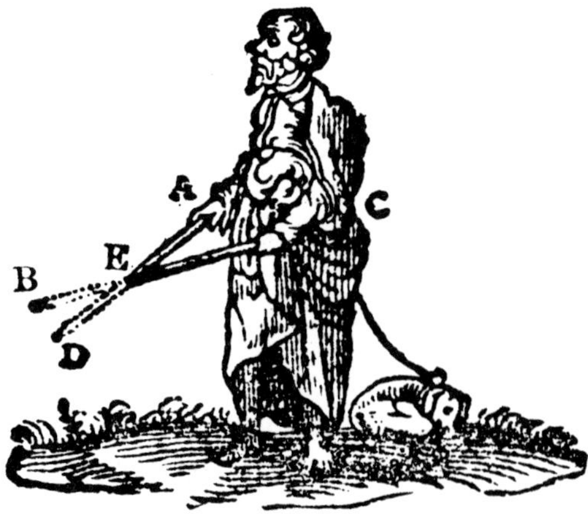

35. *A Man Holding Two Sticks.* Illustration from Réné Descartes, *Dioptrique.* Leiden, 1637.

my hand when I push a stick against hard rock or spongy turf resemble the hardness of the rock or the softness of the turf, it is reasonable to doubt whether the objects I see have qualities that bear any resemblance to my experience of light and color and to entertain the possibility that "colours are nothing other than the various ways in which the bodies receive light and reflect it against the eye."[8] (Remember that light itself is being considered as "a certain movement, or very rapid and lively action.")

Finally, and most important for our purposes, Descartes capitalizes on these two results to show that optics can dispense with "those images flitting through the air . . . which so exercise the imagination of the philosophers."[9] For if the production of light by luminous bodies and its reflection by illuminated bodies can be explained without supposing that anything actually travels through the air, and if our visual experience need not match the physical objects we see in the way that a picture matches what it represents, then there is no need to postulate pictorial intermediaries that could transport the appearances of visible objects to our eyes:

> There is no need to suppose that something material passes from objects to our eyes to make us see colors and light, or even that there is something in the objects which resembles the ideas or sensations that we have of them. In just the same way, when a blind man feels bodies, nothing has to issue from the bodies and pass along his stick to his hand; and the resistance or movement of the bodies, which is the sole cause of the sensations he has of them, is nothing like the ideas he forms of them. By this means, your mind will be delivered from all those little images flitting through the air, called "intentional forms."[10]

In the first discourse, Descartes does not attempt to disprove the imagist hypothesis, but the walking stick analogy holds out the promise of a purely mechanical optical theory, which can dispense with it. The attack on the imagist hypothesis occurs later in the *Optics,* but it takes a subtler form than the first discourse might lead us to expect. For Descartes accepts—indeed he insists—that an image of what surrounds us *is* produced on each of our retinas and that this image, like a drawing or an engraving, "can stimulate our mind to conceive the objects depicted in it." Moreover, he concedes that retinal images do in fact resemble the objects that produce them. But he argues at length in the fourth and sixth discourses that "it is [not] by means of this resemblance that the picture causes our sensory perception of these objects."[11] His argument begins as follows: "We must take care not to assume—as our philosophers commonly do—that in order to have sensory perceptions the soul must contemplate certain images transmitted by objects to the brain, or at any rate we must conceive the nature of these images in an entirely different manner from that of the philosophers."[12]

The manner in which images were traditionally conceived, Descartes explains, was "confined to the requirement that they should resemble the objects they represent." But, he claims, if we accept this conception of images, it will be impossible to explain how they are produced by objects, received by the eye, and transmitted to the brain. This claim is somewhat peremptory since the imagist hypothesis had been combined with ideas about the production and transmission of images that are similar to Descartes's own—by Roger Bacon, for example. But the passage that follows contains his principal argument against the imagist hypothesis and introduces his novel conception of an image: no longer a likeness that can act as a surrogate for a visible object but merely a stimulus that can produce a distinctive kind of psychological effect:

> [The philosophers'] sole reason for positing such images [that is, images that are produced by objects, received by the eye, etc.] was that they saw how easily a picture can stimulate our mind to conceive the objects depicted in it, and so it seemed to them that, in the same way, the mind must be stimulated, by little pictures formed in our head, to conceive the objects that affect our senses. We should, however, recall that our mind can be stimulated by many things other than images—by signs and words, for example, which in no way resemble the things they signify. And if, in order to depart as little as possible from accepted views, we prefer to maintain that the objects which we perceive by our senses really send images of themselves to the inside of our brain, we must at least observe that in no case does an image have to resemble the object it represents in all respects, for otherwise there would be no distinction between the object and its image. It is enough that the image resembles its object in a few respects. Indeed the perfection of an image often depends on its not resembling its object as much as it might. You can see this in the case of engravings. . . . Now we must think of the images formed in our brain in just the same way, and note that the problem is to know simply how they can enable the soul to have sensory perceptions of all the various qualities of the objects to which they correspond—not to know how they can resemble these objects.[13]

The first thing that is likely to strike us about this passage is that Descartes appears to accept the imagist hypothesis and to reject only the doctrine, which was formerly associated with it, that pictures are likenesses. He seems to be willing to concede that "the objects which we perceive by our senses really send images of themselves to the inside of our brain" and that these images "enable the soul to have sensory perceptions of all the various qualities of the objects to which they correspond," so long as it is not supposed that they do so because they resemble these objects. This may seem disappointing. For in the first discourse, as we have seen, Descartes held out the promise of an optical theory that discards "those images flitting through the air," and now, less than a dozen pages later, it seems that only the flitting is to be discarded. But, as we shall see, his argument is less conservative than it appears to be, whether or not the appearance is contrived "in order to depart as little as possible from accepted views."

In the passage quoted, Descartes argues that the mere presence of images in our eyes or in our brains cannot by itself explain how we see. The problem, he says, is to explain how an image in the eye or the brain can "stimulate the mind to conceive the objects depicted in it," and there is no reason to accept a priori that any sort of resemblance between these images and the things they represent is part of the answer. For we know perfectly well that signs and words stimulate the mind to conceive the objects that they represent, without resembling them at all, and that pictures such as engravings do so without resembling them in any respect except for shape, and in that respect imperfectly. What we know for sure about pictures is that they do have this effect on us: that is, they do "make us think of countless different qualities in [the objects they represent]." But how they do so is an open question. Once we see this point clearly, and no longer assume that resemblance explains depiction, we shall no longer find it tempting to suppose—as philosophers have been accustomed to—that the mere presence of an image in the eye or the brain can explain how we see.

In order to see how radically this argument transforms the orthodox conception of images, we need to compare the role that images play in the theory Descartes attacks and the role that they play in his own theory. The difference is this. Descartes makes the representational content of images depend on the nature of the sensory perceptions they cause us to have instead of the other way round. It is precisely for this reason that the requirement that an image resembles what it represents becomes superfluous. For in order to explain how an image represents objects with such and such colors, sizes, and shapes, what we now need to do, it seems, is to discover what patterns of stimulation in the brain the image causes and what sorts of sensory perceptions are caused by these patterns of stimulation. Hence, the question of whether, to what extent, or in what respects images resemble what they represent has become theoretically irrelevant: "The problem is to know simply how they can enable the soul to have sensory perceptions of all the various qualities of the objects to which they correspond." Reaching for his walking stick again, Descartes concludes the fourth discourse as follows:

> For instance, when our blind man touches bodies with his stick, they certainly do not transmit anything to him except in so far as they cause his stick to move in different ways according to the different qualities in them, thus likewise setting in motion the nerves in his hand, and then the regions of his brain where these nerves originate. This is what occasions his soul to have sensory perceptions of just as many different qualities in these bodies as there are differences in the movements caused by them in his brain.[14]

Descartes's innovative conception of images is wholly subservient to his theory of perception. It was devised to allow him to concede that retinal images enable us to see without jeopardizing his mechanical optics and, thereby, the geometrical theory of matter. For if we conceive of these images as nothing more than complex mechanical stimuli that are, as he puts it, "ordained by nature" to cause sensory perceptions, we remain free to acknowledge that there may be a great disparity between the physical world we inhabit and the appearance in which it is clothed when we perceive it. In effect, Descartes's corrosive scrutiny has dissolved the imagist hypothesis without refuting it directly. For without the corollary that pictures are likenesses, all that remains of the hypothesis is a chain of mechanical causes that leaves us free to doubt the very fact it was meant to explain—namely, that our visual experience reveals the true nature of the objects that we see. The concession Descartes makes "in order to depart as little as possible from accepted views" is therefore not quite what it seems: he permits us to retain a formula but not the substantial doctrine that it was used to express. And in the fifth discourse, it transpires that he did not really make the concession because he acknowledged that there is some virtue in respecting orthodoxy but because it is true: visible objects do "imprint quite perfect images of themselves on the back of our eyes," and Descartes believed that these images "also pass beyond into the brain."[15]

~

Since we are mainly concerned with Descartes's attack on the resemblance theory, we can begin an assessment of his argument by considering two questions. First, was it necessary to disprove the resemblance theory in order to undermine the imagist hypothesis? And second, is the resemblance theory inconsistent with the geometrical theory of matter? I shall argue that in each case the answer is no.

The first question is the simpler one to answer. There was no need for Descartes to disprove the resemblance theory because the mere presence of an image in the eye or in the brain cannot possibly explain how we see objects, any more than having a picture pasted on our foreheads could—regardless of whether our conception of images is "confined to the requirement that they should resemble the objects they represent." In other words, the imagist hypothesis is incapable of explaining vision whatever theory of pictorial representation is right. This point was already understood by Theophrastus, who criticized Empedocles' theory of hearing in the following way: "Empedocles explains hearing by stating that it is due to intra-aural sounds. But it is strange of him to suppose that he has explained how we hear, by merely stating this theory of a sound, as of a gong, within the ear. For suppose that we hear the outer sounds by means of this gong; by what do we hear *the gong itself*, when it rings? This—the very point of the whole inquiry—is neglected by him."[16]

Perhaps Descartes was aware of this argument, for a similar one appears at the beginning of the sixth discourse:

> Now when this picture thus passes to the inside of our head, it still bears some resemblance to the objects from which it proceeds. As I have amply shown already, however, we must not think that it is by means of this resemblance that the picture causes our sensory awareness of these objects—as if there were yet other eyes within our brain with which we could perceive it. Instead we must hold that it is the movements composing this picture that, acting directly upon our soul in so far as it is united to our body, are ordained by nature to make it have such sensations.[17]

In this passage, Descartes comes close to saying that it is futile to postulate images as surrogates for visible objects because doing so implies that we have another pair of eyes with which we see these images. But what he actually says is different. What he actually says is that the resemblance between the images in our brains and the visible objects that produce them cannot explain how we see these objects because if it did we would need another pair of eyes to see the images. This is true. For if images in our brains make us aware of objects by resembling them, their effect on us depends on their appearance and, hence, on being seen. But it is surely an unfortunate point for Descartes to be making because it seems to imply that the resemblance between images and the objects that they represent is not theoretically insignificant where visible pictures, the ones that we do see with our eyes, are concerned. And this evidently contradicts the burden of his argument in the fourth discourse. There, he makes the unargued and ostensibly implausible claim that "we must think of the images formed in our brain in just the same way" as engravings. In other words, he claims that the correct explanation of how we see what engravings represent must be the same as the correct explanation of how we see what the images in our brains represent—despite the fact that we really do see the first kind of picture but not the second. In both cases, he says, "the problem is to know simply how they can enable the soul to have sensory perceptions of all the various qualities of the objects to which they correspond—not to know how they can resemble these objects." In the sixth discourse, however, the argument turns precisely on the distinction between images that we do see and ones that we don't. I shall return to this point shortly.

The second question was whether the resemblance theory is inconsistent with the geometrical theory of matter. Again, the answer is no. If the geometrical theory of matter is true, our sensory perceptions disguise the true nature of material objects. For if matter is nothing more than embodied geometry, the bright and colorful appearance in which it is clothed when we perceive it is our own creation. But in the first place, Descartes confuses the question of whether our perceptions disguise the nature of material objects and the question of whether our perceptions resemble the objects that produce them.[18] That is why he wants to destroy the idea that the links in the chain that runs from the object to the image and from the image to the sensory perception are connected by resemblances. And second, as the metaphor of a chain suggests, Descartes could have disregarded the relationship between objects and images altogether and concentrated his attack on the link between the last image in the chain—the one on the pineal gland—and the perception. There is no need to break a chain in more than one place, and so there is no need for Descartes to argue that the images in our brains do not resemble the objects they enable us to perceive in order to prove that our perceptions themselves do not resemble these objects.

It seems, therefore, that Descartes's revolutionary conception of images was neither a vital part of his attack on the imagist hypothesis nor a corollary of his metaphysics. But there is a deeper problem with his argument than this, for although I have so far gone along with the idea that optical images in our eyes enable us to see, this is in fact a residue of the imagist hypothesis that continued to contaminate Descartes's visual theory.[19] The objects we see produce images of themselves on our retinas because the retina has a reflective surface. These images will be clearly visible if we look into an eye with the right sort of instrument. "Real" images, as they are called in optics, are produced on a surface by a lens; whereas "virtual" images are produced by mirrors. But both kinds of images are caused by reflection, and since retinal images exist because of the light the retina reflects, it is obvious that they do not cause our sensory perceptions. The irradiation of the retina enables us to see, but the light that the retina reflects does not. The retinal image is not irrelevant to visual theory. As Descartes argues in the fifth discourse, its existence and orientation confirm Kepler's description of the geometry of the eye. But retinal images do not enable us to see, any more than echoes in our ears enable us to hear. For example, suppose Lucy can see a tree. If James looks into Lucy's eye with the right sort of instrument, James will also be able to see a tree because an image of a tree will be visible on Lucy's retina. Hence Lucy's retinal image will explain why James can see a tree; but it will not explain why Lucy herself can see one. Aristotle understood this point well: "Democritus is right in his opinion that the eye is of water; not, however, when he goes on to explain seeing as mirroring. The mirroring that takes place in an eye is due to the fact that the eye is smooth, and it really has its seat not in the eye but in the one that sees it, inasmuch as the case is merely one of reflection."[20] Aristotle is referring to the virtual image reflected by the surface of the cornea, the glassy membrane that covers the front part of the eye, and not the real image on the retina; but the principle is just the same.

The fact that retinal images are caused by reflection brings us to the main point. Reflections are called images, but there is a fundamental difference between images of these kinds and engravings or paintings or drawings. For if we see a reflection of something, what we see is the thing itself and not something else—a certain sort of picture—that represents it. For example, I use the mirror in my bathroom to see my own face when I shave. But it really should be obvious that I see my face itself and not a picture of it on the mirror's surface. That is why I direct the light toward my face. As we have seen, Plato's *Republic* is the locus classicus for the analogy between painting and mirroring; and we find the comparison repeated many times in Renaissance art theory, notably by Alberti.[21] It has become an axiom in the theory of art that the analogy misrepresents the nature of art, in general, and of pictorial art in particular. But the root of it is a mistake not about art but about reflections.

Remarkably, the idea that mirrors show us pictures of things and not the things themselves still flourishes in serious academic work. It is possible that Plato did not grasp the difference between mirror images and pictures, although Aristotle evidently did. But our contemporaries should know better. Yet Umberto Eco insists that it is naive for the man who sees his reflection in a mirror to suppose that he is seeing himself: "It would be so," he writes, "only if he, the observer I mean, were the one inside the mirror," implying that there is something inside the mirror, but it is not the observer.[22] In a similar vein, Gombrich describes the bathroom mirror as "an instrument of illusion" and urges the reader to perform an experiment when it is clouded by steam:

> It is a fascinating exercise in illusionist representation to trace one's own head on the surface of the mirror and to clear the area enclosed by the outline. For only when we have actually done this do we realize how small the image is that gives us the illusion of seeing ourselves "face to face." To be exact, it must be

exactly half the size of our head. . . . But however cogently this fact can be demonstrated with the help of similar triangles, the assertion is usually met with frank incredulity. And despite all geometry, I, too, would stubbornly contend that I really see my head (natural size) when I shave and that the size on the mirror surface is a phantom. I cannot have my cake and eat it. I cannot make use of an illusion and watch it.[23]

The assertion in this passage that ought to be met with frank incredulity is that the impression of seeing oneself face to face in a mirror is an illusion. For when I look at myself in my bathroom mirror, I do not see a small image or an illusionist representation of my face on its surface. All that I can see on the surface of the mirror are the blemishes in the glass, some specks of paint, and condensation. The "small area enclosed by the outline" that Gombrich refers to does not contain an image. It is simply the area I need to wipe clear in order to see my head; and, if the mirror is already clear, it is the area I would need to cover—with a piece of paper, for example—in order to occlude it. I may find its size surprising, but that is not because I have been misled by a miniature trompe l'oeil; it is because I am not a good judge of visual angles or occlusion size. As we saw in the previous chapter, the idea that an object's occlusion size is unreal, that the experience of perceiving it is an illusion, has a long and distinguished history; but it is a myth.

The traditional conception of a mirror image as a natural picture that is visible on, in, or behind a mirror—we shift uncertainly from one preposition to another—is confused and paradoxical. There is in fact no such thing. We can speak, innocuously, of seeing a mirror image or a reflection of something, or of seeing something reflected in a mirror. But what a mirror actually reflects is neither an object nor a picture: it is of course simply light. I cannot see this reflection occurring, but the fact that it does occur explains the fact that I can see myself in a mirror, face to face. "I copied this from myself in a mirror," says the inscription Dürer added proudly to his earliest self-portrait drawing (fig. 18). He was right: he had made a drawing of his own face and not of an image of it.

Why does the thought persist, that mirrors merely show us images of things, when we know perfectly well how they work? Part of the reason—this seems to be the case in Eco's text, for example—is that flat mirrors reverse left and right, in the sense that when I am shaving the left side of my face, there seems to be a razor on the right side of the face I see in the mirror. Isn't this is an illusion? And does it not follow that what I am actually seeing is not my face but an image of it?

The short answer is that this does not follow. We can see this, if we think

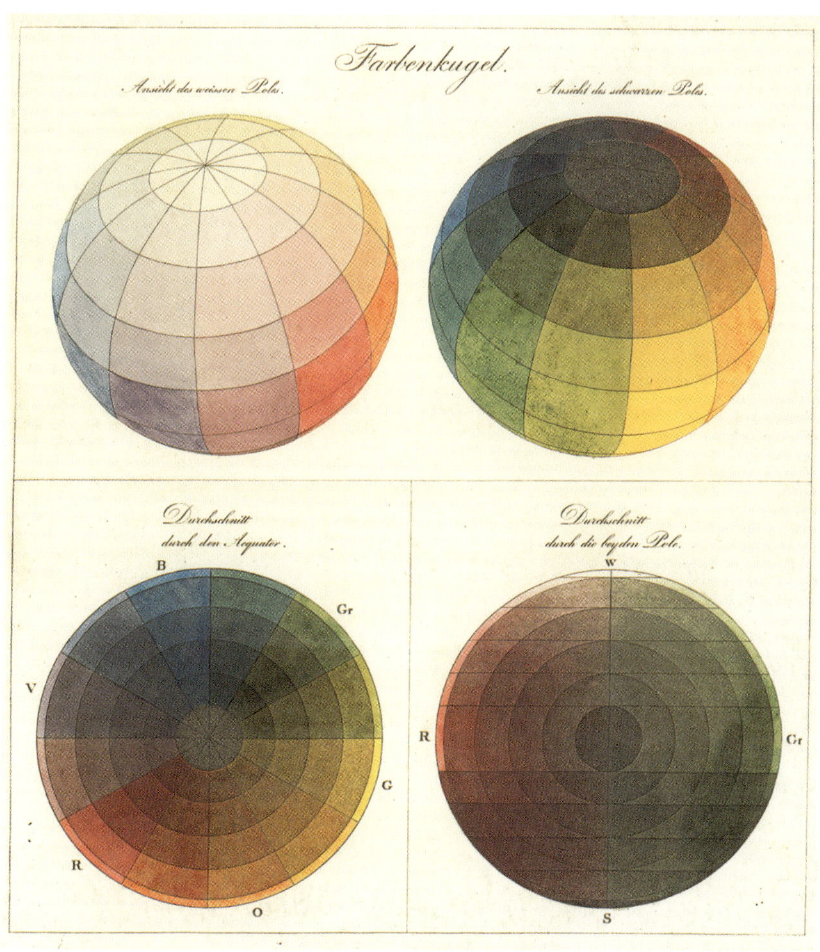

1. Phillip Otto Runge, *Farben-Kugel* (Color-sphere), 1810. Hand-colored etching.

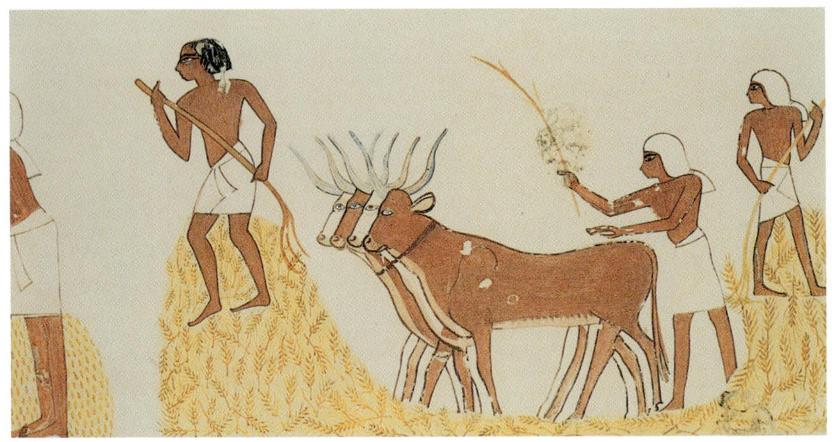

2. *Harvest Scene*, ca. 1420–1411 B.C. (detail). Wall painting on plaster. Deir el-Medina, Thebes. Watercolor copy by Nina M. de Garis Davies.

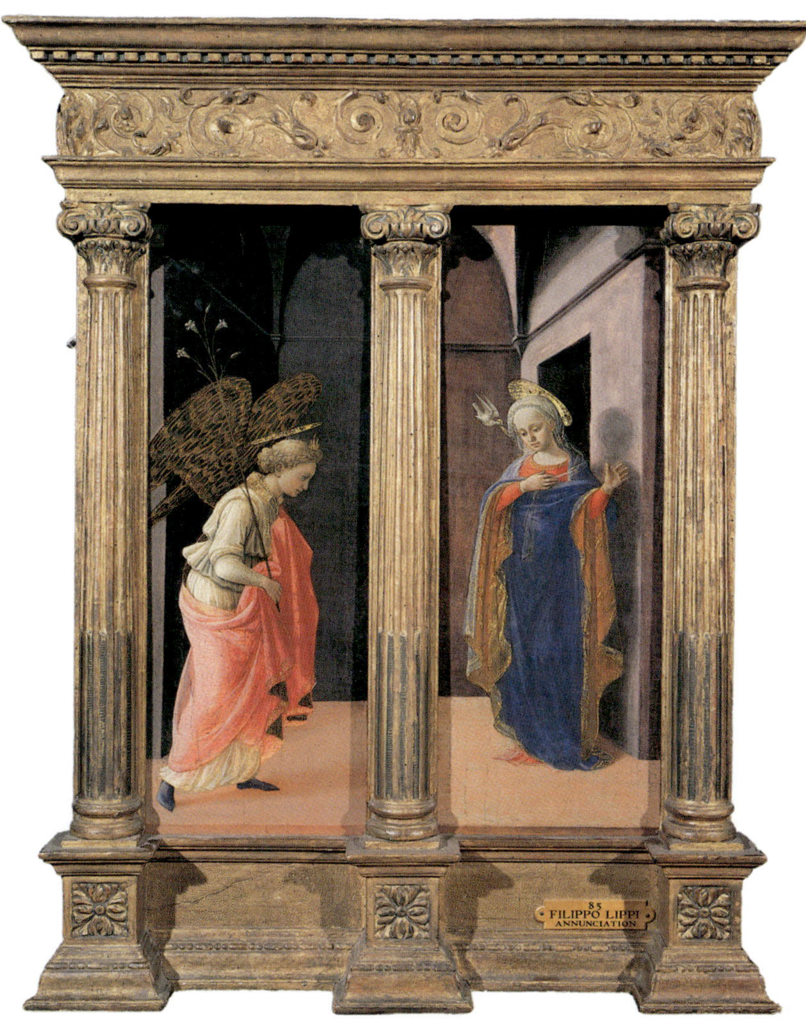

3. Fra Filippo Lippi, *The Annunciation,* ca. 1440. Tempera on wood. The Frick Collection, New York.

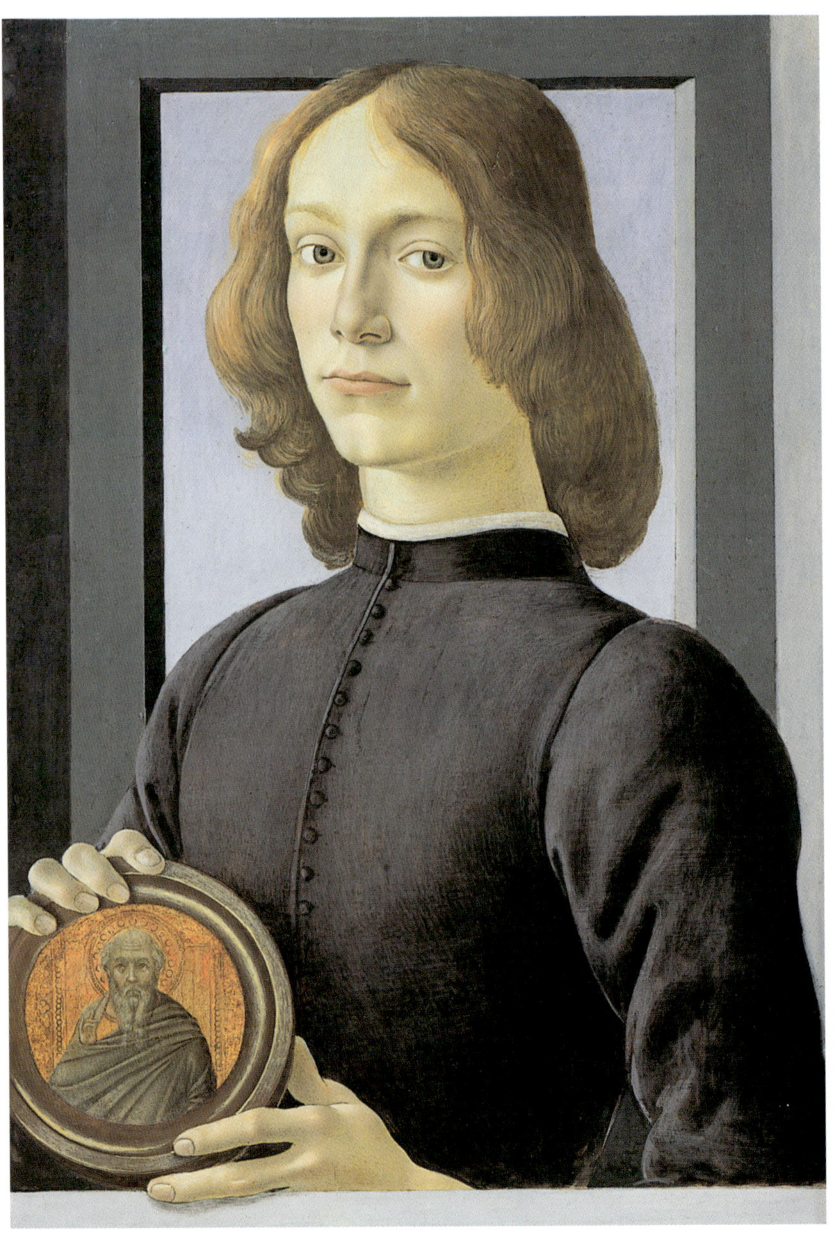

4. Sandro Botticelli, *Young Man Holding a Medallion,* ca. 1485. Tempera on wood. Private collection, on loan to the National Gallery of Art, Washington D.C.

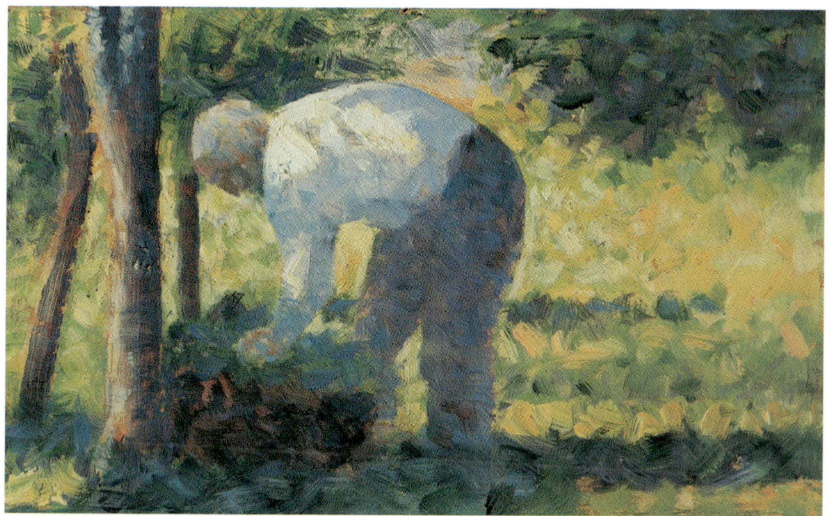

5. Georges Seurat, *The Gardener,* 1882–83. Oil on wood. The Metropolitan Museum of Art, New York.

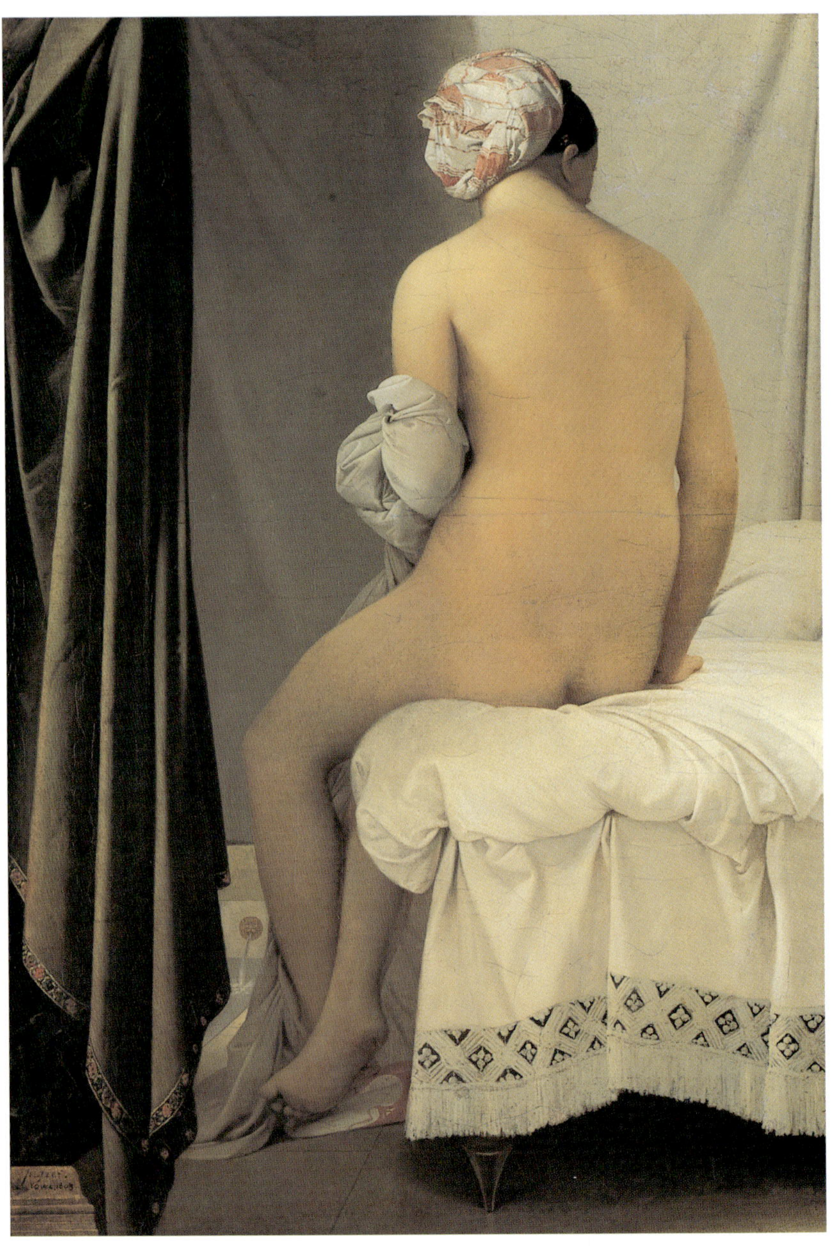

6. Jean-Auguste-Dominique Ingres, *Bather of Valpincon*, 1808. Oil on canvas. Musée du Louvre, Paris.

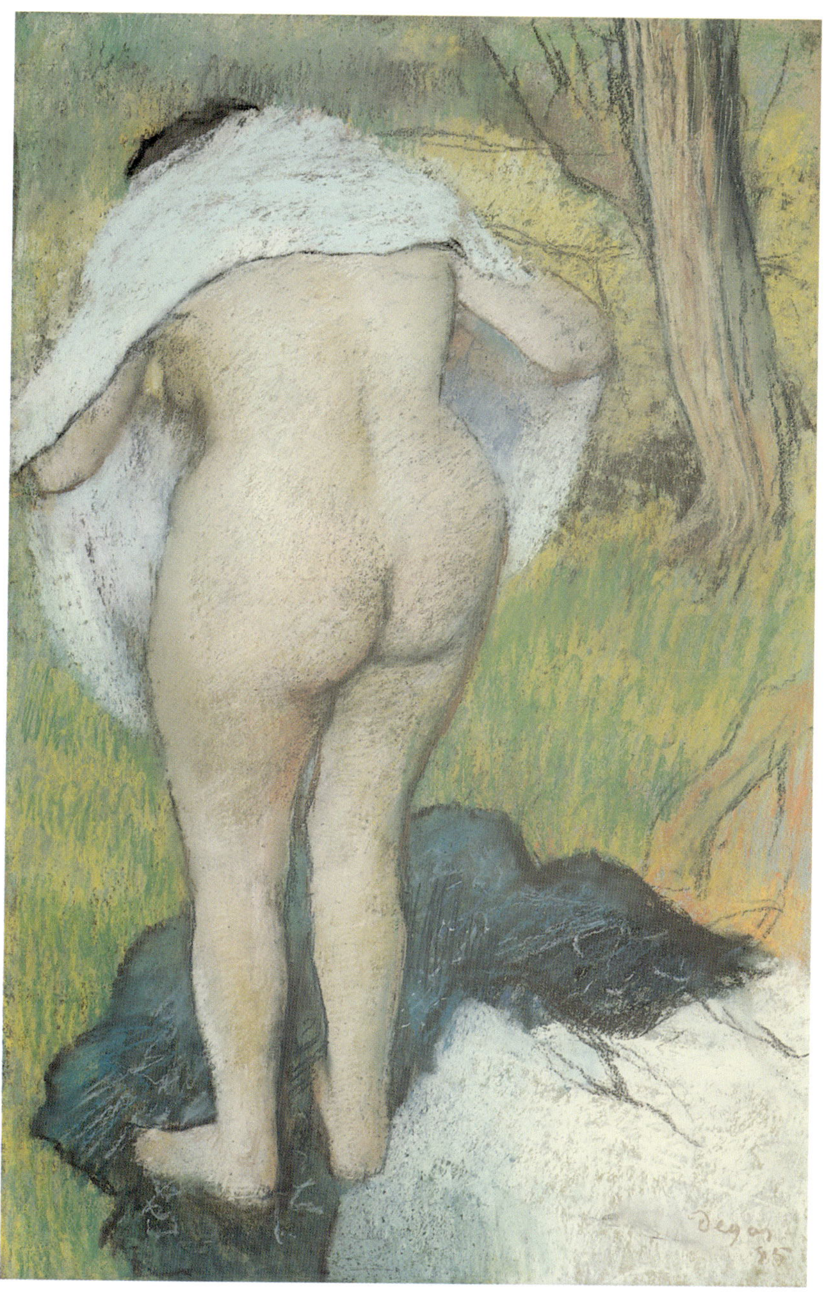

7. Edgar Degas, *Woman Drying Herself*, 1885. Pastel. National Gallery of Art, Washington, D.C.

8. Leonardo da Vinci, *A Copse of Trees Seen in Sunlight,* ca. 1500–1502. Red chalk. Royal Library, Windsor Castle.

about optical inversion. If I replaced the lenses in my spectacles with inverting prisms of clear glass, the scene before my eyes, which looks upright to me now, would look upside down. But I would see the same objects as I do now and not pictures or images of them. Inversion—that is, rotation through 180 degrees—does not imply that we cannot see visible things themselves. Indeed, if it did imply this, the same would presumably be true of the single degree of prism included in many people's spectacles, with the result that these spectacles would not enable people to see the visible objects that surround them better but prevent them from seeing these things at all. The simple fact is that when I see my face in a flat mirror, I see it reversed. But *what* I see is nothing other than my face.

Left-right reversal is part of the reason, but perhaps the main point is just that some errors are resilient. "It would seem," Aristotle says, "that in [Democritus's] time there was no scientific knowledge of the general subject of the formation of images and the phenomena of reflection."[24] If this is correct, we should not find it surprising that Democritus believed that reflections were natural pictures. The curious fact is that as the science of optics progressed, this confused idea was modified but it was not abandoned; and since it lies dormant in the very idioms in which we speak about reflections it is liable to come awake from time to time and perplex us. "Why are grammatical problems so tough and ineradicable?" Wittgenstein once asked: "—Because they are connected with the oldest thought habits, i.e., with the oldest images that are engraved into our language itself."[25]

In short, since retinal images are reflections they do not cause our sensory perceptions, and strictly speaking they are not pictures at all. But how should these facts affect our assessment of Descartes's attack on the imagist hypothesis? The answer is twofold. First, they reinforce the attack by making it doubly plain that we do not see objects by perceiving pictures of them in our eyes. But second, they confirm that there was no need for Descartes to attack the resemblance theory. For the resemblance theory is a theory of depiction, and the images in our eyes are not pictures.

~

The main errors in Descartes's *Optics* are therefore these two: first, the doctrine that the images produced by visible objects in our eyes cause our perceptions and, second, the assumption that reflections are pictures—in other words, that we must explain how pictures represent and how reflections produce perceptions "in just the same way."

Ironically, both of these errors are vestiges of the very hypothesis about vision that Descartes was laboring to disprove: the hypothesis that visual perception is the result of perceiving images that are transmitted from visible objects to the eye. As we have seen, Descartes did not need to argue that the content of a picture depends on the nature of the perception it is apt to produce in our minds, either to disprove the imagist hypothesis or to safeguard his geometrical theory of matter. But when the two errors Descartes makes are combined, it is not merely understandable but actually inevitable that he should have thought it necessary. For if our visual perceptions of objects are produced by pictures of them in our eyes, then it must be true that we see objects by seeing these pictures of them—unless, that is, a picture can make us aware of what it represents without being seen.[26]

Descartes's theory of depiction is designed to show that this paradoxical effect does in fact occur. Pictures, he argues, are simply complex mechanical stimuli "ordained by nature" to cause sensory perceptions. In effect, they are hallucinogens that happen to be administered through the optic nerve. Hence although our visual perceptions *are* mediated by pictures, there is no need for us to see these pictures in order to see the objects they represent. This is, undeniably, an ingenious finesse, but we need to uncover the errors he makes in order to appreciate quite how ingenious it is.

Descartes's principal ideas about pictures—his rejection of the resemblance theory and his idea that the content of a picture depends on the experience it produces in our minds—is the result of applying a theory devised to fit pictures that we do not see to pictures that we do see. So we should not be surprised to discover that his argument leads him to advance a mistaken theory of pictorial art. Nevertheless, these two principal ideas were advanced afresh in *Art and Illusion,* and they have played a central role in the philosophical study of pictorial art since then. As we approach these twentieth-century texts, we should bear in mind that these ideas were first set out in a text that is mainly concerned with the role that retinal images play in perception, that the theory of perception for which they were originally designed was an application of Descartes's geometrical theory of matter, which implies that our experience of light and color is an illusion, and that Descartes's arguments depend on the ancient confusion between pictures and reflections. Let us turn to the twentieth century now.

7

ART AND EXPERIENCE

> The representation . . . is not a replica. It need not be like the motif. The craftsman of Jericho did not think eyes indistinguishable from cowrie shells any more than Picasso thinks baboons indistinguishable from motor-cars, but in certain contexts one can represent the other. They belong to the same class because they release the same response.
>
> E. H. Gombrich

THE RECENT RESURGENCE of subjectivism in the theory of art began some forty years ago, when the resemblance theory became unpopular among philosophers. Since then it has gathered pace in tandem with changing fashions in the philosophy of mind. The initial impetus was provided by the publication of *Art and Illusion.* In this book, and in many subsequent articles and lectures that elaborate its theme, Gombrich argues that the development of Western art—essentially the art of ancient Greece and Rome and the art of Western Europe from Giotto to Cezanne—consists in a series of discoveries about the nature of visual perception and the means by which the effect of visible objects on our senses can be simulated. "What may make a painting like a distant view through a window," he writes, "is not the fact that the two can be as indistinguishable as is a facsimile from the original: it is the similarity between the mental activities both can arouse."[1]

This remark is about a specific artistic tradition and specific pictorial devices, such as foreshortening and shading, which I shall return to in later chapters. But the epigraph at the top of this page, which is from *Art and Illu-*

sion, is about representation in general, and the book as a whole encouraged a search for a general theory of depiction based on the idea that it expresses. This search intensified after the publication of Nelson Goodman's *Languages of Art,* which persuaded the majority of philosophers that the resemblance theory was not viable without providing an alternative to it that commanded general assent. Today there is broad agreement among philosophers that the nature of pictorial art cannot be explained by analyzing the relationship between the marks on the surface of a picture and the objects that they represent. The consensus is that it can only be explained by defining the psychological effect that these marks are intended to produce.[2]

As we have seen, Descartes—whose *Optics* is the original source of this idea—claims that pictures "enable the soul to have sensory perceptions of all the various qualities of the objects to which they correspond" and that a picture "causes our sensory perception of these objects." But these remarks were mainly intended to describe the effect of retinal images, and the sensory perception produced by an engraving of a battle or a storm cannot be defined in the same way. For it is not in fact a perception of a battle or a storm, since that is not what the spectator is perceiving. Nor is it a perception of "all the various qualities" of a battle or a storm, for again the spectator is not actually perceiving these qualities. We may say that we can see a battle or a storm in a picture. But is there a plausible construction we can place on this idiom that makes the remark come out as true? Or is it a vestige of what the French philosopher Charles Lalo called the first aesthetic theory of mankind: the identity of portrait and portrayed?[3]

Perhaps this is the kind of magical idea that Wittgenstein had in mind when he asked the unsettling question: "Is it superstition to think I *see* the horse galloping in the picture?"[4] But although Wittgenstein emphasizes the word "see," the problem is as much about the "in." Does the phrase "in the picture" signify a place? Or should we parse Wittgenstein's sentence differently and construe the expression "see . . . in" as a phrasal verb—like "give in" (yield) and "take . . . in" (deceive)? This maneuver would acquit us of the charge of superstition. But the price is high. For how should we explain what "see . . . in" means? What kind of experience does it describe? This is the main problem that subjectivist theories of depiction have to solve.

The best-known solution in the recent literature is the one proposed by Richard Wollheim in his book *Painting as an Art.* I shall therefore begin this chapter by examining Wollheim's solution in detail and then broaden the discussion to criticize subjectivism in the theory of depiction as a whole.

~

In the introduction, we saw that a subjectivist theory of beauty faces two challenges. In the first place, if we hold that the beauty of an object is explained by the pleasurable sentiment it arouses, this sentiment will need to be defined, since many objects that do not seem beautiful are pleasurable to see or hear. Second, if we deny that beauty is relative to each individual, we shall need to explain what makes one sentiment more apposite than another. Subjectivism in the theory of depiction faces the same challenges. First, the experience produced by a picture of a certain kind of object must be defined, and distinguished from the experience of seeing this kind of object in the flesh. Second, since it is possible to misperceive the content of a picture, a subjectivist theory will also need to define a standard of correctness, that is, it will need to explain what makes the difference between a spectator's correctly perceiving the content of a picture and her misperceiving it.

Wollheim's theory of depiction is designed to meet both of these challenges. He argues that the visual experience that a picture must produce is one that has "a certain phenomenology." He calls this experience "seeing-in," using the hyphen to remind the reader that the phrase is a term of art, which needs defining; and he calls the phenomenology that defines the experience "twofoldness," for a reason I shall explain shortly. Then, in order to meet the second challenge, he proposes that the standard of correctness, which determines whether the spectator has correctly perceived the content of a picture, "is set—set for each painting—by the intentions of the artist in so far as they are fulfilled."[5] In a moment, we shall see what kinds of intentions Wollheim has in mind. But here, to begin with, is the passage in which twofoldness, and thereby seeing-in, is explained:

> Seeing-in is a distinct kind of perception, and it is triggered by the presence within the field of vision of a differentiated surface. Not all differentiated surfaces will have this effect, but I doubt that anything significant can be said about what exactly a surface must be like for it to have this effect. When the surface is right, then an experience with a certain phenomenology will occur, and it is this phenomenology that is distinctive about seeing-in. . . . The distinctive phenomenological feature I call "twofoldness," because, when seeing-in occurs, two things happen: I am visually aware of the surface I look at, and I discern something standing out in front of, or (in certain cases) receding behind, something else. So, for instance, I follow the famous advice of Leonardo da Vinci to an aspirant painter and I look at a stained wall, or let my eyes wander over a frosty pane of glass, and at one and the same time I am visually aware of the wall, or of the glass, and I recognize a naked boy, or dancers in mysterious gauze dresses, in front of (in each case) a darker ground. In virtue

of this experience I can be said to see the boy in the wall, the dancers in the frosty glass.[6]

Wollheim does not suggest that the marks on a frosty pane of glass (photographed by Minor White) depict dancers or that the marks on a stained wall (photographed by Aaron Siskind) depict a boy (figs. 36, 37). We can see these things in these surfaces, but they are not pictures. However, he continues:

> Representation can be explained in terms of seeing-in, as the following situation reveals: In a community where seeing-in is firmly established, some member of the community—let us call him (prematurely) an artist—sets about marking a surface with the intention of getting others around him to see some definite thing in it: say, a bison. If the artist's intention is successful to the extent that a bison can be seen in the surface as he has marked it, then the community closes ranks in that someone who does indeed see a bison in it is now held to see the surface correctly, and anyone is held to see it incorrectly if he sees, as he might, something else in it, or nothing at all. Now the marked surface represents a bison.[7]

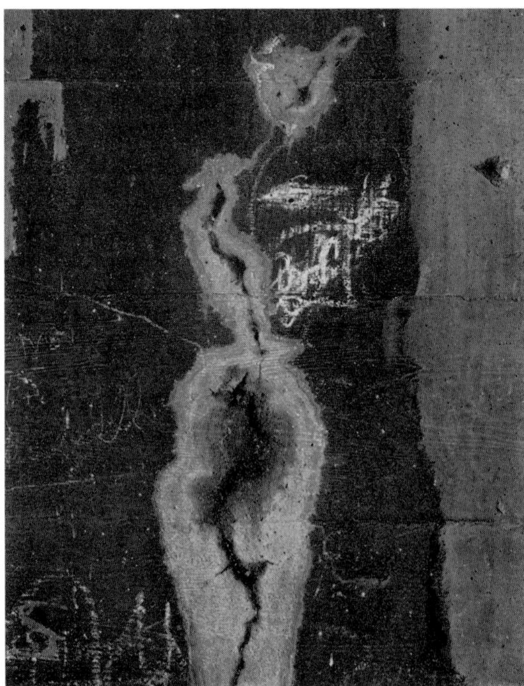

36. Aaron Siskind, *Chicago,* 1948. Photograph.

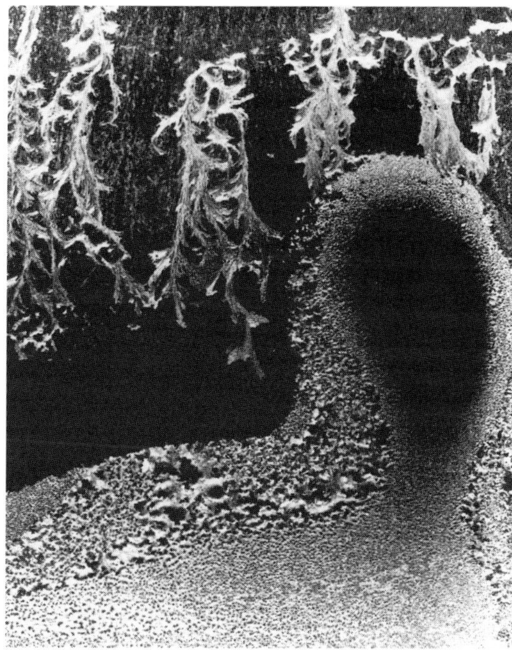

37. Minor White, "Empty Head," frost on window, 1962. Photograph. From *Sequence 14: Sound of One Hand.*

Thus depiction occurs when the marks on a surface are successfully designed to make the seeing-in experience occur. It is not enough that this experience should occur. It must, when it occurs, fulfill the intention of the person who produced the marks.[8]

If Wollheim's theory of depiction is correct, a spectator who perceives the content of a picture must have an experience of the kind he postulates. That is, the spectator must be visually aware of the picture's surface, and she must also discern something standing out in front of something else. I shall discuss the two aspects of the experience Wollheim postulates in turn, before considering the role the artist's intention plays in his theory.

There is an objection to the claim that the spectator must be visually aware of the picture's surface, which concerns trompe l'oeil. The objection is that a trompe l'oeil painting is not designed with the intention that the spectator should be visually aware of its surface. In fact it is designed with the opposite intention—that is, with the intention that the spectator should fail to be visually aware of its surface. Hence, if Wollheim's theory of depiction were correct, a successful trompe l'oeil painting would not be a picture. It would not represent anything at all. And this, the objection concludes, shows that the theory fails.

Now Wollheim accepts that his theory has this implication—namely, that a trompe l'oeil painting is not a representation—but he does not regard this as a defect in the theory: "There are paintings that are non-representational . . . because they do not invoke, indeed they repel, attention to the marked surface. *Trompe l'oeil* paintings, like the exquisite series of cabinets in gouache by Leroy de Barde . . . are surely in this category. They incite our awareness of depth, but do so in a way designed to baffle our attention to the marks upon the surface."[9] But can this be the right test of whether a painting is representational? If so, the canon of representational paintings must be dramatically reduced. For example, paintings by van Eyck and Ingres must be excluded, along with the cabinets in gouache by Leroy de Barde. Of course, van Eyck's *Arnolfini Portrait* and Ingres's portrait of Louis-Francois Bertin are not trompe l'oeil paintings. We reserve the term "trompe l'oeil" for paintings that invite us to imagine that we are seeing the kinds of objects they depict. That is why it is generally confined, in the case of easel painting, by the choice of subject matter (small domestic objects, flowers, insects, etc.) and the scale (approximately 1:1). But the surfaces of van Eyck's and Ingres's paintings are as transparent as the surfaces of trompe l'oeil paintings by van Hoogstraten or Boilly. And so they are also nonrepresentational, according to the test Wollheim himself suggests.

This would be an implausible result. But in fact Wollheim's reply to the objection is mistaken, even on his own terms, because the objection fails to bite unless a trompe l'oeil painting is designed to produce an illusion and to sustain it for as long as the spectator sees the painting—unless, to borrow a phrase from Leibniz, the viewer of a trompe l'oeil painting is like a dog barking at a mirror.[10] And this is really an exaggeration, which distorts the aim and the effect of trompe l'oeil painting. The play element would be lost and the enjoyment of skill and virtuosity, which trompe l'oeil cultivates and caters to, would be frustrated if it were true. That is why, as Ruskin remarks, trompe l'oeil invariably has "some means of proving at the same time that it is an illusion."[11]

This is a point Wollheim seems to acknowledge. For he does not claim that a trompe l'oeil painting is designed to prevent us from being visually aware of the marks on its surface. He claims that it is designed to "baffle our attention" to the marks on the surface. And these are quite different claims. I may, for example, be aware of the color of an object, or its shape, without attending to these properties. To attend to the color or the shape of an object is to make this property the center or the focus of one's engagement with it. But we are not obliged to give this role to whatever we are aware of. Indeed we often cannot do so. I may, for example, be aware of a dozen people talking simultaneously, but I cannot simultaneously attend to what each of them is saying.

However, if Wollheim is right to make only the weaker claim about trompe l'oeil—that is, the claim that it is designed to "baffle our attention" to the surface, and not the claim that it is designed to prevent awareness of it—it follows that his theory does not imply that trompe l'oeil paintings are non-representational. For the theory does not require the spectator to attend to the marked surface of a picture or require that the artist intend that she should do so. Hence, the reason Wollheim gives for denying that trompe l'oeil paintings are representational is an unconvincing one, on his own terms. But by the same token this objection to his theory fails.

I shall turn now to the second aspect of the experience Wollheim defines, that is, to the spectator's discerning something—for example, a naked boy or dancers in gauze dresses—standing out in front of something else. Before we examine the claim that a picture must produce an experience of this kind, we need to disambiguate it. The claim as it stands is ambiguous because Wollheim does not make it clear whether the "something else" that a depicted object must stand out in front of—such as the "darker ground"—is supposed to be the picture's surface, or whether it is supposed to be part of the depicted scene.[12]

Suppose, first, that the claim is that the spectator must discern a depicted object standing out in front of the picture's surface. This seems implausible. For example, Picasso's painting *The Two Brothers* represents a naked boy standing in front of a clay-colored wall (fig. 38). The spectator is, of course, expected to discern this. But is she also expected to discern a boy standing out in front of the painting's surface? I, for one, am not aware of having an experience of this kind. The boy does not appear to me to be standing in any spatial relation to the painting's surface—any more than he seems to be standing inside the frame or in front of the wall on which the painting hangs. Indeed, the only circumstances in which it seems likely that a depicted object will appear to stand out in front of the picture's surface is when a trompe l'oeil element is added to it—as for example when (according to legend) the young Giotto painted a fly on the nose of a face drawn by his teacher Cimabue, which the older man tried to brush away.

A simple ink drawing of a human figure on plain paper is no different from a painting in this respect. The spectator must of course be able to distinguish the ink marks from the unmarked paper. And this distinction can be experienced spatially, so that the ink marks seem to stand above the paper's surface. But this does not appear to be a key fact in the theory of depiction, for three reasons. First, what is experienced here is a relation between the ink marks

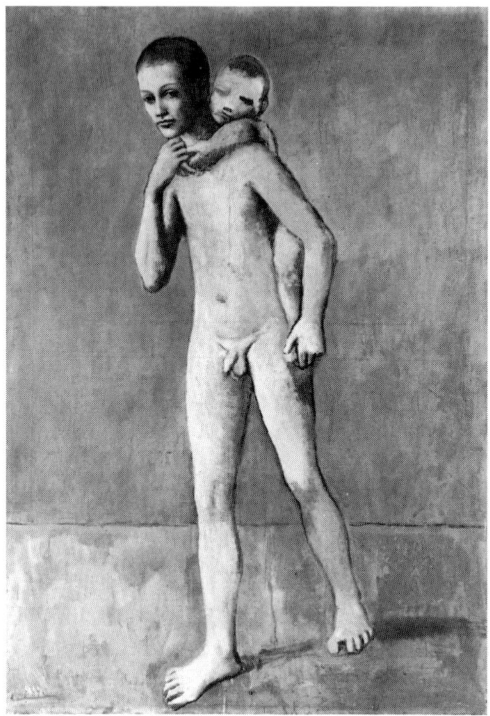

38. Pablo Picasso, *The Two Brothers,* 1906. Oil on canvas. Kunstmuseum, Basel.

and the paper's surface, and not between the human figure represented and the paper's surface. Second, although the ink marks can appear to stand above the paper's surface, there is no reason to suppose they must. And third, if the distinction is experienced spatially in the case of an ink drawing, there is no reason why it should not be experienced spatially when we read a printed text and distinguish the ink marks that form the letters from the paper on which the text is printed.

Suppose now that we interpret Wollheim's claim as meaning that a spectator who sees what a picture represents must discern something standing out in front of something else within the depicted scene, such as a boy standing out in front of a clay-colored wall. If this is the right way to interpret Wollheim's claim, it is open to two decisive objections. First, it implies that every picture depicts something standing out in front of something else. But although this is generally the case, there are many exceptions: the scene of combat in a Mesolithic rock painting, the frieze of mourners on a Geometric vase, even a child's stick-figure drawing (figs. 39–41). All of these are exceptions because of a combination of two factors. First, in each case the surface

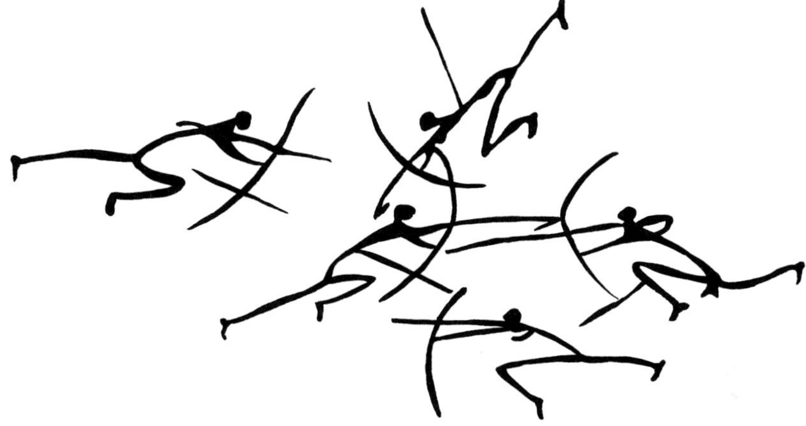

39. *Scene of Archers in Combat,* ca. 8500 B.C. Rock Painting. Morella la Vieja, Castellon de la Plana, Spain.

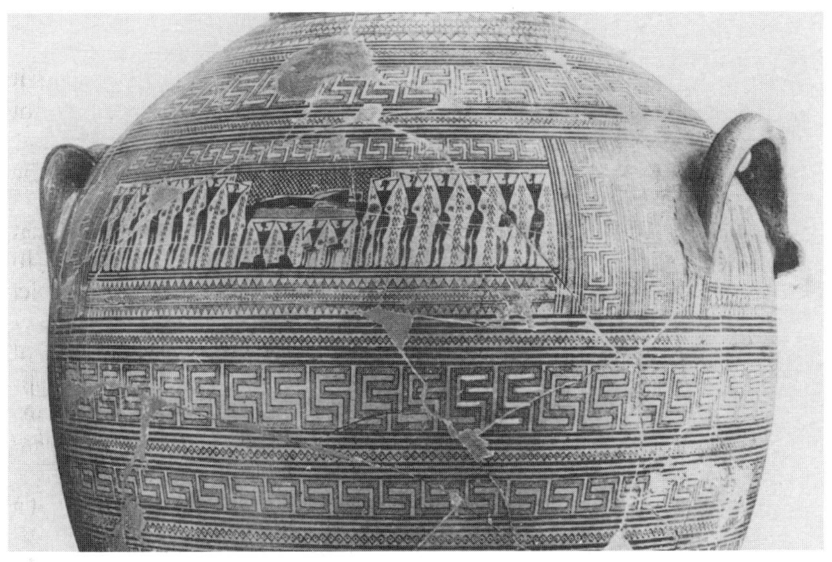

40. Amphora, ca. 750 B.C. Attributed to the Dipylon Master. National Museum, Athens.

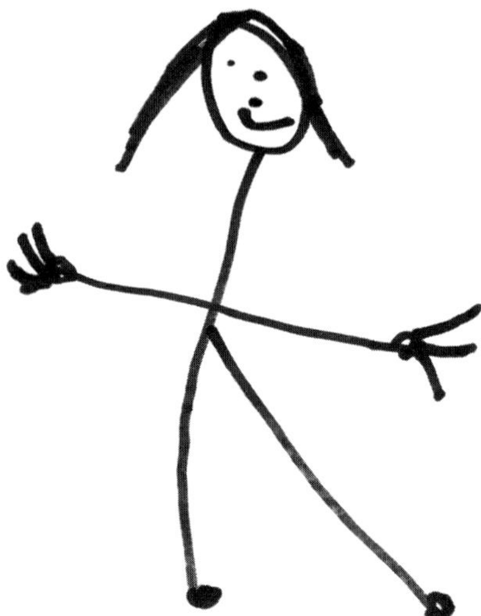

41. Drawing by a four-year-old child.

on which the figures are drawn does not contribute to the picture's content: it is a ground but not a background.[13] Second, the figures themselves are not shown in depth. As it happens, a silhouette can represent depth surprisingly well, as a self-portrait by August Edouart—self-styled silhouettist to the French royal family—shows (fig. 42). But there is no reason why it must.

The second objection is that if it is interpreted in this way, the claim that the spectator's experience involves discerning something standing out in front of something else is a claim about the kind of scene a picture must depict and must be seen to depict—namely, a scene in which something is further from the implicit point of view than something else. But if the experience of seeing-in is defined in this way, it cannot be used to explain how pictures represent, even if the claim about what a picture has to depict is true. For we cannot explain *how* pictures represent by stating a generalization about *what* they represent.

For these reasons, it is doubtful whether a spectator who perceives what a picture represents must have an experience of the kind that Wollheim postulates. A fortiori, it is doubtful whether an artist must intend the spectator to have an experience of this kind. And if the second interpretation of Wollheim's claim is the one that captures what he means, postulating this kind of experience cannot explain depiction, even if it is true that every picture depicts something standing out in front of something else.

I shall now comment on Wollheim's proposal that the standard of correctness, which determines whether the spectator has correctly perceived what a

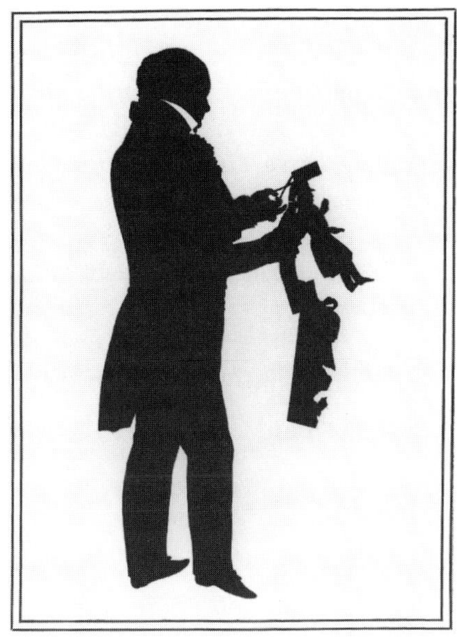

42. August Edouart, *Portrait of the Artist Cutting the Silhouette of Liston the Actor*, 1828.

picture represents, "is set . . . for each painting by the intentions of the artist in so far as they are fulfilled." As we have seen, this proposal is designed to answer a question that a subjectivist theory of depiction is obliged to address if it acknowledges the possibility that a spectator can misperceive the content of a picture.[14]

Wollheim's proposal seems to be mistaken for two reasons. First, it implies that a marked surface cannot depict a kind of object unless the artist has the intention that a spectator should see that kind of object in it. But this seems to be false. For an artist may intend to depict a larch or a man in the uniform of a midshipman. But he may depict a spruce or a man in the uniform of a captain by mistake. Hence, there may be a difference between what a picture depicts and what the artist meant it to depict—just as there may be a difference between what an utterance means and what the speaker meant to say. (In both of the counterexamples mentioned, there are more general terms that apply to the depicted object and that do conform to the artist's intention—for example, "tree" and "man" respectively, and in both cases, "living being." This does not affect the argument.)

Second, Wollheim's proposal implies that if an artist produces a marked surface with the intention that a spectator should see a certain kind of object in it and his intention is fulfilled, then the marked surface depicts that kind of object. But this also seems to be false. For example, Picasso sometimes invites the spectator to see a penis in the part of a picture that depicts a nose or a tongue, or a vulva or anus in the part that depicts a mouth, but it would be inaccurate to say that these things are actually depicted (figs. 43, 44).

These objections do not imply that there is no connection at all between intention and pictorial content. It is plausible that there is some connection here—as the analogy with linguistic meaning suggests. For acknowledging that what an utterance actually means need not be the same as what the speaker means to say is consistent with the view that an utterance means nothing unless the speaker means or intends something by the words he utters; and it is also consistent with holding that a meaningful utterance cannot possibly occur except against a background that includes the custom of making utterances with the intention of saying something. The second idea is relatively uncontroversial, whereas the first is not. Both can be transferred to the case of pictures in a straightforward way, but neither will provide a standard of correctness—that is, a way of distinguishing between the case where someone correctly perceives the content of a picture and the case where she misperceives it.[15]

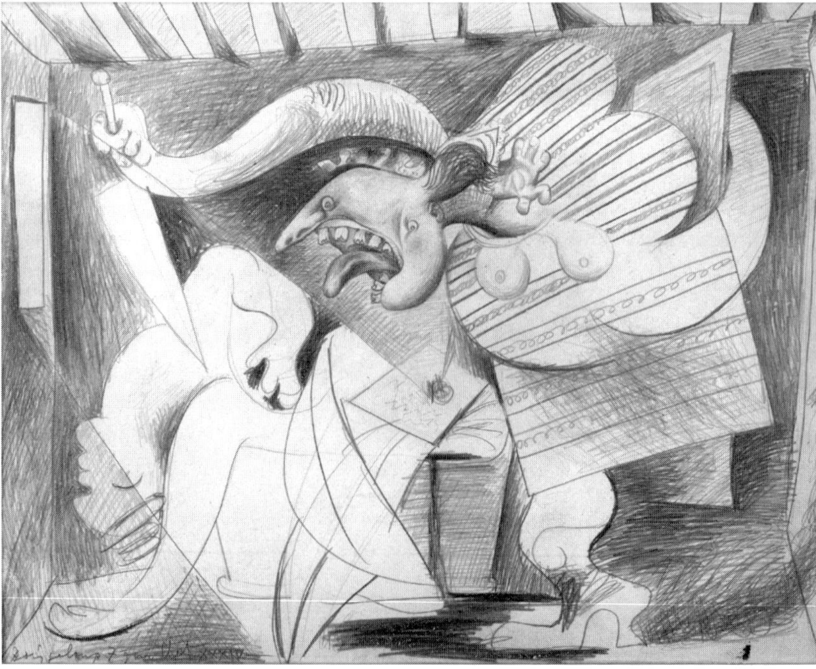

43. Pablo Picasso, *The Murder*, 1934. Lead pencil. Musée Picasso, Paris.

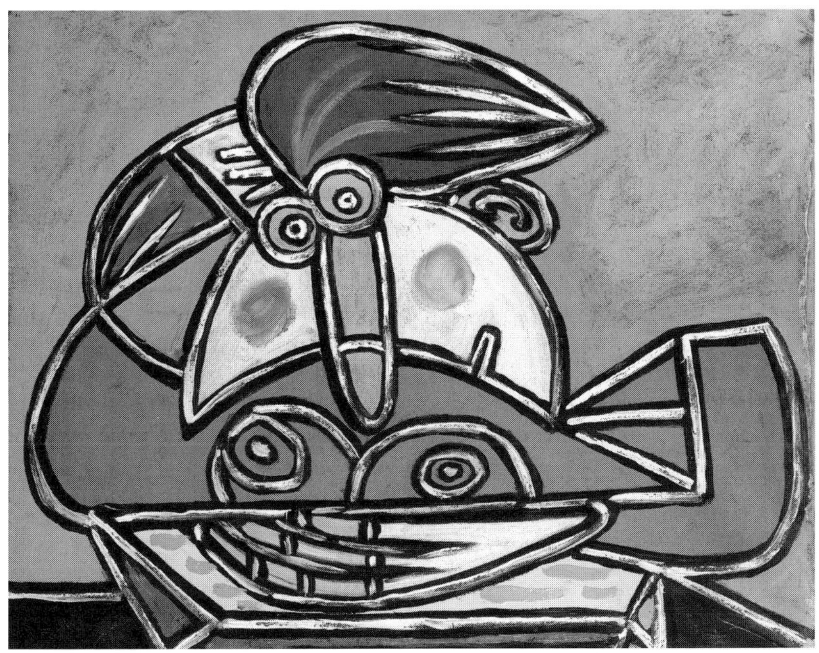

44. Pablo Picasso, *Woman Leaning Over,* 1935. Oil on canvas. Private collection.

The last objection to Wollheim's theory, and the most consequential one, is that he quietly shirks the task he sets himself: defining the kind of perception he calls "seeing-in." If we skate across his remarks quite quickly, we can get a sense of what he has in mind: seeing-in involves being visually aware of a surface and simultaneously "discerning something standing out in front of . . . something else." But what exactly does the phrase "discerning something" mean?

Wollheim offers, as an example, the case where "I recognize a naked boy" in the marks on a stained wall. But I do not really recognize or discern a naked boy in these marks because there is no boy there for me to recognize or discern. Neither is my experience indistinguishable from the experience of recognizing or discerning a boy. If it were, it would be an illusion, but that, as Wollheim himself rightly insists, is not the case. So what kind of experience is this quasi-recognizing of a naked boy supposed to be? It seems to be both like and unlike the experience of really recognizing a naked boy: sufficiently like it to encourage us to borrow the phrase, and sufficiently unlike it to be distinguishable from an illusion. But how should we describe the similarity and the difference?

Wollheim fails to address these questions. And because he fails to address them, he fails to explain how the experience of seeing a boy in something differs from the experience of seeing a tulip in it or a pair of boots and, therefore, how a picture of a boy differs from a picture of a tulip or a pair of boots. In effect, Wollheim tells us something about the generic nature of seeing a boy in a picture: he tells us that it involves "discerning *something* standing out in front of, or . . . receding behind, something else." But he does not tell us anything about its specific nature because the fact that the something is a boy is not explained.

This striking omission raises a larger question. When we considered Hume's doctrine, that the beauty of an object is explained by the pleasurable sentiment it arouses, we found that the pleasurable sentiment Hume postulates cannot be defined except (as I put it there) in terms of a thought that gives it an articulate shape and a direction—the thought *that the thing seems beautiful.* Again, when we examined Locke's theory of colors, we found that sensations of color cannot be defined except by means of color terms themselves, which apply in the first instance to colored bodies, surfaces, and light. It is natural to wonder whether a similar circle is bound to arise if we attempt to explain depiction by defining the kind of perception that a picture must be capable of producing—the experience Wollheim labels "seeing-in."

Now it is simple enough to define the kind of perception that occurs when a spectator with sufficient knowledge, acumen, and visual skill—for short, a qualified spectator—looks at a picture of a kind of object, event, or scene, as long as we use the concept of depiction to define it. For it must be possible for such a spectator to see that a painting of a cow depicts a cow, that an engraving of a battle depicts a battle, and so on. This must be possible because nothing counts as a picture if no kind of knowledge, acumen, and visual skill would suffice to enable a spectator to see what it depicts. Hence it must be possible for a qualified spectator to describe her perception of a picture by saying, "I can see an arrangement of colors that depicts a cow," "I can see a configuration of lines that depicts a battle," and so on. As we have seen, this is true even of trompe l'oeil.

Hence, it is a simple matter to define the perception that a picture must be able to produce: it is the kind of perception that a spectator could describe by means of sentences like these. But in order to break the circle, we need to find some other kind of predicate that ties the marks on the surface of a picture to the kinds of objects they depict, which a spectator could substitute for "depicts a cow" or "depicts a battle" in sentences like the ones above. But it is not difficult to see that no such predicate exists. For our visual imagination is sufficiently plastic to allow a fleck of paint to depict a man, a nail, an eye, or a fleck of paint. It is true that the shape of a mark on the surface of an orthomorphic picture must be the same as the occlusion shape of the object it depicts. But the basic principles of pictorial art reveal how exiguous the relationship between the marks on a picture's surface and the kinds of objects they depict can be. For example, the shape of a configuration of marks that depicts a cow need not even look as if it is an occlusion shape that a cow could have. This condition is satisfied in some cases, such as Paulus Potter's *Cows in a Meadow;* but it is not satisfied in all cases. For example, it is not satisfied in the case of Dubuffet's *Cow with a Subtile Nose* (figs. 45, 46). The shape of the part of Dubuffet's painting that depicts the cow is evidently an occlusion shape that a cow in a picture could have. But this observation reintroduces the concept of depiction, which we were hoping to explain.

The most we can say is that the shape of a configuration of marks that depicts a certain kind of object must look as if it resembles an occlusion shape that an object of that kind could have—whether or not a spectator would spontaneously describe it in these complex terms. But this accommodating condition will also be satisfied by a picture that depicts something intended to resemble an object of a certain kind—without actually being one. For example, there is a watering can in Degas's *Dancers at the Bar,* presumably used to sprinkle sand on the floor, which wittily echoes the shape of a dancer with one leg raised high so that the foot rests firmly on the bar and one arm extended with the hand resting on the raised leg (fig. 47). If the shape of the part of the painting that depicts the watering can looks as if it resembles the occlusion shape a watering can could have, then it also looks as if it resembles the occlusion shape a dancer with one leg raised, and so on, could have. The same point can be made about the works by Picasso mentioned above (figs. 43, 44).

Hence, the final objection to Wollheim's theory of depiction—that it does not explain how the experience of seeing a boy in something differs from the experience of seeing a tulip in it or a pair of boots—cannot be overcome. If we search for a form of words to define the kind of experience that a picture produces in the mind of a spectator, and exclude a word such as "depict" or "represent" itself, there will be nothing useful we can substitute for the vague and unsatisfactory idea that a cowrie shell and an eye "release the same response" or that perceiving the content of a picture involves "discerning something standing out in front of . . . something else."

Curiously, there is one remark in *Painting as an Art* that suggests that Wollheim is aware of this himself:

> We get lost once we start comparing the phenomenology of our perception of the boy when we see him in the wall, or our perception of the wall when we see the boy in it, with that of our perception of boy or wall seen face-to-face. Such a comparison seems easy enough to take on, but it proves impossible to carry

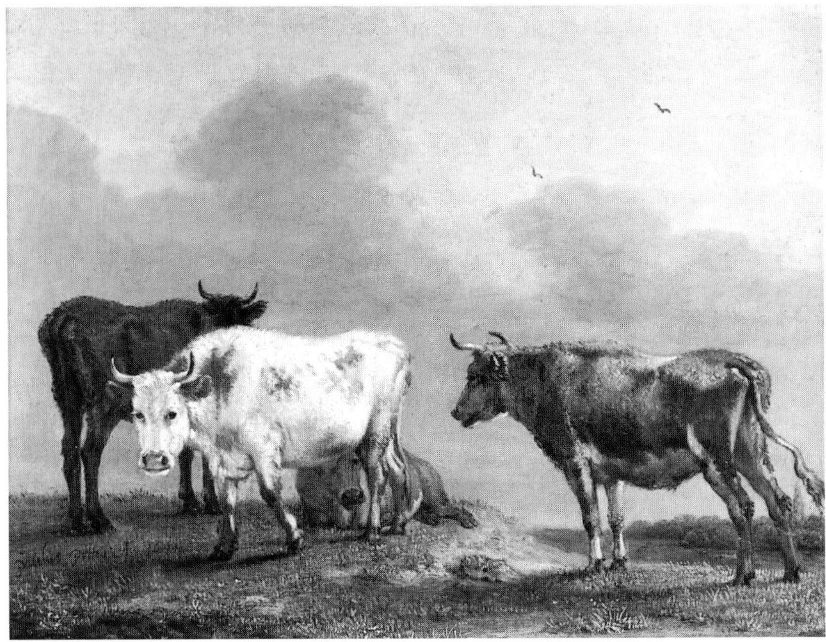

45. Paulus Potter, *Four Cows in a Meadow*, 1651. Oil on canvas. Rijksmuseum, Amsterdam.

> out. The particular complexity that one kind of experience has and the other lacks makes their phenomenology incommensurate.[16]

Complexity is rarely the stumbling block when philosophical invention fails. But the comparison Wollheim refuses to attempt could not be simpler to provide. For, by hypothesis, the boy looks like a boy, and the marks on the surface of the wall look like marks that depict a boy. So the phenomenology of my perception of the boy can be described by saying that it seems to me as if I were seeing a boy. And that of my perception of the boy when I see him in the marks on the surface of the wall can be described by saying that it seems to me as if I were seeing marks that depict a boy. This comparison is easy to make and understand. But of course it explains seeing-in in terms of depiction, which is the opposite of what Wollheim set out to do.[17]

~

The project of explaining depiction by defining the kind of experience that a picture produces in a spectator's mind is therefore bound to fail. For if we conceive of a picture as an artifact that produces a distinctive kind of experience,

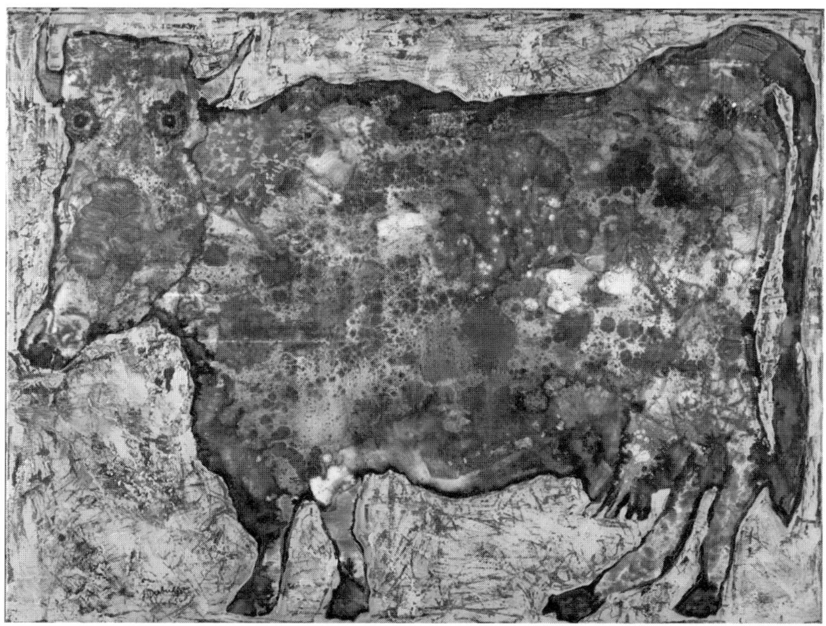

46. Jean Dubuffet, *The Cow with the Subtile Nose*, 1954. Oil and enamel on canvas. Museum of Modern Art, New York.

we shall find ourselves unable to define this kind of experience, except as seeing a picture and seeing what it depicts. It is no more feasible to define it without mentioning depiction than it is to define the pleasurable sentiment Hume postulates without mentioning beauty or to define the experience of seeing something red without mentioning the color red. So instead of pursuing this will-o'-the-wisp, we would do better to explore the reasons that have encouraged philosophers and art theorists to accept this kind of theory.

One reason is that it is easy to confuse two ideas. The first is that a picture is designed to produce a particular kind of experience in a spectator's mind. The second, which is the core doctrine of subjectivist theories of depiction, is that a painting or drawing counts as a picture—in other words, that it *is* a picture—*because* it produces this effect. Subjectivist arguments commonly proceed from the first idea. "The goal which the artist seeks with such self-critical persistence," writes Gombrich, "is . . . a psychological effect." "The artist paints," writes Wollheim, "in order to produce a certain experience in the mind of the spectator." But subjectivism about pictorial content cannot be justified in this way.

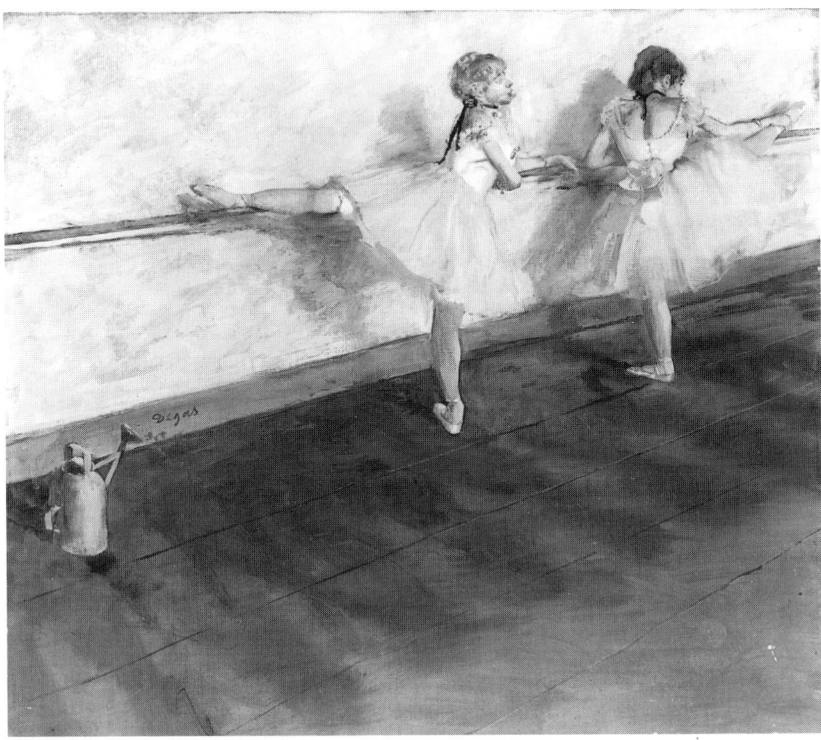

47. Edgar Degas, *Dancers Practicing at the Bar,* 1877. Mixed media on canvas. Metropolitan Museum of Art, New York.

It is true that we can think of a picture as an object designed to produce a psychological effect. But we can think of a beer or a cheese or a sonnet in the same way. Guinness is designed to produce the experience of tasting its smooth malty taste, Roquefort is designed to produce the experience of tasting its tangy taste, and a sonnet is designed to produce the experience we have when we read it or hear it being read. So there is no harm in saying that the goal the brewer, the cheesemaker, or the poet seeks with such self-critical persistence is a psychological effect. But we cannot infer—and in fact it is not true—that something counts as a beer or a cheese or a sonnet because of this effect or that describing the effect is the right way to explain what a beer or a cheese or a sonnet really is. Nor does it follow in the case of pictures. As Picasso said, a picture only lives through the one who is looking at it. But we cannot infer that the inky marks of an engraving and the colored pigments that make up a painting are transformed into an image by "the beholder's share."

This is one reason for the appeal of subjectivism in the theory of depiction, but it is not the main reason. The main reason, I believe, is not a philosophical idea at all. It is an idea that the experience of painting, or of a certain kind of painting, directly suggests. Here are few examples.

First, Diderot's description of a still life by Chardin: "The magic defies understanding. . . . Approach the painting and everything blurs, flattens out and vanishes; step back and everything comes together and reappears." Second, Reynolds describing the "odd scratches and marks" on the surface of a painting by Gainsborough: "This chaos, this uncouth and shapeless appearance, by a kind of magic, at a certain distance assumes form, and all the parts seem to drop into their proper place." Third, Proust, writing about a landscape painting by Monet: "There we are, attentive to the magic mirror, moving back from it, trying to expel all other thoughts, attempting to grasp the meaning of each color, each one evoking past impressions in our memory which come together in an architecture as aerial and as many-coloured as the colours on the canvas to erect in our imagination a landscape."[18] Finally, the earliest observation of this kind occurs in Plato's dialogue *Theaetetus,* although Socrates' tone is noticeably less admiring: "But now that I've got close to what we're saying, Theaetetus, as if it were a modern painting, I do not understand it at all; whereas, as long as I was standing some distance away, it seemed to me that there was something in it."[19]

Each of these writers refers to a kind of magic—Plato does so in a passage from the *Republic,* which I shall comment on in chapter 10—which acts "at a certain distance," when we "step back," and transfigures the brushstrokes on a painting's surface, so that a coherent image, an intelligible picture, appears in the place of mere colors or "odd scratches and marks." Step forward, and the image is replaced by the material substance of the painting and the texture of the artist's work; step back again, and the image reappears. Not every painting affords an experience of this kind, and various terms are used to describe the ones that do: for example, "painterly" and "impressionist"—which does not refer here to a period style. The boundaries of the objects depicted are often imprecise, the brushwork is generally looser, and in oil painting the surface is generally less smooth. But the essential thing is that these are pictures that lie at the opposite pole to trompe l'oeil, in the sense that the visible disparity or difference between surface and content is especially salient.

It is, I suggest, chiefly the experience of this visible disparity or difference that makes it tempting to locate the content of a picture in the spectator's imagination, as Proust does in the passage quoted above, or to attribute its existence to the beholder's share. It is like the experience of looking through a microscope, which encouraged Locke to conceive of colors in the same way.[20]

When we stand at a distance, we see a landscape or a color, but when we scrutinize the surface carefully, this flimsy image or evanescent color disappears, and in its place we see the material structure, which produced the original experience in our minds. These are the two perceptions that Wollheim's "twofoldness" combines, and transferred to the case of sculpture, the experience of disparity or difference lies behind Gombrich's remark, which I used as the epigraph to this chapter: "The craftsman of Jericho did not think eyes indistinguishable from cowrie shells any more than Picasso thinks baboons indistinguishable from motor-cars, but in certain contexts one can represent the other. They belong to the same class because they release the same response."

The response this remark releases in me is: yes, but . . . Yes, it is true that in some respects our response to a picture can resemble our response to the kind of object it depicts. The pattern of eye movements that occurs when we see pictures of faces; feelings of sexual arousal, reverence, or shock; the violent destruction of some images of tyrants; the contagious effect of seeing a yawning figure in a picture, which Leonardo mentions—these are all well-known examples of the phenomenon Gombrich is talking about. But if we return to his own example, it is surely obvious that eyes and cowrie shells do not release exactly the same response in us, and that they would do so only if we were unable to distinguish them from each other. And it is surely also obvious that although eyes are not indistinguishable from cowrie shells, there is a resemblance in shape between them, which we are able to perceive and which the craftsman of Jericho knew how to exploit.

Nevertheless, Gombrich's remark captures the main reason for the continuing appeal of subjectivism, namely, the thought that art colludes with human nature in more ingenious ways than the resemblance theory can acknowledge. For example, when a spectator looks at a painting, she can generally see that it depicts a clove of garlic or a glass of water, as long as she knows, or can imagine, what a clove of garlic or a glass of water looks like, or would recognize one if she saw it. The resemblance theory promises to explain this fact in terms of an objective relationship between the marks on the surface of the painting and cloves of garlic or glasses of water—a relationship that the spectator's experience of the painting registers but that exists quite independently of any facts about this experience. But when the disparity between surface and content is especially salient, it seems that this promise cannot be fulfilled.

Consider another of Gombrich's examples—the gold braid on Jan Six's cloak, in Rembrandt's portrait of his patron (figs. 48, 49). Invoking the familiar trope, Gombrich describes the brushstrokes that depict the braid as "magic simplicity" and "sublime wizardry," and with good reason. But, the subjectivist will argue, the resemblance theory cannot explain how this magic works because, objectively speaking, Rembrandt's brushstrokes do not resemble gold braid more closely than they resemble a flight of stairs or a pile of books. So we need not object to saying that the brushstrokes *look like* gold braid if this means simply that they successfully depict it. But in the final analysis this fact can only be explained by defining the effect the painting has on us—the perception it produces in our minds.

It should by now be obvious how an advocate of the resemblance theory will reply to this argument. She will concede that Rembrandt's painting is designed to have a certain kind of effect on a spectator. But she will insist that the fact that it depicts gold braid cannot be explained by defining this effect because the effect itself can only be defined as the experience of seeing the brushstrokes on the painting's surface and seeing what they depict. So there is no harm in saying that the brushstrokes *produce the effect of* gold braid if this means simply that they successfully depict it. But in the final analysis this fact can only be explained by defining the visible relationship between these brushstrokes and gold braid.

The debate in which these are the opening moves can be adjourned; but if the argument in the previous few chapters is correct, it cannot be decided in favor of one side or the other. What is needed, in order to achieve a resolution, is a willingness to make concessions on both sides. The subjectivist will have to acknowledge that the occlusion shape principle and the other basic principles of pictorial art relate the surface and the content of a picture without referring to its psychological effect. And the advocate of the resemblance theory will have to concede that these same principles indicate the limit of any definition we could give, of the visible relationship between the marks on a picture's surface and the objects they depict. They indicate this limit because they indicate how far the visible properties of an object in a picture that are expressly marked on the picture's surface leave its exact character unfixed. Its occlusion shape is fixed, but whether it is a piece of gold braid or a pile of books is not.

If both points are conceded, there is no prospect either of defining the visible relationship in which the marks on the surface of a picture stand to the kinds of objects they depict or of defining the kind of experience that these marks produce in the mind of a qualified spectator. Furthermore, both kinds of definition are ruled out for the same reason. For although the attempts philosophers have made to formulate them are historically and polemically opposed, in the final analysis they are really bound together—because defining the visual experience of a qualified spectator means comparing the perception that occurs when she sees gold braid with the perception that occurs when she sees a picture of gold braid; because that means comparing how gold

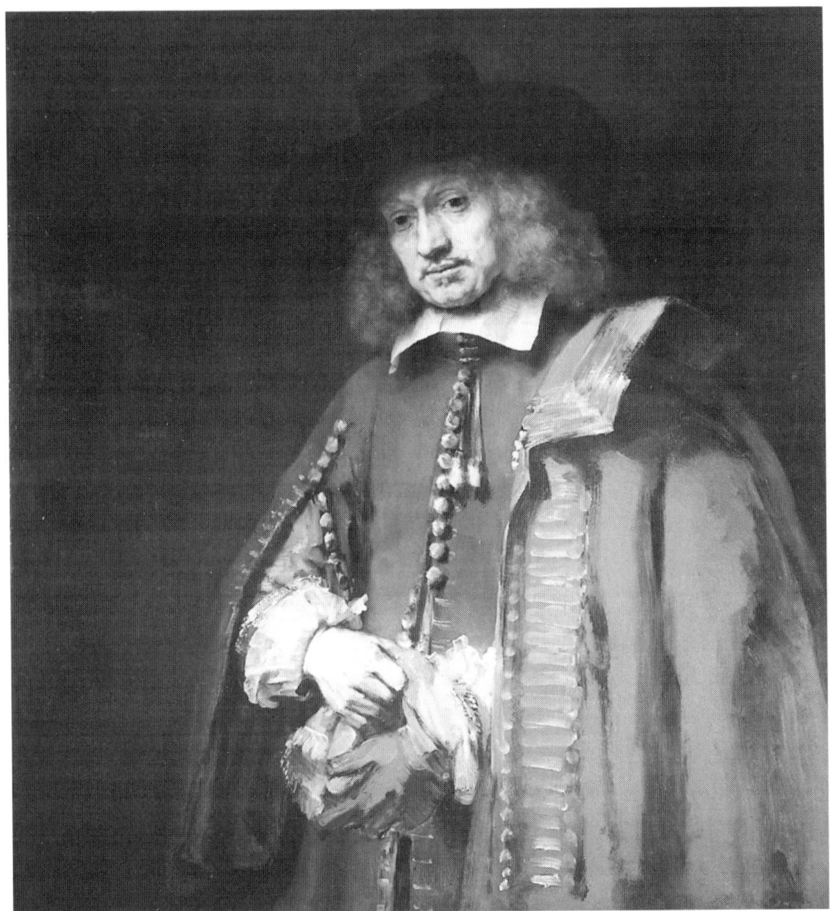

48. Rembrandt van Rijn, *Jan Six,* 1654. Oil on canvas. Six Collection, Amsterdam.

braid looks with how a picture of gold braid looks; and because that means describing the visible relationship between gold braid and a picture of gold braid. The occlusion shape principle and the other basic principles of pictorial art disclose how, and to what extent, the surface of a picture controls our experience when we perceive its content and, hence, how the shapes and colors on the surface of a picture and the spectator's knowledge of appearances jointly explain her perception of its content. But analysis cannot take us any further.

If we acknowledge this limitation, we are not left empty handed. For we can still say, first, that an arrangement of colors on a plane depicts a certain kind

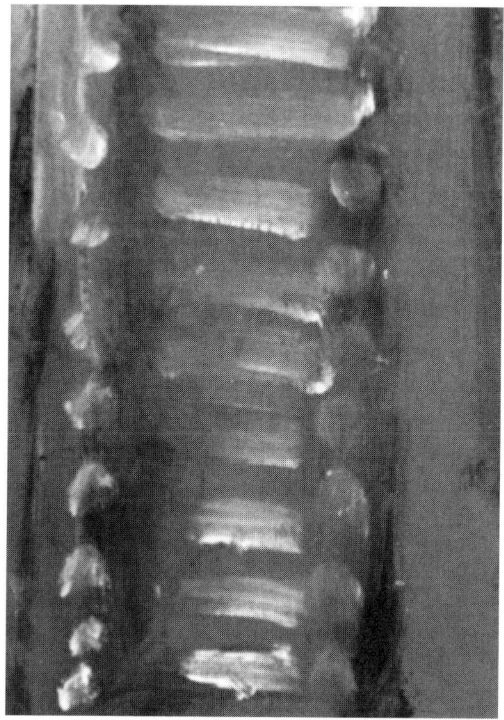

49. Detail of figure 48.

of object if, and only if, a qualified spectator can see that it depicts this kind of object; second, that a qualified spectator can see that a picture depicts a certain kind of object because she can see the occlusion shapes and relative occlusion sizes of the objects it depicts, and their surface colors and aperture colors too, if these are depicted; and third, that she can see these properties because they *are* the shapes, relative sizes, surface colors, and aperture colors of the corresponding parts of the picture's surface. This does not amount to an analysis of the concept of depiction, in the traditional sense, because it does not reduce the concept to a combination of simpler elements. But analysis, in this sense, is an ambition we are forced to renounce, once we have understood that the occlusion shape principle and the other basic principles of pictorial art mark the point at which philosophy must hand the baton on to science.

Beyond this point there are many problems to explore. First, our ability to recognize gold braid must be engaged in some way when we see the gold braid on Jan Six's cloak, as it is when we actually see gold braid. But we do not yet know how these different perceptions are produced. Second, the same is true for the depiction of more abstract qualities and relations, such as shape, tex-

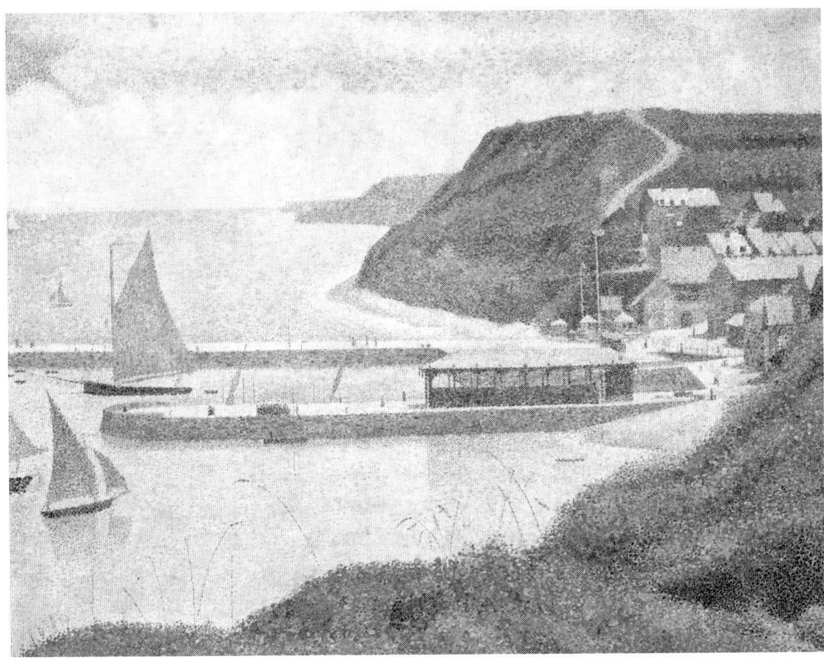

50. Georges Seurat, *Port-en-Bessin, the Outer Port (High Tide)*, 1888. Oil on canvas. Musée d'Orsay, Paris.

ture, depth, solidity, and motion and the direction and quality of light. Third, many drawings depend on the fact, which has not yet been adequately explained, that we can see a line as the boundary of a solid form.[21]

Finally, pictorial art recruits optical effects that are caused by the characteristics of our visual system. For example, optical fusion was used by Byzantine mosaicists to depict penumbra, as we have seen. And in some of Seurat's later paintings he seems to have used partial optical fusion to depict haze or the shimmer of light (fig. 50). Again, the bluish shadow on a mower's shirt, in one of the beautiful small panels Seurat painted in the early 1880s, registers the color of the sky (plate 5). But on a bright day the blue color of the shadow is intensified by the effect of simultaneous contrast, induced by the yellow color of sunlight, which is also recorded on the shirt. And this allows the artist to use chromatic color as a surrogate for brightness.

Taken together, these examples illustrate a claim whose classic formulation is due to the German physiologist, Hermann von Helmholtz: "A careful observation of the works of the great masters will be serviceable, not only to physiological optics, but also because the investigation of the perceptions and the observations of the senses will promote the theory of art, that is, the comprehension of its mode of action."[22] The theory of art cannot be equated with the "comprehension of its mode of action." It includes much more than physiological optics or than physiological optics applied to the works of the great masters. But the main substance of the remark is true. Unfortunately, the record of physiological optics in the theory of art to date is as mixed as the record of philosophy and, as we shall see in chapter 10, Helmholtz himself deserves some of the blame.

REALISM

8

WORDS AND PICTURES

[Picasso and Braque] discovered that the true character of painting and sculpture is that of a *script.* The product of these arts are signs, emblems for the external world not mirrors reflecting the external world in a more or less distorting manner. Once this was recognized, the plastic arts were freed from the slavery inherent in illusionistic styles.

Daniel-Henry Kahnweiler

PICTURES CAN BE COMBINED with written words in many ways. Some of the most familiar ways are to use pictures as illustrations to accompany texts, to use words or names to provide titles, captions, or signatures for pictures, and to include a written text in a depicted scene—either as a self-sufficient object, such as a book or a letter, or as a sign of speech (fig. 51).

Titles are often assigned to pictures for convenience, for example, when an inventory or catalog is prepared. But they can be chosen by the artist to express or encourage a thought about the work. For example, Holman Hunt entitled a painting of a young woman rising from the lap of her would-be (or perhaps has-been) seducer *The Awakening Conscience.* Or they can be used to signal an irony, as in Richard Hamilton's tribute in collage to consumerism, *Just what is it that makes today's homes so different, so appealing?* (fig. 52). Or they can be used to alert the viewer to the artist's aesthetic priorities. For example, Whistler changed the title of a painting from *The Artist's Mother* to *Arrangement in Grey and Black.* "To me it is interesting as a picture of my mother," he explained, "but what can or ought the public to care about the identity of the portrait?"[1]

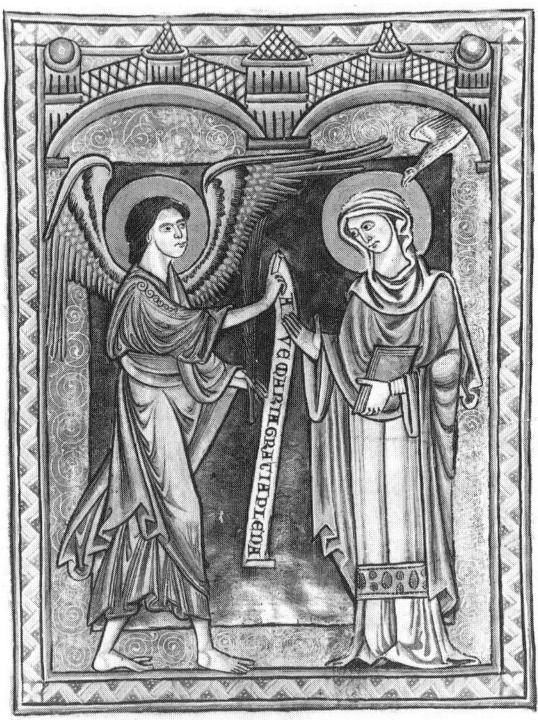

51. *Annunciation.* Glazier Hachette Psalter, fol. 1v, ca. 1225. Pierpont Morgan Library, New York.

Titles are names of works of art, whereas captions are not: they are either integral parts of the works in which they occur or else they are neither exactly inside nor outside them but belong in the space Kant called the "*parergon.*"[2] The tragic litany of captions to Goya's series of prints *The Disasters of War* provides an extraordinary series of examples. Some of them comment on the image; some describe it; some ask a question; some cry out with revulsion. Here are a few, in sequence: "Todo va revuelto." "Tambien esto." "Yo lo vi." "Y esto tambien." "Esto es mal." "Asi sucedió." (Everything is upside down. That too. I saw it. And this too. This is bad. It happened thus.) Very different, both in style and purpose, is the long dedicatory inscription, as if on an ex-voto, to Goya's moving portrait of himself being nursed by his friend and doctor Arrieta, during a near-fatal illness: "Goya agradecido, à su amigo Arrieta: por el acierto y esmero con que le salva la vida en su agúda y peligrosa enfermedad, padecida à fines del año 1819 a los setenta y tres de su edad. Lo pinto en 1820." (From Goya, with gratitude, to his friend Arrieta: for the sureness and solicitude with which he saved his life during his acute and dangerous

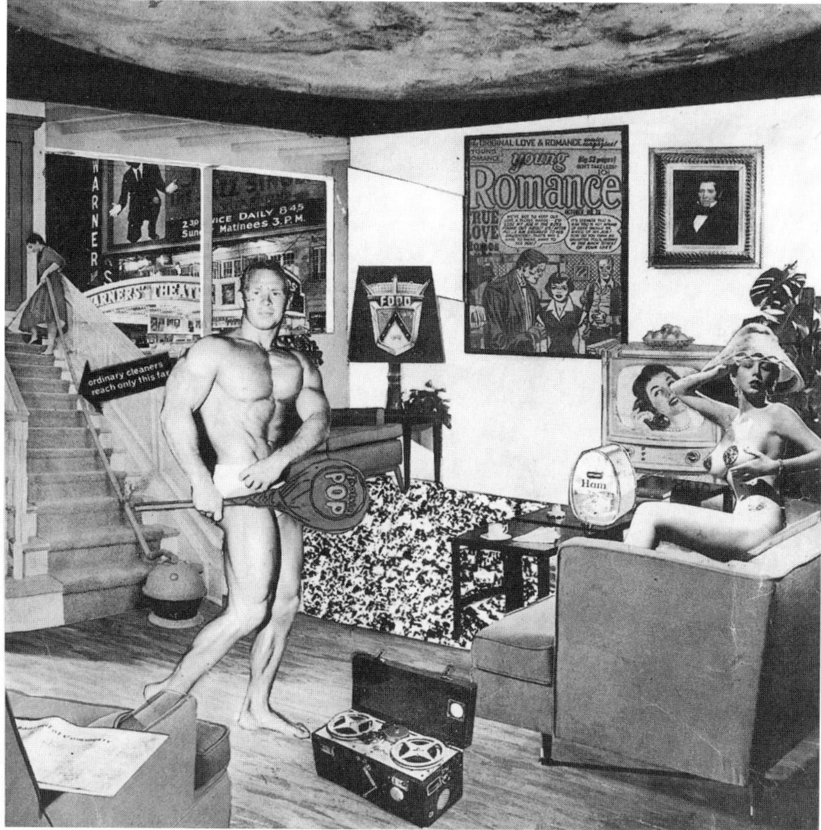

52. Richard Hamilton, *Just what is it that makes today's homes so different, so appealing?* 1956. Collage. Kunsthalle, Tübingen.

illness, suffered at the end of the year 1819, at seventy-three years of age. He painted it in 1820.)

Signatures commonly take the form of a name or monogram, sometimes accompanied by a date. But there are other possibilities. For example, the signatures on Greek vases, which are the earliest surviving marks of authorship on works of art, take the form of a statement that so-and-so "painted it"—or, in the case of the potter, "made it." This custom was eventually dropped, or considered an archaism, in the eighteenth century. But artists have also incorporated a signature into the content of a picture, in a number of ways. For example, Goya (again) portrays the Duchess of Alba pointing toward a phrase

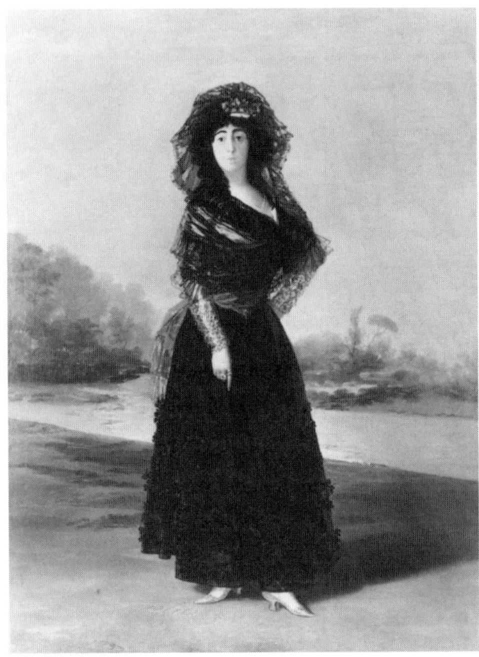

53. Francisco Goya, *Duchess of Alba*, 1797. Oil on canvas. Hispanic Society of America, New York.

marked in the ground before her feet: "Solo Goya." The words, which seem to carry a veiled and potent message, are inverted in relation to the viewer but legible to her (fig. 53). David's *Death of Marat* combines the artist's signature "DAVID" with the dedication "À MARAT" and, in smaller capitals, the year according to the revolutionary calendar, "L'AN DEUX," all shown as painted on the side of an upended box, which stands as a makeshift desk beside the bath (fig. 54). One ingenious device was used in some Japanese erotic prints. The signature appears in the picture as the signature on a respectable painted screen (fig. 55). In this way, the artist tactfully pretended to disguise his authorship of the print.

The last two ways of combining words and pictures I shall mention are of particular theoretical interest. They are, first, that written words can be constructed or composed of pictures and, second, that pictures can be composed of written words (figs. 56, 57). The lesson these examples teach us is that whatever differences exist between a picture and a written text, they cannot be defined in terms of form or appearance, since a single design, with a definite and constant form, may be both a text and a picture. So, is the true character of painting and sculpture that of a script, as Kahnweiler asserted? And if not, how can the difference between a picture and a written text be defined?

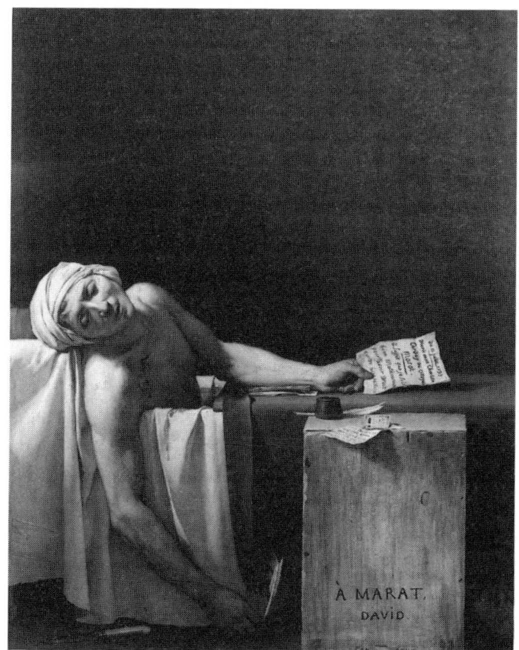

54. Jacques-Louis David, *Death of Marat*, 1793. Oil on canvas. Musées Royaux des Beaux-Arts de Belgique, Brussels.

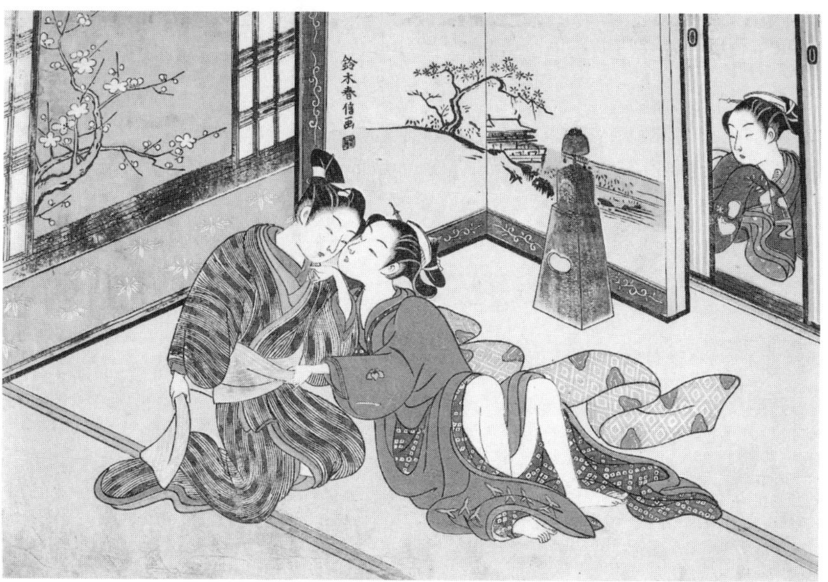

55. Suzuki Harunobu, *Lovers Watched by a Maidservant*, 1767–68. Woodblock print. Museum of Fine Arts, Boston.

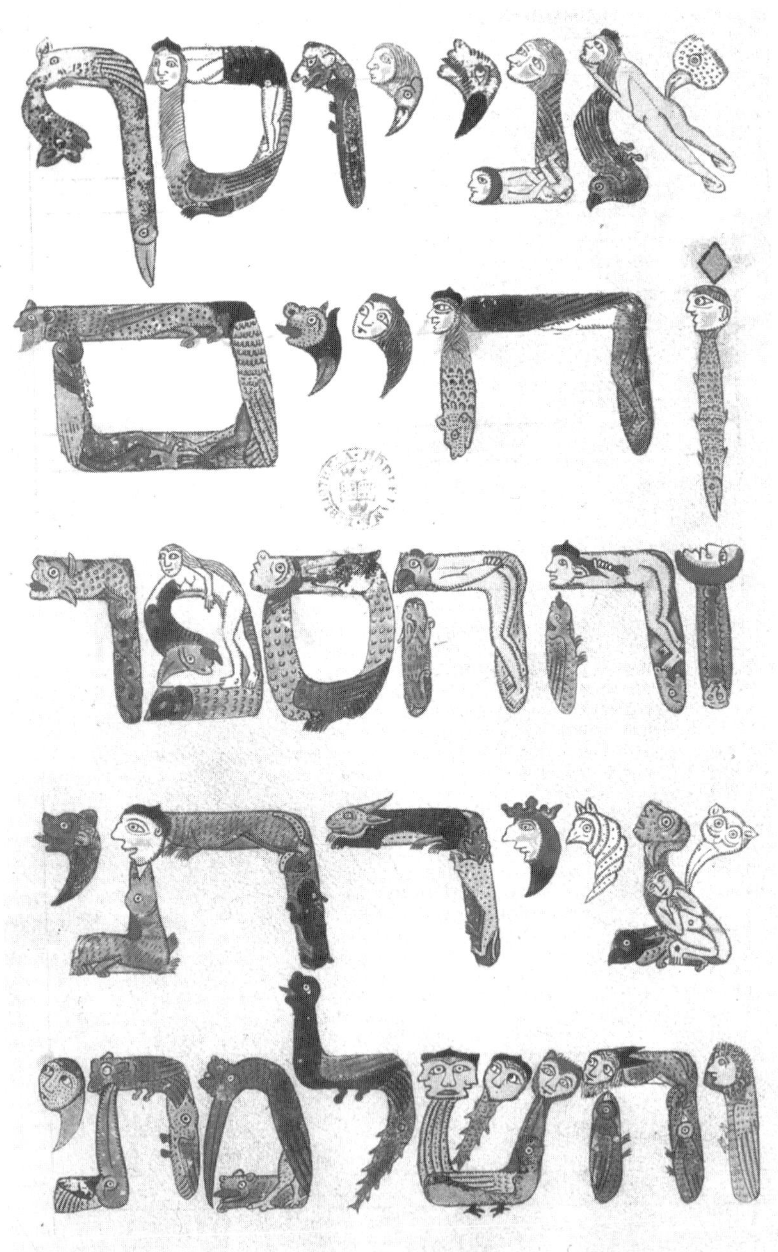

56. The Artist's Colophon. The Kennicott Bible, fol. 447r, ca. 1476. The Bodleian Library.

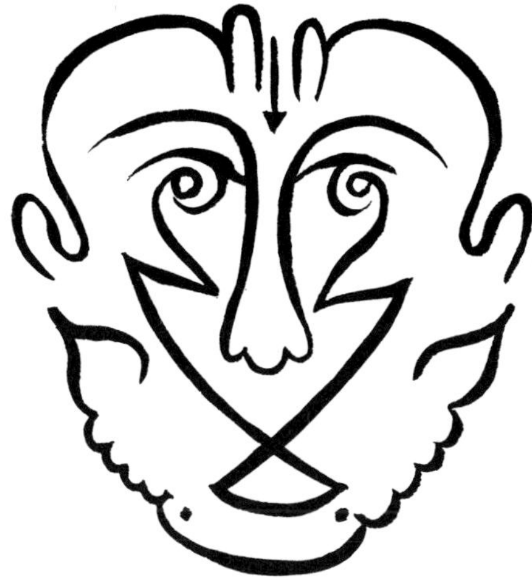

57. A face made up of the names of Allah, Muhammad and the first three imams, in Arabic script. Date unknown.

The argument in the last four chapters provides a simple answer in two parts: first, the occlusion shape principle and the other basic principles of pictorial art govern the content of a picture but not the meaning of a text. Second, a viewer's ability to perceive the content of a picture depends on her knowledge of the appearances of the objects it depicts, whereas in general her ability to read and understand a written text does not. However, in this chapter I shall set this answer to one side in order to explore the popular claim that pictures, like words, are conventional signs of the objects they depict.

The distinction between natural signs and conventional signs stems originally from Plato's *Cratylus.* But the classic exposition of it appears in Augustine's treatise *On Christian Doctrine,* which is the first and most influential patristic work on biblical hermeneutics. Augustine defines a sign as follows: "A sign is a thing which, over and above the impression it makes on the senses, causes something else to come into the mind as a consequence of itself." And he distinguishes between natural and conventional signs as follows: "Natural signs are those which, apart from any intention or desire of using them as signs, do yet lead to the knowledge of something else, as, for example, smoke when it indicates fire. . . . Conventional signs, on the other hand, are those which living beings mutually exchange for the purpose of showing, as well as they can, the feelings of their minds, or their perceptions, or their thoughts."[3]

Both words and pictures are conventional signs by Augustine's definition because they are signs that human beings purposefully exchange to express their thoughts or their perceptions. But when pictures are described as natural or conventional signs by twentieth-century philosophers, what is at issue is not how they are used but the relationship between them and the objects they depict. Causation and resemblance are generally held to be natural relations, which exist independently of human custom or convention; and pictures are therefore classified as natural signs by philosophers who accept the resemblance theory or the illusion theory, in some form. For the resemblance theory claims that a picture depicts the objects it resembles, and the illusion theory claims that a picture depicts the objects whose effect on the senses resembles the effect it has itself. When twentieth-century philosophers defend the claim that pictures are conventional signs, they mean that semantic conventions, rather than resemblances or illusions, explain how pictures represent.

This doctrine has become commonplace in art theory. It is often advanced with a polemical intention—to undermine the hegemony of the so-called traditional Western system of representation (so called by Nelson Goodman) or to free art from the slavery inherent in illusionistic styles. It does not always seem to matter that there is no such thing as *the* traditional Western system of representation, that the hegemony of nineteenth-century academic painting was broken in the 1870s, that the influence of art from Asia, Oceania, and Africa all played a part in transforming European painting between 1880 and 1910, or that Cézanne was no more interested in illusionism than were Picasso or Braque. The safest battles to join are the ones that have already been won.

Sometimes, however, the claim that pictures are conventional signs is advanced with a subtler intention. For example, Leo Steinberg does not use it as a weapon against nineteenth-century art. On the contrary, he uses it to demonstrate that there is no need for painters to abandon the attempt—in Van Gogh's poignant phrase—to be "simply honest before nature," in order to escape the condescension of art historians who disparage "the power that is nothing but a technical capacity in the imitation of nature."[4] "This famous slur," writes Steinberg, "reverberating in the prejudice of almost every modern connoisseur, has become standard critical jargon. The picturing of overt nature is written off as mere factual reportage . . . patently uncreative and therefore alien to the essence of art." But the right way to respond to the slur, he argues, is not to defend the value of the technical capacity that it encourages us to despise. It is to deny that any such skill exists:

> The ineluctable modality of the visible—young Dedalus's hypnotic phrase—is a myth that evaporates between any two works of representation. The encroaching archaism of old photographs is only the latest instance of an end-

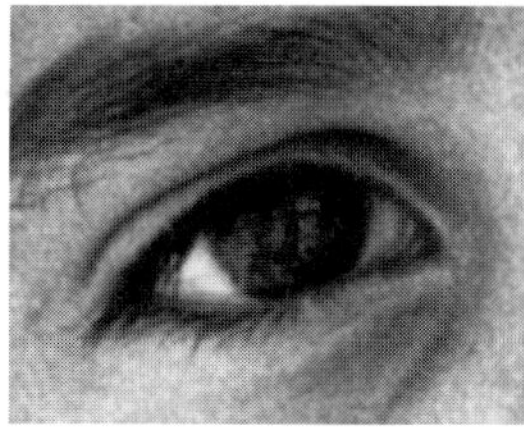 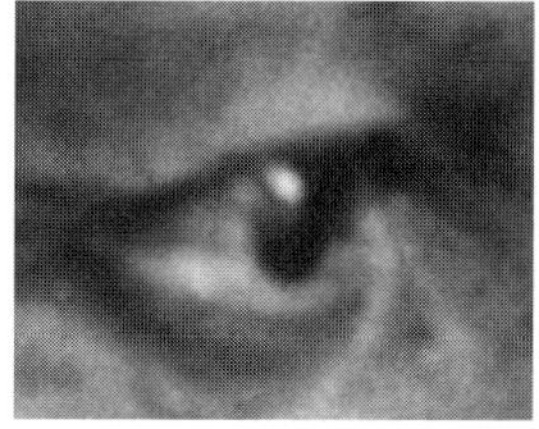 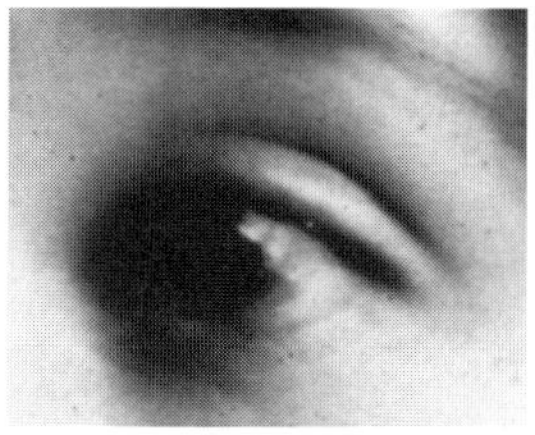

58. Details of photographs from the 1860s, 1930s, and 1980s.

> less succession in which every new mode of nature-representation eventually resigns its claim to co-identity with natural appearance. We can therefore assert with confidence that "technical capacity in the imitation of nature" simply does not exist. What does exist is the skill of reproducing handy graphic symbols for natural appearances, of rendering familiar facts by set professional conventions.[5]

I find this argument unconvincing for two reasons. First, it is true that old photographs look old, but it does not follow that photographs are handy graphic symbols. Here, for example, are three details from photographs taken in the 1860s, the 1930s, and the 1980s, each showing a human eye (fig. 58). Are they so hard to date because the symbols nineteenth-century photographers used to represent a human eye were more durable than the ones nineteenth-century painters used? Or is it because the appearance of the human eye did not change much in a hundred years? The right answer is neither of these facts alone. It is the combination of the second one with the fact that the differences between lenses and emulsions, and the effects of time on paper, are not visible in these reproductions. The stability of professional conventions is neither here nor there.

Second, it is true that what Steinberg calls the picturing of overt nature has sometimes been written off by critics as mere factual reportage, but there is no need to claim that works of art are conventional signs in order to argue against this unconvincing doctrine. For example, Meyer Schapiro, who has no more sympathy than Steinberg for the idea that "representation is a passive mirroring of things," argues as follows: "[This view is] thoroughly one-sided and rest[s] on a mistaken idea of what representation is. There is no passive, "photographic" representation in the sense described. . . . All renderings of objects, no matter how exact they seem, even photographs, proceed from values, methods and viewpoints that somehow shape the image and often determine its contents."[6] Both authors reject the Platonic doctrine that representation is unimaginative and mechanical, but whereas Steinberg argues that it stems from ignoring the fact that pictures reproduce "handy graphic symbols for natural appearances" and "render familiar facts by set professional conventions," Schapiro suggests that it ignores the role of "values, methods and viewpoints" in pictorial art.

Steinberg's ideas are not by any means eccentric, and the jargon he favors—the "handy graphic symbols" and "set professional conventions"—is deeply entrenched. Both the ideas and the jargon can be found in many works by members of the Warburg School, and recent trends in philosophy—and in the humanities in general—have given them a new lease of life.[7] But in this chapter and the next one, I shall argue that Schapiro's diagnosis is the more accurate of the two. In both chapters, however, I shall focus on the argument in Nelson Goodman's book *Languages of Art*, which contains the only serious attempt to explain precisely what kind of system of conventions a general theory of depiction must postulate, if it is committed to these popular ideas. This is not by any means a point of detail. Without this precision, conventionalism can provide historians and critics with a range of convenient and attractive metaphors, but it cannot amount to a testable theory of art. Goodman's arguments show what is involved in taking seriously the popular claim that pictorial styles are systems of conventions, and they offer the only rigorous theoretical foundation so far devised for the now standard view that realism is in the eye of the beholder.

~

Languages of Art is a heterodox product of the philosophical debate about pictorial art that stems from the work of Charles Sanders Peirce. In particular, it stems from Peirce's theory of signs, which was shaped by the pragmatist maxim for which he is best known: "Consider what effects, which might have conceivably practical bearings, we conceive the object of our conception to have. Then, our conception of these effects is the whole of our conception of the object."[8] For example, the whole conception of hardness, Peirce says, is that a hard thing will not be scratched by many other substances: this is the practical effect of being hard; the whole conception of weight is that a heavy thing, in the absence of an opposing force, will fall; and so on. In each case, the idea of something is said to consist wholly in the idea of its practical effects, and these are either observable changes or effects on an observer's sensibility.

Applying this maxim to the concept of a sign, Peirce argues that signification is not a binary relation between a sign and what it signifies but a triadic relation between a sign, the object signified by the sign, and the sign's "sensible effect"—that is, the thought it produces in the mind of a person who interprets it. For example, if I read the name "Socrates" in a text, it signifies Socrates because it makes me think about him. Moreover, according to Peirce, my thought about Socrates is itself another sign, with the same signification as the sign interpreted. And, being another sign, it too will produce a thought about Socrates, for example, when I infer one belief about him (say, that he is mortal) from another (that he is a man).

Peirce's taxonomy of signs is famously complex. But the important distinction, for our purposes, is the one that Peirce himself regarded as most fundamental: between three kinds of sign, whose interpretation depends on three different relations between a sign and an object signified. A sign that signifies an object because of a causal, spatial, or temporal relationship between them is called an index; a sign that signifies an object because they resemble each other is called an icon; and a sign whose significance depends on custom or convention is called a symbol. For example, a low barometer with a moist air is an index of rain; a weathervane is an index of the direction of the wind; and if one says, "There is a fire within a hundred yards of here," the word "here" is an index because it has "exactly the same force as if he had pointed energetically to the ground."[9] "Every picture," Peirce writes, "(however conventional its method) is essentially [an icon]" and, likewise, a diagram or an ideographic hieroglyph.[10] Words, sentences, and books are symbols, and so are the white flag and the Victoria Cross.[11]

The claim that pictures are iconic signs was accepted and disseminated by the principal American philosophers who attempted to bring the theory of art under the aegis of a general semiotic theory, namely, Suzanne Langer and Charles Morris, and by philosophers who drew on the theory of meaning to reform aesthetics, such as John Hospers.

Langer, Morris, and Hospers agree that pictures signify or (modifying Peirce's terminology) symbolize the objects they depict, and they distinguish between pictures and other signs in similar ways to Peirce. Langer argues that a picture "is essentially a symbol," which shares "a certain proportion of parts" with the object that it represents.[12] Symbols, she explains, "lead [us] to conceive their objects," but they are also "vehicles for the conception of [an] object" and, therefore, instruments as well as causes of thought.[13] Morris describes a picture as a *visual* and *iconic* sign, that is, a "visual stimulus . . . which is similar in some respects to what it denotes."[14] And following Peirce, he defines signification in terms of the effects of signs, but he gives this approach a behaviorist inflection that is foreign to Peirce's philosophy. Finally, Hospers is more reticent than either Morris or Langer about the nature of signification. He claims that pictures are symbols that "refer to or stand for" the objects they represent, but he does not explain what "standing for" is, beyond mentioning, as an example, that the word "chair" "refers to or stands for . . . the kind of object that I am now sitting on."[15] Hospers calls a picture a *natural* symbol because (he says) there is "a close natural relationship, namely likeness or resemblance, between symbol and thing symbolized."[16]

The claims made by these authors were challenged on three main grounds. First, Peirce holds that signification is a triadic relation. A sign, he says, is a sensible token that produces a thought about the object that it signifies. So the three relata are the sign, the object, and the thought. (The normal use of the word "sign" may be at odds with this doctrine, but we can treat it as a stipulation.) But, it was argued, nothing can stand in a relation, say, to a chair without standing in that relation to a specific chair, as I now stand in the relation of "sitting on" to the chair that now bears my weight. Whereas if a painting represents a chair, there need not be any chair in particular that it represents. Hence it need not signify a chair, in the stipulated sense of "signify." Reference and denotation are not quite the same thing as signification.[17] But since reference and denotation were also held to be relations, this objection was thought to apply equally to all of the four authors I have mentioned.

Second, it was pointed out that the concept of an iconic sign is too loose and accommodating to pull its weight in a semiotic theory because so many different kinds of things count or are counted by semioticians as iconic signs: onomatopoeic words; sentences that are similar in structure to the circumstances they describe, such as, "the keys are to the left of the vase" (written down) or "the *Sanctus* comes before the *Agnus Dei*" (spoken), graphs, maps, paintings, photographs, shadows, footprints, samples of colors or of cloths, and more. Hence, very little is revealed about the nature of pictorial art by saying that pictures are iconic signs.

Finally, it was argued that iconicity can attach a picture to the wrong thing. For example, Morris held that an iconic sign "denote[s] any object which has the properties (in practice, a selection from the properties) which it itself has."[18] But this implies that if a portrait of Sam is an iconic sign, it denotes Sam's twin as well as Sam himself. And we cannot improve matters by holding that an iconic sign denotes the object that it resembles most, for two reasons. First, a portrait of Sam could prove to be a better likeness of his twin. And second, the modification would imply that an iconic sign denotes itself, if resemblance is a reflexive relation, or the best copy of itself, if it is irreflexive.

Languages of Art addresses each of these three problems. Goodman holds that pictures are symbols, along with letters, words, paragraphs, diagrams, and graphs. But he describes the word "symbol" as "a very general and colourless term," and it carries no theoretical burden in his argument.[19] He also holds that a picture, like a written text, is a *visual* symbol, since what it represents depends on how the visible marks of which it is composed are distributed across its surface. But he denies that pictures are iconic signs and he argues that the pictorial content of a design is no more constrained by its appearance, and no less an artifact of a system of conventions, than the meaning of a text. This, needless to say, is the chief heterodoxy.

Goodman's argument begins with Goya's portrait of the Duke of Wellington. The portrait, he claims, like the name "Arthur Wellesley," denotes the man. Denotation, he explains, is a variety of reference. It is, as we just noted, a relation: specifically, the relation that obtains between a name and its bearer, a label and the thing or things it is attached to, or a predicate (e.g., "*x* is round") and the several members of the corresponding class (e.g., the class of round objects). The assumption that the same relation obtains in each of these cases is substantial and contentious. But for the moment we need only take note of it. I shall return to it later.

Pictures are therefore like labels, names, and predicates. They can, of course, depict many things apart from people—mountains, battles, streets, and cafés, for example. But since the verb "denotes" expresses a relation, a picture cannot be a symbol that denotes without denoting something, any more than a person can be a murderer without a victim or be married without having a spouse.[20] An empty name—that is, a name that has no bearer—a label that is not attached to anything, and a predicate that nothing satisfies, such as the predicate "*x* is both round and square," are said to have null denotation. A painting of Zeus has null denotation, since Zeus does not exist, and a painting of a centaur has null denotation because there are no centaurs.

Goodman claims that denotation is, as he puts it, "the core of representation" and that "a picture that represents . . . an object refers to and, more particularly, denotes it."[21] But just as "Zeus" is evidently a name, despite being an empty name, and the predicate "*x* is part man and part horse" is perfectly intelligible, despite the fact that nothing satisfies it, there are paintings that, as we can readily see, represent Zeus or a centaur.[22] Goodman does not deny this. So what can he mean by the claim that denotation is the core of representation? And why does the existence of pictures with mythological subjects not prove that a picture can represent an object without denoting it?

The answer to the first question is as follows. Goodman argues that a picture, like a text or graph, is composed and interpreted in accordance with a set of rules or conventions that correlate symbols with denotata. For example, the name "Arthur Wellesley" is correlated with a man, the predicate "*x* is red" is correlated with red things, the predicate "*x* is round" is correlated with round things, and so on. Goodman does not say how these correlations are effected.

But perhaps a baptism can correlate a name with a child; agreement among the members of a family or in a community of scientists can decide the name of a pet or a virus; and custom fixes the significance of the bulk of the predicates we use in daily conversation.

If this general pattern is acknowledged, it is easy to see how empty names can arise. For we can imagine that a name is correlated with an individual when in fact it is not, and we can combine predicates to make more complex ones that nothing satisfies. Pictures with null denotation are comparable. They are complex symbols, constructed in accordance with the conventions governing a pictorial system of representation and analogous to names or descriptive passages in works of fiction. The fiction need not involve gods or strange beasts. *Mansfield Park* is as fictional as Ovid's *Metamorphosis*, and Cruikshank's illustrations for *Oliver Twist* are as fictional as any picture of a winged Cupid or a drunken Silenus, with his retinue of satyrs.

The second question was why the existence of pictures with mythological subjects fails to prove that a picture can represent an object without denoting it. The answer to this question follows from the answer to the last one. "Arthur Wellesley" is the name of a duke. "Zeus" is the name of a god. But whereas the phrase "is the name of" expresses a relation in the first sentence, it merely classifies a symbol in the second. It tells us what sort of word we are dealing with, but not by relating it to something else. It cannot possibly express a relation, we are told, because there is nothing to which it can relate the name "Zeus."

In the same way, Goodman argues, the verb "represents" has more than one interpretation. It is, he says, "highly ambiguous."[23] In the sentence "Goya's portrait represents the Duke of Wellington," the verb is a two-place predicate—"*x* represents *y*"—that expresses a relation between two independently existing things, namely, a painting and a man. But in the sentences "Ingres's painting represents Zeus" and "Piero di Cosimo's painting represents a dying centaur," the same verb is being used quite differently. When we look at these sentences on the page, it is easy to construe the verb in the same way as we construed it in the sentence about Goya's portrait. But (Goodman argues) we should instead interpret it as part of a one-place predicate, namely, "*x* represents Zeus" or "*x* represents a dying centaur." Like "*x* is a still life" and "*x* is predominantly green and pink," these predicates can be used to describe or classify a painting but not by relating it to something else.[24]

Hence, texts and pictures are both symbols. But, Goodman argues, texts or parts of texts that differ widely in appearance may still be instances of the same name or predicate. For example, "*Socrates is wise*" and "socrates is wise" are instances of the same sentence and say exactly the same thing. By contrast, pictures that differ in appearance, in any one of many different ways, and however small the difference is, will also differ in what they represent.

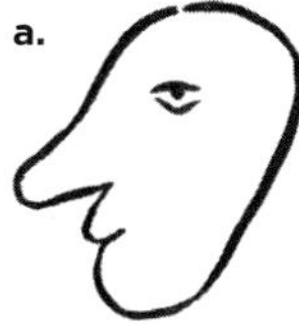

b. A man with a long nose

59. (*a*) Drawing of a man with a long nose.
(*b*) Description of a man with a long nose.

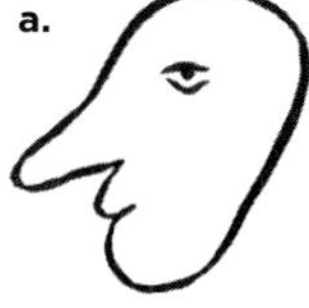

b. A man with a long nose

60. (*a*) Same drawing with elongated nose.
(*b*) Same description with elongated "nose."

For example, compare a drawing of a man with a long nose with the written phrase "a man with a long nose" (fig. 59). If we change the drawing slightly, say by elongating the part that represents the nose, it will depict a longer nose than it did before. But the corresponding change to the phrase will not have the same effect (fig. 60). A small change to the written phrase *may* change its meaning but only if it affects the classification of one or more characters, so that "nose" becomes "hose," for example. But there is no respect—the thickness or color of the line, or the size or shape of any part of the inscription—in which any perceptible change, however small, will change the significance of a written phrase. And the same is evidently true of speech. A single English phrase will vary phonetically from San Francisco to Hong Kong and acoustically from one utterance to the next by the same speaker.

Why do small differences matter in the case of pictures and not in the case of written words? One possible explanation is that a picture is an iconic sign—a sign that signifies an object because of the resemblances between them. For any difference between two pictures will entail a difference between the objects they resemble.[25] But Goodman denies that this is the right explanation. As we have seen, he claims that pictures are conventional signs, and he explains the fact that small differences affect what a picture represents in terms of three properties that pictorial systems of conventions are supposed to have and linguistic systems are supposed to lack, namely, syntactic density, semantic density, and relative repleteness. He writes as follows:

> Consider, for example, some pictures in the traditional Western system of representation: the first is of a man standing erect at a given distance; the second, to the same scale, is of a shorter man at the same distance. A third image in this series may be of intermediate height; a fourth, intermediate between the third and second; and so on. According to the representational system, any difference in height among these images constitutes a difference in height of the man represented. Whether any actual men are represented does not matter; all that

is in question here is how the several images classify into characters, of which the images are marks.[26]

Thus pictures are marks or instances of characters, just as this *A* is an instance of the first letter of the alphabet. A system is syntactically dense if it provides for infinitely many characters such that between any two there is a third. An alphabet is not a dense system since it contains between twenty and thirty signs and since there is, for example, no letter between *A* and *B*. But the "traditional Western system of representation" is syntactically dense, as the example of pictures of men, and in particular the phrase "and so on," is supposed to prove. A system is semantically dense if its characters correspond to an infinite number of compliance classes (i.e., classes of denotata) such that between any two there is a third—in this case classes of men whose height is, potentially at least, infinitesimally graduated. Hence, although the pictures in the example are not meant to denote actual men, the fact that "any difference in height among these images constitutes a difference in height of the man represented" demonstrates that the system in which they are characters is a semantically dense system. Finally, a system is relatively replete if relatively many properties of a character, such as the thickness and color of a line, affect its significance. For example, the Italian caricaturist Pier Leone Ghezzi often indicated shadows merely by a thickening of the line (fig. 61).[27]

"This all adds up to open heresy," Goodman concludes. "Descriptions are distinguished from depictions not through being more arbitrary but through belonging to articulate rather than to dense schemes. . . . Resemblance disappears as a criterion of representation. . . . The often stressed distinction between iconic and other signs becomes transient and trivial."[28]

~

The nominalist heresy was already popular when *Languages of Art* appeared. Back in 1921, Roman Jakobson had claimed: "It is necessary to learn the conventional language of painting in order to 'see' a picture, just as it is impossible to understand what is spoken without knowing the language."[29] But blithe claims like this had never been backed up in convincing detail—or expressed with comparable panache. If the argument in previous chapters is correct, the nominalist theory of depiction cannot be true, and it does not follow from the observation that we need to learn to perceive pictures. But there is much to be gained by setting these arguments to one side and criticizing Goodman's theory on its own terms. This is the task to which I shall turn now, beginning with the claim that denotation is the core of representation. As we have seen, this claim epitomizes Goodman's doctrine that pictures are made

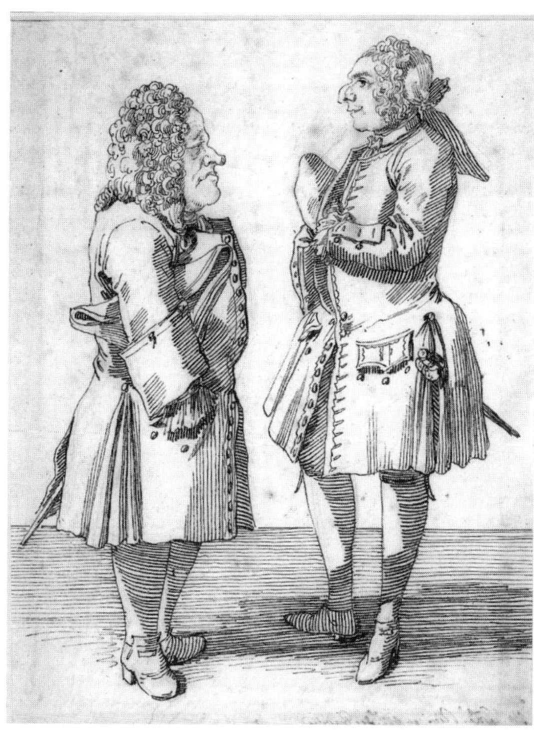

61. Pier Leone Ghezzi, *Cavaliere Ricci and Monsieur de Gravelle,* ca. 1720–30. Pen and brown ink. Huntington Library, San Marino, California.

by artists and interpreted by spectators using a system of rules that correlate symbols with their denotata. But is it true? Certainly, rules and conventions of various kinds are involved in making and interpreting pictures. The question is whether they include any of this specific kind.

Two basic kinds of rule are involved in making and perceiving pictures, which play quite different roles. First, there are iconographic conventions, such as the ones concerning the symbolic attributes of saints: Saint Peter's keys, Saint Catherine's wheel, the palm frond held by a martyred saint, and so on. Second, there are technical rules, such as Alberti's rules for drawing a pavement in perspective, which I shall discuss in chapter 10, or the techniques set out in the classic Chinese manual, *The Mustard Seed Garden Manual of Painting*. The different roles played by these two kinds of rules are quite evident and not difficult to describe.

To begin with, iconographic conventions allow us to make inferences about the subject of a picture. For example, if we know the relevant convention, we can infer that a bearded scholar with a lion at his feet is Saint Jerome, that a pelican fighting a snake represents the crucifixion vanquishing original sin, or that a winged figure is an angel. In each case, an iconographic convention enables a spectator to move from one description of a picture's content to another. But it follows that an iconographic convention cannot explain how the spectator knows that this original description applies. It cannot explain how she can see that a painting depicts a bearded scholar with a lion at his feet, a pelican fighting a snake, and so on.

Technical rules are quite different. Like iconographic conventions, they can be explained in manuals, but more often they are passed directly from one artist or craftsman to another. For example, Greek vase painters used lines of various shapes to depict the anklebone, such as a short L-shaped line, a longer line with a small hook at the end, or a triangle open at one corner. And *The Mustard Seed Garden Manual of Painting* includes specific techniques for painting orchids, bamboo, plum trees, and so on (fig. 62). These are techniques for the application of slip or ink, which are designed to control the appearance of a foot, a stem, a branch, or a leaf and which therefore mediate between the marks on the surface of a picture and its content. But

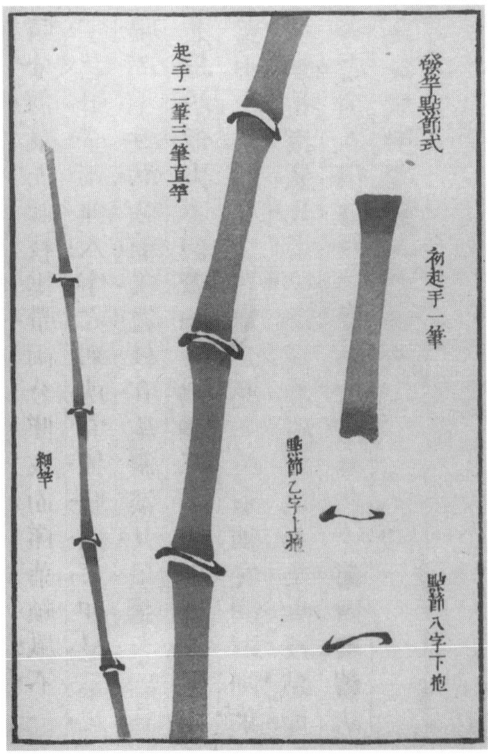

62. *Bamboo.* Page from *The Mustard Seed Garden Manual of Painting,* 1679–1701.

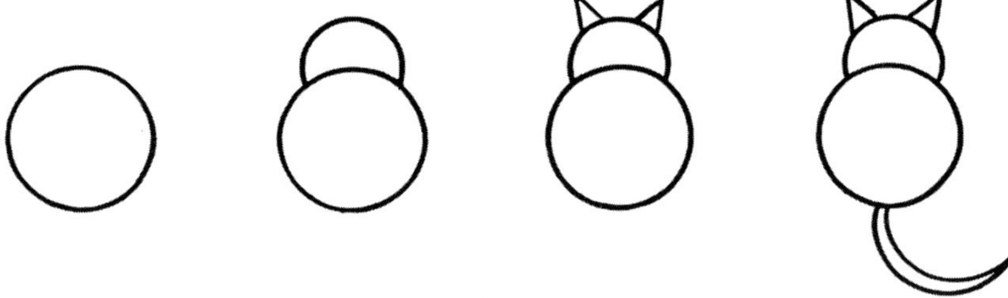

63. Gombrich's method for drawing a cat.

whereas the spectator needs to be aware of an iconographic convention in order to arrive at the specific description it licenses, her ability to identify bamboo in an ink painting need not depend on her knowledge of the techniques that guided its design and execution.

It is easy to confuse these two kinds of rules. For example, Gombrich comments on a method for drawing a cat, which he had learned as a child, as follows (fig. 63): "Whatever can be coded in symbols can also be retrieved and recalled with relative ease. The tricks of how to draw this or that—a cat for instance—. . . can really be described as such simple methods of coding."[30] But in fact the tricks of how to draw this or that are not really methods of coding. For whenever information is encoded in symbols, the person doing the encoding and the person doing the decoding must both know what the code is. This is true of Morse code and semaphore, and it is equally true of an iconographic convention, such as the one that makes it easy to identify the symbolic meaning of the pelican fighting a snake, as long as the spectator knows what the convention is. But the tricks of how to draw this or that are technical rules, which only the artist needs to know.

Goodman does not offer any examples of the kind of rule he postulates, and it is not difficult to see why. For, unlike either iconographic conventions or technical rules, they are supposed to mediate between the patterns of color on the surface of a picture and the members of its compliance class, that is, its one or several denotata. Moreover, the viewer's knowledge of these rules is supposed to be engaged whenever she perceives what a picture represents, even if she would not be able to say what the rules are. But rules of this kind do not play any part in making pictures. We could invent rules mediating between the marks on a picture's surface and its denotata. For example, we could invent a purely geometrical procedure that could be used to make a drawing of the Eiffel Tower because it defines curves with the right shapes. But even in this case, a viewer would not need to know what the rule is, or even that one has been used, in order to identify the picture's subject. Hence, the claim that pictures are both produced and interpreted by applying rules that correlate symbols and denotata is false.

I shall now turn to the claim that pictures are instances of characters in a dense symbol system and, then, to the looser claim that pictures "function in somewhat the same way as descriptions."[31]

The claim that pictures are instances of characters in a dense symbol system is untenable, for the following reasons. A set is dense if, and only if, between any two elements that belong to it there is a third. But without an ordering, nothing is between two other things; and the same set of elements may be dense relative to one ordering but not another. For example, since the set of natural numbers can be mapped onto to the set of rational numbers, and since there is a dense ordering of the set of rational numbers, the set of natural numbers can also be given a dense ordering. But it is not dense relative to the ordering we learn at school, namely, {1, 2, 3, 4, . . . } because here there is no number between 1 and 2, or between 2 and 3, and so forth. So, what is the ordering relative to which a pictorial symbol system is supposed to provide for a dense set of pictures?

Goodman's answer is that "the ordering in question is . . . such that any element lying between two others is less discriminable from each of them than they are from each other."[32] But this proposal involves two questionable assumptions. The first is that for any three pictures one will be less discriminable from either of the other two than they are from each other. This seems to be false. For example, which *Entombment* does the proposed ordering place in the middle: Raphael's, Michelangelo's, or Pontormo's? Which of the three is hardest to distinguish from the other two? And if three two-color prints are printed from the same two blocks, which is between the other two, if the first has cyan and yellow where the second has yellow and magenta and the third has magenta and cyan? The answer, in both cases, is surely none.

The second assumption is that for any four pictures, *a, b, c,* and *d,* if *b* is less discriminable from *a* or *c* than they are from each other, and if *c* is less discriminable from *b* or *d* than they are from each other, then *b* and *c* will both be less discriminable from *a* or *d* than they are from each other. But there are many sequences of simple designs of which this is untrue. For example, consider the following four signs: **X O O X**. The second sign has color in common with the sign to its left, and shape in common with the sign to its right, whereas these two signs have neither shape nor color in common. Hence, the second sign is presumably less discriminable from the first or the third than they are from each other. Similarly, the third sign is presumably less discriminable from the second or the fourth than they are from each other. But by the same criteria neither the second sign nor the third is less discriminable from the first or from the fourth than they are from each other. Hence, no ordering of the kind proposed by Goodman is feasible in any symbol system in which these four signs are characters or parts of characters. But it is easy to imagine four pictures that differ only in that the first has the first sign where the second has the second, and so on.

For these reasons, the ordering Goodman proposes is unfeasible. And no set of pictures is dense relative to any of the orderings we know, such as the ones that are used in exhibitions or museums.

Do pictures function in somewhat the same way as descriptions, as Goodman claims? The phrase "in somewhat the same way" is of course too vague to allow a simple yes or no answer. But Goodman has often been accused of exaggerating the similarity between texts and pictures, and it is possible to decide whether this charge is just. I shall argue that it is.

The two commonest objections to Goodman's theory are concerned with the connection between vision and depiction. Roughly speaking, the first is that only what is visible can be depicted and the second is that if I can recognize the appearance of a certain sort of object—such as a tulip or a pair of boots—then I can recognize a picture of that sort of object. Goodman's theory, it is said, is inconsistent with these facts. I shall argue that each of these objections can be met but only by conceding that if pictures function in somewhat the same way as descriptions, these descriptions must be ones that are couched purely in terms of form and color. I shall then argue that the concession is a fatal one, which implies that Goodman's theory cannot be true.

Languages of Art is best known for the doctrine that the pictorial content of a design is no more constrained by the shapes and colors on its surface than the meaning of a written text and that both are equally the product of a system of conventions. If this were true, it would be possible to depict sounds, smells, or flavors, but this is not possible. For example, we could easily devise a system of conventions that used colors distributed on a plane to represent sounds or sequences of sounds and in which small differences affected what was represented in the same way as they do in pictures. The symbols would in effect be graphs in which, for example, the x-axis represented time; the y-axis, pitch, color represented timbre, and the thickness of the line, volume. But a picture cannot represent a sound, except by incorporating symbols of a different kind, such as words or musical notation (fig. 64). Hence, Goodman's doctrine must be false.

If the objection is stated in exactly these terms, it seems to be open to a decisive rejoinder, namely, that it is possible to depict sounds. For example, a drawing by Saul Steinberg represents the sounds of various musical instru-

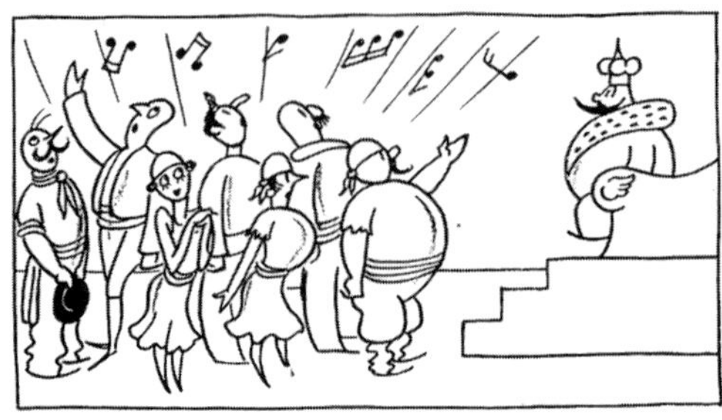

64. Otto Soglow, *"The gypsies have arrived, your majesty!"* 1930s. Detail.

ments using purely pictorial means (fig. 65). But perhaps there is a better way of stating the objection. For if we acquiesce in the conceit that pictures are analogous to descriptions, these drawings are obviously not literal representations of the sounds made by the instruments in the picture. For example, the sound made by a harp can be described as "filigree," but filigree is in fact made out of beads and threads of metal. So this description would be metaphorical. Steinberg's drawing of the sound made by a harp, whose delicate strokes and dots resemble threads and beads, is a pictorial version of the same metaphor. Now it is possible to describe a sound in literal terms, without employing a metaphor of any kind. But a picture of a sound will need to be metaphorical, and that is a fact that Goodman's theory is unable to accommodate. For if pictorial content were no more constrained by the form and color of the design than the meaning of a written text is, this limitation would not exist. Or so the modified objection runs.

There is only one way in which this objection can be met, and that is by conceding that the compliance classes of characters in a pictorial system of representation are defined by shape and color alone. This concession does not imply that tulip-shaped-and-colored and boot-shaped-and-colored things cannot be depicted. But it does imply that literal depiction is limited to things that have shapes and colors and that if pictures are analogous to descriptions, they are analogous to ones in which only shape or color predicates occur. If this concession is made, the fact that a picture of a sound cannot fail to be a metaphor will cease to be an embarrassment to the theory. For although color terms can be used to describe sounds—the composer Olivier Messiaen was notorious for describing chords in this way—these descriptions are bound to be metaphorical ones. Hence, the parity between pictorial art and language that Goodman defends can be maintained in the face of this objection if the concession is made.

The other common objection to Goodman's theory is that the ability to

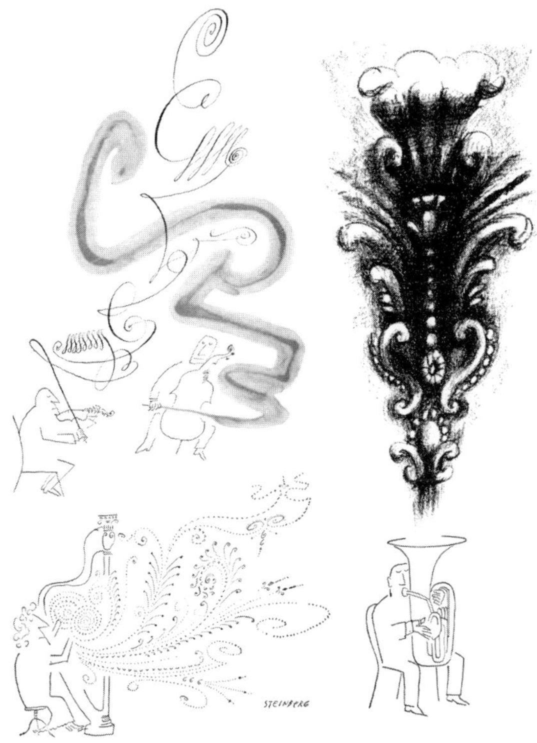

65. Saul Steinberg, *Musical Instruments*, 1955.

recognize an object by its appearance is more closely linked with the ability to recognize a picture of it than with the ability to recognize a description of it in words. Whereas Goodman's theory implies, on the contrary, that neither link is closer than the other.

This objection surely has some plausibility, but it is hard to transform it into a compelling argument. We cannot simply claim that if one can recognize an object of a certain kind by its appearance, then one can recognize a picture of an object of that kind by *its* appearance. For if I recognize, say, a pineapple by its appearance, then it looks to me like a pineapple, and I take it to be a pineapple for that reason. Similarly, if I recognize a picture of a pineapple by *its* appearance, then it looks to me like a picture of a pineapple, and I take it to be one for *that* reason. But it does not follow from the fact I can recognize a pineapple that I am capable of taking *anything* to be a picture. For I may have no notion of what a picture is. So the simple claim is not acceptable. But it is not obvious that we can qualify it in a way that makes it plausible, without weakening it to the point where it is consistent with Goodman's theory. Some critics have attempted to do this, and failed. For example, Richard Wollheim puts the objection in the following terms:

> It is a grave objection to [Goodman's theory] that it cannot account for the evident fact of transfer. By the term "transfer" I mean, for instance, that, if I can recognize a picture of a cat, and I know what a dog looks like, then I can be expected to recognize a picture of a dog. But on [Goodman's] view this ought to be baffling. It should be as baffling as if, knowing that the French word "*chat*" means a cat, and knowing what dogs look like, I should, on hearing it, be able to understand what the word "*chien*" means.[33]

Notice that Wollheim does not claim that if I know what a dog looks like, I can be expected to recognize a picture of a dog. He adds the condition that I can recognize a picture of a cat. This forestalls the objection to the simpler claim. But it also blunts the force of the objection since there are many symbolic systems in which transfer occurs. For example, there is a diagrammatic notation for guitarists that represents the fingering for each chord by marking a grid with dots. It seems obvious that if I can recognize the diagram of a G major chord, and I know the fingering for an E major chord, then I can be expected to recognize the diagram of an E major chord (fig. 66). Hence, Wollheim's argument is unconvincing. He appears to have mistaken a disanalogy between pictures and words for a disanalogy between pictures and conventional symbols generally.

But if transfer is an evident fact about pictures, as it seems to be, and if pictures function in somewhat the same way as descriptions, as Goodman says they do, these will have to be descriptions of a special kind, since transfer will have to be a fact about them, too. For example, it will have to be the case that if I can recognize this kind of description of a cat, and I know what a dog looks

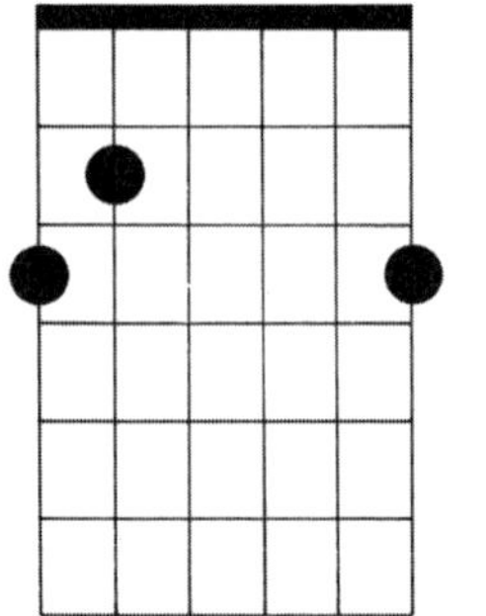
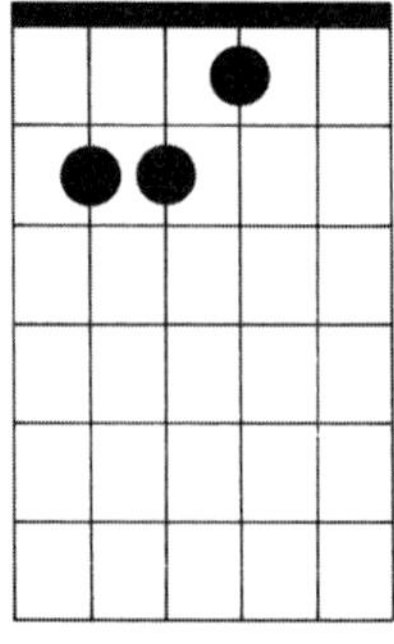

66. G major chord and E major chord in guitar tablature.

like, then I can be expected to recognize this kind of description of a dog. What constraints does this requirement place on the vocabulary in which this special kind of description will be couched?

First, the only kind of description I can be expected to recognize because I know what a dog looks like is a description of a dog's appearance. Second, the only kind of description of a dog's appearance I can be expected to recognize because I can recognize a certain kind of description of a cat is one that makes use of the same vocabulary as this kind of description of a cat. Hence, if pictures function in somewhat the same way as descriptions, these descriptions must be couched in a vocabulary that has a sufficiently broad competence in the description of appearances to handle cats and dogs and that is fully engaged in descriptions of both animals, so that if I understand one I can be expected to understand the other. When we consider how far transfer extends—not merely from cats to dogs but also from clouds to cuckoos—it is obvious that this could only be a vocabulary of color and shape predicates. Hence, if a picture is like a description, then once again it must be like one that consists of form and color predicates alone.

So the two commonest objections to Goodman's theory can be met but only by conceding that if pictures function in somewhat the same way as descriptions, these descriptions must be couched purely in terms of form and color predicates. But if this were true, any attempt to say what a picture represents that goes beyond a description of forms and colors would have to be the result of making an inference or interpretation. This implication of the theory, I suggest, is the rock on which it founders in the end.

Goodman explicitly denies that we need be "aware . . . of making any interpretations at all" when we perceive what a picture represents.[34] But in fact his theory implies that we *should* be aware of making an interpretation when we perceive that a picture represents the sun, as opposed to something round and yellow, or a cherub, as opposed to something pink and bulbous, just as we would be aware of making an interpretation if we realized that a verbal description consisting entirely of form and color predicates was in fact a description of one of these things. Once we know a language well, we come to hear or see words, phrases, and sentences as having the meaning they do. Goodman can therefore comfortably maintain that we need not be aware of interpreting pictures when we perceive what they represent, as long as we do not outstrip their manifest signification. But as soon as we perceive that a picture depicts something of such and such a kind, where "such and such" involves more than just forms and colors, he is bound to admit that we have left behind what visual experience can present us with by means of an inference or interpretation, however rapidly or automatically it is made.

As we saw in chapter 4, Goodman attacks the myth of the innocent eye, the myth that strictly speaking all we can ever see is a patchwork or mosaic of colors and that our perceptions of bodies disposed in space is the result of processing this raw material from the senses. But Goodman's theory, we have discovered, implicitly applies the same mythical picture of perception to the experience of seeing what a picture represents. For if the pictorial content of a design were no more constrained by the shapes and colors on its surface than the meaning of a written text is, any perception of the content of a picture that steps beyond the shapes and colors it depicts would have to be the result of inference or interpretation. This is no more plausible than the mythical idea about visual perception in general, which Goodman sensibly rejects.

There is one further point, which clinches the argument above. We have seen in previous chapters that the occlusion shape principle and the other basic principles of pictorial art reveal how exiguous the visible relationship between the marks on a picture's surface and the objects they depict can be. They relate the forms and colors of these marks to the forms and colors of the objects they depict, but they place no further limits on the kinds of objects that a picture represents. This defines the full extent of their jurisdiction. It therefore also marks the extent to which a system of rules or conventions can mimic depiction. Hence, if we attempt to explain the nature of pictorial art in terms of a system of conventions, the result we should expect is that the visible content of a picture will be confined to shapes and colors. This is precisely what we have found.

9

REALISM AND RELATIVISM

Pluralism—the incommensurability and, at times, incompatibility of objective ends—is *not* relativism, nor, *a fortiori*, subjectivism, nor the allegedly unbridgeable differences of emotional attitude on which some modern positivists, emotivists, existentialists, nationalists and, indeed, relativistic sociologists and anthropologists found their accounts.

Isaiah Berlin

THE USE OF THE TERM "REALISM" in art history is so messy and unclear that perhaps it should simply be abandoned. It was once associated with terms such as "verisimilitude" or "fidelity to nature," which now have a rather antiquated ring and which were in any case never satisfactorily defined. Realistic art is said to include Greek painting and sculpture in the fifth and fourth centuries B.C., late Medieval and early Renaissance art in Italy and in northern Europe, Dutch painting in the seventeenth century, French painting in the mid-nineteenth century, and disparate parts of twentieth-century art. So the term has an extraordinarily broad scope. And it is understood in substantially different ways. Sometimes it is assumed that a realistic work of art is truthful, sometimes that it resembles the kinds of objects that it represents, and sometimes—in the case of painting—that it produces the illusion of seeing these kinds of objects face to face. More than eighty years ago, Roman Jakobson accused historians of art of acting as if the idea of realism were "a bottomless sack into which everything and anything could be conveniently thrown."[1] In the same spirit, the glossary of a recent book about Renaissance art and literature describes the term "realism" as having so many applications as to be almost vacuous.[2]

However, one powerful and original idea about realism in the visual arts was disseminated for the first time in the twentieth century, by Jakobson himself. It is that the representational content of a painting or sculpture, like the meaning of a text, depends on a system of conventions and that the impression of reality some works of art convey more forcibly than others depends on the novelty or the familiarity of the system of conventions that the artist used to represent his subject. To progressive critics, an established system of conventions will seem tired and mechanical, and the impression of reality will be produced by novelty, whereas to conservative critics, an innovative system will seem artificial and meretricious, and the impression of reality will be produced by familiarity. For example: "A contemporary critic [i.e., a progressive] might detect realism in Delacroix, but not in Delaroche; in El Greco and Andrej Rublev, but not in Guido Reni; in a Scythian idol, but not in the Laocoön. A directly opposite judgment, however, would have been characteristic of a pupil of the Academy [i.e., a conservative] in the previous century."[3] Realism is therefore relative to the observer. Critics who describe a work of art as realistic may imagine that they are referring to an objective trait, which is independent of their outlook and their taste. If so, they are mistaken.

In the 1920s, Jakobson's idea about realistic art was liberating and ostensibly in tune with progressive art. As we have seen, Kahnweiler declared that Picasso and Braque had discovered that "the true character of painting and sculpture is that of a *script*" and had thereby freed the plastic arts from "the slavery inherent in illusionistic styles."[4] (He was their dealer at the time.) And in the decades that followed, several influential art historians and philosophers advanced similar views. For example, Leo Steinberg and Nelson Goodman each adopted one aspect of Jakobson's idea. On the one hand, Steinberg claimed that we naively imagine that new and refreshing styles are closer to nature, whereas in fact the impression of reality is caused by novel sets of conventions. And he drew the following conclusion, which I quoted in the last chapter but shall repeat here:

> The ineluctable modality of the visible—young Dedalus's hypnotic phrase—is a myth that evaporates between any two works of representation. The encroaching archaism of old photographs is only the latest instance of an endless succession in which every new mode of nature-representation eventually resigns its claim to co-identity with natural appearance. We can therefore assert with confidence that "technical capacity in the imitation of nature" simply does not exist. What does exist is the skill of reproducing handy graphic symbols for natural appearances, of rendering familiar facts by set professional conventions.[5]

On the other hand, Goodman claimed that the impression of reality is produced by the conventions we are accustomed to: "The literal or realistic or naturalistic system of representation is simply the customary one."[6]

I do not find either of these views convincing. On the one hand, it cannot be true that every new mode of nature representation eventually resigns its claim to co-identity with natural appearance because not every new mode of nature representation makes this claim in the first place. Cubism, for example, never did, and it would not have been plausible if it had. Besides, it does not follow from the fact that there cannot be a final, uniquely successful way of representing nature that what is naively described as a technical capacity in the imitation of nature is really explained by "set professional conventions." There may be as many different ways to skin a cat as there are taxidermists, but they are all constrained by the ineluctable modality of feline anatomy. On the other hand, the realistic system of representation cannot simply be the one to which spectators are accustomed because as an artistic style evolves, spectators are inevitably less accustomed to innovative subjects and techniques than they are to the ones these modify or replace. Hence, if Goodman's claim were true, an artistic style could never become more realistic in the eyes of spectators living at the time. But the historical record proves, on the contrary, that it can.

But if neither of these views is convincing, both are motivated by an interesting thought, which we should not simply brush aside, namely, that comparing artistic styles with conventional systems of representation can teach us to be pluralists about art. If we take the analogy between languages and period styles in the visual arts seriously, it is thought, we shall be forced to give up the idea that nineteenth-century academic painting, or any other favored local style, is the most universal and genuine, sanctioned by reason, and the destiny of all mankind. That is why the plastic arts can be freed from "the slavery inherent in illusionistic styles" by the discovery that "the true character of painting and sculpture is that of a *script*"; and it is why Roman Jakobson claimed that "it is necessary to learn the conventional language of painting in order to 'see' a picture, just as it is impossible to understand what is said without knowing the language."[7] The things we say are not inherently truer or more faithful to reality if we say them in French; and they are not inherently truer if we paint them in French either. As Meyer Schapiro put it, in his 1937 essay on the nature of abstract art: "All renderings of objects, no matter how exact they seem . . . proceed from values, methods and viewpoints that somehow shape the image and often determine its contents."[8]

For my own part, I agree that we should take the analogy between language and representation in the visual arts seriously, and I shall return to it later. But

I do not believe that paintings are handy graphic symbols or that painting and sculpture are like scripts. These ideas are as confused as the old-fashioned ones about verisimilitude and fidelity to nature, which they were intended to replace. I also agree with Schapiro's remark that representation invariably proceeds from values, methods, and viewpoints, but I shall argue that we can be pluralists about art without being relativists about realism.

Schapiro's point is the one that historians of art are—or at least should be—keen to defend. But it can be tempting to embrace more extravagant and less defensible ideas because they would support the principles we really care about, if they were true. For example, Linda Nochlin writes as follows:

> The commonplace notion that Realism is a "styleless" or transparent style, a mere simulacrum or mirror image of visual reality, is another barrier to its understanding as an historical and stylistic phenomenon. . . . The very aspirations of realism, in its old naive sense, are denied by the contemporary outlook that asserts and demands the absolute independence of world of art from the world of reality and, indeed, disputes the existence of any single, unequivocal reality at all. We no longer accept any fixed correspondence between the syntax of language, or the notational system of art, and an ideally structured universe.[9]

The sound point here is that the visible world does not prescribe or sanction any particular style of representation for the world of art. But, as I hope to show in this chapter, this point can be disentangled from the metaphysical ideas it is combined with here and from the claim that art is a system of notation. I shall begin by examining Goodman's views about realism in detail. His is easily the most incisive argument against the traditional idea that realism consists in fidelity to nature, and his positive doctrine proceeds logically from this attack. If the argument fails and the positive doctrine is untrue, it will be instructive to discover why.

~

As I have said, Goodman holds that "the literal or realistic or naturalistic system of representation is simply the customary one." Realism, he argues, is not a matter of fidelity to nature and cannot be measured by resemblance. For our judgments of resemblance are influenced by our visual habits, and our visual habits are influenced in turn by the kinds of pictures we are used to seeing. Hence, resemblance cannot be a "constant and independent" standard against which pictures can be measured because "the criteria of resemblance vary with changes in representational practice."[10] "Realism," Goodman concludes, "is relative, determined by the system of representation standard for a given culture or person at a given time."[11]

Whether or not this claim is true, however, it does not follow from the observation that the art we see modifies our visual habits and influences the resemblances we perceive because fidelity to nature may also be something that we must learn to see and judge correctly and because art may be a source from which we learn. In a similar way, progress in the physical sciences has enabled us to refine our observations of natural effects, and these observations have in turn enabled us to test scientific theories. There is nothing suspicious about this interaction between theory and observation, and nothing that should make us wonder whether we possess a "constant and independent" standard, with which scientific theories can be assessed. Science has sometimes progressed in this way, step by step, placing its weight on one foot while it moves the other one, and there is no reason why art should not sometimes do the same.

Besides, it is easy to exaggerate the extent to which our visual experience is modified by art. Oscar Wilde famously remarked that nobody had noticed the fog in London until it appeared in impressionist paintings. But in fact, writers have generally described optical effects long before painters learned to represent them. For example, the spinning highlights on a chariot wheel were described by the Latin poet Prudentius many centuries before Velazquez captured this effect in paint. The appearance of sunlight on a wall is mentioned by Saint Bernard of Clairvaux, but there is no record of it in twelfth-century painting. And a Babylonian poem describes the sight of the earth as it appears to a man flying up to the heavens on an eagle's back: first it is like an island in a river, then like a garden surrounded by a ditch, and so on, until it finally disappears. When the earliest surviving manuscript of this poem was written, in the seventh century B.C., no observation of this kind had ever been exploited by a painter—whether in Mesopotamia or the Nile valley, China or Greece.[12]

Goodman's claim that "the criteria of resemblance vary with changes in representational practice" must therefore amount to more than this if it is to bear the weight he places on it. And so it does. In fact, it is a sign of his allegiance to a form of nominalism that he summarizes in the claim that "predicates are labels."[13] This claim is not defended with argument in *Languages of Art*, but it is expounded in detail. It is, in effect, the book's seminal principle and éminence grise.

What is meant by the claim that predicates are labels, and what bearing does it have on the theory of realism in art? To begin with, the terms used to state the claim are to be understood as follows.

First, Goodman uses the term "predicate" in an unusually liberal way. For example, the sentence "Socrates is wise" would normally be said to consist of the name "Socrates" and the predicate "*x* is wise." The name is used to refer to the man whom the sentence is about, and the predicate is used to say something about him, to characterize him in some way. But Goodman does not distinguish between the two parts of the sentence in this way, and he calls proper names and other referring expressions predicates, as well as verb phrases. So the doctrine that predicates are labels applies to referring expressions too.[14] Second, Goodman explains his use of the term "label" as follows: "Objects are classified by means of, or under, various verbal labels," and the labels denote "the no or one or several members of that class."[15] Since we can combine things to form a class in any way we please, he points out that an object is "one of countless objects, and may be grouped with any selection of them," and he adds that "for every such grouping there is an attribute of the object."[16] In other words, we can, in principle, attach a label to the members of any group, however large or miscellaneous it may be.

Hence, the doctrine that predicates are labels provides a uniform explanation of the semantic function of referring expressions and predicates: the name "Zeus" denotes nothing because Zeus is a fiction; both the name "Xenophon" and the definite description "the author of the *Anabasis*" denote a single man—the same man in both cases, as it happens; the name "the Ten Thousand" denotes Xenophon's army; and the predicates "*x* is snub-nosed" and "*x* is wise" denote Socrates, plus unknown numbers of other men and women. The point of predication is simply to say that two labels apply to the same individual or group. For example, "Socrates is wise" says that the labels "Socrates" and "*x* is wise" apply to the same individual; "All of the Ten Thousand are courageous" says that the label "*x* is courageous" applies to every individual to whom the label "*x* is one of the Ten Thousand" applies; "only the Ten Thousand are courageous" says that the label "*x* is one of the Ten Thousand" applies to every individual to whom the label "*x* is courageous" applies; and so on.

If we examine judgments about resemblance in the light of this doctrine the results are striking. The significance of the judgment that A resembles B in being snub-nosed remains clear, for it is true if and only if A and B are both snub-nosed, that is, if the label "*x* is snub-nosed" applies to both A and B. But it becomes difficult to explain what the unqualified judgment that A resembles B means, for there is no particular label that applies to each of a pair of things if and only if they resemble one another. If we decide that A resembles B if and only if at least one label applies to both of them, then A and B resemble each other come what may, for if we want a label that applies to A and B, the label "A or B" will do nicely, whatever A and B may be. And we cannot narrow the field by denying that A resembles B unless many labels apply to both of them, since "A or B or C," "A or B or D," "A or B or E," and so forth are bound to apply to A and B. The only option that remains is to prefer some labels to others, and the only basis for preference Goodman is willing to acknowledge is that we are in the habit of using some labels more than others. Hence, he concludes, "the 'natural' kinds are simply those we are in the habit of picking out."[17]

Goodman's doctrine does not imply that we cannot make reliable judgments of resemblance in familiar respects—that we cannot reliably judge that A and B resemble each other in being round or red, for example. But it does imply that the unqualified judgment "A resembles B" is merely an expression of the various needs, customs, and prejudices that fashioned our habitual stock of predicates. And by the same token, it implies that the judgment "A resembles B in form and color" stands in just the same relation to our habitual stock of form and color predicates. "A resembles B in form and color" purports to identify an overall resemblance in appearance between A and B and seems on the face of it to be as objective and categorical as the judgments that A is round or red. But if we accept Goodman's doctrine, "A resembles B in form and color" merely says that the same form predicates and the same color predicates from our favored list or our habitual stock apply to both A and B. So, if this stock of predicates were to change, the judgment would change too.

Since our experience is colored by the predicates we use, we perceive the kinships we invent and tend to imagine that they are independent of us. As Montaigne says, "Whatever is off the hinges of custom, is believed to be also off the hinges of reason."[18] But if Goodman's argument is sound, the truth of the matter is that all affinities are elective; and if we claim to perceive an especially close resemblance between a painting by Giotto, Caravaggio, or Vermeer and the kinds of objects it depicts, we shall only succeed in expressing our allegiance to, and our familiarity with, the system of representation that these artists found congenial and persuaded spectators to accept. Hence, although the doctrine that predicates are labels does not by itself imply that realism is "a matter of habit" or that realism depends (as Goodman puts it) on "how stereotyped the mode of representation is, upon how commonplace the labels . . . have become," it makes these claims difficult to resist, if we start out with the thought that realism is a matter of resemblance.[19]

That is how the doctrine that predicates are labels challenges the traditional view of realism as an objective quality we can perceive in art, rather than a trait that habit encourages us to project. But the doctrine is demonstrably false. In fact, there are just two essential points. First, we can apply a predicate—such as "*x* is wise," "*x* is snub-nosed," "*x* is round", or "*x* is red"—to indefinitely many things. This means that understanding a predicate cannot merely involve knowing what objects it applies to: it must mean knowing why it applies to those objects and not others. If a predicate were simply a label attached to the several members of a class, it would be equivalent to an abbreviated list of names; and so, however many times we witnessed its use, there would be nothing we knew that would entitle us to apply it, or to refuse to apply it, to a fresh case.

Second, if referring expressions and predicates were both labels, as Goodman claims they are, predication would be impossible. For either "A is F" would simply juxtapose two labels—like "Zeus, Socrates," for example—and therefore fail to say anything; or it would be equivalent to a statement of identity, that is, it would purport to tell us that an object denoted by the label A is identical with one denoted by the label F. But in that case, "A is F" would in effect be an abbreviation of the disjunction, "A is identical with one of the following things: . . . or . . . or . . . ," and hence, if it were true, it would be unmasked by analysis as the tautology: "A = A or A = B or A = C or. . . ." "Socrates is wise" may be a truism, but it is not a tautology.

It follows that Goodman's doctrine is not an austere and faithful explanation of what predication involves. It does not explain predication, it abolishes it—by exaggerating the kinship between class membership and predication and by conflating predicates and names.[20] In fact, the predicate "*x* is round" is not a name attached to the several members of the class of round things—any more than it is a name attached to the class of round things or to the property of being round—because it is not a name at all, and it cannot be used grammatically as if it were one. The term we use to refer to the class of round things is "the class of round things," and the term we use to refer to the several members of the class of round things is "the several members of the class of round things." The predicate "*x* is round" is not equivalent to either of these noun phrases. We use it to describe something as round, not to refer.

Since predicates are not labels, the use of resemblance to explain realism cannot be impugned on the grounds that criteria of resemblance are dictated by habits of classification. For there is no reason to demand that the judgment that A resembles B be supplemented by a list of the classes of which A and B are supposed to be joint members. It is true that the judgment will seem equivocal unless it is clear what sort of comparison is intended. But this does not imply that there is nothing more to one thing's resembling another than our choosing to apply the same labels to them, since there is no need for us to indicate the sort of comparison we have in mind with a string of labels: "A resembles B in color" and "A resembles B in shape" are unambiguous as they stand. Resemblance cannot be reduced to comembership of a class, but the concept of resemblance is not discredited by this fact, any more than the theory of classes is.

I have argued that we cannot make predications unless we can both use words to refer to particular things, as, for example, we standardly use proper names, and use words to ascribe properties to these things. For example, the sentence "Socrates is wise" could not be used to say that Socrates is wise if there were not linguistic conventions both for referring to a person (by the use of a personal name) and for attributing a property to the person referred to by attaching a predicate to the name. Conventions of both kinds are needed, and neither kind can be assimilated to the other. Now pictures are not names or predicates. Nor are they combinations of the two. But this basic difference between pictures and predications reflects another that is equally basic, and that deserves more attention than it has received.

A sentence that is capable of being used to say something true or false—for example, one that combines a name with a predicate—can be used to state (or to purport to state) a fact or to tell part of a fictional story. But there is a sense in which the first way of using a sentence of this kind must precede the second. By this, I do not mean that a sentence that is used in a fictional story must first have been used to state, or to purport to state, a fact. What I mean is this: telling fictional stories involves an implicit agreement, or understanding, between the speaker and her audience. Speaker and audience implicitly agree to suspend a pragmatic convention, namely, the convention that a sentence that can be used to state, or to purport to state, a fact is—inter alia—being used to do so. But a convention cannot be suspended unless it first exists. Hence, the use of language that embodies this convention—the fact-stating use of language—must already exist for the custom of telling fictional stories to begin.

In the case of pictures, there is no analogue of the pragmatic convention to which I have referred. For example, there is no convention to the effect that an engraving of a battle represents a battle that was once actually fought or that a painting that depicts a man with a distinctive physiognomy is a portrait. And if a convention of this sort were introduced, for whatever reason, it could subsequently be dropped. Whereas the linguistic convention could not be dropped, except perhaps in a community in which there was no intention to pass on the use of language from one generation to the next. So, what is said is, by default, said to be so; but no similar assumption operates in the field of pictorial art. If it did, the poignant captions to Goya's series of prints *The Disasters of War,* which I mentioned in the last chapter, would be superfluous: "Yo lo vi." "Y esto tambien." "Esto es mal." "Asi sucedió." (I saw it. And this too. It happened thus.)

So we have, on the one hand, the absence of rules or conventions in the field of pictorial art that are analogous to those involved in making predications, and, on the other hand, the absence of a pragmatic convention analogous to the one that accords priority to the fact-stating use of language over its use in fiction. But now it should be obvious that these two absences are not coincidental, because it is first and foremost—and more pertinently, first—in the fact-stating use of language that we are taught rules or conventions for referring to things and for ascribing properties to things that are referred to. That is why I said that the pragmatic convention could only be dropped, if it could be dropped at all, in a community that did not intend to pass on the use of language from one generation to the next. So, the absence of an analogue of the pragmatic convention and the absence of rules analogous to those involved in making predications is not a coincidence, because the second absence follows from the first.

In short, one use of pictures is analogous to the use of words to describe particular historical events or situations and particular persons, but this is not the essence of depiction. Reference and predication are rooted in reportage, and the purely imaginative use of words is secondary or dependent, but this is not true of depiction, which is at root an imaginative act. No theory of art that disregards this fundamental difference can be right. Jakobson and his followers did disregard it, because they exaggerated the affinity between language and pictorial art. By and large, they did so in a rather sketchy way, as when Jakobson made the assertion I quoted earlier, that "it is necessary to learn the conventional language of painting in order to 'see' a picture, just as it is impossible to understand what is spoken without knowing the language." The great merit of *Languages of Art* is that Goodman formulated this assertion in a precise and testable way for the first time. As a result, however, we can see exactly why the idea of a "conventional language of painting" cannot play the role in art history traditionally assigned to "verisimilitude" or "fidelity to nature."

~

Let us return now to the general question of how the concept of realism is to be understood. As we have seen, Goodman argues that realism is relative—determined by the system of representation standard for a given culture or person at a given time. Goodman's nominalism makes this idea difficult to resist, if we start out by assuming that a realistic picture is one that resembles what it represents especially closely. Like many philosophical ideas, it gets a leg up from the doctrine that it clamorously rejects. But although I have argued that Goodman's theory of realism is false, I do not want to support the view that he opposes. The truth, I believe, is less simple and more interesting than that.

If the term "realism" does not merely record how stereotyped or novel the mode of representation is, or how commonplace the labels have become, we can begin to map the ground it covers by drawing a rough distinction between subject matter and technique. Consider subject matter first. In their book *Romanticism and Realism,* Charles Rosen and Henri Zerner argue that the great achievement of nineteenth-century realist painters was to make art out of trivial or banal material, without ennobling or idealizing it, or making it picturesque.[21] And they point out that this is something novelists attempted, too. Flaubert comments on this in a letter to Louise Colet: "To write the *mediocre* beautifully, and at the same time to have it retain its aspect, its shape, its very words, this is truly diabolical."[22]

Realism, in this sense, is about the choice of subject matter and the manner in which it is treated. For example, compare Ingres's painting of 1808, *The Valpincon Bather* and Degas's inaccurately titled pastel of 1885, *Woman Drying Herself* (plates 6, 7). One salient difference between them is that the surface of Ingres's painting is almost transparent—the brushstrokes are barely visible at all—whereas Degas compels the spectator to attend to the individual strokes that were deposited on the surface of the paper as the pastel crayon was rubbed back and forth. But if we set this difference in the use of materials to one side and focus on the way in which the theme of the nude was treated by the two artists—if, in particular, we consider the ungainly pose of the woman in Degas's drawing, her feet planted steadily on the ground, her bottom sticking out just enough to balance the weight of her head, and the rapid gesture with which she pulls her shift over her head—there is a sense, although it is not the only available sense, in which this is the more realistic treatment of the theme.

I do not mean to imply that realism in subject matter is confined to nineteenth-century European art. On the contrary, it is ubiquitous. To take two examples more or less at random, J. D. Beazley describes the Foundry Painter, who decorated red-figure cups in the first quarter of the fifth century B.C., as a Greek realist; and although he apologizes for not wanting to discuss or define realism as such, this is evidently what he has in mind.[23] One of Beazley's examples is a small skyphos decorated with a boy running off with a plate of cakes or fruits, carrying his hoop so that he can run faster. We can contrast this boy with the golden-haired Ganymede on a Bell krater by the Berlin Painter (to whom I shall return shortly) gracefully trundling his hoop and carrying a rooster, a love gift, in his outstretched hand (figs. 67, 68). Again, Murillo's *Four Figures on a Step* is a realistic painting in this sense, whereas Poussin's *The Holy Family on the Steps* is not (figs. 69, 70). As it happens, when Murillo's painting

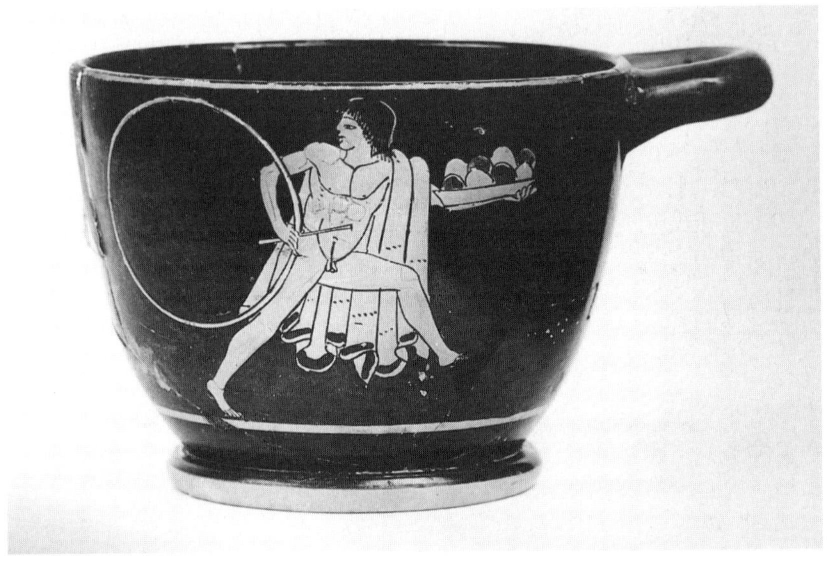

67. Skyphos, ca. 490 B.C. Attributed to the Foundry Painter. Athens, National Archaeological Museum.

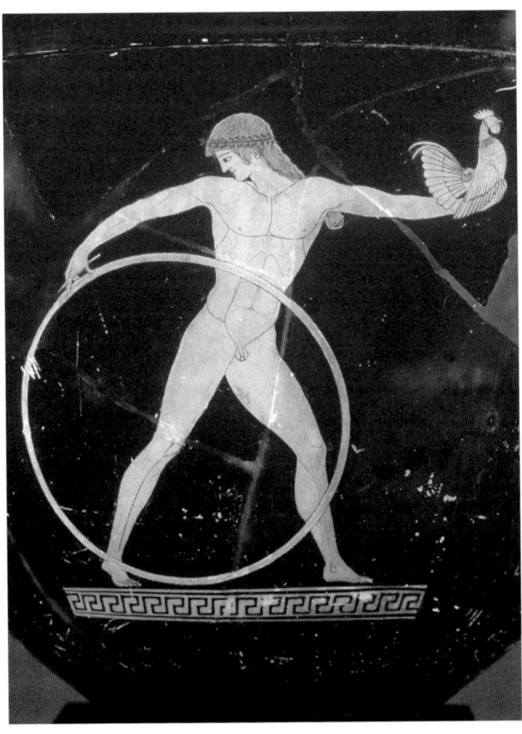

68. Bell-krater, ca. 490 B.C. Attributed to the Berlin Painter. Musée du Louvre, Paris.

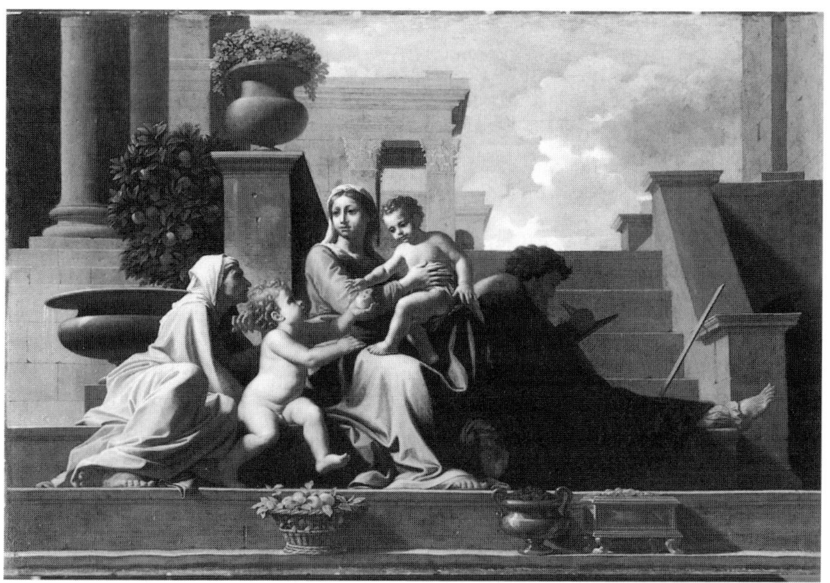

69. Nicolas Poussin, *The Holy Family on the Steps*, 1648. Oil on canvas. Cleveland Museum of Art.

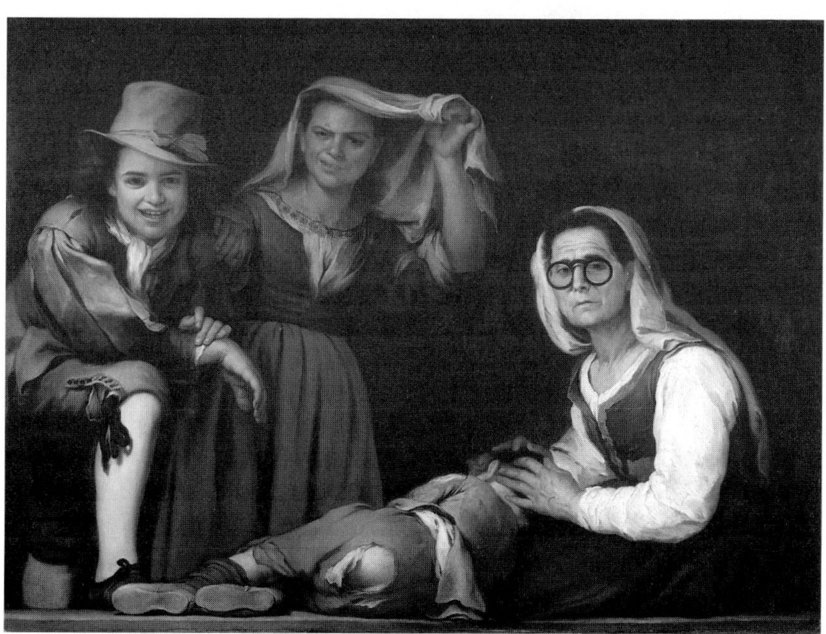

70. Bartolomé Esteban Murillo, *Four Figures on a Step*, ca. 1655–70. Oil on canvas. Kimbell Art Museum, Fort Worth, Texas.

was exhibited in New York in 1925, it was described as "A Family Group [Presumed to be Doña Beatriz, wife of Murillo, and their three children.]" (The tear in the boy's trousers had been overpainted.) There was not a shred of evidence for this identification of the group. Perhaps it seemed the only way of doing justice to the impression of reality the scene conveyed.

Turning now to realism in technique, let us compare the paintings on two Panathenaic vases, which were made about fifty years apart (figs. 71, 72). On the earlier vase, which was decorated by the Euphiletos Painter in about 530 B.C., the artist conveys the exertion of the burly runners in a marvelously vivid way and (as Michael Podro pointed out to me) conveys an impression of rapid motion with their flickering limbs. But their anatomy is sketchy and their posture is wrong. The second vase is very different. The Berlin Painter prefers grace to exertion, and these men look as if they are setting out for a gentle jog. But their anatomy is depicted with a plausible economy of means and the forward arm is placed, as it is in nature, opposite the forward leg. So the differences we would have in mind if we described the Berlin Painter as a more realistic artist than the Euphiletos Painter are not differences in subject matter. They are differences in the technical resources he was able to control. The same would be true if we described Masaccio's *Maestà* as more realistic than Duccio's. The differences that would encourage us to describe the later artist's work as more realistic are a more precise control of anatomy and a more accurate depiction of posture in the case of the vase paintings and more successful modeling and perspective in the case of altarpieces.

The distinction between subject matter and technique is rough, and paintings that are realistic by these two criteria have traits in common. For example, rather as the Berlin painter rejected the archaic formula for the running man, French realist painters rejected the academic repertoire of idealizing poses and gestures—which, ironically, were ultimately derived from classical Greek art. But the distinction is useful because it is mainly in the study of realism in technique that nominalism has sown confusion. In the remainder of this chapter, I shall describe the main elements of realism in Greek painting and the general terms in which the evolution of realistic techniques in pictorial art should be understood. From now on, "realism" means realism in technique.

The first main element of realism is accuracy, but accuracy in a specific form. Accuracy in general takes three forms: narrative accuracy, which is the accurate representation of a story or an episode within a story; iconic accuracy, which is the accurate representation of a particular individual or place; and pictorial accuracy, which is the accurate depiction of a kind of material or object or activity—such as water or satin, a palm tree or a dove, sleeping, galloping, or making love.

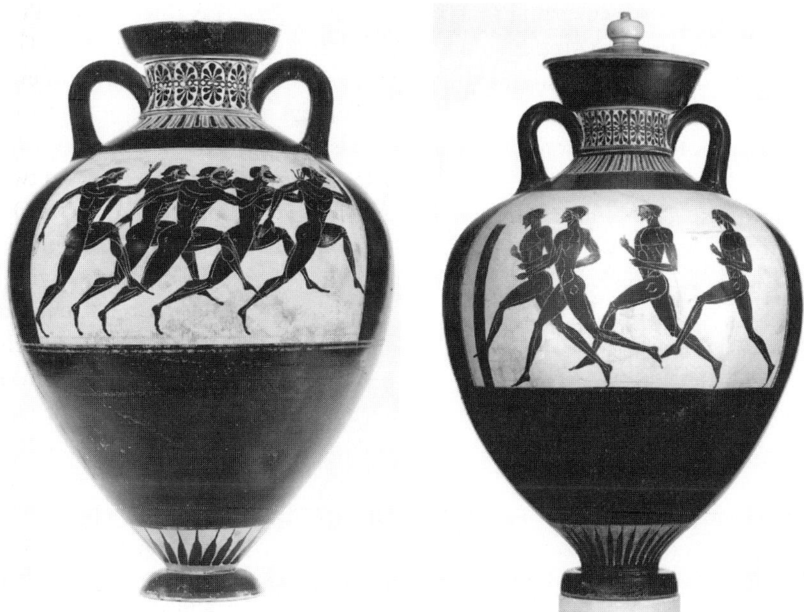

71. (left) Panathenaic amphora, ca. 530 B.C. Attributed to the Euphiletos Painter. Metropolitan Museum of Art, New York.
72. (right) Panathenaic amphora, ca. 480 B.C. Attributed to the Berlin Painter. Metropolitan Museum of Art, New York.

In each of these three forms, accuracy combines a degree of individuation or precision with the avoidance of idealization, fantasy, error, and deceit. The history of these forms of accuracy is of course entwined. But neither narrative accuracy nor iconic accuracy alone is a reliable measure of realistic art. For example, the scene of the Last Supper in Monreale Cathedral is as accurate a representation of the gospel story as Leonardo's painting in Milan, but the second work is more realistic than the first; and Giotto's *Expulsion of the Money-Lenders* is a realistic painting, but it is not an accurate representation of Herod's temple.

However, pictorial accuracy is a salient characteristic of realistic art. For example, the subject of each of the vase paintings I mentioned earlier can be recognized with equal facility or speed and neither of these paintings is artificial or unskilled. But the depiction of anatomy and posture on the later vase is more accurate. By this I do not mean that it is more accurate by fifth-century standards. For when a man runs, his forward arm is in fact opposite his forward leg. This was just as true in 530 B.C. as it was in 480 B.C. and as it is today.

It was not necessary to use a camera with a rapid shutter speed in order to discover this, as it was necessary in order to discover how a horse gallops. But both of these discoveries made it possible for artists to represent particular kinds of motion with greater accuracy than before.

If I seem to be laboring an obvious point, I hope the reader will accept that what is obvious to some people needs to be proved to others. In fact, "accuracy" has become a suspect term in the eyes of many historians of art. The following passage from a recent study of Greek vase painting is a representative example of a way of thinking that is now widespread:

> Most stylistic histories treat Attic vase-painting as a quasi-scientific adventure in accurate description. It is commonplace to celebrate the objectivity of the artists, their powers of observation, and their tireless curiosity. In this way, representational systems take on all the authority of science: dispassionate observation, not historical milieu, determines stylistic development. The key maneuver here is not so much the equation of accuracy with quality, but the establishment of accuracy as a supposedly objective criterion in the first place. For obviously there are many ways of making an "accurate" picture.[24]

It is debatable whether it is more common today to celebrate the objectivity of artists or to deny it. But in any case, this passage is unconvincing for two reasons: first, if there are many ways of making an accurate picture, it does not follow that a judgment about the accuracy of a picture cannot be objective. The plurality of ways does not imply the subjectivity of judgments or results. Second, if observation plays an important role in art, it does not follow that stylistic development is unaffected by historical milieu. We are not forced to choose between these explanations of stylistic change.

In fact, observation is at the heart of painting and sculpture at all times and in every culture, even if it is mainly the observation of other works of art. But the particular objects, qualities, and structures that are observed, and the techniques that are used to observe them, are influenced both by forces within the artistic tradition itself and by forces beyond it. This is true of painting and sculpture, and it is true of other human pursuits as well: farming, warfare, and navigation, for example. In particular, it is surely a truism that while science depends on observation, it does not depend on observation alone, and observation alone does not determine how science evolves, any more than it determines the development of art. Hence, the sharp distinction this author proposes, between the motor of development in science and the motor of development in art, misrepresents the history of both. The opposition between "dispassionate observation" and "historical milieu" is false.

In short, accurate observation is not a solitary or sovereign principle in art any more than it is in science. For example, six-pack abdomens and superficial veins did not appear on male figures because a sculptor noticed for the first time that they exist (figs. 73, 74). Furthermore, Greek art was not a department of Greek science. The elaborate musculature of the figure of Sarpedon on Euphronios's Calyx krater has much more to do with the aesthetics of the gymnasium than with anatomy in sixth-century Greece. Nevertheless, the clarity, consistency, and precision with which Sarpedon's muscles and the veins of the Riace warriors are represented are unprecedented; and their accuracy can be objectively assessed with an anatomy textbook or with a photograph of Mr. Universe (fig. 75).[25]

The second main element of realistic art is animation, which combines mobility with the expression of emotion, character, or thought. For example, the first painful grimace on a surviving vase appears in the tondo of a cup from about 500 B.C., which represents Achilles binding the wound on Patroclus's arm (figs. 76, 77). The tense expression on Patroclus's face is delicately marked by three curved lines between his mouth and cheek. The vase painter has added a little white pigment to show him bearing his teeth with pain. And he has also depicted him turning away from Achilles, and bracing his foot against the tondo's frame. (It looks as if Patroclus's mouth is turning down, but this is the effect of the moustache. It works in same way as the moustache in Frans Hals's mistitled *Laughing Cavalier*, but in the opposite direction [fig. 78].)

Xenophon records a conversation on this topic between Socrates and the painter Parrhasios, whom Pliny describes as "the first to give liveliness to the face."[26] Parrhasios is at first doubtful whether "the character of the soul" can be represented in a painting: "How could that be imitated, O Socrates, which has neither proportions, nor colour . . . and is, in fact, not even visible?" But he is rapidly persuaded that it is possible to represent both *ethos* and *pathos*—both character and emotion—by showing their physical expression in the gaze, the face, and the posture of the body, "both stationary and in movement." We do not have to believe that this conversation actually took place. But the story reflects a lively interest among both artists and philosophers in the expression of character and emotion, which painting and sculpture amply document.

Animation deserves to be mentioned separately because paintings that are more realistic by other criteria, such as the accurate depiction of anatomy or the control of modeling and perspective, are commonly less realistic by this one. For example, compare Cimabue's *Crucifixion* with Simon Vouet's *Christ on the Cross*—bravely maintaining his *contrapposto* to the bitter end; or compare the fresco of the *Lamentation* in Saint Panteleimon, Nerezi with William-

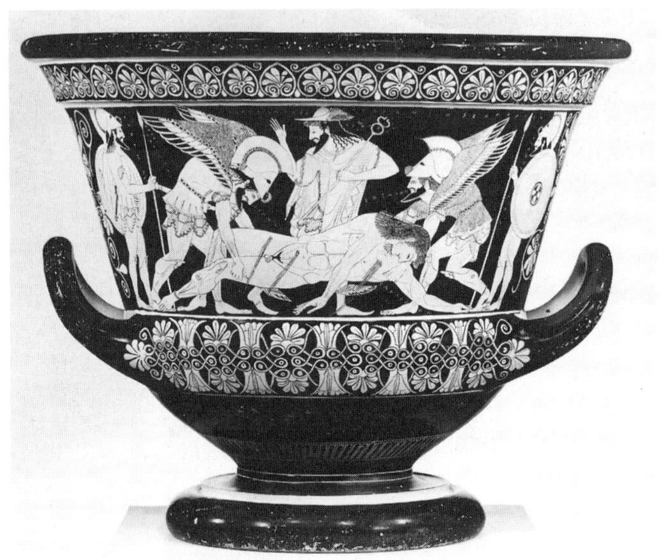

73. (left) Calyx crater, ca. 515 B.C. Attributed to Euphronios. Metropolitan Museum of Art, New York.
74. (below left) Riace Warrior A, ca. 460–450 B.C. Bronze. Detail of hand. Museo Nazionale di Reggio Calabria.
75. (below right) Tony Lanza, *Leo Robert, Mr Universe 1955*. Photograph.

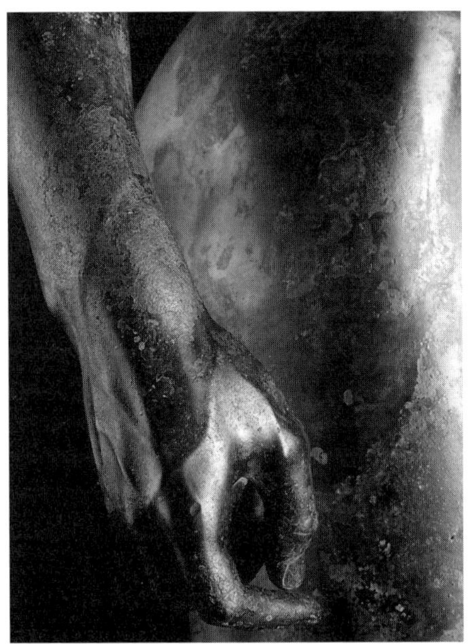

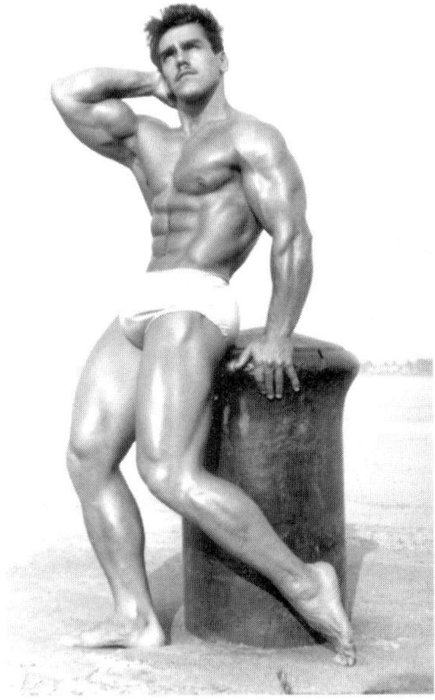

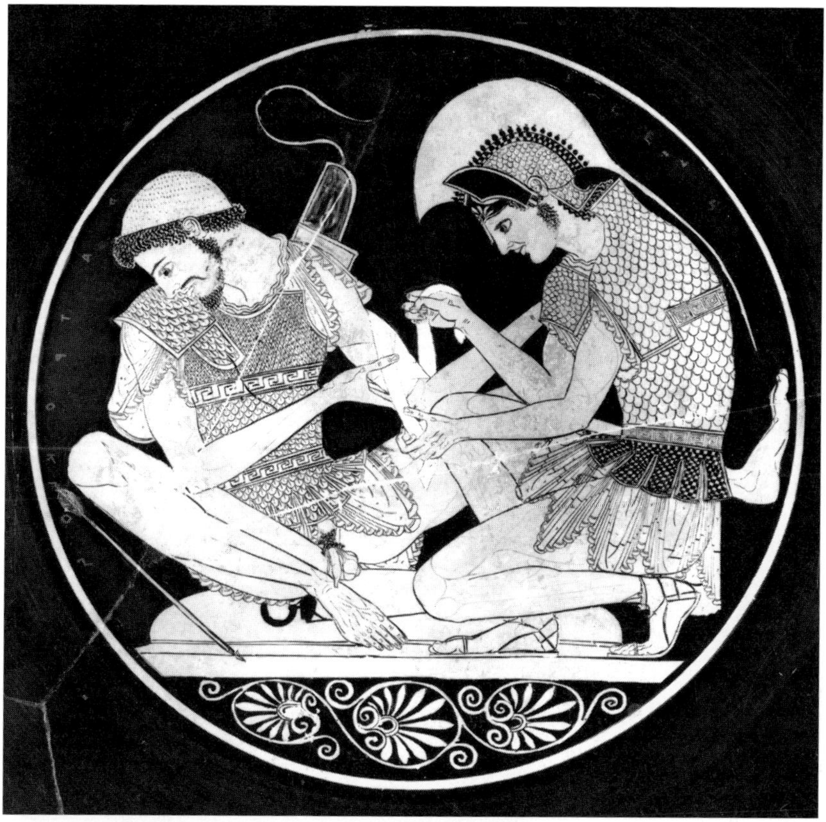

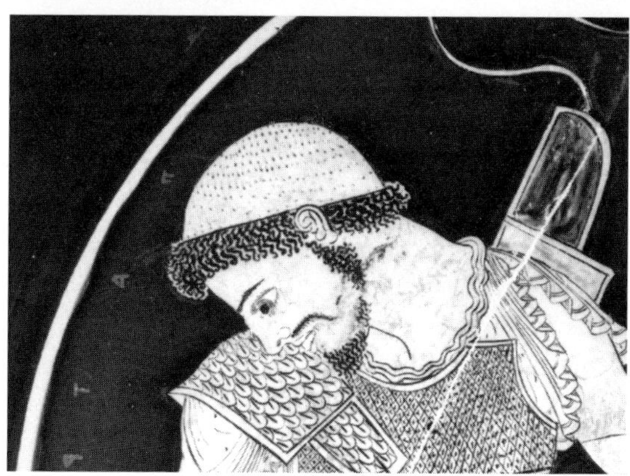

76. (above) Kylix, ca. 500 B.C. Name vase of the Sosias Painter. Staatliche Museen zu Berlin, Antikensammlung.
77. (left) Detail of figure 76.

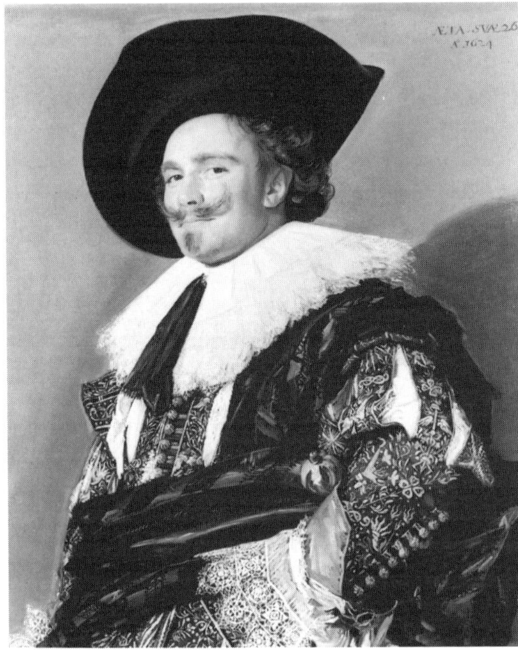

78. Frans Hals, *The Laughing Cavalier,* 1624. Oil on canvas. The Wallace Collection, London.

Adolphe Bouguereau's *Pietà* (figs. 79–82). However, animation also points toward a much more general measure of realism, namely, the extent of the range of questions it is possible to ask about a depicted scene: modality, as I shall call it.

The overarching idea of modality is the key to understanding the evolution of realism in pictorial art. For the principal measure of realism—that is, realism in technique—is the range of questions we can ask about a picture's content: Is this man angry or impassive? Is he despondent or alert? Is he Semitic or Egyptian? Is he young or old? Is he fat or thin? Is his cloak made of linen or of wool? Is he standing in the shade or in the sun? Is he running, walking, jumping, or standing still?

Consider the problem of depicting motion. As I have said, Socrates persuades Parhassios that character and emotion can be represented by showing their physical expression in the posture of the body "both stationary and in movement." But if Xenophon had made Socrates ask Parrhasios whether motion can be represented in a painting, it is not difficult to imagine the artist's reply: "How could that be imitated, O Socrates, which has neither proportions, nor colour . . . and is, in fact, not even visible without change?" In fact, however, four solutions to this problem are particularly well known, and

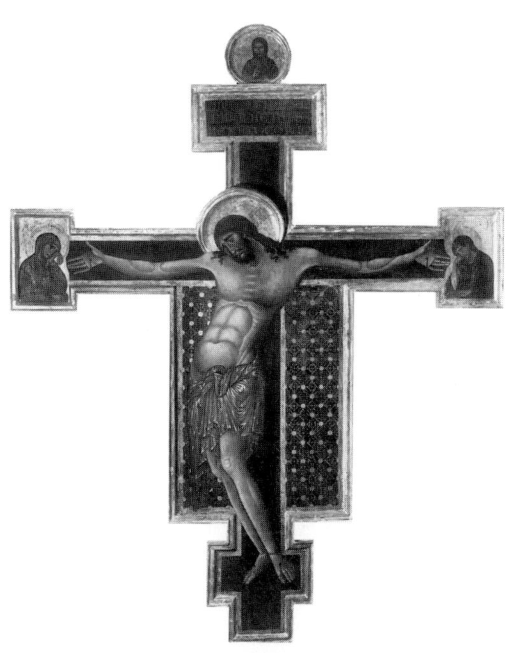

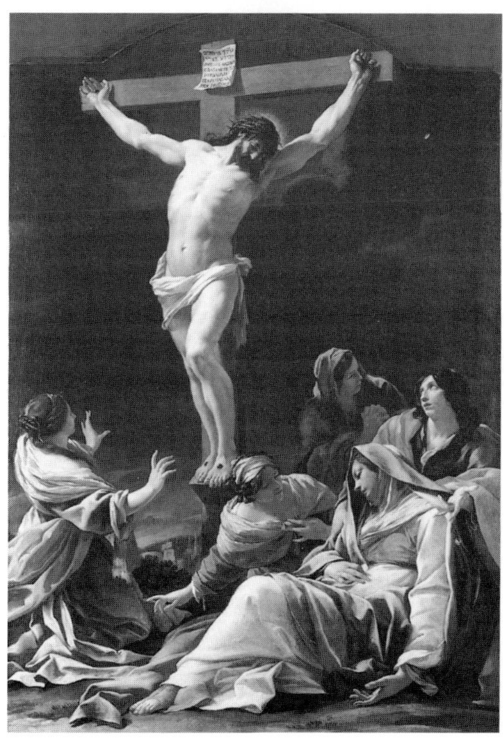

79. (above) Cimabue, *Crucifixion*, ca. 1268–71. Tempera on wood. Church of San Domenico, Arezzo.
80. (left) Simon Vouet, *Crucifixion*, 1620s. Oil on canvas. Musée des Beaux Arts, Lyon.

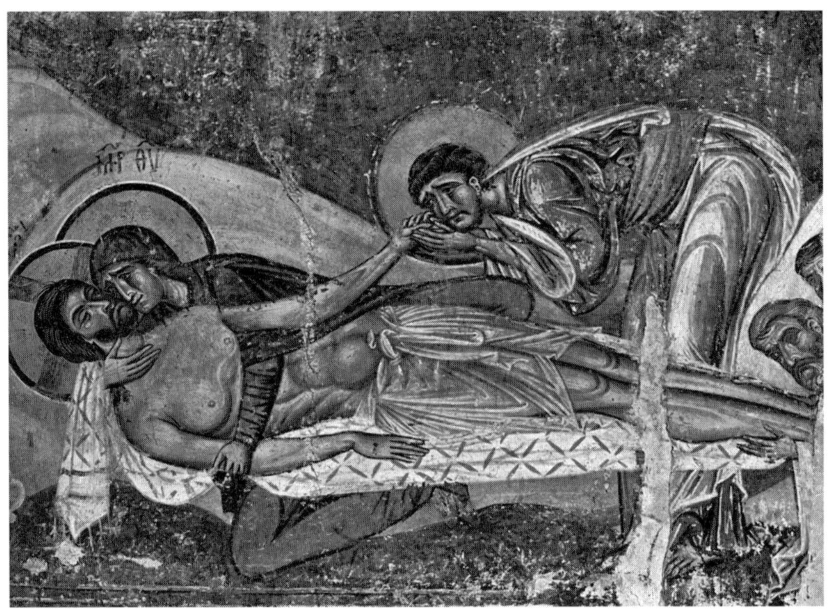

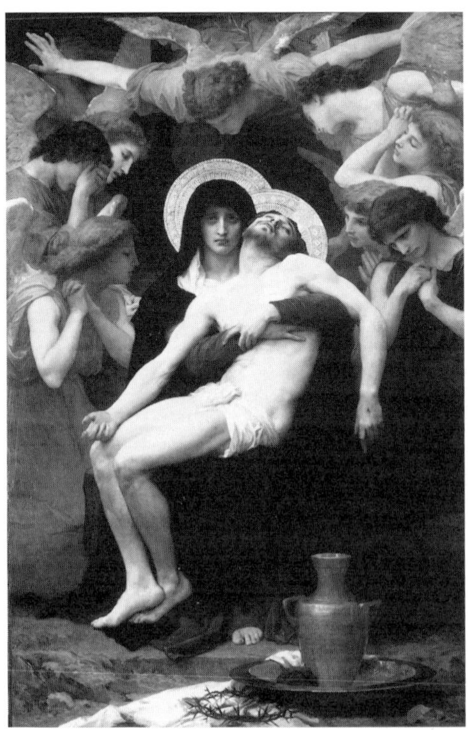

81. (above) *Lamentation,* 1164. Fresco. Church of St. Panteleimon, Nerezi. Detail.
82. (left) William-Adolphe Bouguereau, *Pietà,* 1876. Oil on canvas. Private Collection, United States. On loan to the Legion of Honor, San Francisco.

Parrhasios himself certainly knew three of them. First, motion is generally not depicted as such but merely implied by a familiar pose, as it is on the Panathenaic vases mentioned above. Second, a painter can also depict the physical effects of motion, as the painter of a fifth-century skyphos did when he showed a girl's hair and the fabric of her dress pulled back by her motion on a swing (fig. 83). Third, a painter can depict the side effects of producing motion, as opposed to the effects of motion itself. For example, Parrhasios himself is said to have painted a man in a race in soldier's armor dripping with sweat.[27] Finally, an artist can depict the appearance of motion, as Leonardo did in a beautiful red chalk drawing of a copse of trees (plate 8). Blur and shimmer are of course also effects of motion, but they are optical effects and not mechanical ones.[28]

The last technique is worth dwelling on for a moment because only in this case is motion shown and not merely implied. One famous example is Velazquez's *Fable of Arachne,* in which the shimmering highlights on the spokes of a spinning wheel float in the space within its rim (fig. 84). This remarkable painting is commonly described as producing the illusion of movement. For

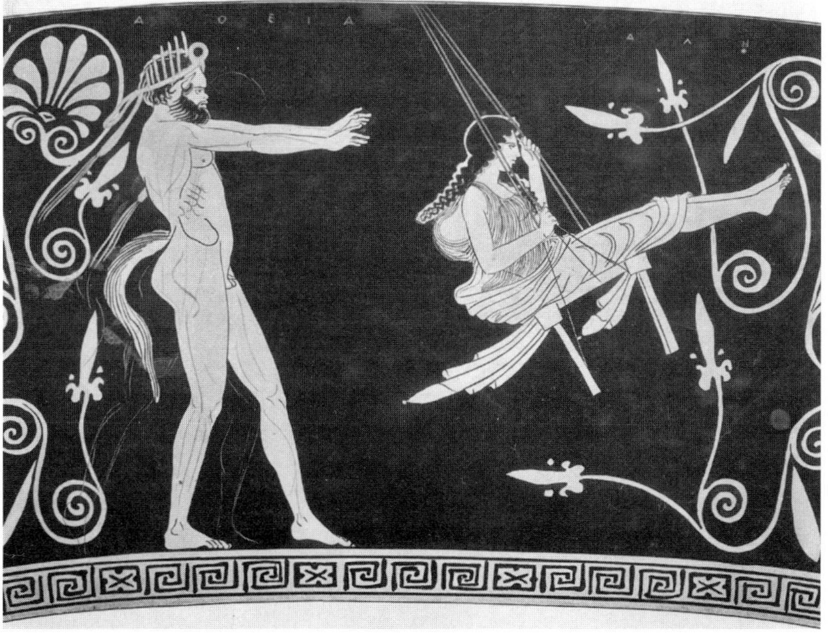

83. Skyphos, ca. 440 B.C. Attributed to the Penelope Painter. Staatliche Museen zu Berlin, Antikensammlung.

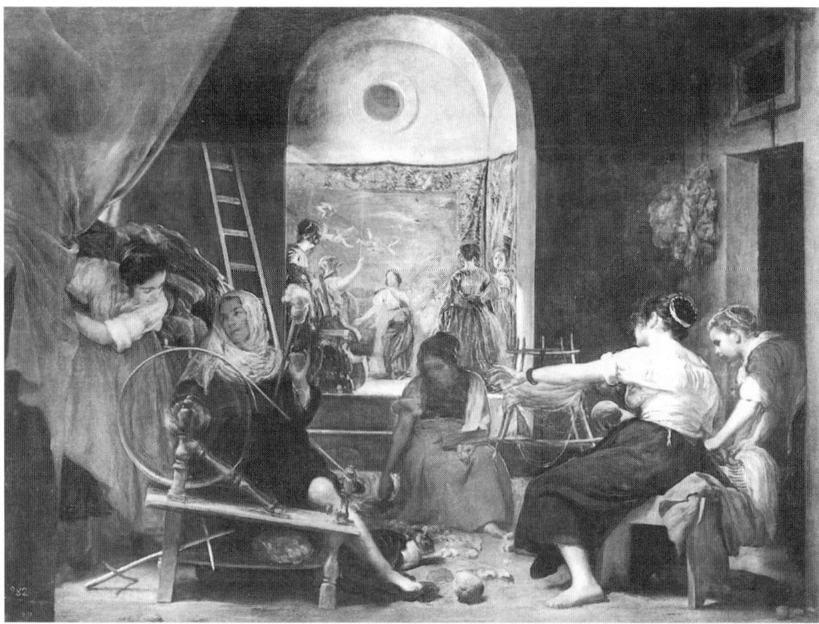

84. Velazquez, *The Fable of Arachne (The Spinners)*, ca. 1657. Oil on canvas. Museo del Prado, Madrid.

example, Gombrich describes it that way.[29] But the word "illusion" is being used carelessly here. For there is no illusion: nothing appears to be other than it is. On the one hand, the wheel appears to be spinning, and it is spinning—just as the woman behind the wheel appears to be teasing wool from the ball on her distaff and is. On the other hand, the surface of the painting does not appear to shimmer or move. If the word "illusion" is used to describe this painting, this is really a kind of hyperbole, which is quite misleading. What is remarkable about the painting is that the motion of the wheel can actually be seen and need not be inferred from any other cues.

Gombrich's description of Velazquez's painting as producing "the illusion of movement" is not a slip. In *Art and Illusion,* he defines realism in terms of a picture's psychological effect, and he thinks of this effect as an illusion. "The history of art . . . ," he writes, "may be described as the forging of master keys for opening the mysterious locks of our senses to which only nature herself originally held the key."[30] I shall comment on this view in more general terms shortly. But Gombrich is also aware of the idea of modality, and he illustrates it with characteristic simplicity and flair:

> As soon as the Greeks looked at the Egyptian figure type from the aspect of an art that wants to "convince," it undoubtedly looks unconvincing. It is the reaction we express when we speak of its "rigid posture." It might be argued that this reaction itself is due to our Greek education; it was the Greeks who taught us to ask "*How* does he stand?" or even "Why does he stand like that?" Applied to a pre-Greek work of art, it may be senseless to ask this question. The Egyptian statue does not represent a man standing rigidly or a man standing at ease—it is concerned with the what, not the how. To ask for more might have struck an Egyptian artist as it would strike us if someone inquired the age or mood of the king on the chessboard.[31]

I do not want to endorse the idea that Egyptian art was not intended to convince. Indeed, I am not sure what the word "convince" here is supposed to mean. But the principal idea in this passage—that there are questions we can address to some works of art that it would be senseless to address to others—is clear and, I believe, correct. The key word here is "senseless." Animation combines mobility with expression, but once these qualities can be depicted, immobility and absence of expression can count as much as their opposites, as, for example, the slack body and mute face of the dead Christ in the *Lamentation* in Nerezi confirm. The fundamental division, where the depiction of the passions is concerned, is between cases in which the question "What is this person feeling?" makes sense and cases in which it cannot properly be raised at all.

~

If modality is the key to understanding the development of realistic art, two important results follow. First, we can turn the analogy between language and representation in the visual arts against Goodman's claim that "the literal or realistic or naturalistic system of representation is simply the customary one" and Steinberg's view that a realistic style is merely a novel set of conventions for making graphic signs. Second, we can show that realism and illusionism are fundamentally different concepts. I shall enlarge on these two points in turn.

First, if artistic styles are compared to languages, it is possible to assume that they differ in the way that different systems of rules do, when they provide different ways of recording information, without differing in the information they can be used to record. This mistake can result from confusing a comparison between two languages with a comparison between two scripts or codes. For example, the hieroglyphic and hieratic Egyptian scripts do not differ in the information they can be used to record and neither do Morse code and semaphore. When Kahnweiler says that "the true character of painting and sculpture is that of a script" and when Gombrich describes "the tricks of how to draw this or that—a cat for instance" as "simple methods of coding," their remarks can therefore dispose us to assume that the modality of pictorial art is always essentially the same.[32] But if we distinguish between languages, on the one hand, and scripts or codes, on the other, we should not be tempted to make this false assumption. For languages differ widely in their expressive powers. For example, the Psalms are not inferior as poetry to Shakespeare's sonnets, but the language at Shakespeare's disposal was much richer than the language available to the Psalmist. Again, "All happy families are alike" can probably be translated into every human language that is known, but the same is not true of "Energy is equivalent to mass."

Hence, the analogy between styles and languages or between paintings and texts should not encourage us to accept that realism is relative to a spectator or a community of spectators or that it is, as Goodman says, "determined by the system of representation standard for a given culture or person at a given time." For if pictorial styles are compared to languages, we should not compare the difference between the pictorial techniques available to a contemporary of Polygnotus or Giotto and to a contemporary of Apelles or Leonardo to the difference between Morse code and semaphore or to the difference between English and French. We should compare it to the difference between the English of *Beowulf* and the English of *Paradise Lost.* The technical resources of pictorial art are always limited in their expressive range, as languages are also bound to be, and these technical resources, like languages, can expand to express new ideas and new observations. Naturally, they can also expand in different directions. For example, the series of questions I used to introduce the idea of modality was chosen with Greek painting specifically in mind and would not help us to describe the development of Chinese landscape painting in the Song dynasty. Hence, there is no single trajectory that realistic traditions in pictorial art are bound to follow and no single destination toward which they must all progress. But in any artistic tradition, the periods of rapid expansion in modality are the periods in which the realistic motive is especially marked.

Turning to the second point, realism and illusionism are sometimes equated, as we have seen. This is one of the main themes of Gombrich's book *Art and Illusion,* and Clement Greenberg's influential essay "Modernist Painting" is founded on the same idea: "Realistic, naturalistic art had dissembled the medium, using art to conceal art; Modernism used art to call attention to art. The limitations that constitute the medium of painting—the flat surface, the shape of the support, the properties of the pigment—were treated by the old masters as negative factors that could be acknowledged only implicitly or indirectly."[33] One could be forgiven for finding this remark puzzling. For anyone who has wandered through a gallery of European art will be aware that painting did not invariably aspire to the condition of trompe l'oeil before Courbet. Not every painter drew the spectator's attention to the surface as emphatically as Titian, El Greco, Rembrandt, or Frans Hals; but equally, few were as intent on erasing it as, say, Pieter Claesz or Gerrit Dou. In any event, the theoretical point that needs to be emphasized is that although the illusionistic potential of realistic painting has at times been greatly admired, illusionism is not the same as realism itself. Constable once said that art pleases by reminding, not deceiving. The old masters can be assumed to have known this, too.

A painting is illusionistic to the extent that a spectator finds herself unable to see its surface *as* a surface. In some cases, a painting's appearance may not even disclose the fact that it is a painting until the spectator moves around it or looks at it closely, although we should not forget Ruskin's percipient remark that trompe l'oeil invariably has "some means of proving at the same time that it is an illusion."[34] But there is generally no difficulty in seeing the surface of a realistic painting as a surface, and most realistic paintings do not use art to conceal art, even at first glance. Furthermore, it is a familiar fact that a painting that is generally found to be illusionistic in one time or place may not be found to be so in another. But we are misrepresenting the significance of modeling and perspective if we say, for example, that Masaccio's *Maestà* was realistic relative to a spectator in fifteenth-century Pisa, but is not realistic relative to a spectator in twentieth-century London, or that it has become less realistic with the passage of time.

Consider perspective. It is obvious in the case of the bronze reliefs by Donatello and Lorenzo Ghiberti, which are among the earliest examples of Renaissance perspective, that trompe l'oeil cannot be in question. The same is evidently true of prints. But it is generally true also of paintings, because the use of perspective does not prevent the flatness of the painted surface and the substance of the pigment from being visible to a spectator. For example, Tintoretto's dramatic paintings of the discovery and theft of the body of Saint Mark are at the same time elaborate exercises in chiaroscuro and perspective and vivid records of the motion of the brush (fig. 85). These two aspects of the paintings are perfectly consistent, and perspective is not being used here to dissemble. Perspective is an indispensable tool for certain kinds of illusionistic painting, especially for large-scale architectural trompe l'oeil. But of course the end is not the same thing as the means.

In short, the principal measure of realism in pictorial art is not the ten-

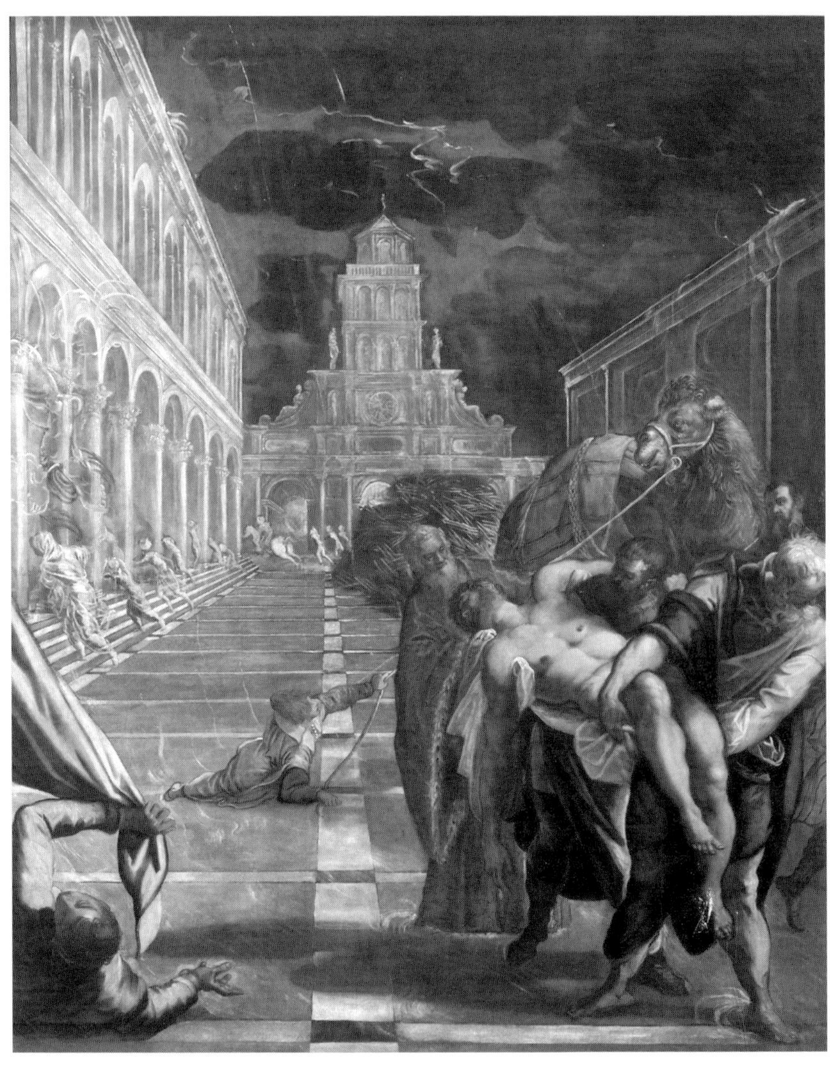

85. Tintoretto, *Transport of the Body of St. Mark,* 1562–66. Oil on canvas. Accademia, Venice.

dency of a picture to deceive the eye or to elicit the same kind of response as the scene in the picture would if we saw it face to face. It is not the quantity of information a picture records or the ease or rapidity with which this information is retrieved by the spectator. And it is not how novel the "labels" or the "handy graphic symbols" used by artists are or how commonplace they have become. The development of realism involves accuracy, animation, and, above all, the extension of the modality of art, the technical expansion of its expressive range.

~

When Kahnweiler announced that painting is a script, his principal aim was to advance the cause of cubism. But the idea eventually gained wide support because it seemed to disprove a false conception of the realistic tradition in European art as the gradual approximation to a predetermined goal that artists have sought to attain at all times in all places and because this false conception was an obstacle to the appreciation of progressive art and a hindrance in the historical study of art—both art that did not belong to a realistic tradition or develop along realistic lines and art that did.

Relativism is the simplest alternative to the monistic idea that there is a single model of truth and perfection in the visual arts, and it has generally been accepted for this reason. Relativists deplore the provincialism that makes European art seem to embody all of the timeless truths about what art should be. They know how our perceptions can be dulled and our sympathies narrowed by an exclusive attachment to the methods and techniques that our own artistic tradition has inherited. They know that societies have used art for different purposes and to express ideas of very different kinds. They know that the values embodied in art and demanded in criticism in a particular place and time are not more valid because they resemble our own. And they know that what looks like technical progress from one point of view can look like decline into empty virtuosity from another.[35]

For at least a century, none of this has been seriously denied. But the claim that "realism" is an honorific term, which we bestow on the style to which we are accustomed, is a poor way of summarizing what it means. It is often true, as Montaigne says, that "the common fancies we find in repute everywhere about us, and infused into our minds with the seed of our fathers, appear to be the most universal and genuine."[36] But it is one thing to believe that realistic art is the most universal and genuine, sanctioned by reason and the destiny of all mankind, and it is another to believe that the concept of realism corresponds to an intrinsic difference between one kind of art, or one kind of artistic tradition, and another, and not merely their relation to our own. The second belief does not imply the first. So if we reject relativism, we are not bound to succumb to the illusion that Montaigne describes: we can still acknowledge Meyer Schapiro's point, that "all renderings of objects, no matter how exact they seem . . . proceed from values, methods and viewpoints that somehow shape the image and often determine its contents," and we can accept that the plurality of values, methods, and viewpoints encompassed by art cannot be ordered in a timeless hierarchy or judged by a single standard that is valid at all times and in all places.

Relativism is a glib reaction to the monism, provincialism, and historicism that art historians in the twentieth century uniformly condemned. It is now accepted as a truism that there is no single model of perfection in the visual arts. But the nominalist philosophy that underpins the relativist claims about realistic art is false. Painting is not the skill of reproducing handy graphic symbols, and referring to differences between "set professional conventions" for "rendering familiar facts" is the wrong way to explain what realism involves. It is possible to admire the realistic spirit in art without idealizing or misrepresenting the various different values, methods, and viewpoints it has embodied, at different times and in different places. And it is possible to admire cubism without imagining that it exposes the false consciousness of realistic art. Realistic art does not have a unique sanction or a unique ability to express the truth. But it does not follow that the realistic style is whichever we know best or find it easiest to absorb and understand. The opposite of monism is pluralism, not relativism. We can be pluralists about art without being relativists about realism.

10

THE CANVAS OF THE BRAIN

And by-and-by, when the mind has grown too large for its lodging, it often finds difficulty in breaking down the walls of what has become its prison instead of its home.

J. Tyndall

WHEN LEONARDO DESCRIBED perspective as the rein and rudder of painting, he was referring in general terms to the use of a geometrical method for depicting space. The original invention was made by the Florentine architect and sculptor Filippo Brunelleschi, sometime between 1413 and 1425, and a simplified method, which I describe below, was disseminated by Leon Battista Alberti in the mid-1430s. Perspective has attracted a great deal of scholarly attention for three reasons. First, it is the most spectacular result of applying mathematical or scientific ideas to the problems of pictorial art, and it had a major reciprocal influence on science, both practically, by transforming the way in which information is communicated by pictorial means—for example, by architects and engineers—and theoretically, by representing bodies disposed in three dimensions in a uniform and comprehensive geometrical scheme.[1]

Second, perspective has seemed to many scholars to epitomize the humanistic philosophy of the Renaissance because it defines pictorial space in relation to an individual observer in a particular place. Alberti's *De pictura*, which contains the first exposition of the system, mentions Protagoras's famous remark that man is the measure of all things, and many writers have seen this thought as being implicit in some way in the system itself. For example, John White claims that perspective carries humanism "into the pictorial world itself" because it expresses "man's central position as observer of a pictorial world of which he himself is the measure." I am skeptical about this idea, but I have confined my reasons to the notes.[2]

The third reason, which I mentioned in the last chapter, is that perspective was used to produce unprecedented illusionistic effects, mainly in intarsia and in fresco. Again, many historians have thought of perspective as illusionistic in its essential form and purpose, and there is an unfortunate tendency to use the word "illusionistic" when what is meant is that a painting uses chiaroscuro or perspective. In fact, as we have seen, it is a mistake to suppose that every perspective painting is designed to produce an illusion: the vast majority are not. Nevertheless, illusionism has fascinated artists, historians, and spectators since antiquity, and this is evidently another reason for the wide interest in perspective.

In this final chapter, I shall discuss some twentieth-century ideas about Renaissance perspective. I shall not review the history of pictorial space, and it is not part of my intention to contribute to the large body of literature about Renaissance art. My interest in perspective is not so much in the thing itself as in some of the things that have been written about it. And the main reason why these writings are of importance here is that perspective is one of the focuses of the intimate and confusing relationship between the theory of vision and the theory of painting, which has been one of the main themes of this book.

As we have seen, this relationship has not been a one-sided affair. It is well known that painters have been influenced by the scientific study of light, color, and visual perception, at least since the Renaissance. But science has been affected at least as much as painting because the formative and governing idea in the theory of vision, from its inception in fifth-century Greece right up to the present day, is that vision depends on the existence of an image in the eye. The principal aim of this chapter is to examine the results of applying a theory of vision conceived under this governing idea to the particular problem of explaining how Renaissance perspective depicts space.

~

Renaissance perspective is a geometrical synthesis of several techniques for depicting nonplanar spatial relations, all of which had already existed for almost two thousand years when Renaissance perspective was invented. There is no need to devise any special techniques to depict planar spatial relations—above, below, to the left of, and to the right of—because they can be reproduced on a marked surface. But in order to depict nonplanar spatial relations, painters invented various techniques, which were eventually harmonized in the geometrical system of perspective. The most interesting, from a theoretical point of view, are overlapping, foreshortening, diminution, and shading. Each is a technique for depicting a property that should be familiar to the reader from earlier chapters: respectively, occlusion, occlusion shape, relative occlusion size, and aperture color.

Overlapping, which is the oldest technique for depicting nonplanar spatial relations, was already used by Egyptian artists in the Old Kingdom (ca. 2650–ca. 2150 B.C.) to depict one object partly occluding another. The object that is partly occluded is only partly depicted, and the part of the picture that would otherwise depict this hidden part depicts instead the part of the object that occludes it. In Egyptian paintings, meticulous overlapping is often used to depict a row of animals, as it is for example in a farming scene from an Eighteenth Dynasty tomb painting in Thebes (plate 2). Virtuoso exercises in overlapping appear on some archaic Greek vases, such as the name vase of the Berlin Painter (fig. 86).

Foreshortening is concerned with what philosophers have sometimes called "apparent shape." As I have explained, I prefer the term "occlusion

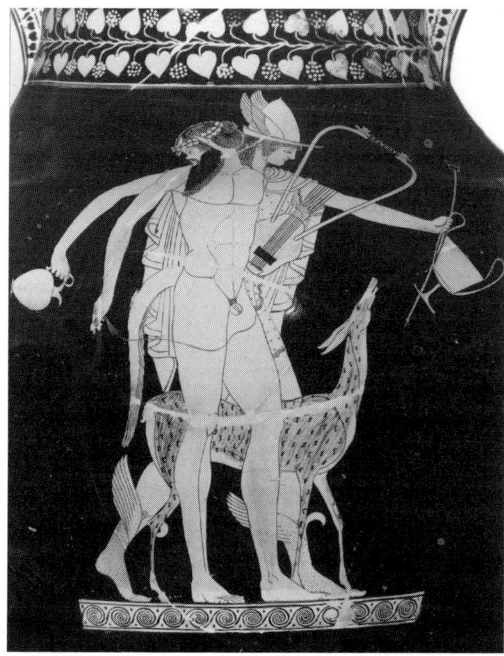

86. Amphora, ca. 490 B.C. Name vase of the Berlin Painter. Staatliche Museen zu Berlin, Antikensammlung.

shape" because "apparent shape" implies mistakenly that we are talking about something that is less than fully real. For example, if a circular shield or the circular rim of a wheel is seen obliquely, it will have an elliptical occlusion shape: the shape of a perpendicular cross section of the solid angle it subtends to the spectator's eye will be an ellipse. An object's occlusion shape, relative to a line of sight, is a product of its three-dimensional shape and its orientation relative to that line. Hence, foreshortening allows a painter to depict orientation by controlling the occlusion shape of an object represented in a picture.

The earliest consistent use of foreshortening is on Greek vases made in the last quarter of the sixth century B.C., and in fact wheels and shields were the first kinds of objects to be foreshortened. Figure 87, which represents a victorious Lapith with one foot resting on a centaur, is from the tondo of a kylix made in the first quarter of the fifth century. (The painter also used a thin slip

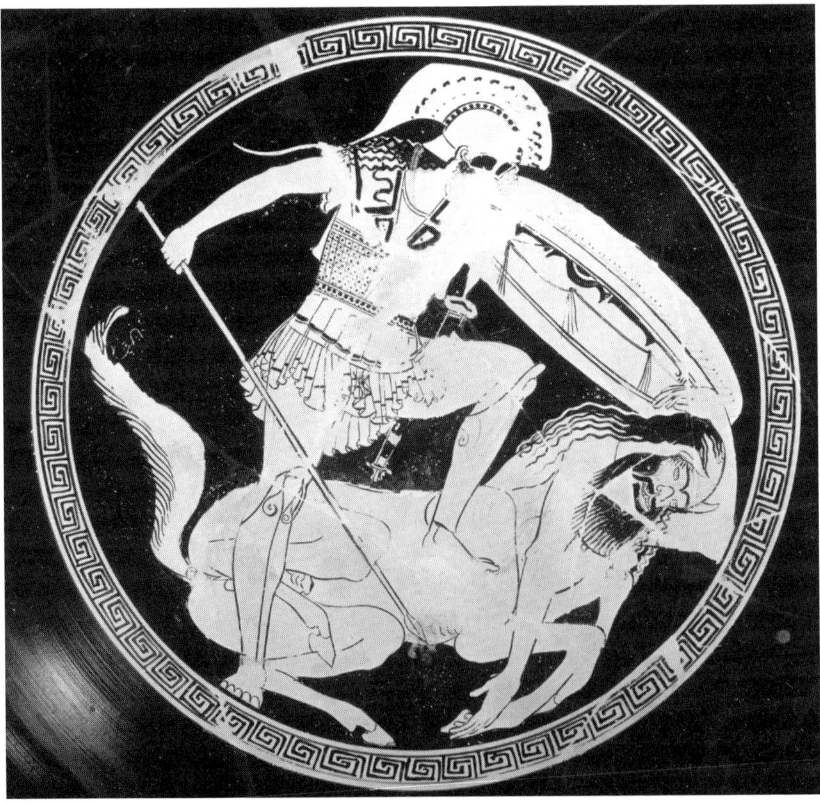

87. Kylix, ca. 490 B.C. Attributed to the Foundry Painter. Antikensammlung, Munich.

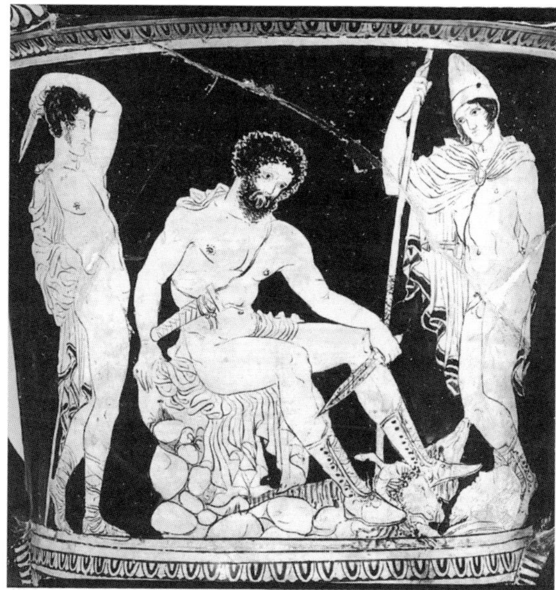

88. Lucanian calyx crater, ca. 380 B.C. Attributed to the Dolon Painter. Cabinet des Médailles et Antiques, Paris.

to add shading to the outer surface of the shield and showed the face of the fatally wounded centaur in the newly invented three-quarter view.) Figure 88, which is shown here for the foreshortening of the thigh, was painted about a century later. It represents Odysseus meeting Tiresias's shade, which prophesies that death will come to Odysseus in old age, far from the sea, and in a gentle way.

Whereas foreshortening is concerned with occlusion shape, diminution is concerned with relative occlusion size. For example, if I look at two similar columns or two similar trees, one of which is farther from me than the other, the occlusion size of the more distant one will be smaller relative to my position. The relative occlusion size of two objects is a product of their relative sizes and their relative distances from the spectator, and diminution therefore enables a painter to depict relative distance from the spectator without partly occluding one of the objects depicted. Diminution seems to have been invented by Greek painters producing backdrops for theatrical productions, and it appears on Greek vases in the second half of the fifth century B.C. Figure 89 shows a wall painting from Pompeii, probably derived from a fourth-century painting by Timanthes, in which the distant figures of Artemis and Iphigenia in the sky are considerably diminished in occlusion size.

Finally, shading is analogous to foreshortening, and it appeared for the first

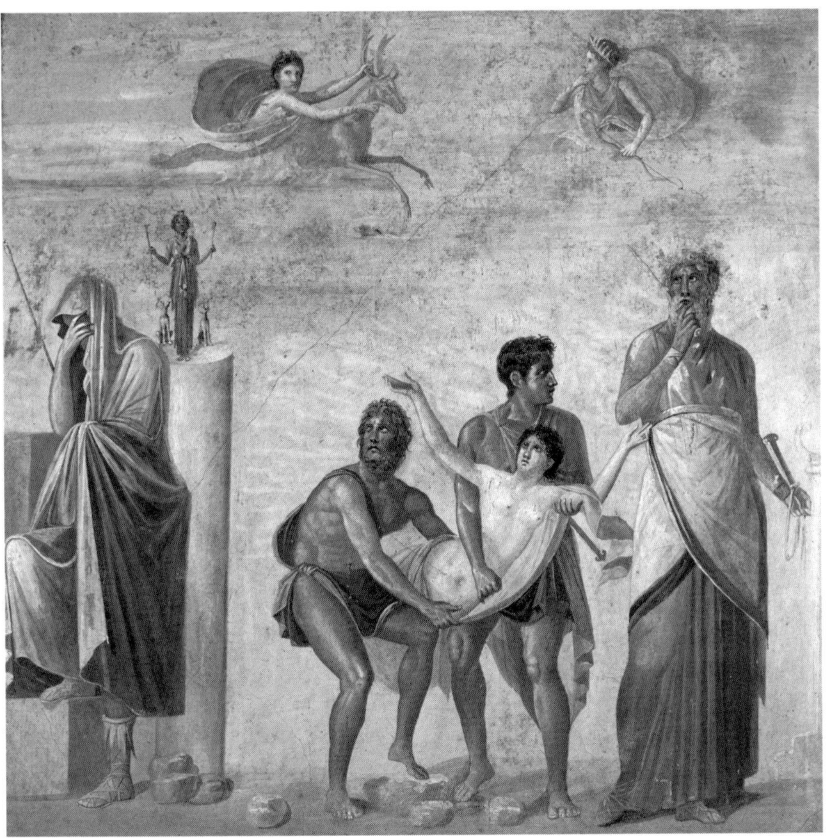

89. *Sacrifice of Iphigenia,* ca. A.D. 62–79. Wall painting from Pompeii. Museo Nazionale, Naples.

time in Greek art a few decades later. As I have explained, foreshortening is a technique for depicting orientation relative to the spectator's line of sight. Shading depicts orientation, too, but relative to a light source rather than to a line of sight. It does so by depicting the varying effect that light has on an object's aperture color, when it radiates predominantly from a particular direction. The altar depicted on a fourth-century Apulian calyx crater provides a simple example of this technique (fig. 90). The *Sacrifice of Iphigenia* is more elaborate. It depicts the light that illuminates the scene as radiating from the left not by depicting the light source itself but by showing the highlights and shaded areas of the objects in the scene and the shadows they are casting on the ground.

~

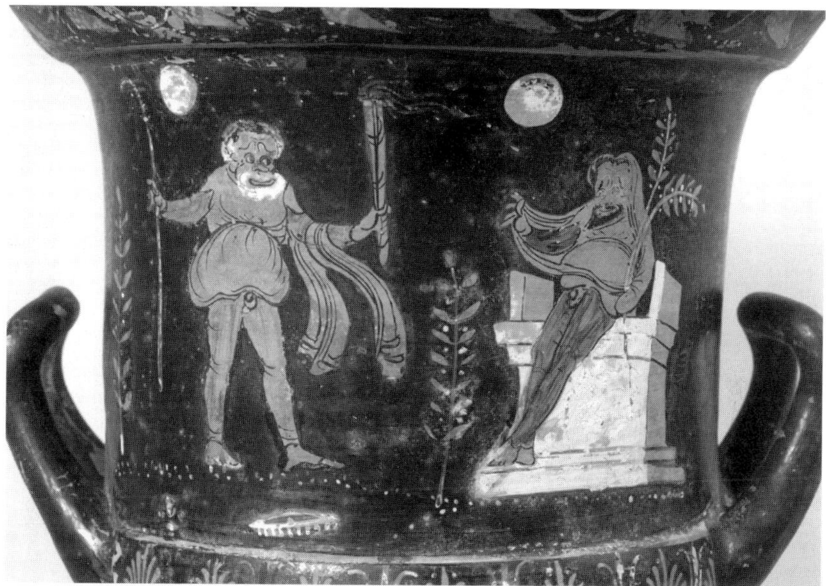

90. Apulian calyx crater, ca. 340–330 B.C. Museo Nazionale, Taranto.

I shall turn now to the system of perspective itself. The geometrical method described for the first time in Alberti's treatise is, in effect, a method for drawing a tiled floor in correct perspective and placing figures on it. It depends on first fixing the position of the picture plane and the spectator's eye. A simplified version of the method can be explained in the following six steps (fig. 91):

- Draw a horizontal line on the picture plane, at the same height as the spectator's eye. This line is called the horizon.
- Mark a point on the horizon, where a line drawn from the spectator's eye will meet the picture plane at right angles. This is called the vanishing point.
- Draw a series of lines from the vanishing point to a series of points at equal intervals on the line along the base of the picture. These lines are called orthogonals.
- Extend the horizon to a point that lies at the same distance from the edge of the panel as the viewing point. This point is called the distance point.
- Draw a series of lines from the distance point to the points already marked on the baseline. These lines are called diagonals.
- Draw a series of horizontal lines that intersect the edge of the panel at the same points as the diagonals do. These lines are called transversals.

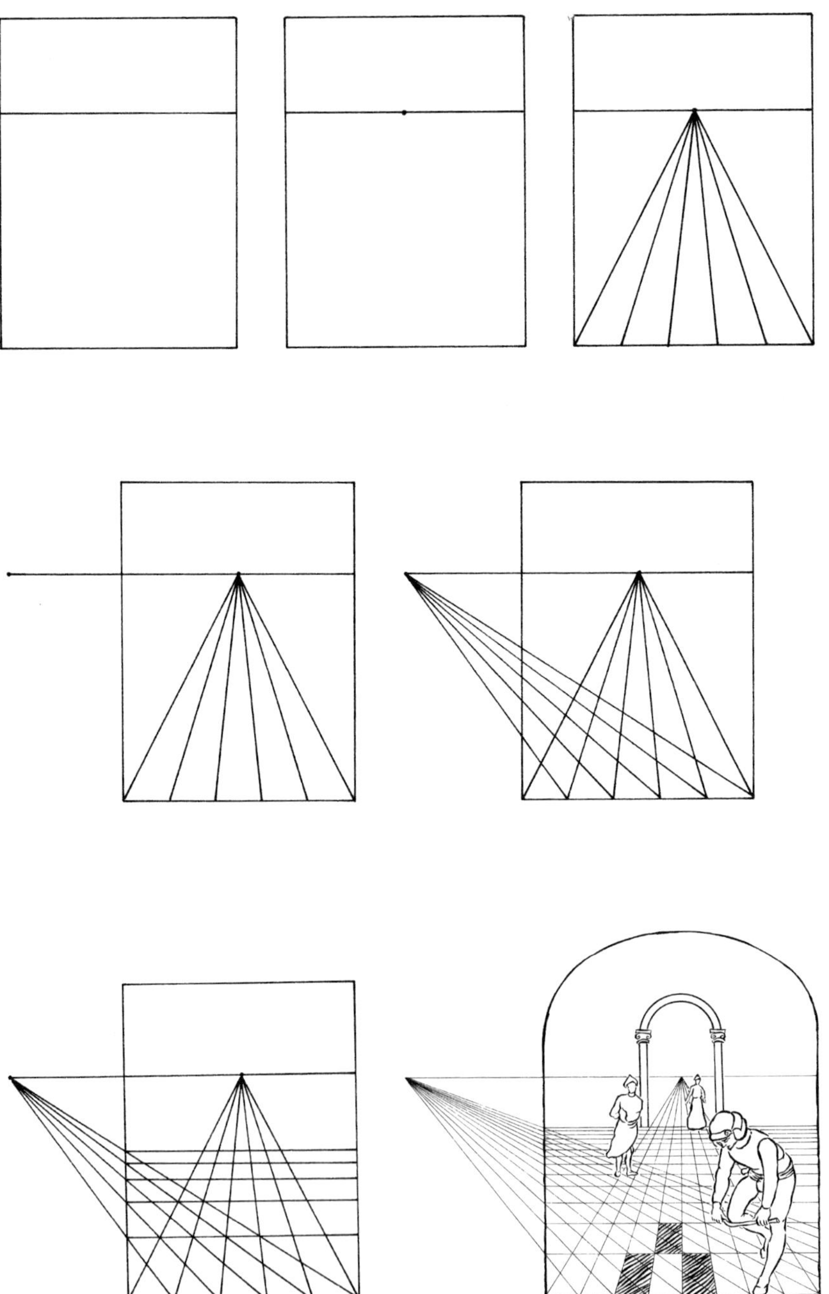

91. A simple perspective construction.

In effect, this procedure produces a horizon and the outlines of tiled floor, or *pavimento.* When figures have been added, the elements of a picture are in place. Anything that appears above the horizon is represented as being higher than the spectator's eye, and anything that appears below it is represented as being lower than the spectator's eye. So the heads of standing figures will appear close to the horizon, but their feet will appear at different distances beneath it, depending on how far they are meant to be from the spectator. The method is simple and practical, and it can easily be incorporated into the workshop practice of a painter. I have only described rudiments of it, which are set out at the end of the first book of *De pictura.* And even this bare skeleton can be used with extraordinary force (fig. 92). But it was rapidly extended to include multiple vanishing points for sets of lines depicting parallel edges that are not perpendicular to the picture plane; the geometrical treatment of shading, cast shadows, and foreshortening—both of complex geometrical solids with plane surfaces and of heads and bodies; and lines of sight that are not horizontal.

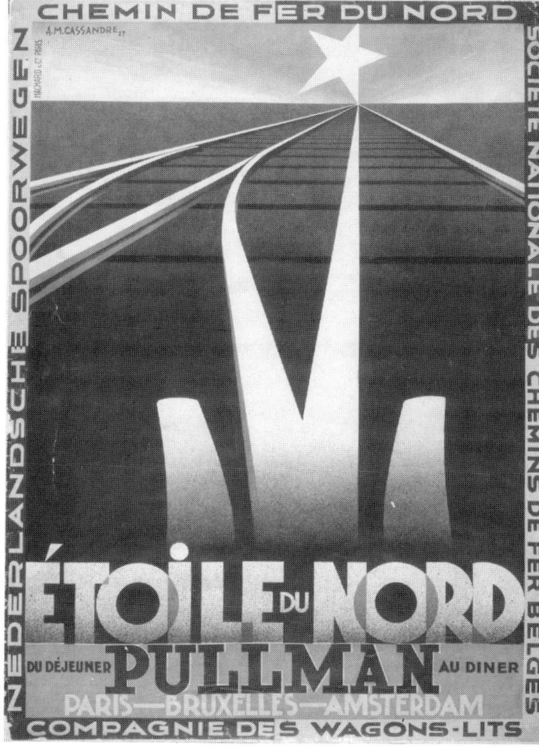

92. Cassandre (Adolphe Mouron), *Etoile du nord,* 1927. Poster.

Two fifteenth-century examples will stand for many. The first is a graceful panel from Ghiberti's *Porta del Paradiso*, on the East side of the Baptistery in Florence, which represents the story of Esau and Jacob (fig. 93). It was made at about the same time as Alberti wrote his treatise—in about 1435. Notice the heads arranged along the horizon, the orthogonals receding to a point in the very center of the panel, and the height of the figures decreasing proportionately with their distance. The figure of Esau is an exception: he is shown climbing a hill, outside the well-ordered and harmonious scene below, and larger than the perspective scheme permits. The second is Mantegna's oculus in the ceiling of the Camera degli Sposi, in the Ducal Palace in Mantua (fig. 94). This was painted thirty years later, in about 1465, and is the earliest example of perspective being used to break the surface of a vaulted ceiling. Here, of course, the orthogonals fan out in a complete circle, and the foreshortening of the

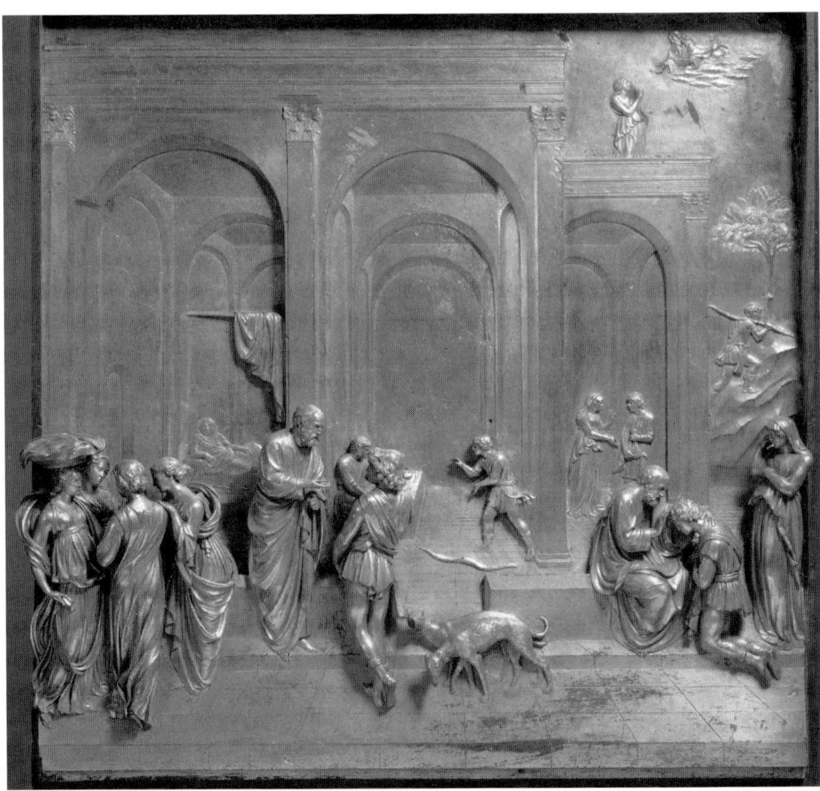

93. Lorenzo Ghiberti, *Jacob and Esau,* panel from the *Gates of Paradise,* Baptistery, Florence, ca. 1435. Gilded bronze. Museo dell'Opera del Duomo, Florence.

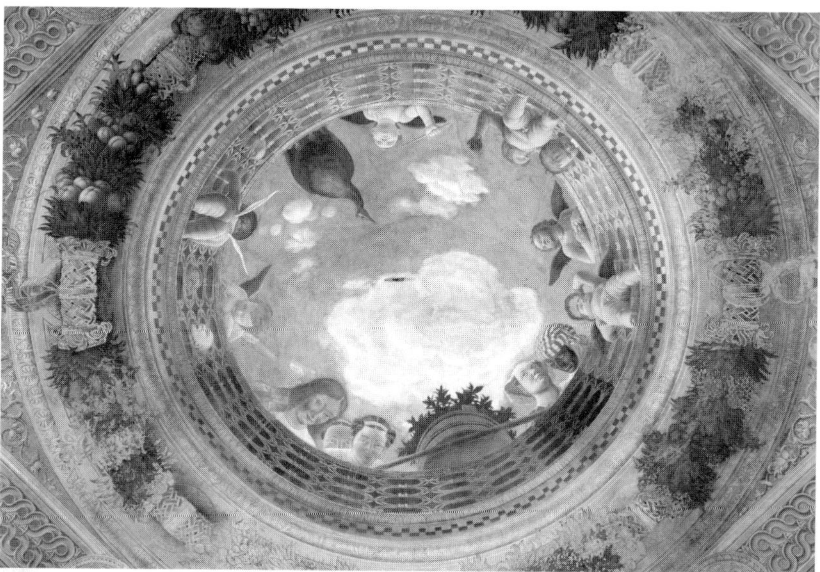

94. Andrea Mantegna, oculus in the ceiling of the Camera degli Sposi, ca. 1471–74. Fresco. Ducal Palace, Mantua.

putti in the painting—the cousins of the stucco putti on the ceiling—may have been constructed by a method of geometrical projection.

That is how Alberti's method works in practice. But if paintings that make use of this technique depict space more successfully than paintings by Giotto, Duccio, or the Lorenzetti brothers, why do they do so?

Alberti's own explanation is geometrical, and it involves little of substance that is not already contained in Euclid's *Optics*. Vision, he explains, depends on a tightly packed bundle of rays, which extends in the form of a pyramid from the eye to the surfaces of the objects that are seen. The apex of this pyramid of rays is in the eye, and its base is on the surfaces of these objects. The rays that enclose the contours of an object define its shape; the rays that strike its surface transmit its color to the eye; and at the very center, the centric ray will strike a plane perpendicular to the eye at right angles. He says that we should think of a painting in perspective as a cross section of a pyramid of visual rays, which pass through it as if it were made of glass until they reach the opaque surfaces of the objects that it represents.[3]

Alberti did not add any figures or illustrations to his text to explain this idea, but a woodcut by Dürer, which was made about a century later, conveys the sense of it precisely (fig. 95). One man holds the tip of a stylus to the point

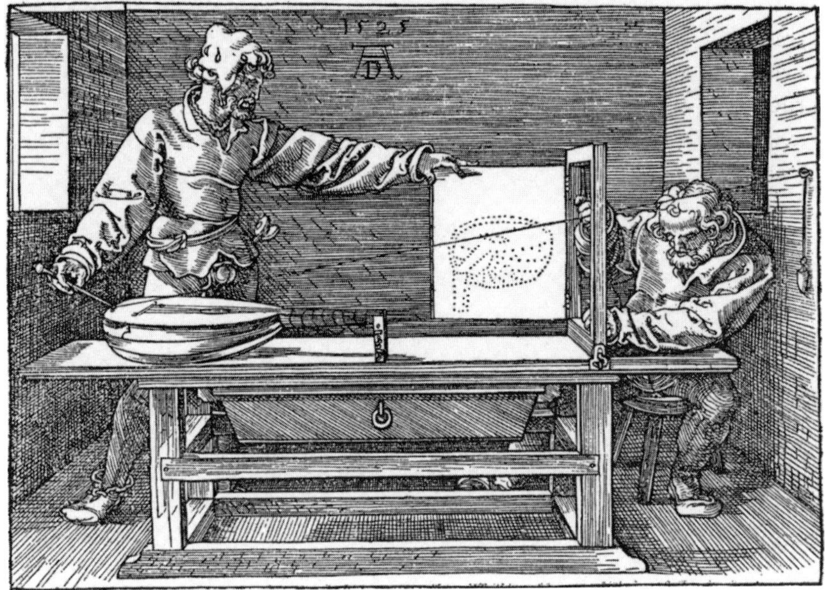

95. Albrecht Dürer, illustration from *Unterweysung der Messung.* Nuremberg, 1525.

on a lute that is about to be recorded in a picture. The other, seated on a stool, aligns a thread to the place where a string attached to the stylus traverses the picture plane. The string passes through a hook on the wall and is held taut by a small lead weight. The picture itself is being drawn on a shutter, which has already been marked with sufficient number of points to show the lute, precisely foreshortened, as it would appear from the apex of the pyramid—the point where the string passes through the hook.

This leaves us with two questions. First, why is constructing a cross section through a visual pyramid a successful way of depicting space? Second, why is Alberti's method equivalent to constructing a cross section?

Alberti's answer to the first question is based on two ideas: first, that each pair of points on a cross section of a pyramid of rays will subtend the same angle to the eye as the corresponding pair of points on the surface of the objects at its base and, second, that the perception of size, shape, and distance are the result of trigonometric operations in which the visual rays are used by the eye to measure angles "as with a pair of compasses." It follows from these two principles that if a painting is a cross section of a pyramid of rays, the geometrical equivalence between the lines on the surface of the painting and the edges of the planes they represent will entail a visual equivalence between the appearance of the painting and the appearance of the scene that it represents.

According to Alberti, that is why constructing a cross section through a pyramid of rays is a successful way of representing space. The other question is why Alberti's method produces the same result as the point-by-point construction of a cross section through a pyramid of rays. In particular, why must the orthogonals converge at the single point on the horizon, opposite the spectator's eye? And why do the transversals foreshorten the pavement at the correct rate?

Alberti does not attempt to answer these questions. He writes: "We have talked, as much as seems necessary, of triangles, pyramids and the cross-section. I usually explain these things to my friends with certain prolix geometric demonstrations that in this commentary it seemed to me better to omit for the sake of brevity."[4] But in the present context, this omission is less interesting than the fact that Alberti deliberately ignores the physics, the physiology, and the psychology of vision. He mentions the controversy over whether visual rays travel from the eye to the object or vice versa, but he says that, for his purposes, this problem can be ignored. He says the same about the function of the eye itself: "This is not the place to discuss whether vision, as it is called, resides at the juncture of the inner nerve or whether images are formed on the surface of the eye as on a living mirror. The function of the eye in vision need not be considered in this place."[5]

This is a highly significant remark because it indicates that although Alberti was partly familiar with medieval visual theory, and took the idea of the visual pyramid and the centric ray from this tradition, he believed that the system of perspective could be fully explained, and fully justified, purely in terms of the bare mathematical skeleton of visual theory.[6] This contrasts sharply with the way in which historians and psychologists in the twentieth century thought about the system, as we shall see.

~

I said at the beginning of this chapter that the formative and governing idea in the theory of perception is that vision depends on the existence of images in our eyes. This idea stems originally from the earliest Greek philosophers and was explained clearly for the first time by Democritus, who believed that these images are thin skins or membranes that stream off the surfaces of objects and enter our eyes. But the idea has undergone several mutations, and the modern version of it dates from the beginning of the seventeenth century when Kepler discovered the geometry of the eye. In chapter 6, I examined Descartes's partial attempt to eradicate the idea from visual theory. We now need to consider how much of it still survives.

In the illustration of Kepler's theory that appears in Descartes's *Optics*, the back of an eye has been cut away and replaced with a thin piece of paper so

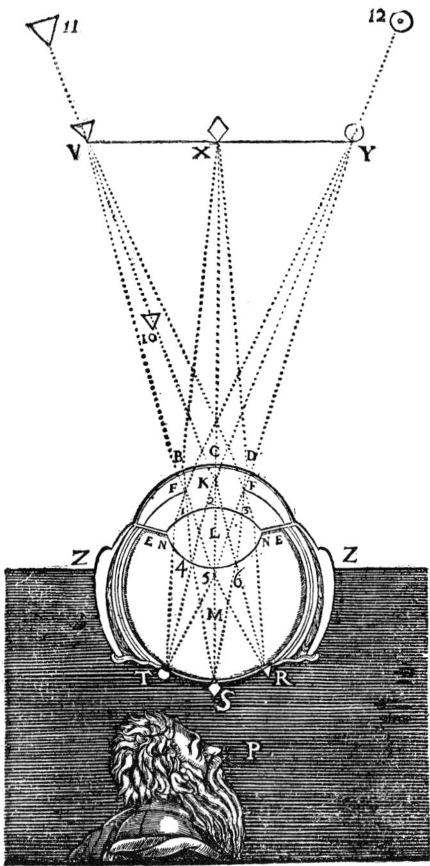

96. Illustration from Réné Descartes, *Dioptrique*. Leiden, 1637.

that a retinal image can be observed (fig. 96). Points *V*, *X*, and *Y* are three points on a visible object, which are approximately equidistant from the eye. The diagram is simplified, of course, and it only shows a few rays traveling to the eye. But light radiates in every direction, so many rays enter the eye from each point on the visible surface of the object. The refractive properties of the eye pull all of the rays proceeding from a single point together, and they converge on a single point on the retina. Point *R* is where the rays from *V* are focused; *S* is the point that corresponds to *X;* and *T* corresponds to *Y.* Thus, the line *RT* is the central part of a retinal image, in cross section, and as the figure shows, it resembles a cross section of Alberti's pyramid of rays. But it is transposed behind the apex, which appears here just behind the cornea. The image is inverted because the rays have crossed, and it is projected onto a curved surface.

When Kepler discovered the geometry of the eye, he thought that the image on the retina is the object that we see, when vision occurs, so that this photographic picture—for which he used the Latin word *pictura*—conveys the appearances of objects to us in the way that a painting does. In fact, this view was implicit in the entire tradition of visual theory that originates with Alhazen, in the eleventh century, and that Kepler brought to a conclusion. The most telling sign of it is the assumption, which was accepted universally for six hundred years, that the retinal image has to be upright because visible objects do not look upside down to us when we see them. Kepler himself made this assumption and abandoned it only with the greatest reluctance after "torturing himself," as he put it, to find a second intersection of the rays that would produce a retinal image the right way up.[7]

As we have already seen, Descartes was acutely conscious that we do not see objects by perceiving pictures of them in our eyes. But the comparison between a retinal image, which is not seen, and a picture, which is seen, played a crucial role in his *Optics*. Its influence has persisted, both in visual theory and in the theory of art.

Since we are concerned with the depiction of depth, distance, and solidity, the question in the theory of vision that concerns us is how depth, distance, and solidity are perceived by sight. The approach to this question that has had the greatest influence in the twentieth century is due to Helmholtz. Here is the way in which Helmholtz presents the question: "Each of our eyes projects a two-dimensional image on its own retina. In whatever way we suppose the conducting nerves to be arranged, the two retinal images when united in the brain can only reappear as a two-dimensional image. But instead of the two two-dimensional retinal images, our experience presents us with a solid image of three dimensions. . . . How can this experience of depth come about?"[8]

Part of Helmholtz's own answer to his question concerns the differences between the two images in our eyes. But he points out that the world does not look flat to us when we close one eye, and this is obviously correct. As it happens, the first pilot to fly solo around the world only had one eye, and he landed his plane successfully a number of times on the trip. Furthermore, few animals apart from primates and cats can use binocular disparity to perceive distance. So how do we perceive depth, distance, and solidity with a single eye? This is Helmholtz's answer: "The means we possess in this case are just the same as those the painter can employ in order to give the objects represented on his canvas the appearance of being solid objects, and of standing at different distances from the spectator." Helmholtz goes on to mention perspective, shading, and foreshortening and the representation of things with plane surfaces, such as walls and pavements, and things with well-known shapes and sizes, such as men and cattle.[9]

So, this is Helmholtz's model of the monocular perception of solidity and depth: the immediate visual stimulus is a retinal image produced by the ambient light. The ultimate effect of this stimulus is a "solid image of three dimensions." And there is an intricate process in between, which somehow exploits the properties that retinal images share with perspective paintings, in order to produce our familiar visual experience of depth, distance, and solidity. Helmholtz himself thought of this process as being similar to reasoning or making inferences, in which the logical steps are governed by laws of association that are drawn from the experience, beginning in infancy, of moving our limbs and bodies with our eyes open and touching or bumping into things. Psychologists today generally think of it as making computations, in which the logical steps are governed by algorithms that are partly innate and partly the result of learning.[10] But if we describe it in this abstract way, Helmholtz's model is still generally accepted.

For example, here is a passage from an article by Colin Blakemore: "There are many aspects of the monocular retinal image that can be used by the brain to judge distance. They have been classified by psychologists, who use very simplified situations to study these clues to distance. But what better way to consider them than to see how they have been used by the great artists, since these are the only conventional devices by which a painter can create a sense of distance on a flat canvas."[11] Blakemore goes on to list and illustrate the same techniques as Helmholtz: perspective, shading, and foreshortening, the size of familiar objects, and so on. He adds that the mechanisms that produce perceptions of distance are not yet understood. But of course this does not invalidate the idea that our visual experience of depth and solidity depends on the properties of the retinal image that he mentions.

Here is a similar passage from an article by V. S. Ramachandran: "Our visual experience of the world is based on two-dimensional images: flat patterns of varying light intensity and colour, falling on a single plane of cells in the retina. Yet we come to perceive solidity and depth. We can do this because a number of cues about depth are available in the retinal image: shading, perspective, occlusion of one object by another and stereoscopic disparity. In some mysterious way the brain is able to exploit these cues to recover the three-dimensional shapes of objects."[12] The view expressed in these passages was not accepted universally in the twentieth century: J. J. Gibson was the chief heretic.[13] However, it was, and it remains, deeply entrenched; and since Gibson's death in 1979, the challenge has been muted and widely ignored.

How should we explain the fact that perspective, shading, and foreshortening are successful techniques for depicting depth if the perception of depth is explained by the properties that retinal images share with perspective paintings?

The natural answer to this question is that the resemblance between retinal images and perspective paintings provides the explanation, and in fact this is the commonest answer that we find. For example, Richard Gregory claims that "when an artist employs geometrical perspective he does not draw what he sees—he represents his retinal image." Blakemore claims that in the Renaissance "artists must have learned that their task was to challenge the viewer just as he is tested by the image in his own eye." Irving Rock claims that "photographs and drawings are comprehensible to us because they more or less resemble the image of a scene as it appears on our retinas." And many similar remarks are scattered through the psychological literature.[14] According to these writers, pictures that resemble retinal images will tend to produce the same experience of depth, distance, and solidity as retinal images do themselves. As Gregory explains: "A picture is essentially like a retinal image—both are flat projections of three-dimensional space . . . the brain is so familiar with the problems of adding the third dimension from information given by the flat retinal image that we might expect it to cope with pictures."[15] Artists can therefore represent depth and solidity successfully by reproducing the geometrical structure of a retinal image and the patterns of light and dark that occur in it—and this is exactly what painters who use perspective, foreshortening, and shading do. When they use these techniques, artists somehow bypass the mechanisms in their own brains, which transform their retinal images into perceptions—that is, into the solid images of three dimensions Helmholtz referred to—and copy their retinal images instead.[16]

When we turn to the art historical literature, the attitude to perspective is more mixed. On the one hand, several influential writers have defended the same theory as the psychologists I have quoted. An early sign of the influence of Helmholtz's physiological optics on the theory of perspective is the treatise *Die Subjektive Perspektive* by Guido Hauck, a professor of applied geometry in Berlin, which was published in 1879: "Geometrical perspective is still based on the physiology of Kepler and Scheiner, who regarded the eye as a stationary camera obscura, and assumed a direct psychological [*seelisches*] understanding of the retinal image as a whole".[17]

Hauck's ideas eventually fed into the mainstream of art history because of their influence on Panofsky; but Emanuel Löwy was the first historian of art to argue that the resemblance between retinal images and pictures that use foreshortening, shading, and diminution explains how these techniques represent solidity and depth. Referring to the development of Greek painting, he wrote: "Where we are able to follow up an entire development of art, we find that its morphological progress is from the psychical image to the physical, that is, to the image on the retina." The great authority on Egyptian art Heinrich Schäfer, also referring to Greek painting, claimed that "perspective . . . reproduces visual impressions faithfully, basing itself on the visual image built into the structure of the human eye." And Panofsky applied the same idea to the Renaissance system of perspective: "The painter, however, who has to render three-dimensional objects on a flat surface, that is, to reproduce a visual image appearing in the eye, and not an object existing as a real thing, had to be made familiar with a method of establishing this visual image on a general and scientific basis. . . . This is the purpose of the discipline which more than anything else deserves the title of a specific Renaissance achievement: perspective."[18]

Thus the Helmholtzian conception of perspective was embedded in art theory during the first decades of the twentieth century. It is one of the main sources of Gombrich's book *Art and Illusion,* which owes much to Löwy and more to Gombrich's sympathetic reading in psychology belonging to the Helmholtzian tradition.[19] And its influence on art theorists interested in the theory of vision has not abated.[20]

However, it has also been quite widely argued by theorists of art that perspective has no mathematical, physical, or physiological justification and no basis independent of the habits instilled in us by our cultural history. If we find that it looks right, this is an effect of acculturation, and if we believe that it *is* right, this is an effect of cultural bias. Many writers have held this view and have defended it with the nominalist arguments criticized in chapters 8 and 9, but the original source of the relativist position is Panofsky's main publication on perspective, the article "Die Perspektive als 'symbolische Form,'" which appeared in 1927.[21]

Unlike Helmholtz, Panofsky was deeply influenced by Kant's theory of space, and in order to understand Panofsky's argument about perspective we need to be aware of the two main doctrines about space and time that Kant defends in the *Critique of Pure Reason.* The first doctrine is that space and time are modifications of our sensibility, and the second is that they are pure forms of all sensible intuition. The first doctrine means that space and time are formal, or structural, features of our perceptions: they are not intrinsic structural features of the world, and physical objects and events do not have spatial and temporal properties independently of their relationship to sentient beings. Kant says this explicitly as follows: "If the subject . . . be removed, the whole constitution and all the relations of objects in space and time, nay space and time themselves, would vanish."[22] However—and this is the second doctrine—they are also pure forms of all sensible intuition. This means that space and time are not a quirk of human psychology because any perceptual experience by any kind of creature would necessarily be organized in the same way.

The most important direct influence on Panofsky's argument was his colleague in Hamburg, the neo-Kantian philosopher Ernst Cassirer. Cassirer accepts Kant's first doctrine, that space and time are modifications of our sensibility, but he does not accept the second doctrine.[23] That is, he does not accept that space and time are the pure and unvarying forms of intuition that Kant postulates. On the contrary, he argues that they are historically contingent. He argues that our experience of space and time depends on the ways in which we have learned to represent them—both pictorially, in art, and by means of language, in mythical narratives, in history, and in geometry and science. Hence, the forms in which we experience space and time—and therefore, we are bound to add, the forms of space and time themselves—vary from one society and one epoch to another. They are not "pure forms of all sensible intuition": they are varied and parochial "symbolic forms."

Panofsky's article defends the idea that perspective is not a uniquely valid method for representing space—as Alberti and the Helmholtzians had claimed, albeit for different reasons—but a historically contingent *symbolic* form. It is, he says, "comprehensible only for a quite specific, indeed specifically modern, sense of space."[24] He describes this modern sense of space in terms that combine the different—and mutually inconsistent—views about space held by Newton, Descartes, and Leibniz, between two and three centuries after the invention of perspective. He calls it "an infinite, unchanging and homogeneous space," recalling Newton; a space that reduces "'body' and 'nonbody' to a common denominator of *substance étendue,*" recalling Descartes; and "a homogeneous and infinite system of dimensional relationships," recalling Leibniz.[25]

What solid evidence does Panofsky offer to support this mixture of Kantianism, relativism, and intellectual history in the *longue durée?* The principal piece of evidence, which Panofsky acquired from Guido Hauck, is this: "Perspectival construction ignores the crucial circumstance that the retinal image—entirely apart from its subsequent psychological 'interpretation,' and even apart from the fact that the eyes move—is a projection not on a flat surface but on a concave surface. Thus already on this lowest, still prepsychological level of facts there is a fundamental discrepancy between 'reality' and its construction."[26] So Panofsky does not reject the idea that the right way to decide about the status of perspective is to compare perspective pictures with retinal images. Rather, he points out that the result of making this comparison is not the one that the Helmholtzians claim it is. He argues that perspective pictures do not in fact resemble retinal images because the retina is curved. Hence, whereas the Renaissance system of perspective represents straight lines as straight, retinal images represent straight lines by curves. A curvilinear system of perspective would therefore eliminate the fundamental discrepancy he refers to, between what he calls "reality"—presumably, the scare quotes are there to remind us of the neo-Kantian theory of space that he accepted—and its construction on the surface of a painting: "The orthogonals of a building, which in normal perspective construction appear straight, would, if they were to correspond to the factual retinal image, have to be drawn as curves. Strictly, speaking, even the verticals would have to submit to some bending."[27]

Panofsky is of course right to point out that the retina is curved. However, the real mistake of the Helmholtzians was not to ignore this fact. Their real mistake, which Panofsky also made, was to explain how a pictorial technique works by comparing a painting, which we do see, with a retinal image, which we do not see. I shall argue that they made this mistake because they did not really succeed in escaping the influence of the idea that the image on the retina is the object that we see, when vision occurs. Some of the writers I have quoted explicitly deny that we see our retinal images, and perhaps they would all deny it, if they were asked. But it is one thing to deny a proposition and quite another to break the grip that it exerts on the imagination and to destroy its influence on scientific ideas.[28]

The idea that painters in the Renaissance copied their retinal images is like the idea that the retinal image has to be the right way up. It seems to make sense, as long as we think of the retina—as Blakemore actually describes it—as a kind of canvas for the brain. But if we reject this way of thinking about the retina completely, it is obviously untenable because a painting that really did resemble a retinal image would be painted upside down on the inside of a sphere; it would flicker and change four or five times each second, which is the rate at which the eyeball jumps from one fixation to another; some parts of it would be blurred and some parts of it would be in focus; it would have a blurry wedge in the corner where the nose is; there would be a blank patch near the middle for the blind spot; and so on.

Once the idea that we perceive our retinal images has been abandoned, it is surely obvious that the right way to explain how perspective works is to think about the geometrical relationship between the marks on the surface of a painting and the objects that these marks represent and that we should not be thinking about the retina at all. The woodcut by Dürer, which I described earlier, shows why (fig. 95). If the pattern of ambient light to the eye from the closed shutter is similar to the pattern of ambient light to the eye from the lute, its effect on the retina will be similar as well because similar causes produce similar effects. Hence, the significant relationship—which explains why the perspective picture of the lute drawn on the shutter foreshortens the lute successfully—is the geometrical relationship between the two objects we can see: the lute and its projection on the shutter. It is not the relationship between the marks on the shutter and the retinal image of an observer.

As Gregory explains, the doctrine defended by the Helmholtzians is, in the final analysis, that we are able to perceive the subject of a picture—and especially a picture painted in perspective—because visual perception is always the result of perceiving what a picture represents. Vision, as David Marr asserts, is "the process of discovering from images what is present in the world and where it is," and it is natural to infer that pictures that resemble retinal images will be nicely attuned to our natural visual skills.[29] "The brain," as Gregory puts it, in the passage quoted above, "is so familiar with the problem of adding the third dimension from information given by the flat [*sic*] retinal image that we might expect it to cope with pictures."

This explanation is evidently confused. For it implies that the brain stands in the same relation to a picture, when we perceive what it represents, as it does to a retinal image, when we perceive the sunlit world before our eyes, and this is tantamount to thinking of the retinal image as a picture. If we compare what happens in my eyes and in my brain when I look onto the street outside my window with what happens when I look at a painting, it should be obvious that the analogue of the retinal image produced by light reflected by the street is the retinal image produced by light reflected by the painting. It cannot be the painting itself. If we imagine that it is the painting, we have in effect replaced the retinal image produced by the painting with the painting itself, and this is plainly a mistake. But if we begin by comparing a retinal image with a painting, as Helmholtz does, in the passage quoted above, we shall sooner or later compare a painting with a retinal image, and the mistake will be difficult to avoid.

The main sources of this confusion are the promiscuous use of the word "image" and the failure to keep the idea of one kind of image from influencing our conception of another. Paintings, photographs, reflections, screen images, perceptions, thoughts, and memories have all been called images at one time or another. This has proved to be extremely confusing. When Newton said that the rays of light reflected by an object "paint the Picture of the object upon that skin called the *Retina*," he misled us; and when Gregory claimed that "it is the light-paintings of images in the eyes that give us visual knowledge of objects," the confusion was evidently still deeply entrenched.[30]

For the presence of pictures in our eyes cannot enable us to discover anything about the world if we cannot see them. The retinal image is a screen image: it is caused by light that has been focused by a lens and then reflected by a screen. But in the first place, whether it is in an eye or on a wall, a screen image can only reveal the appearance of an object if it is seen; and second, the light that the retina reflects does not cause the changes in the nervous system that enable us to see.[31]

It may seem recalcitrant or literal minded to insist on these obvious facts. But it is necessary to insist on them because the theory of perspective proposed by psychologists in the Helmholtzian tradition demonstrates that if the immediate visual stimulus is thought of as an image, they will be ignored. It is true that the screen image that the retina reflects reveals the structure of the ambient light, and that vision depends on the effect of this structured ambient light on the retinal cells. But history proves that if these facts are elided or abbreviated in the thought that vision is caused by an image in the eye, confusion ensues.

When we see the visible objects that surround us, light radiates toward our eyes, the lenses in our eyes focus radiation from each point in the visual field, and a field of photoreceptors in each eye shifts back and forth across the focused beam of light and reacts to the radiation its encounters. The history of visual theory shows that it is extremely difficult to describe this as a process of image formation without imagining that the image functions like a picture. Kepler, Newton, and Helmholtz all made this mistake, and psychologists in the twentieth century made it in spades. It did not only affect the way they explained perspective. In a perfectly general way, it governed how they thought and reasoned about visual perception. This kind of mistake is a common one in science, and there is a good explanation of why it occurs in the book John Tyndall wrote about his friend and colleague Michael Faraday:

> In our conceptions and reasonings regarding the forces of nature, we perpetually make use of symbols that, when they possess a high representative value, we dignify with the name of theories. Thus, prompted by certain analogies, we ascribe electrical phenomena to the action of a peculiar fluid, sometimes flowing, sometimes at rest. Such conceptions have their advantages and their disadvantages; they afford peaceful lodging to the intellect for a time, but they also circumscribe it, and by-and-by, when the mind has grown too large for its lodging, it often finds difficulty in breaking down the walls of what has become its prison instead of its home.[32]

The idea that vision depends on the existence of an image in the eye guided Kepler when he discovered the geometry of the eye. By encouraging him to search for an upright image, it misled him, but it also enabled him to arrive at the correct solution. That is the moment at which the idea should have been abandoned, but it became the kind of prison that Tyndall mentions here instead. Tyndall also mentions that Faraday wanted to eradicate the word "current" from electrodynamics: "We can hardly divest it sufficiently of its meaning, or prevent our minds from being prejudiced by it," Faraday wrote.[33] Perhaps it would be best if the phrase "retinal image" were dropped altogether, at least until neurophysiology has matched the achievements of Faraday, Maxwell, and Hertz. But since this phrase is unlikely to be dropped, art historians and art theorists should consider texts in visual theory with great caution: in this case, the healthy dose of skepticism is large.

~

Thus, one source of confusion in the Helmholtzian tradition is muddled thinking about retinal images. The other is muddled thinking about visible objects and their properties. As I said, when I introduced the elementary techniques that perspective combines and coordinates, a circular wheel or shield has an elliptical occlusion shape, relative to an oblique line of sight; if two similar trees or columns are located at different distances from the spectator, the occlusion size of the nearer one will be greater; and if a uniformly colored object is illuminated from one side, that side will be brighter than the other. These properties are not merely appearances, if appearances are in the eye or in the mind. We can perceive them accurately or inaccurately; and when we perceive them inaccurately, we can correct our mistakes. Mistakes about occlusion shape and relative occlusion size can be corrected by measurement and calculation; and mistakes about brightness can be corrected with a light meter.

For example, when the photograph reproduced as figure 97 was taken, in the courtyard of the Palazzo Strozzi in Florence, the occlusion shapes of the arches were visible, and so were the relative occlusion sizes of the columns, the light and shade across their surfaces, and the shadows they cast. We do not always pay attention to these properties, as we do not always pay attention to the movements our fingers make when we tie our shoes. But the occlusion shapes and relative occlusion sizes of objects enable us to perceive their orientation and relative distance, and the variations in aperture color on their surfaces that are caused by variations in illumination enable us to perceive their solid forms.

Nevertheless, there is a long tradition in philosophy that says that occlusion shape, relative occlusion size, and aperture color belong in the mind or in the eye of the observer or that the experience we have when we see these properties is an illusion. This idea, like so many other seminal ideas in the the-

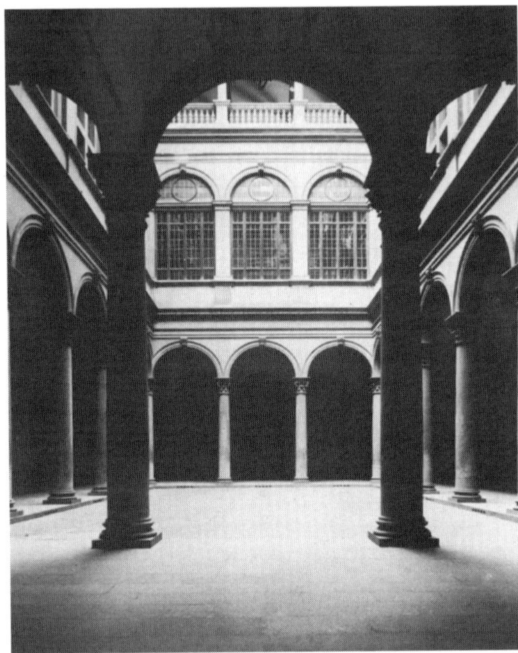

97. *Courtyard of the Palazzo Strozzi, Florence,* 1950s. Photograph.

ory of art, begins with Plato, who mentions it precisely to explain his disapproval of the new style of painting that used foreshortening and shading—the style he called *skiagraphia,* that is, shadow painting. Thus, in book 10 of the *Republic,* Socrates says this: "The same magnitude, I presume, viewed from near and from far does not appear equal . . . and the same things appear concave and convex, owing to similar errors of vision about colours. . . . So *skiagraphia,* which exploits this weakness of our nature, is a kind of witchcraft. . . . But the arts of measuring and numbering and weighing come to the rescue of the human understanding . . . and the apparently greater or less, or more, or heavier, no longer govern us, but are defeated by measurement and calculation."[34] Here, for comparison, is Hume: "All objects seem to diminish by their distance: But tho' the appearance of objects to our senses be the original standard, by which we judge of them, yet we do not say, that they actually diminish by the distance; but correcting the appearance by reflexion, arrive at a more constant and establish'd judgement concerning them."[35]

The prevailing tendency today is to identify what Hume calls "the appearance of objects to our senses" with the retinal image; to identify Hume's "constant and establish'd judgement" with Helmholtz's solid image in three dimensions; and to identify Hume's "reflexion" with the inferences or computations that transform the flat image in the eye into the solid one in the mind. (This is the view of Blakemore and Ramachandran, for example, as we have seen.) But Plato's basic idea—that occlusion shape, relative occlusion size, and relative brightness are literally or metaphorically in the eye of the observer—still soldiers on.

The influence of this idea on the theory of painting is not difficult to trace. For if we accept it, then we are likely to infer either that foreshortening and shading are used to represent objects *as they appear to us* rather than *as they are* or, alternatively, that they are used to represent retinal images, which we do not see, instead of the kinds of objects that we do see. The first inference was made by Plato. Winckelmann repeats it when he claims that "the earliest essays, especially in the drawing of figures, have represented, not the manner in which a man appears to us, but what he is." Panofsky repeats it again when he concludes his influential essay on perspective by describing it as "transforming the *ousia* (reality) into the *phainomenon* (appearance)." It has also become a familiar trope in art history, diligently repeated from one book to the next.[36] The second inference has dominated reflection on perspective in the Helmholtzian tradition, where occlusion shape, relative occlusion size, and relative brightness are attributed to the retinal image and described, as they are in the remarks by Blakemore and Ramachandran quoted above, as "clues to distance" or "cues to depth."

It is a nice irony that Plato's basic idea was originally used as a stick with which to beat modern painters. But whether it casts them in a poor light, for exploiting human weakness, or in a good light, for anticipating physiological optics, it is false. The relationship between an object's occlusion shape and its three-dimensional shape is an example neither of the relationship between appearance and reality nor of the relationship between the retinal image an object produces and the object itself. It is a geometrical relationship between two properties, both of which are real and both of which belong to the same object. As we have seen, an object's occlusion shape is relative to a line of sight, whereas its three-dimensional shape is not. But this does not impugn the reality or objectivity of its occlusion shape in the least—any more than the reality or objectivity of its three-dimensional shape is impugned by the fact, discovered by Einstein in 1905, that this property is relative to the inertial frame in which the object is observed.

The Helmholtzian theory of perspective can therefore be traced to the persistent influence of two ideas: first, that the function of our visual system is to enable us to perceive what an image represents and, second, that the properties of objects that foreshortening, diminution, and shading are used to depict are properties of these images. If we reject these ideas, we can see these techniques clearly and for what they are, namely, techniques for depicting the occlusion properties and the aperture colors of objects and parts of objects at different distances from an implicit point of view and from a source of light. Painters who use these techniques do not abandon reality for the shifting sands of mere appearance. And the system of perspective, which coordinates and harmonizes these techniques, is not an effective method for depicting space because sight is mediated by photographic pictures in our eyes. It is an effective method because the properties of real objects, whose depiction the system enables the artist to control, depend on their spatial relations to one another, to the spectator, and to the light.

CONCLUSION

I SHALL NOW BRING this book summarily to an end. In the first part, I examined the main evidence that is thought to support the doctrine that colors do not exist, or that they are relative to systems of concepts or to observers, or that they are subjective—in the sense of being dependent on the psychological effect that colored objects produce in our minds when we perceive them. I argued that the evidence is unconvincing and that there are conclusive reasons for refusing to accept that these doctrines are true. Since colors are the basic visible properties of objects—for whatever we see, we see by seeing colors—this removes the main obstacle to a reflective endorsement of the natural belief that sight enables us to perceive and, therefore, also to represent in art the objective world that we inhabit and not merely the effects it produces in our minds.

In the second part, I argued that it is possible to define the basic principles of pictorial art in objective terms, that is, without referring to the psychological effect that a picture produces in a spectator's mind, and that the nature of pictorial art cannot be explained subjectively, that is, by defining this effect. If this argument is correct, it is possible to conceive of pictures as conventional signs, in the sense Augustine gave this term, that is, as signs that human beings mutually exchange for the purpose of showing the feelings of their minds, or their perceptions, or their thoughts, without implicitly regarding the theory of pictorial art as a branch of optics or psychology—as Descartes, Helmholtz, and their successors in the twentieth century did.

Both of these parts of the book were concerned with ideas that were developed with great force in the seventeenth century and that have cast a long shadow across the theory of art since then. The ideas I discussed in the third part are more recent, but they have become equally well entrenched. There, I argued that a correct understanding of realistic art is threatened from two sides: from one side, by a form of nominalism that misrepresents the role that conventions can legitimately play in the theory of art and, from the other side, by a misconception of the process of visual perception itself, which underlies the dominant tradition in twentieth-century visual theory. I argued that realistic art is neither a familiar repertoire of conventions nor a series of techniques for trompe l'oeil and that Renaissance perspective is not a means by which painters match the images in our eyes. Rather, the evolution of realistic techniques extended the modality of pictorial art, as the evolution of languages has extended the range of meanings they are capable of expressing, and Renaissance perspective was a geometrical synthesis of the principal realistic techniques invented by Greek artists in the sixth and fifth centuries B.C.

The arguments with which I supported these various conclusions proceeded in the way that philosophy generally does, by drawing and examining distinctions. For the most part, these distinctions are well known to philosophers, and many have been the subject of intense debate. This is especially true of the distinctions between appearance and illusion, between relativism and pluralism, between three-dimensional shapes and occlusion shapes, between pictures and optical images, between names and predicates, between languages and codes—and, of course, it is true above all of the distinction between appearance and reality itself. I suppose it is unlikely that my arguments are satisfactory at every point. But I hope at least to have convinced the reader that the basic problems about pictorial art I have addressed cannot be solved unless these distinctions are thoroughly understood. This is my main reason, and the only reason of which I feel completely sure, for believing that philosophy can contribute to the theory of art at all.

NOTES

INTRODUCTION

1. *The Philosophical Writings of Descartes,* trans. J. Cottingham et al. (Cambridge: Cambridge University Press, 1985), 1:166.

2. Aristotle *Metaphysics* 1072a29; B. Spinoza, *Ethics,* pt. 3, prop. 9; Augustine *De vera religione* 32.59; Aquinas *De div. nom.* 4.10; D. Hume, *Enquiry concerning the Principles of Morals,* ed. L. A. Selby-Bigge (Oxford: Oxford University Press, 1957), app. 1, p. 294.

3. It is now widely believed that this attribution is false. See W. Burkert, *Lore and Science in Ancient Pythagoreanism,* trans. Edwin L. Minar, Jr. (Cambridge, Mass.: Harvard University Press, 1972). For a defense of the traditional view, see L. Zhmud, *Wissenschaft, Philosophie und Religion im frühen Pythagoreismus* (Berlin: Akademie Verlag, 1997).

4. Voltaire, "Beauté," *Philosophical Dictionary,* trans. T. Besterman (London: Penguin Books, 1972).

5. Pascal, *Pensées,* 473, in *Oeuvres Complètes,* ed. J. Chevalier (Paris: Gallimard, 1954), p. 1221.

6. "The Sceptic," in D. Hume, *Essays Moral, Political and Literary,* ed. E. F. Miller, rev. ed. (Indianapolis: Liberty Classics, 1987), p. 163.

7. I. Kant, *Critique of Judgement,* trans. W. Pluhar (Indianapolis: Hackett, 1987), §34, p. 149.

8. Lawrence Sterne, *The Life and Opinions of Tristram Shandy, Gentleman* (Oxford: Oxford University Press, 1998), 3:12.

9. "Of the Standard of Taste," in D. Hume, *Essays Moral, Political and Literary,* p. 235.

10. *Fernando Pessoa: Selected Poems,* trans. J. Griffin, 2d ed. (Harmondsworth: Penguin, 1982), p. 82.

CHAPTER ONE

The epigraph for this chapter comes from W. K. C. Guthrie, *A History of Greek Philosophy* (Cambridge: Cambridge University Press, 1962), 1:2.

1. Diels-Kranz 68 B 125 (Galen, *De medic. empir.*), H. Diels and W. Kranz, *Die Fragmente der Vorsokratiker,* 7th ed. (Berlin: Weidmann, 1954).

2. On the historical roots of the myth about colors, see E. J. Dijksterhuis, *The Mechanization of the World Picture,* trans. C. Dikshoorn (Oxford: Oxford University Press, 1961).

3. *Il Saggiatore* [The assayer], in *Le opere de Galileo Galilei,* ed. Antonio Favaro (Florence: S. A. G. Barbèra Editore, 1929–39), 6:347–48.

4. J. Gage, *Colour and Meaning* (London: Thames & Hudson, 1999), p. 46; S. Palmer, *Vision Science: Photons to Phenomenology* (Cambridge, Mass.: MIT Press, 1999), p. 95; S. Zeki, "Colour Coding in the Cerebral Cortex: The Reaction of Cells in Monkey Visual Cortex to Wavelengths and Colours," *Neuroscience* 9 (1983): 764. Similar claims can be found in R. L. Gregory, *Eye and Brain,* 3d ed. (London: Weidenfeld & Nicolson, 1977), pp. 77–78; I. Rock, *Perception* (New York: Scientific American Books, 1984), p. 4; H. Rossotti, *Colour* (Harmondsworth: Penguin, 1983), p. 16; F. Malin, *Understanding Paintings* (Oxford: Phaidon, 1980), p. 96; and in most psychology textbooks. When Palmer claims that "colour is a psychological property of our visual experiences," he means that we are aware of colors when we have these experiences and not that these experiences themselves are colored. Similarly, when Zeki says that color is a property of the brain, and not of the world outside, he means the same as Palmer does and not that the brain is colored but the rest of the world outside the skull is not.

5. W. V. O. Quine, "Two Dogmas of Empiricism," reprinted in Quine, *From a Logical Point of View* (Cambridge, Mass.: Harvard University Press, 1961), p. 36. It would be more accurate to say that whether the thought or proposition expressed by a sentence is true or false depends both on what the sentence means and on the facts. But Quine repudiated thoughts and propositions and held the controversial view that truth is a property of sentences.

6. Many philosophers have commented on the relationship between being yellow and looking yellow without appreciating that the idea of looking a certain way, or having a certain look, is already implicit in the thought that something *is* yellow—and that the relationship between being yellow and looking yellow is therefore comparable to the relationship between, say, having a lean and hungry look, as Cassius did, and looking as if one has a lean and hungry look, as a plump man in a sharp and slanting light or an actor made up for the role of Cassius might. As Grice pointed out, someone might look tough looking in the dim light of the passage, although as soon as he moved into the room it could be seen that really he looked quite gentle (Paul Grice, "Some Remarks about the Senses," reprinted in *Studies in the Way of Words* [Cambridge, Mass.: Harvard University Press, 1989], p. 258). The popular claim that an object is yellow if, and only if, it looks yellow to a standard observer in standard conditions has an obvious parallel here. For while it is not true that a man is tough if and only if he looks tough to a standard observer in standard conditions, it is approximately true that a man is tough looking if, and only if, he looks tough looking to a standard observer in standard conditions.

7. I owe this nice phrase to Jonathan Bennett.

8. J. C. Maxwell, "Theory of Compound Colors and the Relations of the Colors in the Spectrum," *Proceedings of the Royal Society* (1860), pp. 404–9. Compare J. C. Maxwell, "On Colour Vision," *Proceedings of the Royal Institute of Great Britain* 6 (1872): 260–71.

9. P. M. S. Hacker, *Appearance and Reality* (Oxford: Basil Blackwell, 1987), pp. 139–40.

10. In a similar vein, John Campbell has proposed that colors are "the grounds of the dispositions of objects to produce experiences of colour" ("A Simple View of Colour," in *Reality, Representation and Projection,* ed. J. Haldane and C. Wright [Oxford: Oxford University Press, 1993], p. 258). But this proposal fails for the same reason. It is true that

colored objects have a disposition to produce experiences of seeing colors. But this is not because an object's color is the ground, or origin, or cause of the disposition; it is because the color and the disposition have the same cause, namely, the object's tendency to absorb some wavelengths of light and to reflect or transmit others.

11. In particular, it would examine the neo-Platonist idea that only properties that are quantifiable are real. See above, n. 2.

12. Bernard Williams, *Descartes: The Project of Pure Enquiry* (Harmondsworth: Penguin, 1978), p. 242.

13. Thomas Nagel, *The View from Nowhere* (Oxford: Oxford University Press, 1986), p. 76.

14. J. L. Mackie, *Problems from Locke* (Oxford: Oxford University Press, 1976), p. 20.

15. There is sometimes a trade-off between simplicity and parsimony; but there is no exchange rate by which to regulate the trade. Hence, if objective methods for measuring simplicity and parsimony were devised, it still would not follow that a rational choice between two competing theories could always be made.

16. I. Kant, *Critique of Pure Reason,* A327/B384.

17. It has been argued that (1) if colors do not cause our perceptions, then these perceptions could have taken place without the colors existing and been just the same; but (2) we cannot be perceiving something if our experience could have been just the same without it; hence (3), if colors do not cause our perceptions, they cannot be properties we perceive. Howard Robinson (*Perception* [London: Routledge, 1994], p. 65) considers this argument and rejects it. Frank Jackson (*Perception* [Cambridge: Cambridge University Press, 1977], pp. 125–26) accepts that it is sound. If it were sound, our basic conception of colors would be contradictory because the principle that colors are inert and the principle that colors are visible would be inconsistent. But in fact both premises of the argument are false. Premise 1 is false because if A does not cause B, it does not follow that B could have taken place without A existing and been just the same. To return to an example I have already discussed, the color a hut is painted does not affect how quickly it heats up, but it would not have heated up so quickly if it had been painted a paler color. Premise 2 is false because one object—such as a star or the top sheet of paper on a pad—may precisely occlude another similar object. Hence, if the nearer star vanished suddenly, or if the sheet of paper were removed, our experience would be unaltered. But it does not follow that we were never really seeing the nearer star or the top sheet of paper at all.

18. Aristotle *De Anima* 2.7.419a12–13.

CHAPTER TWO

The epigraph for this chapter comes from R. B. Angel, *Relativity: The Theory and Its Philosophy* (Oxford: Pergamon, 1980), p. 109.

1. Both phrases are quoted from P. F. Strawson, "Perception and Its Objects," in *Perceptual Knowledge,* ed. J. Dancy (Oxford: Oxford University Press, 1988), pp. 109–10. Nagel claims, in a similar vein, that how something looks, feels, smells, tastes, or sounds is relative to a "general human perceptual point of view" (*The View from Nowhere* [Oxford: Oxford University Press, 1986], p. 14). Relativist claims about color are also made in M. A. E. Dummett, "Common Sense and Physics," in *Perception and Identity,* ed. G. F. Macdonald

(London: Macmillan, 1979), p. 16; D. Wiggins, *Needs, Values, Truth,* 3d ed. (Oxford: Oxford University Press, 1998), p. 107; Bernard Williams, *Descartes: The Project of Pure Enquiry* (Harmondsworth: Penguin, 1978), p. 243; C. McGinn, *The Subjective View: Secondary Qualities and Indexical Thoughts* (Oxford: Clarendon Press, 1983), p. 9.

2. However, we are able to make the simplest spatial and temporal judgments—e.g., about which of two remembered events occurred before the other—without using a ruler or a clock. I return to this point below.

3. On Runge, see J. Gage, *Colour and Culture* (London: Thames & Hudson, 1993), chap. 11, and *Colour and Meaning* (London: Thames & Hudson, 1999), chap. 13; R. G. Kuehni, *Colour Space and Its Divisions* (Hoboken, N.J.: John Wiley, 2003), pp. 59 ff. On Maxwell, see P. M. Harman, *The Natural Philosophy of James Clerk Maxwell* (Cambridge: Cambridge University Press, 2001), chap. 2.

4. The most prominent recent use in metaphysics of the notion of a point of view is made in Thomas Nagel's book *The View from Nowhere.* But Nagel's conception of objectivity involves a serious misunderstanding about the role that frames of reference play in physical theories. A note on this point may be of interest to readers familiar with Nagel's book.

In broad terms, Nagel argues that we can attain a more objective picture of the physical world by transcending the human point of view from which physical objects appear to have colors, by abandoning traditional ideas about space and time, and by moving toward a "view from nowhere"—a view from no point of view at all. Discarding the idea that physical objects have intrinsic colors is part of one step we have taken in this direction, under the guidance of Galileo and Descartes. And since special relativity implies that space and time are relative to an inertial frame, discarding shapes is part of another step. Nagel describes Einstein's "huge step" toward an objective view of the world as follows (p. 76):

> What formerly seemed to be an objective conception of absolute space and time was revealed to be a mere appearance, from the perspective of one frame of reference, of a world whose objective description from no frame of reference is not given in a four-dimensional coordinate system of independent spatial and temporal dimensions at all. Instead, objects are objectively located in relativistic space-time, whose division into separate spatial and temporal dimensions depends on one's point of view.

These remarks involve three issues: first, the contrast between Newton's conception of absolute space and absolute time and Einstein's discovery that spatial and temporal intervals are relative to inertial frames; second, the contrast between a description of the world from the perspective of one frame of reference or another and a description from the perspective of no frame of reference at all; and third, the idea expressed in Minkowski's famous remark, "Henceforth, space by itself, and time by itself, are doomed to fade away into mere shadows," which I comment on below.

The issue that is immediately relevant to Nagel's notion of objectivity is the second. Special relativity, he suggests, is an advance toward an objective view of the world because Newtonian physics describes physical phenomena "from the perspective of one frame of reference," whereas special relativity describes them "from no frame of reference". But this could not be further from the truth. The principle of special relativity is indeed that physical laws, including the laws of electrodynamics, are the same in all inertial frames. But it does not follow that special relativity enables us to describe the world from no frame of reference. No such description is possible. There is no description of the world in which "objects are objectively located" from no frame of reference because without a reference frame we cannot assign spatial or temporal quantities to natural phenomena at all. It is therefore a mistake to think of any physical theory as providing a view from nowhere of the physical world.

5. W. V. O. Quine, *The Roots of Reference* (LaSalle, Ill.: Open Court, 1973), p. 71.

6. The pioneering work was published in B. Berlin and P. Kay, *Basic Color Terms: Their Universality and Evolution* (Berkeley: University of California Press, 1969). The basic color terms they identify are black, white, red, green, yellow, blue, brown, purple, pink, orange, and gray. Some aspects of their work remain controversial, but the simple point that basic colors are not linguistic artifacts is not.

7. Except that there is no contraction orthogonal to the direction of its motion.

8. J. L. Austin, *Sense and Sensibilia* (Oxford; Oxford University Press, 1962), p. 66. C. L. Hardin, *Colour for Philosophers* (Indianapolis: Hackett, 1988), pp. 67 ff.) discusses several other less familiar cases where the idea of standard conditions is inapplicable.

9. The assumption is necessary because a suitably designed color chart will enable a trichromat to assign gross colors belonging to a dichromatic system, although not the reverse.

10. E. R. Dodds suggests that the antithesis was first explicitly discussed in the field of medicine: "Are health and sickness determined mainly by a man's phusis, his 'constitution' as we say, or mainly by his nomos, i.e., his customary regime of diet, exercise, and so forth? But very soon the problem assumed an ampler scope. When law and human nature conflict, which ought we to follow? Is the social restraint which law imposes on nature a good or a bad thing? For the Sophists that was the grand question" ("The Sophistic Movement and the Failure of Greek Liberalism," in *The Ancient Concept of Progress and Other Essays* (Oxford: Oxford University Press, 1973), p. 99.

11. D. Hume, "Of the Standard of Taste," in *Essays Moral, Political and Literary,* ed. E. F. Miller, rev. ed. (Indianapolis: Liberty Classics, 1987), p. 234.

12. Williams, *Descartes,* p. 242. Williams also describes the *term* "green" as "relative, relating to human tastes and interests" (p. 243), and says that *concepts* of secondary qualities are "peculiarly relative to our experience" (p. 244). For the full argument, see Williams, *Descartes,* pp. 240–46. My general impression of this complex argument is that Williams fails to distinguish with sufficient care between the question of which truths are "peculiarly relative to our experience" and which concepts are anthropocentric. This leads him to infer from the anthropocentricity of our system of gross color concepts, to which he rightly draws attention, that objects do not "'really' have one color rather than another."

13. Strawson, "Perception and Its Objects," p. 112.

14. The thought that agreement provides this guarantee can also be founded on a general commitment to the notion that truth cannot outstrip best opinion. There are compelling reasons to reject this idealistic doctrine, but they are not relevant here since, if it were true, it would have no special application in the case of colors. On this topic, see W. Künne, *Conceptions of Truth* (Oxford: Oxford University Press, 2003), chap. 7.

15. But human nature does not leave us a totally free hand. Rules of pronunciation are constrained by the shape of the human mouth and tongue, and norms of politeness by

natural reactions of disgust. For example, it could not be a conventional expression of gratitude for a meal to vomit on one's host.

16. D. Armstrong, *Perception and the Physical World* (London: Routledge & Kegan Paul, 1961), p. 182.

17. I ignore the point that in many states the highest court of appeal will not decide questions of fact.

18. Precisely this kind of mistake has led some physicists and philosophers to embrace an idealist interpretation of special relativity. They have mistakenly supposed that the basis of the theory does consist in hypotheses about the behavior of clocks and measuring rods. There is an excellent discussion of such an interpretation (namely, Eddington's) in Angel, *Relativity: The Theory and Its Philosophy,* pp. 104 ff.

19. H. Minkowski, "Space and Time," reprinted in A. Einstein et al., *The Principle of Relativity* (1923; reprint, New York: Dover, n.d.), p. 75.

20. Something similar can also be said about the colors of physical objects and their spectral reflectances. It is true that surface colors are caused by reflectances, and that reflectances have a broader explanatory competence than colors; but it does not follow that colors are less real. Equally, the shapes of planets are caused by mechanical forces and the shapes of crystals are caused by electrical forces; but it does not follow that the shapes are less real than the forces.

21. Plato *Phaedrus* 265d–266a.

CHAPTER THREE

1. John Ruskin, *Modern Painters I* (1843), complete edition (Sunnyside: G. Allen, 1888), pt. 2, sec. 1, chap. 5, §3.

2. Descartes, *Principles of Philosophy,* 1.68, in *The Philosophical Writings of Descartes,* trans. J. Cottingham et al. (Cambridge: Cambridge University Press, 1985), 1:217. John Locke, *An Essay concerning Human Understanding,* ed. R. Woodhouse (London: Penguin, 1977).

3. See above, p. 17. There are also passages, both in the *Optics* and in the *Principles of Philosophy,* which would support a reductionist interpretation of Descartes's view about colors. See, for example, pp.70 and 218 in *The Philosophical Writings of Descartes.*

4. Newton expresses a similar idea as follows, although he is speaking about light, rather than the bodies that reflect it: "The homogeneal Light and Rays which appear red, or rather make Objects appear so, I call Rubrifick or Red-making; those which make objects appear yellow, green, blue and violet, I call Yellow-making, Green-making, Blue-making, Violet-making, and so of the rest. . . . For the rays to speak properly are not coloured. In them there is nothing else than a certain Power and Disposition to stir up a Sensation of this or that Colour" (*Opticks,* 4th ed. (London, 1731), bk. 1, pt. 1, definition).

5. Locke avoids the controversial question of how light interacts with colored bodies. Writing of porphyry, he simply claims that "it has, indeed, such a configuration of particles, both night and day, as are apt, by the rays of light rebounding from some parts of that hard stone, to produce in us the idea of redness, and from others the idea of whiteness" (2.8.19). There is an excellent discussion of the controversy in A. I. Sabra, *Theories*

of Light from Descartes to Newton (Cambridge: Cambridge University Press, 1981), chaps. 9–11.

6. I owe the useful phrase "blank sensory effects" to Michael Ayers (*Locke* [London: Routledge, 1991], vol. 1, chap. 7.

7. Locke also writes: "Yellowness is not actually in gold, but is a power in gold to produce that idea in us by our eyes, when placed in a due light" (2.13.10). In this remark, he seems to deny that gold is actually yellow; but it is probably best understood as meaning that yellowness (being a power) is a potentiality, and not an actuality, in gold. He also claims that bodies would not be colored if there were no sentient animals with eyes to see them: "Were there no fit organs to receive the impressions fire makes on the sight and touch, nor a mind joined to those organs to receive the ideas of light and heat by those impressions from the fire or sun, there would yet be no more light or heat in the world than there would be pain if there were no sensible creature to feel it" (2.31.2). This is plainly inconsistent with what I have identified as his key idea. Finally, he also writes: "What is Sweet, Blue, or Warm in *Idea,* is but the certain Bulk, Figure and Motion of the insensible Parts in the bodies themselves, which we call so" (2.8.15). This remark is not pellucid, but it seems to identify the colors of bodies not with powers to produce sensations or ideas but with the physical structure that explains why bodies have these powers.

8. J. McDowell, *Mind, Value and Reality* (Cambridge, Mass.: Harvard University Press, 1998), p. 134.

9. This view was quite widely held in Oxford in the twentieth century. W. Kneale, for example, writes as follows: "When Locke said that the secondary qualities were powers in things to produce sensations in us, he stated the fact correctly, but he did not realize that his statement was only an analysis of the plain man's use of secondary quality adjectives" ("Sensation and the Physical World," *Philosophical Quarterly* 1 [1951]: 123). I am grateful to Keith Allen for drawing this remark to my attention.

10. B. Stroud, *The Quest for Reality* (Oxford: Oxford University Press, 2000), p. 41.

11. Whether it actually is contradictory is another matter. Locke thought it was not. He claims that "one may truly be said to see Darkness. For supposing a hole perfectly black, from whence no light is reflected, 'tis certain one may see the Figure of it, or it may be Painted" (2.8.3, 2.8.6).

12. I owe some of the points in this passage to Colin McGinn, who argues cogently against his own earlier position on the nature of colors in "Another Look at Colour," reprinted in *Knowledge and Reality* (Oxford: Oxford University Press, 1999). See esp. pp. 300 ff.

13. A famous argument in Wittgenstein's *Philosophical Investigations* (trans. G. E. M. Anscombe [Oxford: Basil Blackwell, 1953], §293) demonstrates that if color words were, in the first instance, names of sensations, we could not use them to communicate. The argument is explicitly about bodily sensations, such as aches and pains. But it applies with equal force to sensations of color or of taste.

Suppose each person has a box and uses the word "beetle" as the name of whatever it contains, but nobody has access to the contents of another person's box. If the word "beetle" is construed as a name of what is in a person's box, the object it names can play no role whatever in the transactions we conduct with words. For no one can know what the word "beetle" is the name of, when another person uses it. It could be the name of any kind of thing that fits into his box or of nothing at all, if his box is empty. In the same way, if we construe the word "red" as the name of a sensation, the sensation drops out of consideration as irrelevant. Whatever this experience is, and whatever it is like, it is powerless to affect our use of words, when we communicate. Hence, we cannot consistently maintain that "red" is the name of a sensation and that we use this sensation to define the property of being red.

It is easy to imagine that if we describe something we perceive as red, this must be the result of comparing it—subliminally, perhaps—with a memory image of redness, stored in the mind. Hence, the meanings of "red" must, in the final analysis, depend on the nature of this mental image. Wittgenstein addressed the premise of this argument as follows:

> If I give someone the order "fetch me a red flower from that meadow," how is he to know what sort of flower to bring, as I have only given him a *word*?
>
> Now the answer one might suggest first is that he went to look for a red flower carrying a red image in his mind, and comparing it with the flowers to see which of them had the colour of the image. . . . To see that the process of obeying the order [need not] be of this kind, consider the order "*imagine* a red patch." You are not tempted in this case to think that *before* obeying you must have imagined a red patch to serve as a pattern for the red patch which you were ordered to imagine. (*The Blue and Brown Books*, 2d ed. [Oxford: Basil Blackwell, 1969], p. 3)

14. C. McGinn, *The Subjective View* (Oxford: Oxford University Press, 1983), p. 7. Similar arguments appear in J. McDowell, "Values and Secondary Qualities," reprinted in *Mind, Value and Reality*, p. 134; and D. Wiggins, "A Sensible Subjectivism," in *Needs, Values, Truth*, 3rd ed. (Oxford: Oxford University Press, 1998), p. 189.

15. Immanuel Kant, *Critique of Pure Reason*, A42/B59.

16. For example, Alex Byrne and David Hilbert identify the colors of bodies and surfaces with types of reflectance; and David Armstrong identifies colors with the microphysical structures of bodies that explain their reflectances. See Alex Byrne and David R. Hilbert "Colors and Reflectances" and David M. Armstrong, "Smart and Secondary Qualities," both in *Readings on Color*, ed. Alex Byrne and David R. Hilbert (Cambridge, Mass.: MIT Press, 1997), vol. 1.

17. *The Philosophical Writings of Descartes*, 1:216.

18. Aristotle *Metaphysics* 1072a29; B. Spinoza *Ethics* 3.9.

19. See, e.g., McGinn, *The Subjective View*, p. 6, n. 2.

20. Wiggins, "Truth, Invention and the Meaning of Life," pp. 106–7.

CHAPTER FOUR

In the original French, the epigraph to this chapter reads: "L'essence et la définition de la peinture, est l'imitation des objets visibles par le moyen de forme et des couleurs" (Roger de Piles, *Cours de peinture par principes* [Paris, 1708], p. 3). For our purposes, this serves as a pithy expression of an orthodox view. Its significance in de Piles's theory of art is discussed in T. Puttfarken, *Roger de Piles' Theory of Art* (New Haven, Conn.: Yale University Press, 1985), chap. 2.

1. D. Davidson expresses the same idea with a physical metaphor instead of a political one, when he says that concept are sometimes "sustained in equilibrium by a number of conceptual pressures" ("Mental Events," reprinted in *Essays on Actions and Events* [Oxford: Oxford University Press, 1980], p. 221).

2. See, e.g., Roger Scruton, "Representation in Music," reprinted in *The Aesthetic Understanding* (London: Methuen, 1983); and P. Kivy, *Sound and Semblance* (Ithaca, N.Y.: Cornell University Press, 1991), pp. 146 ff.

3. Roger Scruton, "Photography and Representation," reprinted in *The Aesthetic Understanding*, pp. 103 and 114.

4. G. W. F. Hegel, *Aesthetics: Lectures on Fine Art*, trans. T. M. Knox (Oxford: Oxford University Press, 1975), 2:799.

5. Recent scholarship supports the revisionist opinion that the attitude to painting Plato expresses here is less dismissive, more nuanced, and more colored with irony than was formerly thought. Two recent studies to which I am indebted are C. Janaway, *Images of Excellence* (Oxford: Oxford University Press, 1995); and S. Halliwell, *The Aesthetics of Mimesis* (Princeton, N.J.: Princeton University Press, 2002).

6. Leon Battista Alberti, *On Painting*, trans. J. R. Spencer, rev. ed. (New Haven, Conn.: Yale University Press, 1966), p. 43. The verb translated here as "represent" is *imitari;* the Italian text has *fingiere*. Both of these verbs are intended to express the Greek concept of mimesis.

7. This formulation implies that if Brutus killed Caesar by stabbing him, the killing and the stabbing are distinct actions. This claim is defended in detail in M. Alvarez and J. Hyman, "Agents and Their actions," *Philosophy* 73 (April 1998): 219–45.

8. Basic representation is therefore similar to the representation of what E. Panofsky calls the "primary or natural subject matter" of a picture (see *Studies in Iconology* [Oxford: Oxford University Press, 1939], p. 5).

9. A. N. Prior (*The Doctrine of Propositions and Terms* [London: Duckworth, 1976], p. 29) remarks that the general notion of a many-termed relation seems to be a relatively recent one and suggests that it was formed by about 1870. Notice that *being the same man [or ship, etc.] as* is not a way in which one thing can stand to another thing and, therefore, not a relation, in my view. On the question of whether identity is a relation, see n. 11 below.

10. The verb "portray" was given its modern sense of a likeness of an individual only in the seventeenth century, by André Félibien. The French engraver Abraham Bosse still used "portraiture" as a term for painting and engraving in general. The phrase "namely rider" was coined by G. Ryle (see "Heterologicality" reprinted in *Collected Papers* [London: Unwin Hyman, 1971], 2:250–57). Beginning with Nelson Goodman, most writers on this subject have drawn a similar distinction. For example Malcolm Budd, who follows Goodman on this point more closely than I do, writes: "When an item is said to be a picture of a man or a boy or anything else, there are two ways in which this remark can be understood: it can be understood to license existential generalization or not to license it. If the remark is intended to license existential generalization, it follows from the fact that something is a picture of a man that there is or was a man of whom it is a picture; if the remark is understood otherwise, this conclusion does not follow (although it may in fact be true)"

(*Values of Art* [Harmondsworth: Penguin, 1995], p. 66). How exactly this distinction relates to mine depends on how the phrase "there is" is to be understood. If it is to be understood in a way that licenses the inference from "it is a picture of the Styx" to "there is a river of which it is a picture," then Budd's distinction and mine are, in effect, the same. Otherwise, they are not.

11. Wittgenstein denied that identity is a relation (see *Tractatus Logico-Philosophicus*, trans. D. F. Pears and B. F. McGuinness [London: Routledge & Kegan Paul, 1961], 5.5303). A detailed argument supporting this position can be found in C. J. F. Williams, *What Is Identity?* (Oxford: Oxford University Press, 1989).

12. This still leaves the case where a picture represents a particular fictional character, river, etc., which calls for a different reply to the objection because if something is said to resemble Malvolio or the Styx, one thing *is* being related to another. But the objection is unconvincing in this kind of case as well because it is possible to argue either that fictional characters, rivers, etc. do exist or, alternatively, that they do not but that this does not prevent them from resembling something.

The most plausible defense of the view that fictional characters exist is in a series of unpublished lectures by Saul Kripke (Reference and Existence, John Locke Lectures, Oxford University, 1973.) Kripke argues that a fictional character is a kind of abstract entity, which exists in virtue of more concrete activities that human beings engage in, such as telling stories, performing plays, writing novels, and so on. He mentions, by analogy, a nation, "which exists in virtue of concrete relations between people." Nations certainly exist. But a true statement about a nation "is true in virtue of, and solely in virtue of, the activities of the people," although there is no guarantee that every true statement about a nation can be exactly paraphrased by a series of statements about the activities of particular people, which do not mention any nations. Similarly, a true statement about Malvolio is true solely in virtue of what Shakespeare wrote, although there is no guarantee that every true statement about Malvolio can be exactly paraphrased by a series of statements about Shakespeare. Moreover, just as it is an empirical question whether a certain nation existed—the Edomites, say—it is an empirical question whether such and such a fictional character exists: "Was there a fictional character who married her uncle?" If there was, this will be true in virtue of appropriate works of fiction having been written, or at least told orally, or something of the kind. If there is such a fictional work, then there is such a fictional character.

The second option is to concede that fictional characters do not exist but to insist that they can still resemble things. According to this view, there cannot be predication without reference. For example, it is not possible to state that JH resembles Malvolio without referring both to Malvolio and to me. But reference does not require existence. What it does require is that the speaker be able to identify whatever she is referring to, with a gesture, for example, or by name, or by means of a description. And this is not ruled out if one of the things being referred to is a fictional character. On the contrary, identifying a fictional character is something we can do quite easily. For example, we can identify Malvolio by saying that he is the character in *Twelfth Night* who wears yellow stockings with cross-gartering. Hence, the statement that JH resembles Malvolio cannot be disputed on the grounds that Malvolio is a fictional character; and if I am wearing yellow stockings with cross-gartering, the statement is true.

My own view is that some fictional characters, places, etc. are more fictional than others. For example, Augie March is more fictional than Abe Ravelstein. The mark of a completely fictional character, as the conventional disclaimer attests, is that any resemblance to an actual person, living or dead, is (at the time of writing) coincidental: it is not that none is possible. (The parenthetical qualification is needed because fictional characters can be imitated.) A character is therefore fictional to the extent that this condition is satisfied. For this reason, I accept that one of the two positions outlined is correct; but I shall not adjudicate between them here. I shall only add this. The difficulty one has to confront in order to decide between them is that philosophers associate existence with the denominable, the denumerable, and the nonfictional. But these concepts do not coincide, because fictional characters can be named and counted. For example, there are nine characters in *Uncle Vanya,* and all but one of them have names. Hence, in order to decide between the two positions we would need to decide which of these associations to give up.

13. For example, Panofsky quotes the following remark by Guido Hauck—a far from casual writer on perspective: "To express ourselves entirely correctly, we must say: parallel lines are represented in a picture thus that if we could extend them sufficiently, their extension within the picture would intersect at one and the same point" (*Lehrbuch der malerischen Perspektive* [Berlin: Springer, 1910], p. 24, quoted in E. Panofsky, *Perspective as Symbolic Form,* trans. C. S. Wood [New York: Zone Books, 1991], p. 103, n. 22). "Thus Guido Hauck, quite correctly," Panofsky adds. On Panofsky and Hauck, see chap. 10 in this volume.

14. Jacques Derrida—closer to Plato at this point than to Magritte—describes the proposition that "shoes are shoes, be they painted or 'real'" as a dogma, which "cannot withstand the slightest scrutiny" (*The Truth in Painting* [Chicago: University of Chicago Press, 1987], pp. 313–14). This remark occurs in the course of Derrida's discussion of Meyer Schapiro's celebrated article "The Still Life as Personal Object—a Note on Heidegger and Van Gogh," reprinted in *Theory and Philosophy of Art: Style, Artist, and Society* (New York: George Braziller, 1994). Perhaps the best assessment of the Heidegger/Schapiro/Derrida controversy is in Michael Kelly, *Iconoclasm in Aesthetics* (Cambridge: Cambridge University Press, 2003).

15. Augustine *In Joannis Evangelium* 24.2.

16. L. Wittgenstein, *Remarks on the Philosophy of Psychology,* ed. G. H. von Wright and Heikki Nyman, trans. C. G. Luckhardt and M. A. E. Aue (Oxford: Blackwell, 1980), vol. 2, §447.

17. Locke writes: "When we set before our eyes a round globe of any uniform colour, v.g. gold, alabaster, or jet, it is certain that the idea thereby imprinted on our mind is of a flat circle, variously shadowed, with several degrees of light and brightness coming to our eyes" (*An Essay concerning Human Understanding,* 2.9.8). Berkeley writes: "In a strict sense, I see nothing but lights and colours, and their several shades and variations" (*An Essay towards a New Theory of Vision,* §130). Compare Bertrand Russell, *Our Knowledge of the External World* (Chicago: Open Court, 1914), pp. 84–85.

18. Nelson Goodman, *Languages of Art: An Approach to a Theory of Symbols* (London: Oxford Univeristy Press, 1969), p. 8.

19. Quoted in John Gage, *Colour and Culture* (London: Thames & Hudson, 1993), p. 209.

20. Quoted in E. H. Gombrich, *Art and Illusion*, 5th ed. (Oxford: Phaidon, 1977), pp. 250 ff.

21. H. von Helmholtz, *Populäre Wissenschaftliche Vorträge*, 3 vols. (Braunschweig: Friedrich Vieweg & Sohn, 1865–76), 3:58.

22. M. Merleau-Ponty, "Cezanne's Doubt," reprinted in *Sense and Non-Sense*, trans. H. L. Dreyfus and P. A. Dreyfus (Evanston, Ill.: Northwestern University Press, 1964), p. 11.

23. M. Schapiro, *Impressionism: Reflections and Perceptions* (New York: George Braziller, 1997), p. 56. This explanation of impressionist painting was already proposed by Jules Antione Castagnary in 1874: "They are *impressionists* in the sense that they render not the landscape, but the sensation produced by the landscape" ("L'exposition du boulevard des Capucines: Les impressionistes," reprinted in *Centenaire de L'impressionisme*, ed. H. Adhemar and A. Clark [Paris: Edition des Musées Nationaux, 1974], p. 265). There is a good discussion of Castagnary's response to impressionism in R. Shiff, *Cézanne and the End of Impressionism* (Chicago: University of Chicago Press, 1984), pp. 3 ff.

24. Goodman also argues that "A resembles B" does not imply "A represents B":

> An object resembles itself to the maximum degree but rarely represents itself; resemblance, unlike representation, is reflexive. Again, unlike representation, resemblance is symmetric: **B** is as much like **A** as **A** is like **B**, but while a painting may represent the Duke of Wellington, the Duke doesn't represent the painting. Furthermore, in many cases neither one of a pair of very like objects represents the other: none of the automobiles off an assembly line is a picture of any of the rest; and a man is not normally a representation of another man, even his twin brother. (*Languages of Art*, p. 4)

Arguably, resemblance is not reflexive because "A resembles B" implies that A can be compared with B—although of course it does not imply that A has actually been compared with B—and nothing can be compared with itself. More precisely, Jimmy at the age of seven can be compared with Jimmy at the age of five, and Guinness in Dublin can be compared with Guinness in Cork; but A in a certain place and at a certain time cannot be compared with A in the same place and at the same time. Staring intently at an object or studying a description of it will not count as comparing it with itself, whatever the purpose of the exercise, and whatever the thoughts accompanying it are. Hence "A resembles A" is not true. It is a difficult question whether it is false or whether it is neither false nor true, and one that need not be decided here.

Apart from this, the passage quoted is convincing, and Goodman is right to conclude that "resemblance in any degree is no sufficient condition for representation" (*Languages of Art*, p. 4). To my knowledge, no philosopher before Goodman entertained the possibility that it is.

CHAPTER FIVE

The epigraph for this chapter comes from Pliny, *Natural History*, trans. H. Rackman (London: Loeb Classical Library, 1952), 35.15.

1. *The Philosophical Writings of Descartes*, trans. J. Cottingham et al. (Cambridge: Cambridge University Press, 1985), 1:165.

2. The locus classicus for this use of the idea of a point of view is Bernard Williams,

Descartes: The Project of Pure Enquiry (Harmondsworth: Penguin, 1978), chap. 8. John McDowell criticizes Williams's metaphorical extension of the idea of a point of view in "Aesthetic Value, Objectivity and the Fabric of the World," reprinted in *Mind, Value and Reality* (Cambridge, Mass.: Harvard University Press, 1998). But he is content to introduce the distinction between appearance and reality by means of the example of occlusion shape because in this case no metaphor is involved: "The way the world really is must be distinguished from the way the world appears to be only because the recipient of the appearance occupies some local or parochial point of view. An illustration of this distinction, with a literal application of the notion of a point of view, is afforded by the way we correct for the angle from which we are observing a plane surface when we form a judgment about its true shape" (p. 117). Compare the following remark by D. Hume: "All objects seem to diminish by their distance: But tho' the appearance of objects to our senses be the original standard, by which we judge of them, yet we do not say, that they actually diminish by the distance; but correcting the appearance by reflexion, arrive at a more constant and establish'd judgement concerning them" (*A Treatise on Human Nature*, ed. L. A. Selby-Bigge, 2d edition ed. P. H. Nidditch (Oxford: Clarendon Press, 1978), 3.3.3; I comment on this remark in the text, p. 99).

3. A novel variant on the idea that occlusion shapes are not "real qualities in the subject" is defended in C. Peacocke, *Sense and Content* (Oxford: Oxford University Press, 1983), chap. 1. I have criticized Peacocke's argument in "Subjectivism in the Theory of Pictorial Art," *Monist: Art and the Mind* 86 (October 2003): 676–701.

4. G.W.F. Hegel's analysis of the difference between painting and sculpture and his general theory of painting are partly founded on a confusion between the implicit line of sight and the line of sight of a notional spectator: "[In painting,] the spectator is as it were in it from the beginning," he writes, "is counted in with it, and the work only exists for this fixed point, i.e. for the individual apprehending it." (*Aesthetics: Lectures on Fine Art*, trans. T. M. Knox [Oxford: Oxford University Press, 1975], 2:806). Hegel's principal claim about painting is that since it "renounces the totality of space" (because it consists of marks on a surface), its subject matter is "only a pure appearance of the spiritual inner life which art presents for the spirit's apprehension" (2:805). This claim is difficult to interpret, but it seems to be the result of injecting a spiritual meaning into Descartes's claim that depiction must be explained subjectively because pictures "represent to us bodies of varying relief and depth on a surface which is entirely flat."

5. L. Wittgenstein, *Philosophical Grammar*, ed. Rush Rhees, trans. Anthony Kenny (Oxford: Basil Blackwell, 1974), p. 76; cf. G. Frege, *The Foundations of Arithmetic* (Oxford: Basil Blackwell, 1953), 2, §56.

6. There is an excellent discussion of the frontal and profile views in European medieval art, to which I am indebted here, in Meyer Schapiro, *Words and Pictures* (The Hague: Mouton, 1973), chap. 4.

7. So-called reversed perspective representations were made in the same way, and "composite" would therefore be a more accurate term. We should therefore be skeptical about the more speculative interpretations of so-called reversed perspective, such as the one advanced by Pavel Florensky (see *Beyond Vision*, ed. N. Misler [London: Reaktion, 2002]). In fact, there is no more reason to invest it with a religious meaning than there would be to interpret Master Betram's pavement in this way.

8. Erwin Panofsky's claims that the "vanishing axis principle was . . . crucial in antique

spatial representation" and that Master Bertram "constructs his tile floors entirely according to the vanishing-axis principle" are unsupported (*Perspective as Symbolic Form,* trans. C. S. Wood [New York: Zone Books, 1991], pp. 39, 59.). We cannot infer from the fact that it is possible to provide a certain kind of geometrical description of a painting that a corresponding method of construction was employed.

9. Julien Levy, *Memoir of an Art Gallery* (New York: Putnam, 1977), p. 177.

10. There is a good discussion of the use of single and multiple vanishing points as organizing principles in fifteenth-century painting in J. White, *The Birth and Rebirth of Pictorial Space,* 2d ed. (London: Faber & Faber, 1967), pp. 196 ff.

11. Melissa Hyde, "The 'Make-Up' of the Marquise: Boucher's *Portrait of Pompadour at Her Toilette,*" *Art Bulletin* 82 (September 2000): 453–75. The distinction between a portrait of the artist and a self-portrait is discussed in V. Stoichita, *The Self-Aware Image,* trans. A.-M. Glasheen (Cambridge: Cambridge University Press, 1997), chap. 8.

12. Charles Harrison drew my attention to this example. Other examples are discussed in R. Wollheim, *Painting as an Art* (London: Thames & Hudson, 1987), chap. 3. Perhaps the first occurrence of an implicit spectator in art is in self-portraiture because here it can be produced by accident, before it is consciously observed. The idea was developed in art history as a theoretical tool in A. Riegl's analysis of Rembrandt's *The Staalmeesters.* Riegl himself said that he owed the idea to Théophile Thoré-Bürger, who "correctly presumed the presence of an unseen party in the space of the viewer, with whom the syndics are negotiating" (*The Group Portraiture of Holland,* trans. E. M. Kain [Los Angeles: Getty Research Institute, 1999], p. 285).

13. Shakespeare, *Richard II,* act 2, scene 2, lines 18–19.

14. A concise discussion of anamorphosis in Greek art can be found in E. C. Keuls, *Plato and Greek Painting* (Leiden: E. J. Brill, 1978), pp. 111 ff.

15. Note that caricature is not an exception to the occlusion shape principle because the principle is about the relationship between the marks on a picture's surface and the objects we see in the picture—i.e., the objects it depicts. It is not about the relationship between the marks on a picture's surface and the persons or events that it portrays. If we lose sight of this distinction, a portrait caricature may seem to disprove the principle because the subject's features are distorted in the drawing. Surely, we may think, the occlusion shape of his nose did not have quite the same shape as this part of the drawing. Perhaps not. But if this seems like an exception to the occlusion shape principle, it is because we are confusing the face depicted and the face portrayed. The former is a distorted version of the latter, but the correspondence that is prescribed by the occlusion shape principle, between the picture's surface and the face that it depicts, still holds.

16. *The Philosophical Writings of Descartes,* 2:27.

17. Hume, *A Treatise on Human Nature,* 3.3.3.

18. L. Wittgenstein, *Remarks on Colour,* ed. G. E. M. Anscombe (Oxford: Basil Blackwell, 1977).

19. J. L. Austin, *Sense and Sensibilia* (Oxford: Oxford University Press, 1962), pp. 65–66.

20. E. H. Gombrich, *Shadows: The Depiction of Cast Shadows in Western Art* (London: The National Gallery, 1995), is an attractive introduction to the topic. See also M. Baxandall, *Shadows and Enlightenment* (New Haven, Conn.: Yale University Press, 1995), esp. chap. 2.

21. Coleridge observed nicely that "the difference . . . must blend with and balance

the likeness, in order to constitute a just imitation" (S. T. Coleridge, *Biographia Literaria,* ed. J. Engell and W. Jackson Bate [Princeton, N.J.: Princeton University Press, 1983], 1:76n).

22. Plato *Cratylus* 432b–c.

23. C. S. Peirce noted this qualification: see *Elements of Logic*, §2, 230, in *Collected Papers*, ed. C. Hartshorne and P. Weiss, 8 vols. (Cambridge, Mass.: Harvard University Press, 1960), 2:136.

CHAPTER SIX

1. On this topic, see A. I. Sabra, *Theories of Light from Descartes to Newton* (Cambridge: Cambridge University Press, 1981), esp. chap. 1.

2. See chap. 1, this volume.

3. Descartes, *Philosophical Writings* 1:152.

4. Ibid., 1:153.

5. Descartes, *De placitis Hippocratis et Platonis,* 7.7.

6. Descartes, *Philosophical Writings* 1:153.

7. Aristotle *De anima* 418b21.

8. Descartes, *Philosophical Writings* 1:153. This is similar to Galileo's fallacious argument about the tickle a feather produces in my nose, which I discussed in chapter 1. It is true that the sensation of hardness does not resemble something present in the rock, and the sensation of sponginess does not resemble something present in the turf. That would only be the case if the rock and the turf had sensations of their own. Similarly, nothing in a blade of grass resembles the experience of seeing the color green, and nothing in a flame resembles the experience of seeing light. But there is no reason to infer that our experience of light and color disguises the real nature of the bodies we perceive or that colors can be reduced to the ways in which bodies absorb and reflect light. Equally, nothing in the blade of grass or the flame resembles the experience of seeing its shape. But we do not infer that the experience of shape is an illusion. In every case, the question of whether our experience resembles something in the objects we perceive is irrelevant to the question of whether the qualities we perceive really exist.

9. Ibid., 1:153–54.

10. Ibid., 1:153; cf. Aristotle *De sensu* 440a15.

11. Descartes, *Philosophical Writings,* 1:165–66.

12. Ibid., 1:165.

13. Ibid., 1:165–66.

14. Ibid., 1: 166.

15. Ibid., 1: 166–67. In the fifth discourse, Descartes describes an experiment with the eye of a dead ox that will confirm the existence of the retinal images and postulates a mechanism to combine them, so that a single image will appear on the surface of the pineal gland, the part of the brain that he believed interacts immediately with the soul.

16. Theophrastus *De sens.* 21, quoted in J. I. Beare, *Greek Theories of Elementary Cognition* (Oxford: Oxford University Press, 1906), p. 97.

17. Descartes, *Philosophical Writings* 1:167.

18. See n. 8 above.

19. Further evidence that Descartes did not succeed in breaking the grip of the imagist hypothesis entirely can be found in *The Passions of the Soul,* which was composed about

fifteen years after the *Optics:* "There must necessarily be some place where the two images coming through the two eyes . . . can come together in a single image or impression before reaching the soul, so that they do not present to it two objects instead of one" (*Philosophical Writings,* 1:340).

It is also striking that an illustration in the *Treatise on Man* shows the retinal image being reinverted before it reaches the surface of the pineal gland (*Philosophical Writings,* 1:105). However, this work was published posthumously and Descartes cannot be held responsible for the plates.

20. Aristotle *De sensu* 438a5–8. The phrase translated here as "it really has its seat not in the eye but in the one that sees it" is not perfectly clear, but J. I. Beare's gloss (*Greek Theories of Elementary Cognition* [Oxford: Oxford University Press, 1906], p. 82) is helpful: "[The mirroring] does not find its full explanation merely in the reflecting surface of the eye in which the image is seen, but requires account to be also taken of the spectator's eye which alone sees this image."

21. Plato *Rep.* 596; cf. Plato *Soph.* 239d. Plato explains the formation of mirror images in *Timaeus* 46a. Eva Keuls and Stephen Halliwell argue independently that Plato's use of the analogy is unserious (Keuls) or satirical (Halliwell). E. Keuls, *Plato and Greek Painting* (Leiden: E. J. Brill, 1978), chap. 1; S. Halliwell, *The Aesthetics of Mimesis* (Princeton, N.J.: Princeton University Press, 2002), chap. 4. I have commented on it above, p. 62.

22. Umberto Eco, "Mirrors," in *Semiotics and the Philosophy of Language* (Bloomington: Indiana University Press, 1984), p. 205. A similar view is defended in R. Brandt, *Die Wirklichkeit des Bildes* (Munich: Carl Hanser, 1999), pp. 37 ff. (The correspondence with me on pp. 40–41 is entirely the author's own invention.)

23. E. H. Gombrich, *Art and Illusion,* 5th ed. (Oxford: Phaidon, 1977), p. 5.

24. Aristotle *De sensu* 438a8–10.

25. L. Wittgenstein, "The Big Typescript" (MS 213), p. 423, reprinted in *Philosophical Occasions,* ed. James C. Klagge and Alfred Nordmann (Indianapolis: Hackett, 1993), pp. 183–84.

26. M. H. Pirenne quotes Yves Le Grand as saying that the eye is the only optical instrument that forms an image that was never intended to be seen (*Optics, Painting and Photography* [Cambridge: Cambridge University Press, 1970], p. 9).

CHAPTER SEVEN

The epigraph for this chapter comes from E. H. Gombrich, *Art and Illusion,* 5th ed. (Oxford: Phaidon, 1977), p. 94.

1. E. H. Gombrich, "Illusion and Art," in *Illusion in Nature and Art,* ed. E. H. Gombrich and R. L. Gregory (London: Duckworth, 1973), p. 240.

2. The following works of analytical philosophy are among those that attempt to explain depiction in terms of a picture's psychological effect: R. Wollheim, *Art and Its Objects,* 2d ed. (Cambridge: Cambridge University Press, 1980), and *Painting as an Art* (London: Thames & Hudson, 1988); N. Wolterstorff, *Worlds and Works of Art* (Oxford: Oxford University Press, 1980); R. Scruton, *Art and Imagination* (London: Routledge & Kegan Paul, 1982); F. Schier, *Deeper into Pictures* (Cambridge: Cambridge University Press, 1986); C. Peacocke, "Depiction," *Philosophical Review* 96 (1987): 383–410; M. Budd, "On

Looking at a Picture," in *Psychoanalysis, Mind and Art,* ed. J. Hopkins and A. Savile (Oxford: Basil Blackwell, 1992); and R. Hopkins, *Picture, Image and Experience* (Cambridge: Cambridge University Press, 1998). One recent book that is notable for bucking the trend is D. Lopes, *Understanding Pictures* (Oxford: Oxford University Press, 1996).

3. C. Lalo, *L'expression de la vie dans l'art* (Paris: F. Alcan, 1933), cited in E. Kris and O. Kurz, *Legend, Myth and Magic in the Image of the Artist* (New Haven, Conn.: Yale University Press, 1979), p. 74. Compare J.-P. Sartre, *The Imaginary,* trans. J. Webber (London: Routledge, 2004), p. 24.

4. L. Wittgenstein, *Philosophical Investigations,* trans. G. E. M. Anscombe, 2d ed. (Oxford: Basil Blackwell, 1958), p. 202.

5. Wollheim, *Painting as an Art,* p. 48.

6. Ibid., p. 46; cf. Gombrich, *Art and Illusion,* pp. 89 ff. Wollheim adds that being visually aware of the surface and discerning something standing out in front of something else are two aspects of a single experience and not two distinct experiences. But since he does not explain how he believes experiences should be counted it is difficult to assess this claim.

7. Wollheim, *Painting as an Art,* p. 48.

8. Wollheim's concept of seeing-in is derived from Wittgenstein's concept of seeing as, but Wittgenstein does not attempt to explain depiction in terms of seeing as. On the contrary, when considering the Jastrow figure of a duck-rabbit, which illustrates one of the various phenomena that he uses the phrase "seeing . . . as" to describe, Wittgenstein asks, "How would the following account do: 'What I can see something *as,* is what it can be a picture of'?" And then, a few lines later, he adds, "Could I say what a picture must be like to produce this effect? No" (*Philosophical Investigations,* p. 201.) These two comments are consistent with the argument in this chapter. Notice that the Jastrow figure is an ambiguous picture—a design that depicts either a duck or a rabbit, rather as the word "bull" signifies either a male ox or a papal edict. Hence, there is no more prospect of explaining the nature of pictorial art by means of it than there is of explaining meaning in terms of ambiguity. It is noticeable that in one place Wittgenstein says that the Jastrow figure "can be seen as a rabbit's head or as a duck's," while in another, he speaks of seeing a rabbit in the figure, and in another still, he speaks of seeing it "as a picture-rabbit" (ibid., p. 194).

9. Wollheim, *Painting as an Art,* p. 62.

10. G. W. Leibniz, *New Essays on Human Understanding,* trans. and ed. P. Remnant and J. Bennett (Cambridge: Cambridge University Press, 1996), p. 135.

11. John Ruskin, *Modern Painters I,* in *The Complete Works of John Ruskin,* ed. E. T. Cook and A. Wedderburn (London: George Allen, 1903), 3:100. This observation was anticipated by Quatremère de Quincy in his *Essai sur la nature, le but et les moyens de l'imitation dans les beaux-arts* (Paris: Treuttel & Würtz, 1823). See Gombrich, *Art and Illusion,* p. 236.

12. The examples of the naked boy and the dancers suggest the first reading. But Wollheim also suggests that the Pure Wool logo is relatively pictorial, whereas the pictograms on public lavatories are relatively unpictorial, which supports the second reading (*Painting as an Art,* p. 60). It is possible that he did not distinguish between them clearly in his own mind.

13. There is a good discussion of this distinction in Meyer Schapiro, "On Some Prob-

lems in the Semiotics of Visual Art: Field and Vehicle in Image-Signs," reprinted in *Theory and Philosophy of Art: Style, Artist, and Society* (New York: George Braziller, 1994).

14. It should be noted that this proposal may be, but need not be, defended alongside a much bolder claim, either that the meaning of a work of art is governed by the artist's intention, or that the task of criticism is the reconstruction of the creative process. These claims, which I have not examined in this book, are discussed in R. Wollheim, "Criticism as Retrieval," in *Art and Its Objects;* and J. Raz, "Interpretation without Retrieval," in *Law and Interpretation,* ed. A. Marmor (Oxford: Oxford University Press, 1995).

15. Part of what is needed, in order to decide whether the first idea is true, is a distinction between two ways of using the term "utterance." It can be used to refer to an action, i.e., the production of a sound or sequence of sounds, but it can also be used to refer to the action's result, i.e., the sound or sequence of sounds produced. Thus, if an utterance was irresponsible, this was the action; but if it was recorded on a tape, this was the result. If we ask whether an utterance is meaningful, we need to be clear which sense we have in mind. For example, it is more plausible to hold that a parrot's utterance is meaningless qua action—since a parrot means nothing by its utterance—than that the sounds that a parrot utters have no meaning.

Whether the sounds a parrot utters have a linguistic meaning depends on whether they are words, or merely sounds that resemble words. One reason for thinking that they are words is that a parrot mimics utterances of words. A squawk that resembled a word by chance would have a weaker claim to having linguistic meaning. And one reason for accepting that mimicry provides a reasonable ground on which to attribute linguistic meaning is that it follows that the relatively uncontroversial view (the view that linguistically meaningful utterance is impossible except against a background that includes semantic intentions) is true. For if the parrot borrows meaning from the sounds it mimics, some sounds must be in a position to extend the loan.

If this is plausible the corresponding view about pictorial content implies that the stains on the wall in Siskind's photograph do not depict a boy. For although they resemble a picture of a boy, the resemblance is a matter of pure chance. On the other hand, if a counterproof of a print were produced by accident it would qualify as a picture by this criterion.

16. Wollheim, *Painting as an Art,* pp. 46–47.

17. In the text, I have stated the argument supporting this conclusion in informal terms, but I shall state it more formally in this note. To begin with, the following general principle is true. Let F stand for a term that signifies a kind of object that can be depicted—"a cow," "a battle," "a sphere," "a cylinder," etc.: in appropriate circumstances (i.e., a suitable light, an unobstructed view, and the opportunity to examine it with care) the marks on a surface that depict F must be such that a qualified spectator could describe her perception of them by saying that she can see marks that depict F.

The question is whether we can modify this principle, and preserve its truth, by replacing the second occurrence of the predicate "*x* depicts F"—i.e., the last phrase—by another complex predicate in which F occurs as a constituent but in which the concept of depiction is not expressly invoked. Let "*x* is F*" represent this predicate. The asterisk is a predicate-forming operator on predicates: in other words, it is a device that complicates or elaborates a predicate and transforms it into another one. Thus "*x* is F*"—like the predicate "*x* depicts F" itself—is the result of complicating or elaborating the predicate "*x* is F." In order to devise a form of words to replace Wollheim's unsatisfactory formulation: "I am visually aware of the surface I look at, and I discern something standing out in front of . . . something else," we need to find a suitable interpretation of "*x* is F*."

Consider the predicate "*x* has the same shape as F." Is this the predicate we need? If so, a configuration of marks that depicts F must be such that a qualified spectator could describe her perception of it by saying that she can see a configuration of marks with the same shape as F. But this is clearly false. For as Descartes points out, "engravings represent to us bodies of varying relief and depth on a surface that is entirely flat," and since it is normally obvious, when one is looking at an engraving, that one is seeing marks on a flat surface, the marks on the surface of an engraving that depict a sphere or a cylinder will not normally be such that a qualified spectator could describe her perception of it by saying that she can see marks with the same shape as a sphere or a cylinder. On the contrary, she would normally be expected to describe her perception by saying that she can see marks on a flat surface—marks that depict a sphere or a cylinder, to be sure, but not marks that are spherical or cylindrical themselves.

So "*x* has the same shape as F" is not the right predicate. What will the right predicate be like? What do we already know about it? One thing we know is this. The asterisk is, as I have said, a device that complicates a predicate, and when we consider the predicate "*x* has the same shape as F," it is obvious how the complication works. It works, in effect, by introducing a term for a visible relation, in which one object can stand to another, a relation such as *having the same shape as.* This is not merely true of "*x* has the same shape as F," in particular. It is a constraint that a suitable interpretation of the predicate "*x* is F*" is bound to respect. For a qualified spectator could not describe her perception by saying that she can see something F* unless *being F** was a visible property. Hence, the asterisk must introduce a term for a visible relation. For example, if "*x* is F" expresses the property of *being a tulip* or *being a pair of boots,* then "*x* is F*" might express the property of *having the same shape as a tulip* or *being the same color as a pair of boots.*

Now an interpretation of "*x* is F*" can easily be devised that works in the special case where F stands for "an object with such-and-such an occlusion shape"—namely, "*x* has a shape that is the same as the occlusion shape of an F." For example, suppose a configuration of marks depicts an object with an elliptical occlusion shape. This configuration of marks must be such that a qualified spectator could describe her perception of it by saying that she can see a configuration of marks whose shape is the same as the occlusion shape of such an object—namely, an ellipse. But a suitable interpretation of "*x* is F*" cannot be devised that works across the full range of permitted substitutions for F because there is no necessary visible relation between a configuration of marks and the object it depicts beyond the relation defined by the occlusion shape principle and the other basic principles of pictorial art.

18. J. Seznec and J. Adhemar, *Diderot Salons,* vol. 1., *1759, 1761, 1763* (Oxford: Clarendon Press, 1957), pp. 222–23; Joshua Reynolds, *Discourses on Art,* ed. Robert R. Wark (New Haven, Conn.: Yale University Press, 1975), discourse 14; and Marcel Proust, "The Painter. Shadows—Monet," reprinted in *Against Sainte-Beuve and Other Essays,* trans. J. Sturrock (Harmondsworth: Penguin, 1988), p. 328. As Michael Rosenthal has noted, Reynolds's remark echoes Vasari's description of Titian's late style, in a translation available at the

time: "The Works he did about this time, are so full of strokes and spots, after a certain bold Manner, that they seem nothing near, but look very well at a distance. . . . This way, though it seems easie, is the most laborious of all; but is made to hide the pains of the painter" (W. Anglioby, *Painting Illustrated in Three Dialogues: Containing some Choice Observations upon the Art, Together with the Lives of the Most Eminent Painters, from Cimabue, to the Time of Raphael and Michaelangelo: With an Explanation of the Difficult Terms* [London, 1685], pp. 359–40, quoted in M. Rosenthal, *The Art of Thomas Gainsborough* [New Haven, Conn.: Yale University Press, 1999], p. 120).

19. Plato *Theaetetus* 208e. The word translated here as "modern painting" is "skiagraphema." Scholars are divided on the exact significance of this term. Some argue that it refers to optical fusion, but I accept the conventional view that it refers to shading, which was invented by Greek painters in the fifth century. See below, p. 215–16.

20. Locke writes:

> Had we senses acute enough to discern the minute particles of bodies, and the real constitution on which their sensible qualities depend, I doubt not but they would produce quite different ideas in us: and that which is now the yellow color of gold, would then disappear, and instead of it we should see an admirable texture of parts, of a certain size and figure. This microscopes plainly discover to us; for what to our naked eyes produces a certain color, is, by thus augmenting the acuteness of our senses, discovered to be quite a different thing. . . . Thus, sand or pounded glass, which is opaque, and white to the naked eye, is pellucid in a microscope; and a hair seen in this way, loses its former color, and is, in a great measure, pellucid, with a mixture of some bright sparkling colors, such as appear from the refraction of diamonds, and other pellucid bodies. (*An Essay concerning Human Understanding*, 2.23.11)

21. See chap. 10, n. 15.

22. H. von Helmholtz, "The Relation of Optics to Painting," reprinted in *Science and Culture*, ed. D. Cahan (Chicago: University of Chicago Press, 1995), p. 280.

CHAPTER EIGHT

The epigraph is a remark by Daniel-Henry Kahnweiler, quoted in Y.-A. Bois, "Kahnweiler's Lesson," *Representations* 18 (Spring 1987): 33–68.

1. J. M. Whistler, *The Gentle Art of Making Enemies* (London: Heinemann, 1904), p. 128.

2. I. Kant, *Critique of Judgement*, trans. W. Pluhar (Indianapolis: Hackett, 1987), §14.

3. Augustine *De doctrina christiana* 2.1.1–2.

4. The phrase is Riegl's. Both this and Van Gogh's phrase are quoted in Leo Steinberg, "The Eye Is Part of the Mind," in *Other Criteria* (Oxford: Oxford University Press, 1972), p. 292.

5. Steinberg, "The Eye Is Part of the Mind," p. 293.

6. M. Schapiro, "The Nature of Abstract Art," reprinted in *Modern Art: Nineteenth and Twentieth Centuries* (New York: George Braziller, 1978), pp. 195–96.

7. For example, the following passage is from E. Kris and O. Kurz, *Legend, Myth, and*

Magic in the Image of the Artist, new ed. (New Haven, Conn.: Yale University Press, 1979), which was originally published in 1934 and was an important source for Gombrich's influential essay *Meditations on a Hobby-Horse* (2d ed. [London: Phaidon, 1971]): "Likeness . . . has nothing to do with the idea of 'true to nature,' which has the aim of exact photographic reproduction; rather it may be more generally described as the attempt to bring pictorial conventions to life." (p. 78). Steinberg goes a step further by including photography in the scope of these conventions.

8. C. S. Peirce, *Collected Papers,* ed. C. Hartshorne and P. Weiss, 8 vols. (Cambridge, Mass.: Harvard University Press, 1960), 5:5.402. To simplify the exposition as much as possible, I have telescoped Peirce's intellectual development and ignored later revisions to his doctrines. For a detailed account of his views and of the ways in which they changed between the 1860s and the 1900s, see T. L. Short, "The Development of Peirce's Theory of Signs," in *The Cambridge Companion to Peirce,* ed. Cheryl Misak (Cambridge: Cambridge University Press, 2004).

9. Peirce, *Collected Papers,* 2:2.305.

10. Ibid., 2:2.279.

11. Notice that a sign can belong to more than one of these three categories. For example, the word "here" is both an index and a symbol; an onomatopoeia is both a symbol and an icon; and a photograph is both an icon and an index. Since Peirce's doctrines are extremely complex, in particular because of the connection between his semiotic theory and his theory of categories, I have simplified them considerably. Peirce's own explanations include the following: *index* (2.248): "A sign which refers to the Object that it denotes by virtue of being really affected by that Object." But note that an index may refer to an object because of a spatial relation rather than a causal one (2.305)—hence the current use of the term "indexical." *Icon* (2.247, 2.255): "A sign which refers to the Object that it denotes merely by virtue of characters of its own. . . . Anything whatever . . . is an Icon of anything, insofar as it is like that thing and used as a sign of it"; "a sign by likeness purely, of whatever it may be like." *Symbol* (2.249, 2.246): "A sign which refers to the object it denotes by virtue of a law, usually an association of general ideas, which operates to cause the Symbol to be interpreted as referring to that Object"; "this law is usually established by men"—the qualification "usually" is explained in 2.297, where a symbol is said to be "a conventional sign, or one depending on habit (acquired or inborn)." The examples I have given are all Peirce's own, except for the flag and the medal. However, he mentions standards, ensigns, signals agreed on, and badges. The briefest exposition of the trichotomy is given in 2.297.

12. S. K. Langer, *Philosophy in a New Key* (Cambridge, Mass.: Harvard University Press, 1942), pp. 68–69.

13. Ibid., pp. 60–61, 68.

14. C. W. Morris, *Signs, Language and Behaviour* (New York: G. Braziller, 1955), p. 190.

15. J. Hospers, *Meaning and Truth in the Arts* (Chapel Hill: University of North Carolina Press, 1947), p. 29. The use of the terms "refer," "stand for," and "denote" to signify the relation between a picture and the objects that it represents does not mark a departure from Peirce's terminology (*Collected Papers,* 2:2.247, 2.273).

16. Hospers, *Meaning and Truth in the Arts,* p. 29.

17. It does not follow from the fact that A causes a thought about B that A denotes or

refers to B. For example, if an expression on my cousin's face reminds me of her mother, it does not follow that it denotes her; and if the taste of an apricot makes me think about Cairo, it does not follow that it refers to it. Hence, the idea that pictures are signs or symbols cannot simply be equated with the idea that they refer to things or denote them.

18. C. W. Morris, "Aesthetics and the Theory of Signs," *Journal of Unified Science* (*Erkenntnis*) 8 (1939–40): 131–50, esp. 136

19. Nelson Goodman, *Languages of Art* (Indianapolis: Hackett, 1968), p. xi.

20. See above, p. 64.

21. Goodman, *Languages of Art*, p. 5.

22. Some logicians prefer to reserve the term "name" for names with bearers. For arguments against this position, see D. Bostock, *Intermediate Logic* (Oxford: Oxford University Press, 1997), pp. 348 ff.

23. Goodman, *Languages of Art*, p. 22.

24. In *Languages of Art* (p. 21), Goodman injudiciously claimed that a predicate of this sort is not only monadic but also unbreakable, i.e., that its meaning cannot be deduced from the meanings of its parts and the way in which they are combined. There are unbreakable two-place predicates, e.g., "*x* loves *y*"; and there are breakable one-place predicates, e.g., "*x* is red and round." Many idioms are unbreakable, e.g., "blue-chip" or "copper-bottomed." But the claim that "*x* represents Zeus" and "*x* represents a dying centaur" are unbreakable predicates is not true. For if it were true, it would not be possible to deduce that a picture that represents Zeus represents a god from the fact that Zeus is a god or to deduce that a picture that represents a dying centaur represents a centaur from the fact that a dying centaur is a centaur. Goodman subsequently conceded that these predicates are semantically complex (*Problems and Projects* [Indianapolis: Hackett, 1972], p. 122), but he continued to hold that they are monadic.

25. Monroe Beardsley, who argues in favor of the doctrine that resemblance explains depiction, claims that "if two representational designs differ as designs, no matter how little, they must differ in what they depict, even if only trivially" (*Aesthetics: Problems in the Theory of Criticism*, 2d ed. [Indianapolis: Hackett, 1981], p. 295). In fact, this is inaccurate. For if two paintings differ only in absolute size, and not at all in the relative proportions of their parts, there will not be any difference in what they depict. Again, if two drawings differ only in the color of the ink or chalk, they will not necessarily differ in what they depict.

26. Goodman, *Languages of Art*, p. 226.

27. Ibid., pp. 136, 153, 229.

28. Ibid., pp. 230–31. Repleteness is not mentioned here but should be understood.

29. R. Jakobson, "On Realism in Art" (1921), reprinted in *Language in Literature* (Cambridge, Mass.: Harvard University Press, 1987).

30. E. H. Gombrich, *Art and Illusion*, 5th ed. (Oxford: Phaidon, 1977), p. 16.

31. Goodman, *Languages of Art*, 30.

32. Ibid., p. 136.

33. Richard Wollheim, *Painting as an Art* (London: Thames & Hudson, 1988), p. 77. The idea that transfer is a distinguishing mark of pictorial representation was originally proposed by Flint Schier (*Deeper into Paintings* [Cambridge: Cambridge University Press, 1986], chap. 3).

34. Goodman, *Languages of Art*, p. 36.

CHAPTER NINE

The epigraph for this chapter comes from Isaiah Berlin, "Alleged Relativism in Eighteenth-Century European Thought," reprinted in *The Crooked Timber of Humanity* (London: John Murray, 1990), p. 87. I am indebted in this chapter to several essays on Berlin's ideas in S. Lukes, *Liberals and Cannibals* (London: Verso, 2003).

1. R. Jakobson, "On Realism in Art" (1921), reprinted in *Language in Literature* (Cambridge, Mass.: Harvard University Press, 1987), p. 27.

2. This did not prevent the author from using it in the book's title: A. Fowler, *Renaissance Realism* (Oxford: Oxford University Press, 2003), p. 212.

3. Jakobson, "On Realism in Art," p. 23.

4. Daniel-Henri Kahnweiler, quoted in Y.-A. Bois, "Kahnweiler's Lesson," *Representations* 18 (1987), pp. 33–68.

5. Leo Steinberg, "The Eye Is Part of the Mind," in *Other Criteria* (Oxford: Oxford University Press, 1972), p. 293.

6. Nelson Goodman, *Languages of Art* (Indianapolis: Hackett, 1968), p. 38; cf. Goodman, "Realism, Relativism and Reality," *New Literary History* 14 (1983): 269–72.

7. Jakobson, "On Realism in Art," p. 21.

8. M. Schapiro, "The Nature of Abstract Art," reprinted in *Modern Art: Nineteenth and Twentieth Centuries* (New York: George Braziller, 1978), pp. 195–96.

9. Linda Nochlin, *Realism* (Harmondsworth: Penguin, 1971), pp. 14f.

10. Goodman, *Languages of Art*, p. 39, n. 31.

11. Ibid., p. 37.

12. This example is mentioned in H. Schäfer, *Principles of Egyptian Art*, trans. J. Baines, rev. ed. (Oxford: Griffith Institute, 1986), pp. 82–83.

13. Goodman, *Languages of Art*, p. 57.

14. Ibid., p. 30, n. 25.

15. Ibid., pp. 30, 31, n.26.

16. Ibid., p. 32. In Goodman's idiolect, the term "attribute" merely signifies class membership.

17. Ibid., p. 32.

18. Michel de Montaigne, "Of Custom, and That We Should Not Easily Change a Law Received," in *Essays*, trans. C. Cotton, ed. W. C. Hazlitt (London, 1877), 4:xxii.

19. The quoted material is from Goodman, *Languages of Art*, pp. 38, 36.

20. I am indebted here to P. T. Geach, who traces the history of the doctrine in "History of the Corruptions of Logic," reprinted in *Logic Matters* (Oxford: Basil Blackwell, 1972), pp. 44 ff.

21. C. Rosen and H. Zerner, *Romanticism and Realism: Mythology of Nineteenth-Century Art* (London: Faber & Faber: 1984), p. 148.

22. Quoted in ibid., p. 146; the translation is theirs.

23. J. D. Beazley, "A Greek Realist," in *Greek Vases: Lectures by J. D. Beazley*, ed. D.C. Kurtz (Oxford: Oxford University Press, 1989), p. 78.

24. R. T. Neer, *Athenian Vase-Painting* (Cambridge: Cambridge University Press, 2002), p. 28.

25. For an interesting and controversial treatment of the relationship between art, medicine, and physiology in fifth-century Greece, see Guy P. R. Métraux, *Sculptors and*

Physicians in Fifth-Century Greece (Montreal and Kingston: McGill-Queen's University Press, 1995).

26. Pliny *Natural History* 35.67; Xenophon *Memorabilia* 3.10.

27. Pliny *Natural History* 35.71.

28. Leonardo's notebooks contain many remarks about the depiction of motion. The most extensive ones occur when he is describing storms and deluges. See, e.g, *The Notebooks of Leonardo da Vinci,* trans. E. MacCurdy (London: Jonathan Cape, 1938), 2:269–74.

29. E. H. Gombrich, *Art and Illusion* fifth ed. (Oxford: Phaidon, 1977), p. 192.

30. Ibid., p. 304.

31. Ibid., p. 114.

32. Kahnweiler, quoted in Bois, "Kahnweiler's Lesson," p. 40; Gombrich, p. 16.

33. Clement Greenberg, "Modernist Painting," reprinted in *The Collected Essays and Criticism,* ed. J. O'Brian (Chicago: University of Chicago Press, 1993), 4:86. Similar remarks occur frequently in Greenberg's writings.

34. John Ruskin, *Modern Painters I,* in *The Complete Works of John Ruskin,* ed. E. T. Cook and A. Wedderburn (London: George Allen, 1903), 3:100.

35. Some of the sentences in this paragraph are adapted from authors who have argued in favor of relativist ideas.

36. Montaigne, "Of Custom."

CHAPTER TEN

The epigraph for this chapter comes from J. Tyndall, *Faraday as a Discoverer,* 5th ed. (London: Longman & Co., 1894), chap. 6.

1. See S. Y. Edgerton Jr., *The Heritage of Giotto's Geometry* (Ithaca, N.Y.: Cornell University Press, 1991); A. Crombie, *Styles of Scientific Thinking in the European Tradition* (London: Duckworth, 1994), vol. 1, chap. 8. Erwin Panofsky, whose views about perspective I shall discuss later in this chapter, expressed this idea in a memorable way: "Natural science as we still know it, and art as conceived by the Renaissance, can in fact be defined as two parallel attempts at representing the universe in an image based on observation and rationalized by mathematics" (*The Codex Huygens and Leonardo da Vinci's Art Theory* [London: Warburg Institute, 1940], p. 91). Perhaps this remark exaggerates the kinship between painting and science, but it is true that perspective and the depiction of anatomy made art and science partners in the study of the natural world for four centuries, until the invisible structure of matter began to occupy a central place in chemistry and physics. On this topic, see M. Kemp, *The Science of Art* (New Haven, Conn., and London: Yale University Press, 1990), esp. pp. 334 ff.

2. John White, *The Birth and Rebirth of Pictorial Space,* 2d ed. (London: Faber & Faber, 1967), p. 122. Panofsky says something similar, in more colorful terms: "Perspective . . . seems to reduce the divine to a mere subject-matter for human consciousness; but for that very reason, conversely, it expands human consciousness into a vessel for the divine" (*Perspective as Symbolic Form,* trans. Christopher S. Wood [New York: Zone Books, 1991], p. 72).

In fact, Alberti's reason for mentioning Protagoras was to suggest that the objects represented in a picture will seem large or small depending on their relationship to the human figures it includes because "man is the thing best known to man." This was not a philosophical claim about man's place in the cosmos; it was a familiar idea about visual perception, which was repeated by several writers in the medieval optical tradition stemming from Alhazen (965–1040). For example, Roger Bacon (1214–92) made the same observation when he said that size is perceived "by comparison and immediate reference to some definite measure accessible to the memory, like the size of the man measuring" (Leon Battista Alberti, *On Painting*, trans. J. R. Spencer, rev. ed. [New Haven, Conn.: Yale University Press, 1966], p. 55; R. Bacon, *Opus Majus*, trans. R. B. Burke, 2 vols. [Philadelphia: University of Pennsylvania Press, 1928], 5.2.3.5).

Moreover, it seems strange that White attaches this philosophical significance to perspective when (disagreeing here with Panofsky) he also argues persuasively in favor of the hypothesis that "an antique system of perspective, founded on the single vanishing point, existed . . . in at least one of the cultural centres that influenced Pompeii" and in favor of the traditional view that its existence is attested in Vitruvius's *De architectura*. (*The Birth and Rebirth of Pictorial Space*, p. 262 and chap. 16, passim.)

3. *On Painting*, p. 52. Euclid referred to a cone of rays; the pyramid is due to Ptolemy. Both are idealizations, since the face of an object can have any shape. See above, p. 76.

4. Alberti, *On Painting*, p. 59. Alberti may have meant a practical demonstration rather than a formal proof. A formal proof was published two centuries later by the French mathematician Girard Desargues.

5. Ibid. Some of Alberti's remarks suggest that he believed that the eye emits rays: "The eye is like a bud which extends its shoots rapidly and in a straight line to the plane opposite," etc. (p. 46). But this is incidental to the analysis of perspective he defends.

6. Alberti's famous remark that a painting is "una finestra aperta sul mondo" is an elegant way to advertise the pleasures of illusionism. But it is principally a claim about the relationship between painting and geometry. In fact it is essentially the same claim that he makes explicitly when he describes a painting as a cross section of a visual pyramid. (*On Painting*, p. 52.)

7. Johann Kepler, *Ad vitellionem paralipomena quibus astronomiae pars optica traditur*, in *Gesammelte Werke*, ed. W. von Dyck and M. Caspar (Munich, 1937), 1:185. Alhazen had argued that the image in the eye cannot be inverted for this reason: "The form cannot extend from the surface of the glacial humour to the cavity of the nerve in straight lines and at the same time preserve the proper position of its parts. For all these lines converge at the centre of the eye, and once they have been extended in a straight line, their positions beyond the centre will be reversed: what is right will become left and vice versa, and what is above will become below and below above" (*Opticae thesaurus Alhenazi Arabis libri septem*, ed. F. Risner [Basel, 1572], 2.2.2.)

8. H. Helmholtz, *Populäre Wissenschaftliche Vorträge* (Braunschweig: Friedrich Vieweg & Sohn, 1871), 2:71.

9. Berkeley believed that distance is inferred from binocular convergence, by trigonometric calculations, and by the accommodation that occurs when the eye brings the point of fixation to a focus. In both cases, the information is supplied by muscular sensations. However, the convergence of the eyes reaches zero at less than twenty meters; and the far accommodation of the lens approaches a maximum limit at about five meters and becomes progressively weaker in middle age. Binocular disparity was discovered in 1833 by

Charles Wheatstone, who invented the stereoscope to test it, although the discovery was anticipated by Leonardo da Vinci (*Codex urbinas latinus 1270,* 155v). But if the same image is presented to both eyes, a powerful impression of depth is still produced.

10. Helmholtz's "solid image of three dimensions" is still widely thought of as an image. See, e.g., E. R. Kandel and R. H. Wurtz, "Constructing the Visual Image," in *Essentials of Neural Science and Behavior,* ed. E. R. Kandel, J. H. Schwartz, and T. M. Jessell (Norwalk, Conn.: Appleton & Lange, 1995), p. 492. But it is also commonly thought of as a complex of symbols or a description. This idea was defended by Kenneth Craik, who thought of symbolization in the manner expounded in Wittgenstein's *Tractatus*—i.e., as an isomorphism between complexes of signs and the states of affairs they represent (*The Nature of Explanation* [Cambridge: Cambridge University Press, 1943], chap. 5). The idea that Helmholtz's "solid image" is a complex of symbols is defended in detail by David Marr (*Vision* [San Francisco: Freeman, 1982], chap. 1 and passim).

11. Colin Blakemore, "The Baffled Brain," in *Illusion in Nature and Art,* ed. R. L. Gregory and E. H. Gombrich (London: Duckworth, 1973), p. 40.

12. V. S. Ramachandran, "Perceiving Shape from Shading," *Scientific American,* August 1988, p. 76.

13. See J. J. Gibson, *The Senses Considered as Perceptual Systems* (Westport, Conn.: Greenwood, 1966), *The Ecological Approach to Visual Perception* (Boston: Houghton Mifflin Co., 1979), and *Reasons for Realism: Selected Essays of James J. Gibson,* ed. E. Reed and R. Jones (Hillsdale, N.J.: Lawrence Erlbaum Assocs., 1982). M. Merleau-Ponty is also critical of the Helmholtzian tradition: see *Phenomenology of Perception,* trans. C. French (London: Routledge & Kegan Paul, 1962), pt. 2, chap. 2, esp. pp. 258–61.

14. R. L. Gregory, *Eye and Brain,* 3d ed. (London: Weidenfeld & Nicolson, 1977), p. 174; C. Blakemore, *Mechanics of the Mind* (Cambridge: Cambridge University Press, 1977), p. 66; and I Rock, *Perception* (New York: Scientific American Books), p. 19. An extraordinary variant on the idea occurs in a review of David Marr's book, *Vision,* by Israel Rosenfeld. As well as the final "solid image in three dimensions," which he calls the "3-D model" or an "object-centered description," Marr postulates a "primal sketch" and a "2½-D sketch." Referring to these intermediate stages in visual perception, Rosenfeld proposes that "we can make sense of artists" sketches [because] they are similar to the symbols computed in our brains" ("Seeing through the Brain," review of *Vision* by David Marr, *New York Review of Books,* 11 October 1984.) This hypothesis is developed at greater length in A. Hayes and J. Ross, "Lines of Sight," in *The Artful Eye,* ed. R. Gregory et al. (Oxford: Oxford University Press, 1995). "The visual system," they suggest, "is so good at interpreting ordinary line drawings because it itself computes a line-drawing-like representation" (p. 345).

Although ideas of this kind in the twentieth century can be traced to Helmholtz's influence on visual theory, the ideas themselves are foreshadowed in earlier writing about art. Svetlana Alpers finds a related conception of pictorial art in seventeenth-century Holland: "In defining the human eye itself as a mechanical maker of pictures and in defining 'to see' as 'to picture,' [Kepler] provides the model we need for that particular binding of finding and making, of nature and art, that characterizes the picture in the north" (*The Art of Describing* [Chicago: University of Chicago Press, 1983], p. 33). This is not quite the idea that pictures are directly comparable to retinal images, although it is close. But

Michael Baxandall has found the direct comparison in an eighteenth-century text, and for a seventeenth-century example, see n. 27 below (M. Baxandall, *Patterns of Intention* [New Haven, Conn.: Yale University Press, 1985], p. 93). In the case of photography, the comparison is as old as the technology itself, for the French physicist Jean Baptiste Biot described the daguerreotype as an "artificial retina" in 1839 (quoted in H. Gernsheim and A. Gernsheim, *L. J. M. Daguerre: The History of the Diorama and the Daguerrotype,* 2d ed. [New York: Dover, 1968], p. 84).

15. R. L. Gregory, *Concepts and Mechanisms of Perception* (London: Duckworth, 1974), p. 335.

16. Colin Blakemore writes: "The painter who strives to represent reality must transcend his *own* perception. He must ignore or override the very mechanisms in his mind that create objects out of images" (*Mechanics of the Mind* [Cambridge: Cambridge University Press, 1977], p. 67). I. Rock takes a slightly different view or, at least, expresses it with a different emphasis, for he claims that the perspectival properties of retinal images are reflected to some degree in conscious experience ("In Defence of Unconscious Inference," in *Stability and Constancy in Visual Perception,* ed. W. Epstein [New York: Wiley, 1977]).

17. G. Hauck, *Die Subjektive Perspektive und die Horizontalen Curvaturen des Dorischen Styls* (Stuttgart: Konrad Wittwer, 1879), p. 4. Hauck was a professor of descriptive geometry, and his ideas about perspective seem to have been influenced by the invention of non-Euclidian geometries in the nineteenth century. He argues in favor of a curvilinear system of perspective on the grounds that the surface of the retina is curved. As we shall see, this argument was one of the chief sources on which Panofsky drew in his article, "Die Perspektive als 'symbolische Form'" (*Vorträge der Bibliothek Warburg* 1924–25 [Leipzig and Berlin, 1927]: 258–330).

18. E. Löwy, *The Rendering of Nature in Early Greek Art,* trans. J. Fothergill (London: Duckworth, 1907), p. 33; H. Schäfer, *Principles of Egyptian Art,* trans. J. Baines (Oxford: Oxford University Press, 1974), p. 269; Panofsky, *The Codex Huygens and Leonardo da Vinci's Art Theory,* p. 92.

19. Gombrich's exact view about the relationship between perspective pictures and retinal images is difficult to pin down. On the one hand, his discussion of ancient art is deeply indebted to his teacher Emmanuel Löwy. His theory of realism is founded on the analogy between seeing what a picture represents and visual perception as such, and he conceives of visual perception just as the Helmholtzians do, as a matter of formulating hypotheses about the cause of a stimulus in the eye, which admits, he says, "of an infinite number of possible interpretations" (*Art and Illusion,* 5th ed. [Oxford: Phaidon, 1977], p. 278) Thus, we find the following remark: "In the course of time, artists have in fact succeeded in simulating one after the other of the clues on which we mainly rely in one-eyed vision" (p. 233). This adds up to the view that Gregory and Blakemore explicitly endorse. Yet we also find remarks, such as the following one, which are signs of Gibson's influence: "To the artist the image in the unconscious is as mythical and useless an idea as was the image on the retina" (p. 303; see also pp. 57, 217.) I suspect that Gibson's own review of *Art and Illusion* was on the mark: "The formulas he finds helpful in one chapter are not always consistent with the hypotheses he finds illuminating in the next" (in *Psychological Review* 76 [1960]: 654).

20. John Willats, *Art and Representation* (Princeton, N.J.: Princeton University Press, 1997), is a recent example. Willats recruits Marr's theory of vision to defend the Helmholtzian theory of perspective. He points out that there is "a persistent tradition that pictures are derived more or less directly from retinal images" (p. 18), and he continues as follows: "The problem with this kind of purely optical theory of pictures is that it makes it very difficult to account for a wide range of pictures . . . except in terms of some kind of deficit theory: lack of skill on the part of children, and a similar lack of skill on the part of artists in earlier periods and other cultures." Pictures by children and pictures of animals in Northwest Coast Indian art cannot, he says, "be easily accounted for in terms of retinal images, or internal descriptions which correspond to possible views. I shall argue, instead, that they are derived from internal *object-centered* descriptions." Willats's position is that perspective pictures derive from retinal images or, perhaps, from "internal descriptions which correspond to possible views"—i.e., the 2½-D sketches postulated by Marr (see above, n. 14). But pictures by children and pictures of animals in Northwest Coast Indian art derive from Marr's 3-D models or object-centered descriptions.

21. Panofsky, "Die Perspektive als 'symbolische Form,'" pp. 258–330, and *Perspective as Symbolic Form.* Writers who have defended the relativist position include Herbert Read, Leo Steinberg, Rudolf Arnheim, Nelson Goodman, W. J. T. Mitchell, and Norman Bryson. The proponents of the opposite view include J. J. Gibson, E. H. Gombrich, M. H. Pirenne, Michael Kubovy, and Margaret Hagen, as well as the authors I have quoted in the text.

22. Hume, *Critique of Pure Reason,* A42/B59.

23. E. Cassirer argues that in order to obtain a correct understanding of culture, we must "accept in all seriousness what Kant calls his 'Copernican Revolution'" (*Language and Myth,* trans. S. K. Langer [New York: Harper, 1946], p. 8).

24. Panofsky, *Perspective as Symbolic Form,* p. 34.

25. Ibid., pp. 29, 44. It is interesting to note that Ernst Cassirer accepted Panofsky's analysis: "One of the most important tasks of Renaissance philosophy and mathematics was the creation, step by step, of the conditions for a new concept of space. . . . Panofsky has shown that this discovery was made not only in mathematics and in cosmology but in the plastic arts and in the art theory of the Renaissance as well; and, in fact, that the theory of perspective anticipated the results of modern mathematics and cosmology" (*The Individual and the Cosmos in Renaissance Philosophy* [New York: Dover Publications, 2000], p. 182 and note).

26. Panofsky, *Perspective as Symbolic Form,* p. 31. Panofsky found a seventeenth-century precedent for this argument. He quotes the German mathematician, Wilhelm Schickhardt, who wrote: "I say that all lines, even the straightest, which do not stand *directe contra pupillam* . . . necessarily appear somewhat bent. Nevertheless, no painter believes this; this is why they paint the straight sides of a building with straight lines, even though according to the true art of perspective this is incorrect. . . . Crack that nut, you artists!" (pp. 33–34). However, Panofsky's own source for the argument was Guido Hauck, who had argued in favor of a curvilinear system of perspective on these grounds. Interestingly, Panofsky's reliance on Hauck's argument is at odds with the view about space he inherited from Cassirer because Hauck's position implies that a curvilinear system of perspective would not be a historically contingent symbolic form, "comprehensible only for a

quite specific . . . sense of space." It would have a unique and transhistorical status because it would correspond to the geometry of the retinal image.

27. Panofsky, *Perspective as Symbolic Form,* p. 33. The last sentence (which on its own terms is perfectly correct) qualifies Panofsky's support for Hauck's system, which introduces curvature only along the horizontal axis.

28. Not all psychologists deny that we see our retinal images in a consistent manner. For example, in the space of twenty lines, Blakemore claims that "the subjects of seeing are not objects themselves, but the flat, intangible images of them which hide within the pupil of the eye"; he describes the retina as "the canvas of the brain"; and he points out that "we do not perceive our retinal image" (*Mechanics of the Mind,* pp. 66–67).

29. Marr, *Vision,* p. 3.

30. "The Light which comes from the several points of the Object is so refracted as to . . . paint the Picture of the object upon that skin called the *Retina.* . . . And these Pictures, propagated by motion along the Fibres of the Optick Nerves into the Brain, are the cause of Vision. For accordingly as these Pictures are perfect or imperfect, the Object is seen perfectly or imperfectly" (I. Newton, *Opticks* [New York: Dover, 1952], p. 15). R. Gregory, *Mirrors in Mind* (Harmondsworth: Penguin, 1997), p. 74.

31. Compare J. J. Gibson: "The common belief that vision necessarily depends on a retinal image is incorrect, since the eye of a bee, for example, does not have a retinal image. What eyes do is to pick up all the useful information in light of which they are capable; retinal images are merely incidental in the process" ("Pictures, Perspective, and Perception," reprinted in *Reasons for Realism,* p. 261). More generally, see Gibson, *The Senses Considered as Perceptual Systems,* esp. chap. 11.

32. Tyndall, *Faraday as a Discoverer.* Tyndall adds, in a footnote: "I copy these words from the printed abstract of a Friday evening lecture, given by myself, because they remind me of Faraday's voice, responding to the utterance by an emphatic 'hear! hear!'"

33. Ibid., chap. 6, note 2.

34. Plato *Republic* 602d.

35. D. Hume, *A Treatise on Human Nature,* ed. L. A. Selby-Bigge, 2d ed. edited by P. H. Nidditch (Oxford: Clarendon Press, 1978), 3.3.3.

36. J. J. Winckelmann, *History of Ancient Art,* trans. C. H. Lodge (London: Sampson Low & Co., 1881), p. 134; Panofsky, *Perspective as Symbolic Form,* p. 72. See also H. Schäfer, *Principles of Egyptian Art,* p. 269; C. Aldred, *Egyptian Art* (London: Thames & Hudson, 1980), p. 15; E. H. Gombrich, *The Story of Art,* 12th ed. (London: Phaidon, 1972), p. 36; W. S. Smith, *The Art and Architecture of Ancient Egypt,* 2d ed., rev. by W. K. Simpson (Harmondsworth: Penguin, 1981), p. 15.

BIBLIOGRAPHY

Adhemar, H., and A. Clark, eds. *Centenaire de l'impressionisme.* Paris: Edition des Musées Nationaux, 1974.

Alberti, Leon Battista. *On Painting.* Translated by J. R. Spencer. Rev. ed. New Haven, Conn.: Yale University Press, 1966.

Alhazen (Ibn al Haitham). *Opticae thesaurus Alhenazi Arabis libri septem.* Basel, 1572.

Alpers, S. *The Art of Describing.* Chicago: University of Chicago Press, 1983.

Angel, R. B. *Relativity: The Theory and Its Philosophy.* Oxford: Pergamon, 1980.

Anglioby, W. *Painting illustrated in Three Dialogues, containing some Choice Observations upon the Art, together with the Lives of the most Eminent Painters, from Cimabue, to the Time of Raphael and Michaelangelo: With an explanation of the Difficult Terms.* London, 1685.

Armstrong, D. M. *Perception and the Physical World.* London: Routledge & Kegan Paul, 1961.

Austin, J. L. *Sense and Sensibilia.* Edited by G. J. Warnock. Oxford: Oxford University Press, 1962.

Ayers, M. *Locke.* London: Routledge, 1991.

Bacon, Francis. *The Essays; or, Counsels Civil and Moral.* Edited by B. Vickers. Oxford: Oxford University Press, 1999.

Bacon, Roger, *Opus Majus.* Translated by R. B. Burke. 2 vols. Philadelphia: University of Pennsylvania Press, 1928.

Baxandall, M. *Patterns of Intention.* New Haven, Conn.: Yale University Press, 1985.

———. *Shadows and Enlightenment.* New Haven, Conn.: Yale University Press, 1995.

Beardsley, M. C. *Aesthetics: Problems in the Theory of Criticism.* 2d ed. Indianapolis: Hackett, 1981.

Beare, J. I. *Greek Theories of Elementary Cognition.* Oxford: Oxford University Press, 1906.

Berlin, B., and P. Kay. *Basic Color Terms.* Berkeley: University of California Press, 1969.

Berlin, I. *The Crooked Timber of Humanity.* London: John Murray, 1990.

Blakemore, C. *Mechanics of the Mind.* Cambridge: Cambridge University Press, 1977.

Bois, Y.-A. "Kahnweiler's Lesson." *Representations* 18 (Spring 1987): 33–68.

Bostock, D. *Intermediate Logic.* Oxford: Oxford University Press, 1997.

Brandt, R. *Die Wirklichkeit des Bildes.* Munich: Carl Hanser, 1999.

Budd, M. *Values of Art.* Harmondsworth: Penguin, 1995.

Burkert, W. *Lore and Science in Ancient Pythagoreanism.* Translated by E. L. Minar Jr. Cambridge, Mass.: Harvard University Press, 1972.

Byrne, A., and D. Hilbert, eds. *Readings on Color.* Cambridge, Mass.: MIT Press, 1997), 2 vols.

Cassirer, E. *Language and Myth.* Translated by S. K. Langer. New York: Harper, 1946.

———. *The Individual and the Cosmos in Renaissance Philosophy.* New York: Dover, 2000.

Chieh Tzu Yuan Hua Chuan. *The Mustard Seed Garden Manual of Painting.* Edited by Mai-Mai Sze. Princeton, N.J.: Princeton University Press, 1977.

Coleridge, S. T. *Biographia Literaria.* Edited by J. Engell and W. Jackson Bate. Vol. 1. Princeton, N.J.: Princeton University Press, 1983.

Craik, K. *The Nature of Explanation.* Cambridge: Cambridge University Press, 1943.

Crombie, A. C. *Styles of Scientific Thinking in the European Tradition.* 3 vols. London: Duckworth, 1994.

Dancy, J. ed. *Perceptual Knowledge.* Oxford: Oxford University Press, 1988.

Davidson, D. *Essays on Actions and Events.* Oxford: Oxford University Press, 1980.

Derrida, J. *The Truth in Painting.* Chicago: University of Chicago Press, 1987.

Descartes, R. *Philosophical Writings.* Translated by J. Cottingham et al. 2 vols. Cambridge: Cambridge University Press, 1985.

Diderot, Denis. *Salons.* Edited by J. Seznec, and J. Adhemar. 4 vols. Oxford: Oxford University Press, 1957–67.

Diels, H., and W. Kranz. *Die Fragmente der Vorsokratiker.* 7th ed. Berlin: Weidmann, 1954.

Dijksterhuis, E. J. *The Mechanization of the World Picture.* Oxford: Oxford University Press, 1961.

Dodds, E. R. *The Ancient Concept of Progress and Other Essays.* Oxford: Oxford University Press, 1973.

Dummett, M. A. E. *Truth and Other Enigmas.* Cambridge, Mass.: Harvard University Press, 1978.

Eco, U. *Semiotics and the Philosophy of Language.* Bloomington: Indiana University Press, 1984.

Edgerton, S. Y. *The Heritage of Giotto's Geometry.* Ithaca, N.Y.: Cornell University Press, 1991.

Florensky, P. *Beyond Vision.* Edited by N. Misler. London: Reaktion, 2002.

Fowler, A. *Renaissance Realism.* Oxford: Oxford University Press, 2003.

Freedberg, D. *The Power of Images.* Chicago: University of Chicago Press, 1989.

Frege, F. *The Foundations of Arithmetic.* Oxford: Basil Blackwell, 1953.

Gage, J. *Colour and Culture.* London: Thames & Hudson, 1993.

———. *Colour and Meaning.* London: Thames & Hudson, 1999.

Galilei, Galileo. *Il Saggiatore* [*The Assayer*]. Vol. 6 of *Le opere de Galileo Galilei.* Edited by Antonio Favaro. Firenze: S.A.G. Barbèra Editore, 1929–39.

Geach, P. T. *Logic Matters.* Oxford: Basil Blackwell, 1972.

Gernsheim, H., and A. Gernsheim. *L. J. M. Daguerre: The History of the Diorama and the Daguerrotype.* 2d ed. New York: Dover, 1968.

Gibson, J. J. Review of *Art and Illusion* by E. H. Gombrich. *Psychological Review,* vol. 76 (1960).

———. *The Senses Considered as Perceptual Systems.* Westport, Conn.: Greenwood, 1966.

———. *The Ecological Approach to Visual Perception.* Boston: Houghton Mifflin Co., 1979.

———. *Reasons for Realism.* Edited by E. Reed and R. Jones. Hillsdale, N.J.: Lawrence Erlbaum Assocs. 1982.

Gombrich, E. H. *Meditations on a Hobby Horse.* 2d ed. London: Phaidon, 1971.

———. *The Story of Art.* 12th ed. London: Phaidon, 1972.

———. *Art and Illusion.* 5th ed. Oxford: Phaidon, 1977.

———. *The Image and the Eye.* Oxford: Phaidon, 1982.

———. *Shadows: The Depiction of Cast Shadows in Western Art.* London: National Gallery, 1995.

Gombrich, E. H., and R. L. Gregory, eds. *Illusion in Nature and Art.* London: Duckworth, 1973.

Goodman, N. *Languages of Art.* Indianapolis: Hackett, 1968.

———. *Problems and Projects.* Indianapolis: Hackett, 1972.

———. "Realism, Relativism and Reality." *New Literary History* 14 (1983): 269–72.

Greenberg, C. *The Collected Essays and Criticism.* Edited by J. O'Brian. 4 vols. Chicago: University of Chicago Press, 1986–93.

Gregory, R. L. *Concepts and Mechanisms of Perception.* London: Duckworth, 1974.

———. *Eye and Brain.* 3d ed. London: Weidenfeld & Nicolson, 1977.

———. *Mind in Science.* Harmondsworth: Penguin, 1984.

———. *Mirrors in Mind.* Harmondsworth: Penguin, 1997.

Gregory, R. L., et al., eds. *The Artful Eye.* Oxford: Oxford University Press, 1995.

Grice, H. P. *Studies in the Way of Words.* Cambridge, Mass.: Harvard University Press, 1989.

Guthrie, W. K. C. *A History of Greek Philosophy.* 6 vols. Cambridge: Cambridge University Press, 1962–81.

Hacker, P. M. S. *Appearance and Reality.* Oxford: Basil Blackwell, 1987.

Haldane, J., and C. Wright, eds. *Reality, Representation and Projection.* Oxford: Oxford University Press, 1993.

Halliwell, S. *The Aesthetics of Mimesis.* Princeton, N.J.: Princeton University Press, 2002.

Hardin, C. L. *Color for Philosophers.* Indianapolis: Hackett, 1988.

Harman, P. M. *The Natural Philosophy of James Clerk Maxwell.* Cambridge: Cambridge University Press, 2001.

Hauck, G. *Die Subjektive Perspektive und die Horizontalen Curvaturen des Dorischen Styls.* Stuttgart: Konrad Wittwer, 1879.

———. *Lehrbuch der malerischen Perspektive.* Berlin: Springer, 1910.

Hegel, G. W. F. *Aesthetics: Lectures on Fine Art.* Translated by T. M. Knox. 2 vols. Oxford: Oxford University Press, 1975.

Helmholtz, H. von, *Populäre Wissenschaftliche Vorträge.* 3 vols. Braunschweig: Friedrich Vieweg & Sohn, 1865–76.

———. *Science and Culture.* Edited by D. Cahan. Chicago: University of Chicago Press, 1995.

Hopkins, J., and A. Savile. *Psychoanalysis, Mind and Art.* Oxford: Basil Blackwell, 1992.

Hopkins, R. *Picture, Image and Experience.* Cambridge: Cambridge University Press, 1998.

Hospers, J. *Meaning and Truth in the Arts.* Chapel Hill: University of North Carolina Press, 1947.

Hume, D. *A Treatise of Human Nature.* Edited by L. A. Selby-Bigge. 2d ed. edited by P. H. Nidditch. Oxford: Clarendon Press, 1978.

———. *An Enquiry concerning Human Understanding.* Edited by T. Beauchamp. Oxford: Oxford University Press 1999.

———. *An Enquiry concerning the Principles of Morals.* Edited by T. Beauchamp. Oxford: Oxford University Press, 1998.

———. *Essays Moral, Political and Literary.* Edited by E. F. Miller. Indianapolis: Liberty Classics, 1985.

Hyde, M. "The 'Make-up' of the Marquise: Boucher's *Portrait of Pompadour at Her Toilette.*" *Art Bulletin* 82 (September 2000): 453–75.

Hyman, J. "Subjectivism in the Theory of Pictorial Art." *Monist,* vol. 86 (October 2003).

Jackson, F. *Perception.* Cambridge: Cambridge University Press, 1977.

Jakobson, R. "On Realism in Art" (1921). Reprinted in *Language in Literature.* Cambridge, Mass.: Harvard University Press, 1987.

Janaway, C. *Images of Excellence.* Oxford: Oxford University Press, 1995.

Kandel, E. R., J. H. Schwartz, and T. M. Jessell. *Essentials of Neural Science and Behavior.* Stamford, Conn.: Appleton & Lange, 1995.

Kant, I. *Critique of Judgement.* Translated by W. Pluhar. Indianapolis: Hackett, 1987.

Kelly, M. *Iconoclasm in Aesthetics.* Cambridge: Cambridge University Press, 2003.

Kemp, M. *The Science of Art.* New Haven, Conn., and London: Yale University Press, 1990.

Kepler, Johann, *Gesammelte Werke.* Edited by W. von Dyck and M. Caspar. Munich: C. H. Beck, 1937–.

Keuls, E. C. *Plato and Greek Painting.* Leiden: E. J. Brill, 1978.

Kivy, P. *Sound and Semblance.* Ithaca, N.Y.: Cornell University Press, 1991.

Kneale, W. "Sensation and the Physical World." *Philosophical Quarterly* 1 (1951): 109–26.

Kripke, S. "Reference and Existence." John Locke Lectures, Oxford University, 1973.

Kris, E., and O. Kurz. *Legend, Myth and Magic in the Image of the Artist.* New Haven, Conn.: Yale University Press, 1979.

Kuehni, R. G. *Color Space and Its Divisions.* Hoboken, N.J.: John Wiley, 2003.

Künne, W. *Conceptions of Truth.* Oxford: Oxford University Press, 2003.

Lalo, C. *L'expression de la vie dans l'art.* Paris: F. Alcan, 1933.

Langer, S. K. *Philosophy in a New Key.* Cambridge, Mass.: Harvard University Press, 1942.

Leibniz, G. W. *New Essays on Human Understanding.* Translated and edited by P. Remnant and J. Bennett. Cambridge: Cambridge University Press, 1996.

Levy, J. *Memoir of an Art Gallery.* New York: Putnam, 1977.

Locke, J. *An Essay concerning Human Understanding.* Edited by R. Woolhouse. London: Penguin, 1977.

Lopes, D. *Understanding Pictures.* Oxford: Oxford University Press, 1996.

Löwy, E. *The Rendering of Nature in Early Greek Art.* Translated by J. Fothergill. London: Duckworth, 1907.

Lukes, S. *Liberals and Cannibals.* London: Verso, 2003.

MacCurdy, E., trans. *The Notebooks of Leonardo da Vinci.* 2 vols. London: Jonathan Cape, 1938.

Macdonald, G. F. ed. *Perception and Identity.* London: Macmillan, 1979.

Mackie, J. L. *Problems from Locke.* Oxford: Oxford University Press, 1976.

Malin, F. *Understanding Paintings.* Oxford: Phaidon, 1980.
Marr, D. *Vision.* San Francisco: Freeman, 1982.
Maxwell, J. C. "Theory of Compound Colors and the Relations of the Colors in the Spectrum." *Proceedings of the Royal Society of London* 10 1860: 404–9.
———. "On Colour Vision." *Proceedings of the Royal Institution of Great Britain* 6 (1872): 260–71.
McDowell, J. *Mind, Value and Reality.* Cambridge, Mass.: Harvard University Press, 1998.
McGinn, C. *The Subjective View.* Oxford: Oxford University Press, 1983.
———. *Knowledge and Reality.* Oxford: Oxford University Press, 1999.
Merleau-Ponty, M. *Phenomenology of Perception.* Translated by C. French. London: Routledge & Kegan Paul, 1962.
———. *Sense and Non-Sense.* Translated by H. L. Dreyfus and P. A. Dreyfus. Evanston, Ill.: Northwestern University Press, 1964.
Métraux, G. P. R. *Sculptors and Physicians in Fifth-Century Greece.* Montreal and Kingston: McGill-Queen's University Press, 1995.
Minkowski, H. "Space and Time." Reprinted in A. Einstein et al., *The Principle of Relativity.* 1923. Reprint, New York: Dover, 1959.
Misak, C. ed. *The Cambridge Companion to Peirce.* Cambridge: Cambridge University Press, 2004.
Montaigne, Michel de, *Essays.* Translated by C. Cotton. Edited by W. C. Hazlitt. 4 vols. London, 1877.
Morris, C. W. *Signs, Language and Behavior.* New York: G. Braziller, 1955.
Nagel, T. *The View from Nowhere.* Oxford: Oxford University Press, 1986.
Neer, R. T. *Athenian Vase-Painting.* Cambridge: Cambridge University Press, 2002.
Newton, Isaac. *Opticks.* New York: Dover, 1952.
Nochlin, L. *Realism.* Harmondsworth: Penguin, 1971.
Palmer, S. *Vision Science: Photons to Phenomenology.* Cambridge, Mass.: MIT Press, 1999.
Panofsky, E. *Studies in Iconology.* Oxford: Oxford University Press, 1939.
———. *The Codex Huygens and Leonardo da Vinci's Art Theory.* London: Warburg Institute, 1940.
———. *Perspective as Symbolic Form.* Translated by C. S. Wood. New York: Zone Books, 1991.
Pascal, Blaise. *Oeuvres Complètes.* Edited by J. Chevalier. Paris: Gallimard, 1954.
Peacocke, C. *Sense and Content.* Oxford: Oxford University Press, 1983.
———. "Depiction." *Philosophical Review* 96 (1987): 383–410.
Peirce, C. S. *Collected Papers.* Edited by C. Hartshorne and P. Weiss. 8 vols. Cambridge, Mass.: Harvard University Press, 1960.
Pessoa, F. *Selected Poems.* Translated by J. Griffin, 2d ed. Harmondsworth: Penguin, 1982.
Piles, R. de, *Cours de Peinture par Principes.* Paris, 1708.
Pirenne, M. H. *Optics, Painting and Photography.* Cambridge: Cambridge University Press, 1970.
Pliny the Elder. *Natural History.* Loeb Classical Library. London: William Heinemann; Cambridge, Mass.: Harvard University Press, 1940–86.
Prior, A. N. *The Doctrine of Propositions and Terms.* London: Duckworth, 1976.

Proust, M. *Against Sainte-Beuve and Other Essays.* Translated by J. Sturrock. Harmondsworth: Penguin, 1988.

Puttfarken, T. *Roger de Piles' Theory of Art.* New Haven, Conn.: Yale University Press, 1985.

Quine, W. V. O. *From a Logical Point of View.* Cambridge, Mass.: Harvard University Press, 1961.

———. *The Roots of Reference.* La Salle, Ill.: Open Court, 1973.

Ramachandran, V. S. "Perceiving Shape from Shading," *Scientific American,* August 1988.

Reynolds, Joshua. *Discourses on Art.* Edited by R. R. Wark. New Haven, Conn.: Yale University Press, 1975.

Riegl, A. *The Group Portraiture of Holland.* Translated by E. M. Kain. Los Angeles: Getty Research Institute, 1999.

Robinson, Howard. *Perception.* London: Routledge, 1994.

Rock, I. "In Defence of Unconscious Inference," in *Stability and Constancy in Visual Perception,* edited by W. Epstein, pp. 321–73. New York: Wiley, 1977.

———. *Perception.* New York: Scientific American Books, 1984.

Rosen, C., and H. Zerner. *Romanticism and Realism: Mythology of Nineteenth-Century Art.* London: Faber & Faber: 1984.

Rosenfeld, I. "Seeing through the Brain." *New York Review of Books,* 11 October 1984

Rosenthal, M. *The Art of Thomas Gainsborough.* New Haven, Conn.: Yale University Press, 1999.

Rossotti, H. *Colour.* Harmondsworth: Penguin, 1983.

Ruskin, J. *The Complete Works of John Ruskin,* edited by E. T. Cook and A. Wedderburn. London: George Allen, 1903.

Russell, B. *Our Knowledge of the External World.* Chicago: Open Court, 1914.

Ryle, R. *Collected Papers.* 2 vols. London: Unwin Hyman, 1971.

Sabra, A. I. *Theories of Light from Descartes to Newton.* Cambridge: Cambridge University Press, 1981.

Sartre, J.-P. *The Imaginary.* Translated by J. Webber. London: Routledge, 2004.

Schäfer, H. *Principles of Egyptian Art.* Translated by J. Baines. Rev. ed. Oxford: Griffith Institute, 1986.

Schapiro, M. *Words and Pictures.* The Hague: Mouton, 1973.

———. *Modern Art: Nineteenth and Twentieth Centuries.* New York: George Braziller, 1978.

———. *Theory and Philosophy of Art: Style, Artist, and Society.* New York: George Braziller, 1994.

———. *Impressionism: Reflections and Perceptions.* New York: George Braziller, 1997.

Schier, F. *Deeper into Pictures.* Cambridge: Cambridge University Press, 1986.

Scruton, R. *Art and Imagination.* London: Routledge & Kegan Paul, 1982.

———. *The Aesthetic Understanding.* London: Methuen, 1983.

Shiff, R. *Cézanne and the End of Impressionism.* Chicago: University of Chicago Press, 1984.

Sibley, F. *Approach to Aesthetics.* Oxford: Oxford University Press, 2001.

Smith, W. S. *The Art and Architecture of Ancient Egypt.* 2d ed. Revised by W. K. Simpson. Harmondsworth: Penguin, 1981.

Spinoza, B. *Ethics.* Translated by R. H. M. Elwes. New York: Dover, 1955.

Steinberg, L. *Other Criteria.* Oxford: Oxford University Press, 1972.

Sterne, L. *The Life and Opinions of Tristram Shandy, Gentleman.* Edited by Ian Campbell Ross. Oxford: Oxford University Press, 1998.

Stoichita, V. *The Self-Aware Image.* Translated by A.-M. Glasheen. Cambridge: Cambridge University Press, 1997.

Stroud, B. *The Quest for Reality.* Oxford: Oxford University Press, 2000.

Tyndall, J. *Faraday as a Discoverer,* 5th ed. London: Longman & Co., 1894.

Voltaire, *Philosophical Dictionary.* Translated by T. Besterman. London: Penguin Books, 1972.

Whistler, J. M. *The Gentle Art of Making Enemies.* 3d ed. London: Heinemann, 1904.

White, J. *The Birth and Rebirth of Pictorial Space,* 2d ed. London: Faber & Faber, 1967.

Wiggins, D. *Needs, Values, Truth,* 3d ed. Oxford: Oxford University Press, 1998.

Willats, J. *Art and Representation.* Princeton, N.J.: Princeton University Press, 1997.

Williams, B. A. O. *Descartes: The Project of Pure Enquiry.* Harmondsworth: Penguin, 1978.

Williams, C. J. F. *What Is Identity?* Oxford: Oxford University Press, 1989.

Winckelmann, J. J. *History of Ancient Art.* Translated by C. H. Lodge. London: Sampson Low & Co., 1881.

Wittgenstein, L. *Philosophical Investigations.* Translated by G. E. M. Anscombe. Oxford: Basil Blackwell, 1953.

———. *Tractatus logico-philosophicus.* Translated by D. F. Pears and B. F. McGuinness. London: Routledge & Kegan Paul, 1961.

———. *The Blue and Brown Books.* 2d ed. Oxford: Basil Blackwell, 1969.

———. *Philosophical Grammar.* Edited by Rush Rhees. Oxford: Basil Blackwell, 1974.

———. *Remarks on Colour.* Edited by G. E. M. Anscombe. Oxford: Basil Blackwell, 1977.

———. *Remarks on the Philosophy of Psychology.* 2 vols. Edited by G. H. von Wright and Heikki Nyman. Oxford: Blackwell, 1980.

———. *Philosophical Occasions.* Edited by James C. Klagge and Alfred Nordmann. Indianapolis: Hackett, 1993.

Wollheim, R. *Art and Its Objects.* 2d ed. Cambridge: Cambridge University Press, 1980.

———. *Painting as an Art.* London: Thames & Hudson, 1988.

Wolterstorff, N. *Worlds and Works of Art.* Oxford: Oxford University Press, 1980.

Wright, C. *Truth and Objectivity.* Cambridge, Mass.: Harvard University Press, 1993.

Xenophon. *Memorabilia.* Translated by E. C. Marchant. Loeb Classical Library. Cambridge, Mass.: Harvard University Press, 1997.

Zeki, S. "Colour Coding in the Cerebral Cortex: The Reaction of Cells in Monkey Visual Cortex to Wavelengths and Colours." *Neuroscience* 9 (1983): 767–81.

Zhmud, L. *Wissenschaft, Philosophie und Religion im frühen Pythagoreismus.* Berlin: Akademie Verlag, 1997.

CREDITS

PLATES: **1.** Research Library, The Getty Research Institute, Los Angeles. **2.** The Queen's College, Oxford. **3.** © The Frick Collection, New York. **4.** Image © 2004 Board of Trustees, National Gallery of Art, Washington, D.C. **5.** The Metropolitan Museum of Art, New York, Bequest of Miss Adelaide Milton de Groot (1876–1967), 1967. (67.187.102). Photograph © 1990 The Metropolitan Museum of Art, New York. **6.** Réunion des Musées Nationaux/Art Resource, New York. **7.** Gift of the W. Averell Harriman Foundation, in memory of Marie N. Harriman. Image © 2004 Board of Trustees, National Gallery of Art, Washington, D.C. **8.** The Royal Collection © 2004, Her Majesty Queen Elizabeth II.

FIGURES: **1.** M. Vorobyev, "Ecology and Evolution of Primate Colour Vision," *Clinical and Experimental Optometry* 87 (2004): 230–38. **2.** © 2005 C. Herscovici, Brussels/Artists Rights Society, New York/Banque d'Images, ADAGP, Paris/Art Resource, New York. **3.** The Cloisters Museum, Metropolitan Museum of Art, New York. **4.** Sarah Blair. **5.** Erich Lessing/Art Resource, New York. **6.** By permission of The Governing Body of Christ Church College, Oxford. **8.** The Queen's College, Oxford. **9.** Scala/Art Resource, New York. **10.** Réunion des Musées Nationaux/Art Resource, New York. **11.** Bildarchiv Preussischer Kulturbesitz/Art Resource, New York. **12.** Staatliche Antikensammlungen und Glyptothek, München. **13, 14.** Bildarchiv Preussischer Kulturbesitz/Art Resource, New York. **15.** Staatliche Antikensammlungen und Glyptothek, München. **16.** © 2005 Estate of Pablo Picasso/Artists Rights Society, New York. Réunion des Musées Nationaux/Art Resource, New York. **17.** Scala/Art Resource, New York. **18.** © Albertina, Wien. **19.** The Metropolitan Museum of Art, New York, Robert Lehman Collection, 1975 (1975.1.862). **20.** Courtesy of The Fogg Art Museum, Harvard University Art Museums, Bequest of Charles E. Dunlap. **21.** Scala/Art Resource, New York. **22.** Erich Lessing/Art Resource, New York. **23.** © The National Gallery of Art, London. **24, 27.** O. Demus, *Byzantine Mosaic Decoration* (London: Routledge & Kegan Paul, 1976). **25.** Bodleian Library, University of Oxford. Vet. E4 e.31, opp. p. 184. **28.** National Portrait Gallery, London. **29.** © The National Gallery of Art, London. **30.** Arthur M. Sackler Gallery, Smithsonian Institution, Washington D.C. By kind permission of Christopher Dutton. **31.** The Royal Collection © 2004, Her Majesty Queen Elizabeth II. **32.** Ashmolean Museum, Oxford. **33.** Bildarchiv Preussischer Kulturbesitz/Art Resource, New York. **34.** The Civic Museums, Venice. **35.** The Queen's College, Oxford. **36.** © Aaron Siskind

Foundation/courtesy Robert Mann Gallery. **37.** Reproduction courtesy of the Minor White Archive, Princeton University Art Museum, Princeton, N.J. © Trustees of Princeton University. All Rights Reserved. **38.** Kunstmuseum Basel, permanent loan of the City of Basel 1967. Photograph Kunstmuseum Basel, Martin Bühler. **39.** Sarah Blair. **40.** The National Archaeological Museum, Athens. **41.** Tally Hyman. **42.** The Queen's College, Oxford. **43.** © 2005 Estate of Pablo Picasso/Artists Rights Society, New York. © Succession Picasso/Art Resource, New York. **44.** © Succession Picasso/DACS 2005. **45.** © Collection of the Rijksmuseum, Amsterdam. **46.** © 2005 Artists Rights Society, New York/ADAGP, Paris. Digital Image © The Museum of Modern Art/Licensed by Scala/Art Resource, New York. **47.** The Metropolitan Museum of Art, New York. **48, 49.** Six Art Promotion bv, Amsterdam. **50.** Réunion des Musées Nationaux/Art Resource, New York. **51.** The Pierpont Morgan Library, New York. MS. G.25, f. 1 verso. **52.** © 2005 Artists Rights Society (ARS), New York/DACS, London. Kunsthalle, Tübingen. Sammlung Zundel. **53.** Courtesy of The Hispanic Society of America, New York. **54.** Royal Museum of Fine Arts, Brussels, Belgium. **55.** The Museum of Fine Arts, Boston. William Sturgis Bigelow Collection. Photograph © 2005 Museum of Fine Arts, Boston. **56.** Bodleian Library, University of Oxford. MS. Kennicott 1 folio 447r Colophon. **57.** Sarah Blair. **61.** Courtesy of the Huntington Library, Art Collections and Botanical Gardens, San Marino, Calif. **62.** Bodleian Library, University of Oxford. Sinica 3838/8 Bamboo. **64.** © The New Yorker Collection 1931 Otto Soglow from cartoonbank.com. All Rights Reserved. **65.** © 2005 The Saul Steinberg Foundation/Artists Rights Society (ARS), New York. **67.** The National Archaeological Museum, Athens. **68.** Réunion des Musées Nationaux/Art Resource, New York. **69.** © The Cleveland Museum of Art, Leonard C. Hanna, Jr. Fund, 1981.18. **70.** © 2004 Kimbell Art Museum, Fort Worth, Tex. **71.** The Metropolitan Museum of Art, Rogers Fund, 1914 (14.139.12). **72.** The Metropolitan Museum of Art, New York, Lent by Gregory Callimanopulos, 1982 (L.1982.102.3). **73.** The Metropolitan Museum of Art. Purchase, Bequest of Joseph H. Durkee, Gift of Darius Ogden Mills and Gift of C. Ruxton Love, by exchange, 1972 (1972.11.10). **74.** Su concessione n. 48 del 16/11/2004 del Ministero per i Beni e le Attività Culturali. Museo Nazionale Archeologico di Reggio Calabria. **75.** Courtesy of Leo Robert. **76, 77.** Bildarchiv Preussischer Kulturbesitz/Art Resource, New York. **78.** Reproduced by kind permission of the trustees of The Wallace Collection, London. **79.** Scala/Art Resource, New York. **80.** Musée des Beaux-Arts de Lyon © Studio Basset. **82.** Courtesy of Hirschl and Adler Galleries, Inc., New York. **83.** Bildarchiv Preussischer Kulturbesitz/Art Resource, New York. **84.** © Museo Nacional del Prado. **85.** Cameraphoto Arte, Venice/Art Resource, New York. **86.** Bildarchiv Preussischer Kulturbesitz/Art Resource, New York. **87.** Staatliche Antikensammlungen und Glyptothek, München. **88.** Bibliothèque nationale de France. **89.** Erich Lessing/Art Resource, New York. **90.** Scala/Art Resource, New York. **91.** Sarah Blair. **92.** Victoria and Albert Museum, London/Art Resource, New York. **93, 94.** Scala/Art Resource, New York. **95.** Bodleian Library, University of Oxford. Figure on penultimate page of Vet. D1 c.24(1). **96.** The Queen's College, Oxford. **97.** Scala/Art Resource, New York.

INDEX